ADVANCED EDUCATIONAL PSYCHOLOGY

Advanced Educational Psychology

Edited by
Tara Chand
Ravi Prakash

KANISHKA PUBLISHERS, DISTRIBUTORS
NEW DELHI-110 002

KANISHKA PUBLISHERS, DISTRIBUTORS
4697/5-21A, Ansari Road, Daryaganj
New Delhi -110 002
Phones: 2327 0497, 2328 8285
Fax: 011-2328 8285
E-mail: kanishka_publishing@yahoo.co.in

Advanced Educational Psychology

First Published 1997

Edition 2018

PRINTED IN INDIA

Published by Madan Sachdeva for Kanishka Publishers, Distributors, 4697/5-21A, Ansari Road, Daryaganj, New Delhi-110 002, Typeset by Sunshine Graphics, Delhi, and Printed at Rajdhani Printers, Delhi.

Preface

Public policy statements on vital indicators of development, such as, health, education, child development and family welfare have been welcome in recent years. They supplement, and in most cases, complement broad-based and generally focussed schemes, including Operation Blackboard, Literacy Mission, Health Cover for All by 2000, Navodaya Schools and others designed for the specific benefit of the millions of the country's poor, deprived, isolated and neglected masses. The efforts of planners and policy-makers has been motivated by the broad principles of the welfare state. Inputs need to be conceived, structured and channellised into the development mainstream. The present publication is a modest attempt in this direction.

It deals with the critical segment of educational psychology and covers such valuable aspects as: learning theories, race and intelligence, intelligence and attainment, personality determinants, personality development, and personality and cognition. The book fulfills a long-felt need in the field of educational research and training.

TARA CHAND
RAVI PRAKASH

Contents

1

Contemporary Learning Theories

The two most prominent families of contemporary learning theory are *stimulus-response associationisms* and *Gestalt-field* theories. These have been in process of development throughout the twentieth century and have roots which extend back into earlier centuries. Their immediate fore-runners were mental discipline and apperception. In a sense, both families were protests against inadequacies and inconsistencies of earlier psychological systems.

This chapter develops "background thinking" which underpins the positions of the two families in regard to learning. It traces how they developed historically, their philosophical implications, and their chief assumptions about the role of psychology. It then shows how adherents of the two families differ in their interpretations of perceptive and motivational processes.

During the 1920s and 1930s, teachers' colleges moved away from Herbartianism as such. This is not to say that Herbartian ideas were completely dead. They were then, and are today, accepted and practiced by many teachers. However, before the twentieth century had been under way long, a new form of associationism had become popular. This was a nonmentalistic, or physiological, associationism. Its chief exponents during the first third of the century were John B. Watson (1878-1958) and

Edward L. Thorndike (1874-1949). Watson's psychology was known as behaviourism. Thorndike's was called connectionism, but it too, in the broadest sense of the term, was "behaviouristic." Although the psychological systems of Thorndike and Watson no longer are advocated in their original form, many contemporary psychologists have a sufficiently similar orientation properly to be termed "neobehaviourists". The psychological theories supported by these persons may be identified as stimulus-response associationisms.

The second major family of contemporary learning theories originated in Germany. In 1912 a German psychologist-philosopher, Max Wertheimer, presented a body of theory which came to be known as Gestalt psychology.

Gestalt is a German noun for which their is no English word equivalent, so the term was carried over into English psychological literature. The nearest English translation of *Gestalt* is "configuration." Various other persons who had been thinking along similar lines contributed to this new school of thought. As Gestalt psychology evolved, other names such as *field, phenomenological, and organismic psychology* became associated with it. In this book, we refer to related theories which originated from Gestalt psychology as Gestalt-field or cognitive-field psychology. Gestalt-field psychology was introduced into the United States in the middle 1920s. It has gathered a large number of exponents and now can be considered the leading rival of S-R associationism. However, a great many psychologists are eclectic in the sense that they borrow elements from both schools of thought and identify themselves with neither.

Students should be aware of the fact that within each of the two families of psychological theory there is considerable diversity. For example, in the S-R family, followers of Clark Hull and B. F. Skinner would be in disagreement on many points. Likewise, in the Gestalt-field family, followers of Kurt Lewin differ considerably in outlook from followers of Kurt Koffka or G. W. Hartmann. The situation in psychology is somewhat like that in politics; many persons gravitate toward one or the other of our two political parties, but in spite of some common interests, both Democrats and Republicans exhibit a wide range of views. In final analysis, however, S-R associationists have certain key ideas in common, just as do the Gestalt-field psychologists. It is proper to consider each category as a definite grouping which can be discussed in terms of the ideas common to its members.

It students are aware that in spite of variance within each family the two families differ sharply, they will understand the ensuing chapters on learning better. To fundamental issues in psychology the two families provide answers which are often quite incompatible. In dealing with the following questions, a person oriented toward S-R associationism is likely to give a significantly different answer from that given by a Gestalt-field theorist. What is intelligence? What happens when we remember and when we forget? What is perception? What is motivation? What is thinking? What is the role of practice in learning? How does learning transfer to other situations? These and many other questions are controversial in the sense that psychologists with different learnings will offer diverse answers.

Before a student adopts the orientation of one family of psychology or the other, he should recognize that objections may be made to any position one takes in psychology and to any currently available theory of learning. However, although the evidence is not clear enough to warrant dogmatic assertions about learning, he may emerge with the feeling that the ideas central to one family of psychological theory are more tenable and have fewer disadvantages than the ideas central to the other.

Although all modern psychologists, irrespective of their orientation, generally accept the methods and results of experimentation, there is wide divergence in interpretation of experimental results and equally wide divergence on how a given interpretation should be applied in solution of a concrete learning problem. These differences appear to stem from disagreement over the fundamental nature of man, the relationship of man to his environment, and the nature of perception and motivation. In spite of disclaimers by some psychologists, it also appears impossible to detach a number of issues in psychology from related issues in philosophy. A psychologist's philosophical learning may not only determine the kinds of experiments he conducts but also influence the conclusions he draws from experimentation.

WHAT ARE THE ORIGINS OF S-R ASSOCIATIONISM?

Early associationists were interested primarily in mental phenomena; their concern was the association of ideas in minds. Modern associationism is rooted in a different kind of interest—the physiology of bodies.

Nineteenth-century forerunners of modern experimental psychology tended to be philosophical dualists; they considered men to consist of minds and bodies, each genuinely real. There was a good deal of speculation in regard to the nature of the relationship of minds and bodies, but seldom denial of the reality of either. In the transition period between Herbart (1776-1841) and Watson (1878-1958) much vacillation took place between emphasis upon the workings of biological organisms and the functions of minds.

During the first half of the nineteenth century, experimental psychology got its start within experimental physiology. The physiologists Bell and Müller became occupied with testing the workings of the nervous system in seeing and hearing. Thus they became psychologists even though they did not call themselves such.

Wilhelm Wundt (1832-1920) was trained in medicine. He turned from medicine to physiology and from physiology to psychology. In 1879 he established the first psychological laboratory of modern history. His method was introspection; he and his students observed the workings of their respective minds. Students from various parts of the world went to Wundt's laboratory at Leipzig to study introspection. But many became psychological heretics; they turned to study of observable behaviour of other persons and animals.

Interest in bodily functioning became apparent among many psychologists late in the nineteenth century. This group of "physiological psychologists" argued that psychology could become a true science only if it switched its focus to bodily processes. In a century which placed ever increasing emphasis upon experimental science, introspection came more and more to appear a highly unreliable procedure. A person could reflect upon the workings of his own mind, but what did this prove? Scientists were ceasing to be concerned with any kind of evidence which was not "publicly verifiable"—that is, subject to public observation and tests. Thus they began to focus their attention on objects or events which could be observed with the "five senses" and studied in the same manner by any number of trained investigators and lead to uniform conclusions.

To a growing number of psychologists, the only logical alternative to the method of introspection was to focus on observable forms of behaviour. Such behaviour includes not only bodily movement as seen by an observer watching a subject but also the internal physical processes related to overt bodily behaviour. Why adrenalin is secreted and how long it takes a person to react to a pinprick are equally proper to a physiological psychologist. Both can be measured objectively, described in terms of definite mechanical sequences or quantities, and reported statistically. Before the twentieth century was very far along, a large number of psychologists has come to feel that psychology, in time, could be made as "scientific" as physics.

We shall name only a few of the persons who contributed to the development of physiological psychology. Marshall Hall (1790-1857) did pioneering work on the neural basis of reflex behaviour. Pierre Flourens (1794-1867) demonstrated that different parts of the nervous system have different functions and he took important steps toward identifying the function of each part. Flourens also proposed that conclusions drawn from animal experimentation should be equally applicable to man. This notion gained wide acceptance and greatly simplified the work of experimental psychologists: after all, it is much cheaper and more convenient to experiment with rats than with human beings.

Some of the most notable animal experiments of the late nineteenth and early twentieth centuries were conducted by the Russian physiologist Ivan Petrovich Pavlov (1849-1936). Pavlov put food before a hungry dog and sounded a bell or tuning fork. He found that, if this procedure was repeated enough times, the sound alone would cause the dog to salivate. As we shall see, Pavlov's work was extremely influential, and nowhere more so than among the growing group of S-R associationists in the United States. Thorndike's animal experiments, making use of chicks, dogs, and cats, were possibly even more comprehensive than Pavlov's and, over the long run, more influential in the United States. His famous "laws of learning" were derived mainly from his interpretation of how cats behave when placed in a cage from which they do not know how to escape—until they learn. Since Thorndike was a dominant figure in psychology for almost half a century, we describe some of his ideas in detail.

Thorndike's Connectionism

Thorndike was an eclectic in the sense that he retained in his thinking certain elements of Herbartian "idea associationism." At the same time, he was strongly influenced by the new physiological psychology. In his writings he talks of both physical and mental units. He assumed that there are both physical and mental events, and that learning is a process of linking the two in various combinations. A mental unit was something sensed or perceived; a physical unit was a stimulus or a response. Specifically, he saw learning as a process of connecting a metal with a physical unit, a physical with a mental unit, a mental with a mental unit, or a physical with a physical unit.

Thorndike's theory of learning is called S-R bond theory or *connectionism*. It assumes that, through conditioning, specific responses come to be linked with specific stimuli. These links, bonds, or connections are products of a biological change in a nervous system. Thorndike thought that the chief way in which S-R connections were formed was through random trial and error (or selecting and connecting). It is probably because of Thorndike's influence that the term *trial* and *error* became popularized and found its way into the vocabularies of many Americans.

In a typical trial-and-error experiment, Thorndike would place a cat in a cage which could be opened from inside only by striking a latch or button. The cat would claw, bite, and scurry wildly about until it accidentally touched the release and was freed. The experiment would be repeated and the animal would behave the same except that over the course of a number of successive "trials" the total time required by the cat to get out would decrease. Eventually the cat would learn to escape immediately without random activity. Thorndike inferred from the timed behaviour of his cats that learning was a process of "stamping in" connections in the nervous system and had nothing to do with insight or "catching on."

Thorndike formulated a number of laws of learning and classified them as either primary or secondary. We describe here only his three primary laws:

1. *The laws of exercise or repetition* : According to this law, the more times a stimulus-induced response is repeated, the longer it will be retained. As Thorndike put it, "Other things being equal, *exercise strengthens the bond between situation and response.*" Conversely, a bond is weakened through failure to exercise it.

2. *The law of effect* : The law of effect states the famous pleasure-pain principle so frequently associated with Thorndike's name. A response is strengthened if it is followed by pleasure and weakened if followed by displeasure. Or, in Thorndike's words, "..... a modifiable connection being made ..... between an S and an R and being accompanied or followed by a satisfying state of affairs man responds, other things being equal, by an increase in the strength of that connection. To a connection similar, save that an *annoying* state of affairs goes with or follows it, man responds, other things being equal, by a decrease in the strength of the connection."

3. *The law of readiness* : Thorndike termed the neuron (or neurons) and the synapse (or synapses) involved in establishment of a specific bond or connection a *conduction unit*. He assumed that, because of the structure of a nervous system, in a given situation certain conduction units are more predisposed to conduct than others. And *"for a conduction unit ready to conduct to do so is satisfying, and for it not to do so is annoying."*

In his later writings Thorndike disavowed his law of exercise or repetition and one-half—the annoyance aspect—of his law of effect. But he seemed not to have had the courage of his convictions. Through implication, he continued to emphasize repetition in learning. His law of effect shifted its emphasis to pleasure, but the pain aspect was not completely discarded.

Students will readily see that Thorndike's laws of learning are closely related and may operate together. For example, if an organism is ready to respond, then response is pleasurable and this fact in itself will tend to fix the response. Students will also see that the laws appear to be exceedingly mechanical. Furthermore, they seem to leave no room for any sort of thought or insight, and they do not appear to require the assumption of any kind of purposiveness of man or lower animals.

The psychological concept *purposiveness* has no direct relationship to the problem of cosmic or teleological purpose. Within a purposive psychology, as contrasted with a mechanistic one, we assume that each animal or person, whatever his developmental level, is seeking some end or purpose and that we can predict his behaviour most accurately when we anticipate what it is he is trying to accomplish.

Watson's Behaviourism

Watson felt much more strongly than Thorndike the need to base psychology exclusively on the concepts of physics and chemistry. To his way of thinking, mind and all kinds of mentalistic concepts were not only unsusceptible of scientific inquiry but also irrelevant to the real task of psychology. Watson drew heavily upon Pavlov's work and became convinced that learning was as Pavlov described it, namely, a process of building conditioned reflexes through the substitution of one stimulus for another.

Watson and other "pure bahaviourists" came to reject certain of Thorndike's ideas because it seemed impossible to exclude mind and mind-related concepts from them. We have already mentioned that Thorndike talked of "mental units." The pure behaviourists were also bothered by Thorndike's concepts of satisfaction and annoyance. These seemed to behaviourists to be mentalistic concepts and better disregarded in a truly scientific psychology. In the tradition of the earlier physiological psychologists, Watson confined his study to only those aspects of animal life which are sufficiently overt to make possible highly objective observation and measurement.

One of Thorndike's secondary laws of learning, however, seemed very promising to the Watsonians. This was the "law of associative shifting," and it became the keystone for the behaviouristic movement of the 1920s.

According to this law, we may, " *get any response of which a learner is capable associated with any situation to which he is sensitive.*" In other words, any response which is possible can be linked with any stimulus. An animal's "purposes or thoughts" have nothing to do with such learning. In fact, purpose and mentalistic thought supposedly are concepts outside the realm of scientific psychology. We may illustrate this law by using an example involving the training of an animal. Suppose we wish to train a dog to sit up at the verbal command "Sit". It is only necessary to induce the dog to sit up repeatedly by dangling a piece of meat or other food above him at the same time the verbal command is issued. Once this procedure has been repeated enough times, the dog should respond properly—without error—whenever the command is given. In this example, as long as the same "adequate stimulus" is used throughout the experiment, it would not matter if the command were replaced by any other accompanying stimulus to which a dog is sensitive—a light, a bell, snapping the fingers, whistling. Furthermore, by using the same basic procedure, it should be possible to teach a dog to perform any other act of which it is capable—standing on its front legs, rolling over, playing dead, etc. This supposed principle of learning, fundamental to behaviourism, is the principle of stimulus substitution.

Behaviourists defined a living organism as a self-maintaining mechanism. They assumed that the essence of a human machine is a system of receptors (sense organs), conductors (neurons), switching organs (brain and spinal cord), and effectors (muscles) attached to levers (bones)—plus, of course, fueling and controlling organs such as stomach and glands. When an organism is defined in such mechanistic terms, mentalistic concepts can be entirely eliminated. Not only can they be dropped out of the picture but they actually begin to seem rather fanciful. (Can one imagine a *machine* having "tender sentiments" or "soaring on the imagination"?) Among behaviourists, there developed an attitude toward the earlier mentalistic psychologists similar to that of a modern physician toward a primitive witch doctor.

The position of a Watsonian behaviourist can be illustrated amusingly in a morning conversation. Ordinarily, a conventional greeting would go as follows: "Good morning, how are you?" "I'm fine, and yourself?" "Just fine." But such a greeting implies introspection. Each person is "looking into himself" in order to decide what kind of shape he is in. Presumably (according to a behaviourist) this is scientifically impossible; instead the two persons would need to inspect each other. The proper salutation of a behaviourist would be, "Good morning, you appear to be fine; how am I?"

The Neobehaviourists

There is a large group of American psychologists today who assume that life can be explained in essentially mechanistic terms but who have adopted positions somewhat different from that of the Watsonian behaviourists. It might be said that Watsonian behaviourism, in its pure form is all but dead. Probably the best term to apply to contemporary S-R associationists is *neo-behaviourists.*

Contemporary S-R associationists do not place nearly as much emphasis upon the operation of brain and nervous system as did their predecessors. Of course, Watson himself had felt that the precise nature of neural mechanisms was largely irrelevant to learning; but Watson's followers, as well as Thorndike, had exhibited a strong interest in neural physiology and the physical mechanics of S-R linkages. Interests of neobehaviourists lie in analyses of behaviour per se rather than in the neural mechanism behind it. They are still concerned with how S's and R's become linked but they are not greatly concerned with the precise operation of the physiological mechanism which lies between.

Neobehaviourists differ from the original behaviourists in another respect. In their experimentation, they have tended to focus attention upon response modification as well as stimulus substitution. Response modification refers to the fate of responses that have already been made—whether they will be strengthened or weakened by subsequent events. In this connection, continual reference is made in the literature of neobehaviourism to *conditioning*. Conditioning means strengthening of a response. It is achieved by stimulus substitution, i.e., accompanying an adequate stimulus by a new stimulus, or by response strengthening or modification, i.e., following a response with a stimulus which strengthens it.

Since Thorndike's concept of learning as a process of "stamping in" a response which was originally accidental is a form of response modification, one might say that many neobehaviourists have returned to Thorndike's conception of learning. However, most neobehaviourists are better systematizers than Thorndike. This is, they are more consistent, largely by virtue of their building systems, which do not at any point require as assumption of conscious behaviour. Thorndike tried to be highly mechanical, but the neobehaviourists have developed psychological theories which are more consistently mechanical than Thorndike's.

Another feature of neobehaviourism is its attempt to explain behaviour which appears purposive. Purposiveness has always bothered psychologists who are behaviouristically oriented because they have felt that purpose is difficult to explain without slipping into a mind-body dualism. However, what seems purposive must be explained in some way. Neobehaviourists tend to develop mechanical explanations for apparent purposiveness. Purposiveness is regarded as a product of a pattern of stimulation, in which certain stimuli are more potent than the rest and thus lead an organism in one way rather than another. Much purposiveness would be interpreted as "drive reduction," that is, a relieving reaction to the stimulation induced by organic drives such as hunger or sex. Neobehaviourists remain careful to explain apparent purposiveness in a way which does not require the assumption of conscious behaviour or intelligent experience.

We shall mention but one more difference between the contemporary neobehaviourists and old-line pure behaviourists. Historically, behaviourism was "atomistic" in the sense that it focused on the *elements* of a situation. Attempts were made to identify specific stimuli and to describe the behaviour of an organism as a product of numerous discrete and isolable reactions. Today, S-R theorists talk in terms of "stimulus situations," i.e., complex configurations of stimulation, and of "molar behaviour," i.e., the coordinated behaviour of a whole act of an organism.

Well-known contemporary neobehaviourists include Edwin R. Guthrie, B. F. Skinner, K. W. Spence, and D. O. Hebb. All these psychologists and their followers are greatly interested in the psychology of learning. However, at one extreme Spence feels that in its present stage of development psychology has little to offer schools, and at the other extreme Skinner represents his psychology as the means of placing education on an efficient basis. Since Skinner's views are representative and extraordinarily clean-cut, Chapter 5 is devoted to an exposition of a Skinnerian psychology of learning.

WHAT ARE THE ORIGINS OF GESTALT-FIELD PSYCHOLOGY?

As noted earlier in the chapter, the position of Gestalt psychology was formally stated first by the German philosopher-psychologist Max Wertheimer (1880-1943) in 1912. The central idea of Wertheimer's point of view is expressed in the German word *Gestalt*, which, as we have seen, means an organized pattern or configuration, or, more simply, an organized *whole* in contrast to a collection of parts. The notion that a thing cannot be understood by study of its constituent parts, but only by study of it as a totality, is probably very old. Gardner Murphy suggests that it can be found in the literature of pre-Socratic Greece. Various Greek writers proposed that the universe could best be understood through "laws of arrangement" or "principles of order," rather than through study of its basic building blocks, the elements. In contrast, other Greek writers were "atomists," i.e., they sought the key to understanding through a study of individual elements. Just as the former might be called the originators of the Gestalt idea, so might the latter be called the originators of the atomistic idea—which characterized early behaviourism.

Among the nineteenth-century forerunners of Wertheimer we should include Ernst Mach (1838-1916), likewise a German. Although Mach held that the worlds of physics and psychology are essentially the same, he also argued that psychology must take into account those sensations which do not correspond to the physical reality before the viewer. These "nonphysical" sensations are sensations of *relationship*. For example, a person may see three dots on a sheet of paper and think of them as the points of a triangle. There is nothing in individual dots to suggest this; it is their configuration that prompts the relationship.

In the 1890s, following Mach, Christian Von Ehrenfels (1859-1932) pursued the same ideas. He stated that, in all perception, qualities appear which represent more than the physical items sensed. A perceiver tends to confer on the physical objects of perception a form, configuration, or meaning. He tries to organize or integrate what he sees. A school of thought began to form along the lines explored by these two men, and a new term came into use—*Gestaltqualitat*, which means approximately "the quality conferred by a pattern."

Wertheimer and his followers went still farther and formulated a series of "laws" of perception—*Prägnanz, similarity, proximity, closure, good continuation, and membership character.* According to the basic *law of Prägnanz,* if a perceptual field is disorganized when a person first experiences it, he imposes order on the field in a predictable way. The "predictable way" follows the other five subordinate laws. *Similarity* means that similar items (dots, for instance) tend to form groups in perception. *Proximity* means that perceptual groups are favoured according to the nearness of their respective parts.

Closure means that closed areas are more stable than unclosed ones. Draw a 340° arc and ask a viewer what you have drawn. He very likely will say "a circle." This is an example of closure; to achieve closure is satisfying. Closure is an alternative to Thorndike's law of effect. *Good continuation* is closely related to closure. It means that, in perception, one tends to continue straight lines as straight lines and curves as curves.

According to the law of *membership character,* a single part of a whole does not have fixed characteristics; it gets its characteristics from the context in which it appears. As Gardner Murphy puts it, "The Gestaltist insists that the attributes or aspects of the component parts, insofar as they can be defined, are defined by their relations to the system as a whole in which they are functioning." For example, a patch of color in a painting derives its quality from its context—the surrounding picture pattern—rather than from anything inherent in itself.

In perception, organization of a field tends to be as simple and clear as the given conditions allow. A viewer imposes an organization characterized by stability, simplicity, regularity, and symmetry. He groups individual items in a field so they will have pattern. He relates similar items required for completeness, and if present patterns are meaningful he tries to maintain them into the future. Imposing a "good" Gestalt, as happens when the foregoing events occur, is a *psychological* task. It does not necessarily involve any change in the physical environment. Rather, it represents a change in how a viewer *sees* his physical environment. However, problem solving often does require a person to manipulate his physical environment in order to make the various elements fall into proper place for a solution.

Two of Wertheimer's German followers, Wolfgang Köhler (1887—) and Kurt Koffka (1886-1941), were mainly responsible for publicizing Gestalt psychology and establishing it in the United States. Köhler is famous, among other things, for his celebrated study of the learning process in chimpanzees (*The Mentality of Apes*, 1925). He set out to test Thorndike's hypothesis that learning is a matter of trial and error in which correct responses are gradually stamped in. Köhler observed that, in addition to learning which might appear accidental, his apes displayed a type of learning which appeared insightful. Hence, Köhler concluded that Thorndike's laws of learning were inadequate. Koffka's book *Growth of the Mind* (1924) contained a detailed criticism of trial-and-error learning as conceived by Thorndike. Koffka not only criticized Thorndike; his book also was a critique of the major ideas of behaviourism.

Kurt Lewin (1890-1947), also German born, took the spirit of Gestalt theory, added to it some new concepts, and coined a new terminology. He developed a field psychology usually referred to as topological and vector psychology (deriving these terms from the fields of geometry and mechanics). Lewin spent his later years in the United States, where he acquired a considerable following. Because his psychology appears to be the most advanced and systematic field psychology, Chapter 4 is devoted to its expansion especially with reference to learning theory.

As a result of experimentation by the Gestalt-field psychologists, S-R associationists generally are coming to recognize that the earlier atomistic stimulus-response idea, based as it was on the principle of simple reflex arcs, does not explain human behaviour adequately. As previously indicated, there is a tendency among contemporary S-R psychologists to speak of "molar behaviour," i.e., behaviour of the whole organism in contrast to piecemeal, or "molecular," behaviour. Such psychologists characteristically refer to "total responses to patterns of stimulation." However, because these psychologists continue to think in terms of a mechanical linking of stimuli and responses, they are still within the basic pattern of S-R associationism. In spite of their adoption of the concept of molar behaviour, their point of view tends to be fundamentally different from, and incompatible with, that of Gestalt-field psychologists.

WHAT IS THE PHILOSOPHICAL THINKING BEHIND THE TWO FAMILIES?

It is the purpose of this part of the chapter to explore some of the philosophical implications of the two families of psychology. When a contrast is drawn between their underlying philosophical premises, differences between the two families are made much clearer. Although psychologists have tried during the past century to divorce psychology and philosophy, it is doubtful that this is possible. There is no science so "pure" that it lacks philosophical implications. Even physicists find it helpful to make assumptions about the basic nature of their materials and processes; they too become involved in philosophical formulations.

Since any psychological system rests upon a particular conception of human nature, psychology is deeply involved with philosophy from the very start. Of the various positions a person may take on the question of the basic nature of man, we have seen that two—good-active and bad-active—are prescientific in the sense that they render judgments on man's hereditary moral nature. The issue among contemporary psychologists is whether man is an active creature of instincts (as exemplified in Freudian or neo-Freudian psychology), an essentially passive creature in a determining environment (as implied in S-R associationism), or a purposive person interacting with a psychological environment (as implied in Gestalt-field psychology). Each of the two latter positions harmonizes with a broad philosophical outlook: S-R associationism with philosophic *positivism* or *realism*, and Gestalt-field theory with a systematic relativism, also called *pragmatism*, *experimentalism*, or *instrumentalism*.

Realism and S-R Associationism

What is realism? Space permits only the barest treatment. Realists are convinced that the physical world experienced by human beings is real and essentially what it appears to be when observed through the senses. Furthermore, even if there were no human beings around to observe it, it would exist in the same state. Existence is independent of a thing's being known. Realists assume that the physical world is governed by natural laws which operate inexorably and without change. They further assume that a basic principle of the universe is cause and effect; every event is determined by events that have gone before. The universe is a vast mechanism governed by laws which are essentially mechanical in nature.

A realist is likely to assume that there is a kind of hierarchy of the sciences, some being much more objective and reliable than others. He places at the top of the hierarchy physics and chemistry, aided by mathematics. These sciences are regarded as models, which other sciences should emulate. To a consistent realist, nothing should be asserted to be real or meaningful unless, through observation, it can be subjected to objective study, using only publicly verifiable data. If anything exists, it supposedly exists in some amount; if it exists in some amount, it can be measured.

Let us next see how this over-all point of view was transplanted to psychology. Early in human history, people commonly believed in animism, i.e., that all objects, including even rocks, have minds or spirits. Since primitive man had no other way of explaining most types of natural events, animism provided at least some basis for understanding. As people learned more about natural causation, animism declined in popularity. In other words, when human beings came to understand something about gravity, a person no longer needed to attribute a mind and will to a rock to know why it fell on his head.

As time went on, mechanical explanations began to be applied to all sorts of physical events involving nonliving objects. Increasingly the nonliving parts of the universe were believed to consist of atoms in motion, each inert by itself, but subject to the push and pull of lawful forces external to itself.

Living matter, particularly human beings, did not appear to conform to the mechanical concepts applied in the world of nature. Human beings seemed, on the surface at least, to be willful and unpredictable. Thus some kind of mind force was attributed to them. Some persons assumed that all living things have such a nonmaterial life force—a belief referred to as vitalism. Belief in a nonmaterial mind force as applied to human beings (body-mind dualism) led. The idea that learning is a process of disciplining or training minds gave us the classical tradition in education. Although actual teaching under the mind-training approach may appear highly mechanical, the conception of human nature underlying it definitely is nonmechanistic. It assumes a mind substance capable of free will and other spontaneous and "uncaused" behaviour.

All associationist psychologies tend to be mechanistic, in the sense that they describe man and thought in the same physicalistic terms as are used by natural scientists. All four psychologies—apperception, connectionism, behaviourism, and reinforcement began as mechanistic theories of learning. Thus, with their coming there was an accompanying move toward rejection of vitalism or any other conception of life inconsistent with realists' interpretation of the universe. Consequently, with the advent of associationistic psychology, psychologists found themselves in increasing sympathy with the tenets of realistic philosophy.

Mechanistic-realistic psychology was an outgrowth of the attempt by S-R theorists to make psychology as "scientific" as physics. The issue between mechanistic and nonmechanistic psychology is nowhere stated more clearly than by the contemporary neobehaviourist D. O. Hebb. Hebb says flatly that psychology's only hope of remaining scientific is to assume that man is basically a mechanism. He says that there are only two alternatives so far as the basic outlook of a psychologist is concerned—mechanism and vitalism. "*Psychology*," he says, "is the study of the more complex forms of organization in behaviour, and of the processes such as learning, perception or emotion which are involved in the organization. .....*Behaviour* is the publicly observable activity of muscles or glands of external secretion as manifested in movements of parts of the body or in the appearance of tears, sweat, saliva and so forth. The *organization* of behaviour is the pattern or combination, of separate items in relation to each other and to environmental stimulation."

Furthermore, with respect to the type of study which psychologists can undertake, he says, "All one can know about another's feelings and awareness is an inference from what he *does*—from his muscular contractions and glandular secretions." To a psychologist such as Hebb, Gestalt-field psychology would appear to be nothing more than "confusionism." The philosophical orientation of a mechanistic psychologist is so thoroughly realistic that any other outlook seems untenable.

Among S-R theorists, much use is made of the concepts *reflexes, reactions, objective measurement, quantitative data, sequence of behaviour, and reinforcement schedules.* They have used these and similar expressions in an attempt to be rigidly scientific. To them, stimulus and response in psychology are equated with cause and effect in physics.

In his approach to education a realist, and likewise an S-R associationist, is very much an environmentalist and determinist in the sense that he assumes that the surrounding environment should, and inescapably will, control closely the behaviours and learnings of students. Thus, teaching practices advocated by S-R psychologists are closely in tune with the realistic outlook. Such psychologists tend to recommend that subject matter be selected by qualified adults prior to the teaching act, that it reflect facts and skills which are useful in contemporary society, and that it be inculcated into students. There is an implicit assumption that, if a given item of subject matter impinges upon a student, there will be a definite and predictable effect. Only secondary, if any, mention is made of such concepts as *student goals, motives, or problem solving.*

Relativism and Gestalt-Field Psychology

Relativism has emerged during the past 70 or 80 years and is, in a sense, a reaction against the absolutistic ways which have characterized many facets of man's thinking throughout history. Relativism contrasts sharply with realism. The latter is absolutistic in that its exponents assume the existence of an ultimate reality which consists of fixed natural laws and they define truth as that which corresponds to natural law and consequently is unchanging. Relativists do not assert or deny absolute existence. Rather they define *psychological reality* as that which we *make* of what comes to us. They then deal with reality, so defined, in achieving truth and designing behaviour.

Probably the central idea of relativism is that *a thing derives its qualities from its relationship to other things.* A person may look at a patch of grass which is in shadow. Compared with grass in the full rays of the sun, the patch appears dark; but compared with grass at night, it appears light. A homely girl, in the company of girls even more homely, appears pretty. The way we perceive any object or event is colored by the total situation. This principle is actually one with which everyone is familiar. Relativistic philosophy does little more than explore and develop the numerous ramifications and implications of this central idea.

It might appear that if relativism were a valid concept a person could never make a definitive statement about anything, except to say that it "is closer than something else," "is to the left of something else," "is redder than something else," "is smaller than something else."

However, this is not an insurmountable problem. In order to view something relativistically, one simply determines a convenient vantage point—a frame of reference. A man can say that his automobile has 200 horsepower and such an assertion can be quite confident. The unit of measure, one horsepower, is an arbitrary measure—contrived by man and susceptible to future change—but it has definite usefulness as a point of reference. Such relatively fixed points of reference are *relatively absolute*. The word absolute, so used, is an adjective; it means no more than that the point of reference is one of relative fixity or stability.

If one assumes that things have to be dealt with relationally, rather than as things-in-themselves, a distinctive method of defining truth, or knowledge, and an equally distinctive method of arriving at truth are required. A relativist rejects the notion that man is able to find and use final or ultimate truth. Consequently, he has little, if any, interest in "eternal verities." Relativists regard knowledge as insights developed and held by human beings using human methods. As Bayles points out, the development of the notion that knowledge is a matter of human interpretation, and not a literal description of what exists external to man, reflects a shift from a realistic to a relativistic view of science. In physical science, it is no longer commonly said that an atom has certain properties; rather, one says that it *acts as if* it has these properties.

A scientific law (including a principle of psychology) is a statement which seems true to all or most of those who are competent to study the matter. The relativistic test of truth is anticipatory accuracy, not correspondence to ultimate reality. Thus, in a sense, a scientific law is a generalization about which there is considerable agreement among those scientifically competent in its areas; it is a matter of consensus. Its test, however, is not the consensus but its predictive accuracy. Relativists assume that no scientific law is "sacred"; any law may change, and indeed, over the course of time most will. A significant aspect of the thinking of relativists is their expectancy of change. They are much more likely than realists to think of both nature and culture as undergoing continuous modification.

But what grounds does a relativist have for judging anything true? To quote Bayles, an insight is considered true "if, and only if, the deduced behaviour pattern, when tested experientially or experimentally, produces the results which were anticipated." Thus, an insight is true if it proves to be reasonably accurate—if what one supposes will follow from its application actually follows. To put it colloquially, a statement is true if it "pans out." Truth, to a relativist, is not based upon "eternal and universal principles". It is man made, and man will change it as need be. This does not mean that truth is unimportant or ephemeral. It does mean that truth tends to evolve as human experience evolves. It also means that truth sometimes is quite personal and individualistic; what is true for me may not be true for you, even in situations which on the surface look quite similar. However, many relativistic truths are widely agreed upon within groups of various sizes; they are social truths.

Both realists and relativists assume that the most valid method of inquiry is scientific in nature; it is based on testable evidence. But they define scientific method in different ways and, as the foregoing discussion has indicated, seek different ends from it. To a relativist, scientific method is not merely a sequence of steps such as a physicist supposedly uses. Scientific thinking is any form of intellectual pursuit which is based on testable evidence and is productive in relation to the goals of the thinker. To be sure, there are some measuring sticks or criteria of scientific truth; these criteria Bayles has encompassed under the headings of adequacy and harmony. A conclusion, to be properly scientific, must *harmonize* all the data, i.e., it must make the data "jibe," or "add up." If a single pertinent fact seems to "point the other way," if it remains unexplained, then the conclusion is not to be trusted. According to the principle of *adequacy*, all known pertinent facts must be taken into consideration. None may be ignored—no matter how unpalatable it might seem.

A relativist construes science much more broadly than does a realist. He assumes that the scientific way can be applied in a wide range of situations. A relativist does not think in terms of a hierarchy of sciences, with physics, chemistry, and mathematics at the top. He is also more flexible with respect to the kinds of data he will consider. A realist in psychology is likely to admit only data of observable physical objects or substances. Conversely, a relativist in psychology will consider all the data of human experience, including that which may seem introspective.

Why is a relativistic outlook in philosophy in harmony with Gestalt-field psychology? This school of psychology contains strong relativistic elements which naturally align it with relativistic philosophy, as will become clear during our examination of certain aspects of Gestalt-field theory.

Gestalt-field psychology is essentially an emergent synthesis which developed from conflict between the tenets of Roussellian "romantic naturalism" and "scientific realism". As we have seen, Roussellians contend that psychological development is primarily a matter of natural unfoldment. To them, learning is largely equated with unfoldment and is a product of inner urges. It is not imposed by a child's environment. Realistic psychologists see all development as a product of learning and assume that learning comes from the environment; it is conditioning induced by stimuli which impinge upon a child from without.

The only way of bridging the two positions appears to be assume that a child is what he is because of an interaction between him and his culture. With the emphasis upon interaction, the responsibility for development rests neither with the child alone (as Rousseau would have said) nor with the environment alone (as a realist says). It is person and environment coming together—in a psychological field—where Gestalt-field psychologists find the clue to psychological development.

What has this to do with relativism? Since the number of possible culture patterns is infinite, the possibilities for variety in human development become infinite likewise. Within its biological limits, human nature might become anything. Furthermore, if one accepts the premises of Gestalt-field psychology, he must define reality in a manner entirely different from that of a realist. Reality now consists of the *interpretations* a person makes of himself and his surroundings as he interacts. If reality is to be regarded as interpretations or meanings, rather than pre-existent physical objects, as such, it is obvious that reality will be in a constant state of flux. In 1947, Earl C. Kelley published an extraordinarily provocative little book entitled *Education for What Is Real*. By "what is real" Kelley means our *perceptions* of physical and social objects. Kelley's book depicts concisely and sharply many aspects of the issue concerning the definition of reality. Because this issue is of prime importance, the following section explores serval of its facets.

HOW DO THE TWO FAMILIES DEFINE REALITY?

S-R associationists tend to treat reality and existence as identical. The term *existence* refers to what exists or "what is there," i.e., physical objects and processes. The chair on which the reader is sitting may be said to exist, and to an associationist the chair is a good example of reality (not one's impression of the chair, but the chair itself). The chair exists in its own right; the way one perceives it is not relevant to its reality.

Gestalt-field theorists make a distinction between reality and existence. Without denying independent existence of objects, or even of other people's ideas, they insist that each person sizes up or interprets his world in such a way that it will form a meaningful pattern for him, and his interpretation is the reality on which he designs his actions. A Gestalt-field psychologist thinks that a person's knowledge of things is always limited by the impossibility of his ever getting completely "outside himself." He assumes that any perception will be colored to some degree by the purposes and experiences of the observer, as well as by the procedures used in observing the perceived object. None of this should be taken to mean that a person literally makes his world; rather, in any field—science, social relations, morality, even religion—each individual makes, not the world, but his own notions of the world.

In order to understand fully the difference in definitions of reality between the S-R association and the Gestalt-field approaches, it is necessary to explore in some detail the differences between their exponents in their definitions of environment, perception, interaction, and experience. We already have suggested some of these differences. We propose now to dig more deeply. Some repetition of what has been said before is necessary.

How is Environment Defined by the Two Groups of Psychologists?

S-R associationists maintain that a person's psychological and physical environments are identical; his environment consists of all his physical and social surroundings. Because environment is defined in objective, physicalistic terms, presumably anyone can see (or hear, smell, feel, or taste) the environment of anyone else.

In contrast, Gestalt-field psychologists think of a person's environment as psychological, and it consists of what he makes of what is around him. It is that portion of a life space or perceptual field which surrounds a *person* on *self.* A psychological environment includes impressions of parts of the physical environment but not necessarily all of it. It also extends beyond its physical environment. Sometimes a person's psychological environment includes largely memories or anticipations; in this case he is scarcely aware of the physical world currently around him. In Lewin's terminology, he is operating on an "irreality level."

Since each person's perceptual environment is unique, obviously two persons may appear to be in the same location in space and time (or as nearly so as possible) and yet have very different psychological environments. Furthermore, the behaviours of two equally intelligent persons who are confronted with the same "objective facts" may differ drastically because each is different in his purposes and experiential background. Whenever a person has a new experience, he changes his environment and will never again be able to recapture the old environment in its identical form. The Gestalt-field conception of environment explains why in a particular family one son may become a minister and another turn to crime; their interpretations of their world differ radically, even though to an outsider their social and physical environments would appear quite similar.

How do the Two Groups Define Perception?

S-R associationists define perception in such a way as to make it analogous with taking photographs. The sense organs in literal fashion "read" a person's social and physical surroundings and record this "reading" in the nervous system. After sensing something, a person may derive a meaning for it. But note that, according to an associationist, sensation comes prior to meaning and the two acts, sensing and finding meaning, are regarded as separate. An S-R associationist assumes that sensation may be indiscriminate, in that a person tends to "take in" all aspects of the physical world to which his sense organs are sensitive. Such a psychologist defines perception, then, as a two-step process (sensing and deriving meaning) which focuses on particular objects of the environment only insofar as previous conditioning directs.

A Gestalt-field psychologist, on the other hand, does not separate sensation of an object from its meaning. In his view, a person will rarely sense an object unless it has relevance to some purpose of the person. It is this relevance to purpose, this instrumental quality, of an object which constitutes its meaning. Unless a person sees some meaning in an object, he will pay little or no attention to it. Thus, a Gestalt-field psychologist sees perception as a unitary process, in which sensation hinges on meaning and meaning on sensation, and sensing and finding meaning occur simultaneously. Perception, to a field psychologist, is highly selective. It is always related to a person's purposes at the time of perception. In his goal-seeking behaviour, a person actively seeks out those aspects of his environment which will help or hinder him, and usually it is to these that he is primarily sensitive.

Furthermore, to a Gestalt-field psychologist the meaning of a sensation or perception is always related to the total situation. Relationships, and not a summation of individual elements, determine the quality of any event (such as perception). Any psychological event is a result of the interaction of many factors; hence, perception always involves a problem of organization. A thing is perceived as a relationship within a field which includes the thing, the viewer, and a complex background incorporating the viewer's purposes and previous experience. Considering the above notions, it is obvious that to a Gestalt-field theorist the senses do not directly mirror physical objects in their geographical environment. The camera analogy which fits the associationist's idea of perception seems to a field psychologist grass oversimplification.

Is Interaction of Person and Environment Alternating or Simultaneous and Mutual?

The term *interaction* is commonly used in describing the person-environment process through which reality is perceived. Both families of psychology use the term but define it in sharply different ways. Whereas S-R association theorists mean alternating interaction or reaction of organism, then of environment, Gestalt-field psychologists always imply that the interaction of a person and his environment are simultaneous and mutual—both mutually participate at the same time.

Alternating Interaction

Alternating interaction begins with a reaction of a person to a stimulus. The person is regarded as a passive receiver of stimuli; his habitual pose is one of waiting or repose. When he receives a stimulus he reacts in whatever way he must—in accordance with the conditioned or innate reflexes which are called into play. When he reacts, it is likely that he will change his physical or social environment in some way. (The environment is also passive, in the sense that it "waits" for him to do something to it.) To an associationist, the temporal sequence of the interactive process is stimulus-reaction-stimulus-reaction, and so on. The chain of S-R's may continue indefinitely. Consider an example : A dog bites a man; the man kicks the dog. Let us suppose the kick conditions the dog not to bite. The dog is friendly toward the next man he encounters, and the man reacts by patting him on the head. The dog may then react by licking the man's hand. The man may then buy the dog a steak. And so on, ad infinitum.

S-R associationists may think of interaction as involving only physical processes. That is, material objects react to other material objects. Interaction between human being is analogous to the interaction of molecules in a chemical compound. One molecule strikes another, which is deflected against another, which hits another, and so on. The interactive process is regarded as a chain of causes and effects; stimuli are causes and responses are effects.

Simultaneous Mutual Interaction

Interaction, when used by Gestalt-field psychologists, refers to a relationship between a person and his environment in which the person in purposeful fashion tries to see meaning in his environment and use objects in his environment in advantageous ways. As he interprets and uses his environment for his own purposes, both are changed. The person's physical environment may be changed in ways which others may observe; or it may not. In any case, its meaning is changed so that it looks different to the person interacting with it. The person changes in the sense that through interaction he achieves new insights which literally transform him, in however minor ways. Gone from this concept of interaction is the idea of the reaction of a passive organism to a stimulus, and an ensuring chain of S-R's running back and forth from organism to environment. Rather, we now have simultaneous mutual change of person and environment, during which we do not make a sharp distinction between the two. In symbolic terms, this concept is simultaneous mutual interaction—the SMI concept.

Parents and siblings usually constitute important aspects of a child's environment. When a second child arrives in a family, the first child sizes up—perceives—the situation. Whether the first child feels rejected depends not upon the physical stimuli he receives from his parents and the sibling but upon what he makes of the relationship of the parents and the second child. The important question is not Do the parents actually favour child number two? but rather Does child number one "see" child number two as favoured over child number one—himself? In this situation, the parents and the other child are key aspects of each child's and parent's environment. The way child number one perceives the situation has important bearing upon the environments of child number two and the parents. Each person in a situation interacts with the others.

Gestalt-field theorists, in their espousal of the concept of SMI, make a sharp distinction between interaction of physical objects in a physical environment and (the subject of psychology) interaction of psychological realities in a psychological environment. To a field psychologist, it is only what occurs in a person's life space which, at that moment (or a longer unit of time), is important to that person. A person interacts by relating himself (as he understands himself) to his interpretation of what is around him. Of course, while interacting, he may move his body and manipulate objects in his physical environment in ways conspicuous to observers. But psychological interaction and physical reaction are two different processes. A person can interact within a psychological field while he is seated in an armchair in front of a fireplace. Human experience is synonymous with an interactive event. It does not necessarily require any kind of motion which an observer can detect.

Any idea can be ridden too hard, and the reader has probably already thought of cases in which the concept of SMI does not seem to fit. For example, a man who is not aware of danger may be shot in the back. It seems fairly clear that in such a case the man has been a passive victim of a feature of his environment which was active in relation to him. However, all this example suggests is that there are situations in which a person has no control over what happens to him. Gestalt-field psychology and relativistic philosophy do not deny this; instead, they operate on the not inconsistent assumption that, whenever a person can, he seeks to manipulate purposefully all those aspects of his environment which at the time mean anything to him. He may or may not be successful, but whether or not he is, his life space will be different as a result of the attempt.

What is Experience?

Up to this point, we have used the term *experience* without really coming to grips with its meaning. Gestalt-field psychologists regard experience as a pivotal concept in any discussion of the interactive process and the meaning of reality. S-R associationists make little use of the term, especially in connection with any investigation or description which is supposed to be scientific. Most charge that Gestalt-field psychologists use the term *experience* in such a way as to imply a process which does not involve the real physical world but only "mentalistic" copies of it. According to associationists, the concept presupposes a special world of consciousness and, if consciousness does exist, it does not lend itself well to scientific study. An associationist may concede that thought appears to exist, but he is likely to insist that, if human beings are to be studied with true scientific objectivity, most kinds of mentalistic concepts must be ruled out of bounds. The well-known neobehaviourist B. F. Skinner express this notion clearly: "....the private event [i.e., thought or consciousness] is at best no more than a link in a causal chain, and it is usually not even that. We may think before we act in the sense that we may behave covertly before we behave overtly, but our action is not an 'expression' of the covert response [i.e., thought] or the consequence of it. The two are attributable to the same variables."

What Skinner appears to be saying is that, even if a person does think, his thoughts are inconsequential; his actions, whether or not he thinks, will be part of a cause-and-effect, (S-R) sequence which originates and ends outside himself. To Skinner, if thought occurs, it is not a cause of action but rather an irrelevant by-product of stimulation which would have caused the action anyway.

If an S-R associationist were to use the term *experience*, he would have to define it mechanistically. To him, experience could mean no more than the conditioning process by which a person acquires a new response. If a child touches a hot stove and if a link is formed between the sight of a stove and a withdrawal response, then an associationist might say the child has had an experience. No thought needs to have occurred and no insights need to have been developed.

Gestalt-field psychologists use the term *experience* extensively but define it in a way consistent with a relativistic outlook. They regard experience as rooted in insightful behaviour. From this point of view, experience is a psychological event which involves acting purposefully with anticipation of the probable or possible consequences of such action. Experience is interaction of a person and his perceived environment. This is what Dewey means when he says, "An experience is always what it is because of a transaction taking place between an individual and what, *at the time*, constitutes his environment." He states further, in connection with experience and learning, that "To 'learn from experience' is to make a backward and forward connection between what we do to things and what we enjoy or suffer from things in consequence." Experience includes an active and a passive element, combined in a peculiar fashion: "On the active hand, experience is *trying*..... On the passive, it is *under-going*. When we experience something we act upon it, we do something with it; then we suffer or undergo the consequences. We do something to the thing, then it does something to us in return: such is the peculiar combination. The connection of these two phases of experience measures the fruitfulness or value of the experience. More activity does not constitute experience."

The SMI concept implies a continuity of experience. Every experience both extracts something from experience which have gone before and modifies in some way experiences which follow. Furthermore, to some degree every experience influences the conditions under which future experiences may be had. Thus, in the case of a reasonably normal person, successive perceptual fields or life spaces tend to be similar to, though not identical with, one another.

It is easy to see why the Gestalt-field concept of experience is in tune with a relativistic philosophy. If life consist of a series of experiences through which a person and his environment are continuously changing, then it is obvious that we must regard life as constant change with no fixed limits. Furthermore, since perception is considered a creative act, human experience can never lead to discovery and assertion of a fixed, absolutistic truth.

WHAT DOES MOTIVATION MEAN TO EACH FAMILY?

Motivation refers to the "mainsprings" or instigating forces of behaviour; people do what they do because of motivation. As in the case of concepts treated previously in the chapter, S-R associationists and Gestalt-field psychologists hold contrasting and seemingly incompatible ideas about the nature of motivation. These differences go back to the contrasting conceptions of basic human nature held by the two schools of thought. If one views man and the universe mechanistically, he will prefer a theory of motivation compatible with this opinion; if he views man as a purposeful, reflective, and creative individual, he will have a quite different theory of motivation.

What is Motivation to S-R Associationists?

As we have seen, associationists tend to regard man as an intricate machine. Machines operate with blind regularity, according to a set of fixed principles. Even a machine as complicated as an electronic brain does not operate purposefully as we usually use the term. An electronic brain does not know what to do until it has been set by a human being. Even electronic brains which can correct their own errors and do other seemingly fantastic things still behave as they do because some person has designed and regulated them. In a sense, a machine has no more purpose than a falling rock; it acts, but it has no thought-out goal. S-R theorists generally attribute this same quality to human nature.

To an S-R psychologist, all motivation is assumed to rise directly from organic drives or basic emotions or from a tendency to respond established upon prior conditioning of the drives and emotions. Organic drives, such as hunger, thirst, and sexual need, and the emotions, fear, anger, and "love," supposedly produce behaviours which are both predictable and irresistible. The drives and emotions are "built into" the machine and it can do nothing to resist them. Conditioning produces a series of learned reflexes which spring into action whenever relevant stimuli appear. These conditioned responses operate more or less automatically; a person makes them because he must. Through conditioning, the machine, i.e., the body, has been regulated to behave in a predictable manner. To an S-R psychologist, then, all behaviour is stimulus directed, whether the stimulus comes from within the organism or without. Motivation is defined as the urge to act which results from a stimulus. Since behaviour is stimulus directed, it is not related to purpose of any kind.

There are certain obvious aspects of the behaviour of men or lower animals which do not appear to be explained by the mechanical concepts of S-R theory. One of these is attention. At any given time, a person pays attention to one thing rather than another. At this moment, the reader of this book is "attending" to this page rather than to a television programme, a poker game, or a pretty girl. So the fact of attention seems to demonstrate that human behaviour is governed by purpose. S-R theorists concede that a person may often respond selectively to one or a small group of stimuli at a time. However, they argue that what appears to be selective response can be explained according to S-R principles and that the existence of purpose need not be assumed. A person selects one response rather than another, according to an S-R psychologist, because of the articular combination of prior conditioning and present physiological drives and stimuli which are operating at the moment of perception. To an S-R theorist, to introduce purpose as an explanation of motivation is to risk introducing some kind of supernatural guiding force and to make impossible a truly scientific approach to the study of behaviour.

An associationist's theory of motivation has important implications for education. According to his viewpoint, a child does not have to "want" to learn history in order to learn it. He does have to be persuaded to study it, to repeat the verbal responses which we associate with a knowledge of history. Anyone can learn anything of which he is capable if he will only allow himself to be put through the pattern of activity necessary for conditioning to take place. Thus, an associationist does not talk much about such things as "psychological involvement" or "helping students see the point of learning." Instead, he engages students in activity and assumes that activity with reinforcement automatically produces learning. A teacher carefully plans which learnings (responses) he wants students to develop. He then induces these responses and associates them with stimuli.

What is Motivation to Gestalt-Field Theorists?

Within the Gestalt-field frame of reference, behaviour is a function of a total situation, i.e., a person interacting within a field of psychological forces which includes memories, anticipations, purposes, and interpretation of relevant physical objects and events. Motivation cannot be described as merely an impulse to act triggered by a stimulus. Rather, motivation emerges from a dynamic psychological situation, characterized by a person's desire to do something.

A Gestalt-field psychologist regards motivation as a product of dis-equilibrium within a life space. A life space includes goals and often barriers to the achievement of these goals. A goal may be either positive or negative—something one wants to achieve, or something he wants to avoid. When a barrier, i.e., any obstacle to the direct and immediate achievement of a goal, whether physical or psychological, appears, a person feels tension. He tries to relieve tension by surmounting the barrier. The tendency to release tension by proceeding toward a goal, including the overcoming of whatever barriers are in the way, is motivation.

The particular form which motivation takes and its intensity are functions of a field of psychological forces in which no distinction can be made between "inner" and "outer." That is, one cannot identify a category of forces which stems exclusively from physiological drives and another category which stems from the outside environment. Hence, a Gestalt-field psychologist objects to the manner in which an associationist attributes motivation to independently acting organic drives and stimuli which originate wholly from outside an organism.

S-R theorists in the Thorndikean tradition make much of pleasure and pain, or satisfaction and annoyance, as instigators of behaviour. An organism presumably is so put together biologically that it seeks to achieve pleasurable states and to avoid painful ones. Gestalt-field psychologists are more likely to talk about success and failure as motivators, the former being the "reward" for completing an act. Success and failure are not merely achievements as such but represent the relationship between a person's ambitions and his achievements. If he has a certain level of aspiration and is able to achieve this level, he feels good about it. If he attains success at one level of aspiration, he is likely to raise the level, and to continue doing so as long as he is able to perform successfully. Thus, goals tend to be self-set and to change in dynamic fashion with each new experience.

Another feature of the Gestalt-field theory of motivation which sets it apart from S-R theory is the emphasis placed on the present situation. Motivation, to the Gestalt-field theorist, grows out one's contemporary life space—the psychological forces which are operating right then. In contrast, an S-R theorist tends to think of motivation as emerging from an accumulation of historical events, i.e., past conditionings, coupled with currently operating organic drives. An S-R theorist looks backward into a person's life to determine why he behaves as he does now. A Gestalt-field psychologist does not ignore the impact of previous experience on a person's contemporary life space, but in explaining the causes of behaviour he focuses on the present scene as the person experiences it. For these reasons, it is common to think of S-R psychology as embodying a *historical* approach and Gestalt-field psychology as embodying a *situational* approach.

A teacher who accepts the Gestalt-field concept of motivation and a teacher who operates within an S-R framework are likely to approach teaching in fundamentally different ways. For one thing, a teacher with a Gestalt-field orientation is concerned always with the problem of personal involvement, i.e., helping students see a need to learn. The personal goals of students will always be relevant. This does not mean that he will cater to their every whim. Often he will try to help them rethink their goals and discard those which are trivial and whimsical. Much of the time he will attempt to arrange the teaching-learning situation so that students will adopt goals entirely new to them. He will not forget that, unless a child realizes a need to learn something, the child either will not learn it at all or will learn it only in a transitory and functionally useless way.

2

Theory of Learning Process

This chapter continues the analysis begun in Chapter 1 but centers on some of the more technical aspects of the learning theories developed by S-R associationists and Gestalt-field theorists. Some repetition of ideas stated in Chapter 1 is inevitable, but the focus is quite different.

Do animals, including man, learn simply by being conditioned step by step under the tutelage of a teacher or experimenter, or do they learn by surveying their situation and grasping relationship? Let us set up a hypothetical experiment and speculate on how animals will behave. Our subjects will be rats in an elevated maze (see Fig. 2.1). The alleys are formed of strips of wood without sidewalls. They are raised high enough from the floor so that the rats will not jump off. The gate in the maze is made so that the weight of a rat will cause it to lower and permit the rat to run through.

In order to accustom the rats to the maze and to develop in them preferential tendencies with reference to the three possible pathways to food, we give them some preliminary training. We deprive them of food for 24 hours, then place them in the starting box and permit them to find their way to the food box. They are given 10 such trials per day and soon learn (after trying the various paths) to take the shortest, path 1, to the food. We then

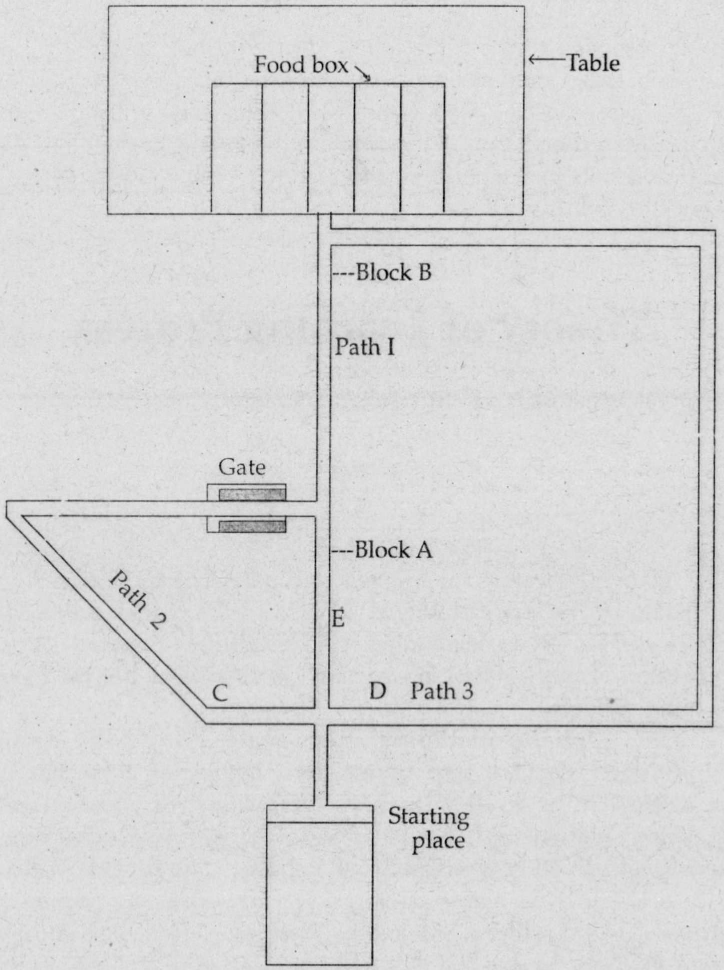

Fig. 2.1 Ground Plan of Elevated Maze Used by Tolman and Hanzik

block path 1 at point A. When this is done, the rats will turn back to the choice point (fork in the road) and almost always (about 93 per cent of the time) take path 2.

Now, what will the rats do when for the first time the block is placed in the common section of paths 1 and 2 (at point B) ? They will return toward the starting place on path 1 and turn at the intersection of the three paths. But will they take path 2 or path 3? Have they sized up the situation and "seen" that the block is on path 2 as well as path 1 ? If so, they will take path 3. On the other hand, if the rats are operating mechanistically they will take the second shortest path to the food, path 2, at least half the time.

We will return to our experiment but first let us consider the significance for man of a learning theory based upon experiments with animals. Such experiments occupy a very important place in modern psychological theory. The chief purpose of studying animal experiments in learning is to give us more effective methods of teaching people.

Do Men Learn Like Other Animals?

Use of results of animal experimentation is governed by the assumptions that the learning process is essentially the same throughout the animal kingdom and that what we discover about animal learning is transferable to human situations. These assumptions would have been thought ridiculous, if not heretical, a few centuries back. Until modern times, philosophers took for granted that there was an unbridgeable gulf between man and the animal kingdom. It was thought that human beings possessed a unique quality: they could reason whereas animals could not. This quality was believed to arise from the existence of a substantive mind; i.e., a mind force, relatively independent of a body, which only man, among the earth's creatures, possesses.

So long as man was considered fundamentally different from other forms of life, animal biology and human psychology remained two sharply separated disciplines. Until a century or so ago, human psychology relied for its source of knowledge solely upon the study of humans—conducted through inspiration, introspection, and intuition, tempered by reason.

There were a few persons of the past who rejected the idea that man and animals are unrelated; of these Rousseau is one of the earliest and most striking. In his book *Emile* (1762) Rousseau strongly implied that a continuity exists between animal and human nature. According to Rousseau's theory of child nature, a human being at birth is a healthy little animal—a creature like other animals of nature.

During the Romantic period (late eighteenth and early nineteenth centuries) many philosophers and literary figures believed that mind permeated the entire universe, including all living things. Furthermore, this universal mind substance was believed to be unitary—everywhere the same. Man possessed more of it than did lower animals, but the difference between human mind and animal mind was one of degree rather than kind. Of course, not all scholars accepted this view. The psychologist Wundt, for example, was convinced that consciousness—a product of mind—was unique to human beings.

It was the work of Darwin and other evolutionists of the nineteenth century that most definitely gave man a place in the animal kingdom. Darwin noticed particularly the close similarity of the bodily structures and functions of man and the lower animals. In his *Descent of Man* he also presented much evidence of the existence of psychological, as well as physical, continuity throughout the animal kingdom. He wrote, "There is no fundamental difference between man and the higher animals in their mental faculties." But in a later section he qualified this opinion by writing, "There can be no doubt that the difference between the mind of the lowest man and that of the highest animal is immense." In spite of the qualification, Darwin appears to have maintained consistently that in their fundamental aspects man and the lower animals exhibit a commonality of both physical and mental characteristics.

Antagonists of the theory of evolution defied Darwin to explain why, if there is a continuity between man and the animal kingdom, man can reason whereas lower animals seem to be governed by instinct rather than reason. Darwin countered with the explanation that much human action, too, is to be interpreted as instinctive in origin and that animals, on their level, exhibit a capacity for reason.

During the latter part of the nineteenth century the idea that there is a continuity among animal species, and that behavioural tendencies, including learning, are broadly similar throughout the animal world, rapidly gained in popularity among biologists and psychologists. Pierre Flourens proposed in the nineteenth century that conclusions drawn from animal experimentation should be equally applicable to man. Pavlov made this assumption also, as did his contemporary, Thorndike, in the United States.

In addition to the cheapness and convenience of using lower animals rather than humans in a psychological laboratory, obviously experiments can be performed on animals which our mores would prevent being tried on people. Furthermore, many persons have felt that it was easier to isolate simple units of behaviour in lower animals than in human beings, although in humans the units may be substantially the same, they are often combined in a manner too complex for ready study. Thus, it was thought that one might learn more about types of behaviour fundamental to the animal kingdom by studying the lower animals than by studying men. For all of these reasons, animal experimentation became extremely popular among psychologists.

In the preceding chapter we describe briefly the general nature of the animal experimentation undertaken by S-R associationists. These psychologists hoped to formulate laws of human learning by observing overt behaviour of laboratory animals placed in various kinds of situations such as puzzle boxes and mazes. By the early 1920s, the manner in which behaviourists conducted their experiments came under the fire of Gestaltists. The nature of the Gestalt criticism is developed in the following section.

Do Other Animals Learn Like Men?

Whereas the behaviourists assumed that men learn like animals, and more specifically like their own experimental animals in their own types of experiment, Gestalt-field psychologists gave the question a reverse twist: Do animals learn like men? Of course, if there is a continuity between man and the lower animals, both ideas should make equal sense and both should be answerable in the affirmative. But Gestalt-field psychologists had something else in mind. While not denying the likelihood of a fundamental similarity in the behaviour of man and other animals, Gestalt-field theorists were interested in raising questions about the whole approach of the behaviourists.

Gestalt-field psychologists noted that behaviourists usually placed their animals in situations entirely foreign to them. There was no place for them to begin a solution and they were permitted a bare minimum of freedom in which to try. Locks, levers, and mechanical devices used were above the animals' level of comprehension. In order for them to achieve the correct procedure it was necessary for them to stumble onto the key by chance. Because lower animals are less discerning of relationships which seem important to men than are human beings, they appear, in a humanly contrived "problem," to make completely random movements. Thus, the nature of their discovery of the relationship between the release mechanism and escaping from a puzzle box, on the surface, appeared to be completely mechanical. Having set the stage against animals displaying genuine problem-solving activity, S-R associationists concluded that learning is a product of a mechanical trial-and-error process.

One of the sharpest criticisms which a Gestalt-field theorist can make of the behaviouristic conception of learning is directed against the tendency of the latter to deny purpose a central role in learning. To a Gestalt-field psychologist, learning always involves purpose. The tension which motivates an animal to learn is tension *toward a goal.* Gestalt-field psychologists feel they have abundant experimental evidence to show that learning is purposive even among animals quite low on the phylogenetic scale.

An animal with purpose does not make random motions—even though it may appear so on the surface. It tries everything at its command, but if the problem is too difficult its trial moves will appear to an observer as random. If one eye of a slug or honeybee is blinded, the animal at first glance appears to go through meaningless motions. However, more careful observation reveals that it is demonstrating something other than mere random response. It assumes a posture which orients its body towards the light source; it flexes its legs on one side and extends them on the other as if it wanted to move in relationship to the light.

Gestalt-field psychologists also criticized experimentation of behaviourists on the ground that it was so arranged that, even if animal learning were insightful, the development of insight would not show. *The real nature of any psychological process can be concealed if the experimenter designs his experiments in line with predetermined conclusions, and this is precisely what the Gestaltists insist S-R associationists are inclined to do.* In an attempt to refute the contention of behaviourists that learning is mechanical—a mere matter of forming the right connections through chance—the Gestaltists designed an entirely different type of animal experiment. Their experiments involved creation of problematic situations which animals might conceivably resolve through development of insight. These situations were geared in difficulty to the presumed potential intelligence of the animals being studied.

Let us now return to the three-path experiment described at the beginning of the chapter. This actually is a classic experiment performed by Tolman and Honzik at the University of California. When the rats backed out of path 1, they did not take path 2 but path 3—the longest path, but the only one now open to the food box. *Of the 15 rats, 14 behaved in this way.* The rats' backing out of path 1 and taking path 3 was an indication of their having "sized up" the situation—of their having developed insight. Using path 3 was a relatively new and creative solution of what, to the rats, was a real problem.

Köhler's famous experiments with chimpanzees further illustrate the Gestalt-field approach to animal experimentation. Kohler spent four years on the island of Tenerife working with chimpanzees. A typical experiment involved suspending food (usually bananas) from the ceiling of a cage and then providing a chimpanzee with a tool or tools with which to knock down or reach for the fruit. The tool might be a pole of adequate length, a pole in sections which had to be joined, or boxes which could be stacked and climbed. Köhler's chimpanzees, rather than gradually acquiring right responses and eliminating wrong ones, seemed at some point in a problem to develop insight into it—to grasp, often rather suddenly, the relationship involved. The chimpanzees seemed to get the idea of "tool use" and to apply it in new situations calling for tool use.

Köhler also experimented with "stupid" chickens and found considerable evidence that even chickens can see relationships and that it is relationship to which they respond rather than specific stimuli. He taught chickens to expect food only from the darker of two papers placed side by side. For the lighter paper he then substituted one even darker than the original dark one. In 70 per cent of the trials the chickens switched their preference from the originally preferred dark paper to the paper which was still darker, suggesting that they had achieved an insight: "If I go to the darker of two surfaces, I will get food." The chickens had "*generalized,*" i.e., sensed the relationship of darker to lighter *as a general principle* in "food getting."

Two American Gestalt psychologists, Raymond Wheeler and Francis Perkins, performed a great deal of animal experimentation in the 1920s and 1930s. Among their most frequently cited experiments was one with goldfish in which the fish received food after responding properly to a configuration of lighting. The fish learned to pick the light of brightest, medium, or dimmest intensity even though the experimenters kept varying the absolute intensity and the serial arrangement of lights. Wheeler and Perkins report numerous other studies made by themselves and others in which animals ordinarily regarded as not very intelligent learned to respond to relationships in an apparently intelligent way.

The question arises, How far down the phylogenetic scale can an investigator go and still observe animals behaving as if they could generalize, i.e., perceive a relationship? To perceive a relationship one must get the feel of how a thing works. At first thought it would seem that to do this an animal must have a certain minimum of sensory and neural equipment—perhaps at least a brain, even if only rudimentary. However, one well-known American biologist, H. S. Jennings, writing in the early 1920s, concluded differently. Jennings spent much time observing the behaviour of protozoa--such as euglenae, paramecia, and amoebae. He found that the actions of protozoa are not only highly variable but also readily modified, and he decided that their behaviour could not be explained merely in terms of simple physiochemical reactions. Jennings thought that insofar as their observable behaviour was revealing, it was as reasonable to infer the presence of conscious behaviour among protozoa as it was among men.

What are we to conclude from all this? One possible conclusion is that an animal experimenter, depending upon his orientation, is likely to arrange his experiment so that animal behaviour appears to be either chancelike and mechanical or insightful. A famous philosopher, Bertrand Russell, noted before the end of the 1920s that psychologists could demonstrate two fundamentally different types of response in their animal experiments, depending entirely on how they arranged the experimental situation. Russell commented humorously: "......Animals studied by Americans rush about frantically, with an incredible display of hustle and pep, and at last achieve the desired result by chance. Animals observed by Germans sit still and think, and at last evolve the solution out of their inner consciousness."

The state of affairs with regard to experimentation with lower animals is probably not as indecisive as Russell's comment would lead one to think. Once a student sets his orientation in either an S-R associationistic or a Gestalt-field point of view, he benefits by the broadest possible knowledge of all available experimental, as well as other, evidence. However, a student's psychological orientation will largely determine how results of each experiment contribute to his interpretation of human learning.

Behaviourists have clearly shown that animals can be put in experimental situations where they demonstrate overt behaviour which seems trial-and-error, chancelike, blind, and mechanical. There seems to be little question but that human experimental subjects could be put in situations which would cause them to appear to demonstrate the same kind of behaviour. The requirement of such experiments seems only to be that the problem presented the learner is one with which his previous experience has in no way equipped him to cope.

On the other hand, the Gestalt-field group of psychologists have demonstrated adequately the one point they wanted to make, namely, that whether one is dealing with the lower animals or man, situations can be arranged in which learning shows an "Aha?" quality. That is, an experimental subject, in learning something, seems to "catch the point" or get the feel of a confronting situation. If man and the lower animals do seem the learn insightfully in situations which permit it, then serious doubt is cast upon the validity of the behaviourist notion that learning is purposeless, mechanical, and chancelike.

Gestalt-field psychologists insist that to describe learning throughout the animal kingdom we do well to begin with human examples. As we examine conscious behaviour of ourselves or others, learning often—and perhaps always—appears to be a matter of *seeing through things, of gaining understanding.* If we start with the assumption that other animals learn in the same way, we devise experiments which will enable them to reveal such learning

This does not mean that if we are studying, a dog, we dare anthropomorphize him, i.e., attribute to him human characteristics; it does mean that we must guard against mechanizing him, i.e., making a machine of him. The way to study a dog is to "dogize" him, just as in studying a child we should "childize" him. In short, we must consider each animal as well as each human being on its own level. If we always keep this in mind, we can probably make some generalized statements about learning which will hold true with respect to most or even all forms of animal life.

WHAT ARE THE TWO MAJOR CONTEMPORARY VERSIONS OF THE NATURE OF LEARNING?

In Chapter 1, we open discussion of the two major contemporary versions of the nature of learning. We now treat in detail these two currently competing descriptions of learning. As already noted, neobehaviourists conceive of learning as *conditioning* or *reinforcement;* Gestalt-field psychologists think of it as *development of insight.*

Is Learning Conditioning—Reinforcement?

Neobehaviourists use *conditioning* or *reinforcement* to describe the learning process as they understand and interpret it. *Conditioning* is so called because it results in formation of conditioned responses. A conditioned response is a response which is associated with or evoked by a new—conditioned—stimulus. Conditioning implies a principle of adhesion, one stimulus or response is attached to another stimulus or response so that revival of the first evokes the second.

Reinforcement is a special kind or aspect of conditioning within which the tendency for a stimulus to evoke a response on subsequent occasions is increased by reduction of a need or a drive stimulus. A need or drive stimulus, in a sense, occurs between the stimulus and the response with which it is associated. A *need,* as used here, is an objective requirement of an organism. A *drive stimulus* is an aroused state of an organism. It is related to the need which sets the organism into action, and may be defined as a strong, persistent stimulus which demands an adjustive response.

The ultimate goal of neobehaviourists is to reduce learning to physio-chemical factors. Learning consists of impressions of new reaction patterns on a pliable, passive organism. Since learning arises in some way from an interplay of organisms and their environment, key concepts of neobehaviourists are *stimulus* (that which is provided by an environment) and *response* (that reaction which is made or given by an organism). Consequently, the problem of the nature of the learning process centres in the relationships of respective stimuli and responses and what occurs between them.

Three representative neobehaviourisms are Edwin Guthrie's *Contiguous Conditioning*, Clark L. Hull's *Deductive Behaviourism or Reinforcement Theory*, and B. F. Skinner's *Operant Conditioning*. These are alike in their emphasis upon a mechanical treatment of stimuli and responses. They agree that at no time is purposiveness to be assumed. Problems of "purposes" must be explained by natural laws or principles whereby organisms mechanically develop "purposes". However, they differ in their interpretations of stimulus-response relationships in learning procedures. Guthrie is convinced that learning occurs when a stimulus and a response happen simultaneously; Hull centered the essence of learning in what occurs between the stimulus and the response; and Skinner places his emphasis upon the stimulus which follows a response. When we express these relationships symbolically, using S for stimulus, R for response, and O for organism, Guthrie holds to an S-R, Hull to an S-O-R, and Skinner, to an R-S learning theory.

Whereas Guthrie's learning theory is conditioning but not reinforcement, Hull's and Skinner's are both conditioning and reinforcement—but of different kinds. Hull called his system deductive because in developing it he, like Newton in physics, deduced or derived a large number of secondary principles of observable phenomena from a small number of primary principles.

Neobehaviourists in education tend not to adhere rigidly to any one of the S-R patterns but to intermix them in applying psychology to teaching procedures. In this way they attempt to achieve an integration of the earlier works of Pavlov, Watson, and Thorndike with that of contemporary S-R associationists. Let us examine very briefly each S-R associationistic theory of learning and see how it would color teaching procedures in a school learning situation.

Guthrie's Contiguous Conditioning

Guthrie's learning theory is conditioning but not reinforcement. Furthermore, it is a special kind of conditioning which we may identify as *simultaneous contiguous conditioning*. *Contiguity* means that stimuli acting *at the time* of a response, on their recurrence, tend to evoke that response. Furthermore, if a stimulus occurs contiguously with a response, the response to that stimulus will continue to occur with it until some other response becomes conditioned to that stimulus.

Strengthening of individual connections of stimuli and response—the actual conditioning—supposedly takes place with a single simultaneous occurrence of a stimulus and response. This does not mean that repetition has no place in learning, but that within repetition an increasing number of stimuli are made into conditioners; there is no strengthening of individual connections, but there is enlistment of more.

Guthrie reasons that, since association can occur with one connection and last for life, there is no need for anything like reward, pleasure, or need reduction to explain learning. Thus, there is no place for reinforcement in contiguity theory. To Guthrie, scientific laws deal with observable phenomena only. In psychology these are physical stimuli, and responses in the form of contractions of muscles and secretions of glands, but there is no place for hypothetical intervening variables between stimuli and responses.

A proponent of contiguous conditioning, in teaching people first gets them to perform in a certain way, then while they are doing so gives them the stimuli which he wants associated with that behaviour. To teach that man is *Homo sapiens*, a Guthriean would induce his student to say *Homo sapiens* and while he was saying it stimulate him with *man* either spelled out, pictured, or both. The more "man" stimuli he could give the student while he was saying *Homo sapiens* the better it would be. In this teaching-learning process *man* is the conditioned stimulus and *Homo sapiens* is the conditioned response.

Hull's Reinforcement Theory

Hull's learning theory also is stimulus-response conditioning, but of a special kind, called *reinforcement*. In presenting his theory of learning Hull stated, "Whenever a reaction (R) takes place in temporal contiguity with an afferent receptor impulse (s) resulting from the impact upon a receptor of a stimulus energy (S), and this conjunction is followed closely by the diminution in a need (and the associated diminution in the drive, D, and in the drive receptor discharge, s_D, there will result an increment $\Delta (S \rightarrow R)$, in the tendency for that stimulus on subsequent occasions to evoke that reaction."

Within Hullian reinforcement, the stimulus and the response are not simultaneous; the stimulus precedes the response. Furthermore, learning does not take place with a single trial; it is stamped in through a process of repeated need or drive stimulus reductions.

Hull thought that learning occurs through biological adaptation of an organism to its environment in a way to promote survival. A state of need means that survival of the organism is not being adequately served. Drive is a general condition of organic privation arising from lack of food, water, or air, from unhealthful temperatures, from tissue injury, from sex-linked conditions, or from other deficiencies. When needs or drive stimuli develop, the organism acts and the action brings reduction in needs or drive stimuli. Actions—responses—which lead to reduction of needs or drive stimuli are *reinforced;* thus reinforcement is centered in adaptation for survival. However, in life situations there are many reinforcers which do not contribute directly to biological adaptation of an organism. Through *higher-order conditioning* many things and actions come to have value and can serve as reinforces. Higher-order conditioning is conditioning based upon previous conditioning.

A child is conditioned to think—say to himself "man" when he sees a man or a picture of a man. This conditioning could have been based upon reduction of drive stimuli. Perhaps he wanted a piece of candy and his parents withheld it from him until he said "man". Now, in ninth grade, "stimulus man" evokes *Homo sapiens*, perhaps through the satisfaction of curiosity, and curiosity is a product of higher-order conditioning; the youth previously had been conditioned to be curious.

Skinner's Operant Conditioning

The unique feature of operant conditioning is that the reinforcing stimulus occurs not simultaneously with or preceding the response but following the response. In operant conditioning, an organism must first make the desired response and then a "reward" is provided. The reward reinforces the response, i.e., makes it more likely to recur. The *response is instrumental* in bringing about its reinforcement. The essence of learning is not stimulus substitution but response modification. In learning, there is a *feedback* from the reinforcing stimulus to the previous response. To illustrate, in the training of pets a desired response is reinforced after it occurs—a dog is fed after it "speaks," and this increases the likelihood of its "speaking" in the future.

Note that in operant conditioning the stimulus which produced the response in the first place is not in any way involved in the learning process. The original response is a result of a stimulus, but the nature of this stimulation is irrelevant to operant conditioning. It is only necessary that some—any—stimulus elicit the response for operant conditioning to function. Emphasis is on reinforcing agents, not on original causative factors.

An operant-reinforcement approach to teaching a ninth-grader that man is *Homo sapiens* would be to show the student *man* along with several other more complicated words, one of which is *Homo sapiens.* If the student chooses *non sequitur* or any expression other than *Homo sapiens,* nothing happens. If he chooses *Homo sapiens,* the teacher says "wonderful." This is reinforcement and they proceed to a new "problem."

Within neobehaviourism, learning is nonpurposive habit formation. Habits are formed through conditioning, which attaches desired responses to specific stimuli. A stimulus triggers an action or response, which can take only one form because of the nature of the stimulus, the condition of the organism, and the "laws of learning" involved. Teachers who adopt this mechanistic approach to learning decide specifically what behaviours they want their students, when finished products, to manifest, and they proceed to stimulate them in such a way as to evoke and fix those behaviours.

Is Learning Development of Insight?

The key word of Gestalt-field psychologists in describing learning is *insight*. They regard learning as a process of developing new insights or modifying old ones. Insights occur when an individual, an pursuing his purposes, sees new ways of utilizing elements of his environment, including his own bodily structure. The noun *learning* connotes the new insights—or meanings—which are acquired.

Gestalt-field theorists attack two weaknesses in the theory that learning is conditioning:

(1) The attempt of S-R associationists to explain complex interrelated organizations in terms of simpler elements, i.e., to insist that learning consists of an accumulation of individual conditioned responses, each relatively simple in itself, but eventuating in a complicated pattern of habits; and

(2) the tendency of S-R associationists to attribute learning to reduction of basic organic drives.

Gestalt-field psychologists view learning as a purposive, explorative, imaginative, and creative enterprise. This conception breaks completely with the idea that learning consists of linking one thing to another according to certain principles of association. Instead, the learning process is linked with thought or conceptualization; it is a nonmechanical development or change of insight.

S-R associationists also sometimes use the term *insight*, but when they do they mean something quite different from what a Gestalt-field theorist means. When used by associationists, the term describes a special and rare kind of learning. To use Woodworth's definition, insight is ".... some penetration into the [absolutely] true nature of things." But to Woodworth and other associationists, the ordinary form which learning takes is conditioning. The most systematic of the associationists would deny that there can be two entirely different kinds of learning; therefore they prefer to describe *all* learning as conditioning. Since insight obviously implies something very different from conditioning, many associationists do not use the term at all. To them it connotes something intuitive and mystical, something which cannot be described operationally. In contrast, Gestalt-field psychologists do not like to use the term *conditioning*; they regard *development of insight* as the most descriptive phrase available to describe the manner in which learning actually takes place.

The Gestalt-field definition of insight is a sense of , or feeling for, pattern or relationships. To state it differently, insight is the "sensed way through" or "solution" of a problematic situation. Insight often first appear as vague "hunches". We might say that an insights is a kind of "feel" we get about a situation which permits us to continue actively serving our purposes, or trying to. When are insights verbalized? Perhaps at once, perhaps never. We probably know many things which we never manage to put into words. This is a problem on which animal experimentation sheds some light. Animals below man cannot talk; they can communicate, but not by putting sounds together in coherent subject-predicate sentences. Yet the evidence indicates beyond much doubt that they learn insightfully when confronted with what to them are problems.

If we define *hypothesis* broadly, we may refer to insights as hypotheses. However, a hypothesis usually is defined as a special kind of verbalized insight. It is a statement which takes the form of a declarative sentence, or in many cases an "if-then" sentence. For example, one might say, "Most redheaded girls have violent tempers" (a declarative statement), or one might say, "If most redheaded girls reach a certain frustration level, they then display a violent temper" (an if-then statement). Hypotheses, defined as verbal statements, are the only kind of insight which we can test in a strictly scientific fashion.

This brings us to a crucial question: Are insights necessarily true? Gestalt-field psychologists do not use the term *insights* in a way to imply that they are necessarily true. Granted, the term sometimes is used this way by others—for example, by Woodworth in the above quotation. But the relativistic orientation of Gestalt-field theorists necessarily leads them to think of insights as trial answers which may or may not help a person toward his goal; they may or may not be true. Truth, relativistically defined, "is that quality of an insight which enables its possessor to design behaviour which is successful in that it achieves what it is designed to achieve." Insights derive from a person's best interpretations of what comes to him; they may be deeply discerning or they may not. They may serve as dependable guides for action or they may prove ruinous. Sultan, one of Köhler's chimpanzees, held a box in the air beneath a hanging banana. He then suddenly released his hold on the box and attempted to jump on it to reach the food. Sultan had an insight, but not a true one.

Insights are to be considered, not as literal descriptions of objective physical-social situations, but as interpretations of one's perceived environment on the basis of which subsequent action can be designed. Although insights are not physicalistic descriptions of objects or processes in the environment, they necessarily take account of the physical environment. Their usability depends in part on how well this is done. Insights may misinterpret a physical environment so badly that they are useless as rules of action, in which case they are to be regarded as false.

It is important to understand that insights are always a learner's own. It is true, of course, that they may become his own through adoption. An insight is usable to a learner only if he can "fit it in." He must understand its significance—for him. A teacher cannot give an insight to a student as we serve a person meat on a platter. He may acquaint students with his insights, but they do not become insights for students until students see their meaning for themselves and adopt them as their own.

One objection frequently raised to the Gestalt-field tendency to construe all learning as insightful is that some learning tasks are performed successfully without apparent development of insight—as, for example, when a child memorizes the multiplication tables. A field psychologist concedes that some learning appears highly mechanical, but he goes on to say that it is not necessarily as mechanical as it appears. He argues that even though a child may repeat the multiplication tables until he appears to have memorized them by rote, what the child actually has done is to get the feel of some pattern which is present in the tables. The pattern may lie in the relationship of numbers or perhaps merely in the order in which the student placed the numbers to "memorize" them.

Insight does not imply that for a person to learn something he must understand all aspects of its use. Any degree of "feel for a pattern" is sufficient to constitute insightful learning. For example, in learning to extract the square root of a number, one might develop insight as to *why* the method works. Or the insight gained might be much more superficial; it might be merely a "feel" for the method—the pattern of steps—with no real understanding of the basic algebraic formula $(x+y)^2 = x^2+2xy+y^2$.

Some Examples of Insightful Learning

Before he can become a sharpshooter, a rifleman must get a "feel" for his rifle. Often a Tennessee squirrel hunter was slow in learning to be an army rifleman. He had an excellent feel for his squirrel gun, but a squirrel gun was not an army rifle. In his army training he had to change old insights as well as develop new ones. On his squirrel gun his sights were fixed immovably to the barrel. To hit a squirrel he had to take wind and distance into consideration and move the rifle away from a line on the target (windward and upward) to give "Tennessee windage" and "Kentucky elevation." He had developed insights to the point that he could behave intelligently without thinking; he could aim his gun and pull the trigger while giving very little attention to what he was doing.

Since his army rifle had movable sights which, prior to aiming, were to be adjusted to allow for windage and elevation, he was supposed to set his sights and then line them directly on his target. But under pressure of target practice he used his new insights to adjusts his sights correctly, then when he began to fire he gave his rifle Tennessee windage and Kentucky elevation. In army terminology he got a "Maggie"—he missed the target completely. He had used two sets of incompatible insights. He could learn to shoot his army rifle accurately only by getting complete feel for his army rifle and leaving most of his squirrel-gun-aiming insights out of the picture.

What is the answer to $\sqrt{(\text{dog})^2} = ?$ How did you know it was "dog"? Had you ever before worked with square root and dog at the same time? If you knew the answer was "dog," you had an insight into the problem. Perhaps you had never put the insight into words, but you knew that $\sqrt{x^2} = x$ and $\sqrt{4^2} = 4\cdot$ Your insight, when verbalized, would run something like, "The square root of anything squared is that thing". Conversely, you may have "learned"—memorized—"The square root of a quantity squared is that quantity" and still not know the answer to $\sqrt{(\text{dog})^2} = ?$

How would students study spelling so as to develop insight? Teaching for insight has definite implication for methods in spelling. Groups or families of words might be studied in such a way that students develop feeling for a certain spelling pattern. Once a pattern is discovered other words will be sought which conform to it. *Cat, fat, and bat* are "at" words. Now what about *hat, mat, pat, rat,* and *sat*? As students, working cooperatively with their teacher, find other word families, they soon will encounter words which apparently should, but do not, fit a certain family—they find some limitations to an insight. They then seek other words with the same divergence from the "rule" and make a family of them. Or in case there is only one divergent word, they think of it as an exception. As the insights into patterns of spelling are put into words, a class can formulate rules. But now rules will be verbalizations of students' insight as contrasted with meaningless statements memorized at the beginning of study.

Insight and Generalization

Often when an insight is first "caught" it applies to a single case. Even so, a person is likely to assume that the insight may work in similar situations. Suppose, for example, that, after studying a particular situation, we hypothesize, "Mary became a shoplifter because she felt unwanted by her parents." The natural next step is to think, "Boys and girls who feel unwanted at home tend to become thieves." Of course, this generalization is only *suggested*. It is not *warranted* by evidence from a single case. Before generalizations become reliable it is usually necessary that they rest on a number of specific insights, all suggesting the same conclusion. In short, dependable generalizations are usually products of considerable experience. Further, they are prone to change in the course of experience, evolving continuously in the direction of greater usefulness as tools of thought.

A tested generalization is assumed to be valid in any future situation similar to the situations in which it was tested. Tested generalizations have the character of *rules, principles,* or *laws.* Syntactically, generalizations are frequently if-then statements: If we take a given action, then the probability is high that a given consequence will follow. We exphasize that tested generalizations should be regarded as *probabilities.* Although, to behave with foresight, we must assume that our generalizations have predictive value, the predictions are to some degree always based on faith.

As suggested earlier, if-then statements usually also may be expressed in present-tense declarative sentences. For example, when a person says, "An increase in the quantity of money is likely to produce a rise in prices," he may mean exactly the same as if he said, "If the quantity of money in circulation is increased, then prices are likely to rise." In using generalizations as hypotheses in scientific procedure, the if-then form often is preferable. It is more likely than is a simple declarative sentence to suggest operations to be performed, and therefore throw emphasis upon experimental tests.

WHAT IS THE RELATIONSHIP OF BEHAVIOUR TO LEARNING?

Behaviouristically defined, "*Behaviour* is the publicly observable activity of muscles or glands of external secretion as manifested in movements of parts of the body or in the appearance of tears, sweat, saliva and so forth." Gestalt-field psychology gives *behaviour* a quite different meaning. It is any change in a person, his perceived environment, or the relation between the two which is subject to *psychological* principles or laws. Psychological behaviour involves purpose and intelligence; hence it is not correlated with physical movement. From a Gestalt-field point of view, psychological behaviour is not directly observable; it must be inferred.

Learning and change in observable behaviour usually occur side by side and obviously are interrelated in some way. Accordingly, S-R associationists contend that any change of behaviour is learning and conversely that learning is a change of behaviour. Thus, the current practice among many educators of defining learning as "change in behaviour" usually reflects an associationist psychology.

Gestalt-field theorists counter that S-R associationists err in making synonymous the observable results of learning and the learning itself. They argue that a change in physiological behaviour does not necessarily mean that learning has occurred. A person who is struck from behind and knocked down may gain from this experience a healthy respect for dark alleys, but the change in behaviour—falling down—is not equivalent to change in insight. Furthermore, a person may use insights he has had for some time as a basis for change in his present behaviour. An author may know that too much coffee is not good for him but persist in drinking coffee until he completes a manuscript and then reduce the amount of coffee he drinks. Probably many changes in the behaviour of school children do not reflect change of insight, or at least not the kind of change which the teacher assumes. Johnny may start saying "please" and "thank you" without an insightful grasp of the implications. He may labour hours every night over homework without having his work produce any change of mind about matters embraced in the homework itself. (Of course, the assignments may cause changes in his attitudes toward teachers and school.)

Gestalt-field psychologists maintain that not only may change in behaviour occur without learning, but also learning may occur without observable changes in behaviour. This is true in any of innumerable situations. There may be no opportunity or occasion for a change in behaviour, as when a person decides it would be nice to give more to charity but doesn't have the money to do so. Now insights may fail to change a person's behaviour if they are competing with old insights which have a stronger hold. Thus one may decide that racial discrimination is bad but continue to practice it. In summary, when a person learns, his behaviour usually changes; but it does not follow that for learning to take place a change in observable behaviour must take place at the same time, or that from a change in overt behaviour we can always accurately infer the full nature of the insight behind it.

Many people with a behaviouristic orientation think that doing something a number of times will necessarily affect future behaviour. Thus, if one smokes a pack of cigarettes a day for a few weeks he is likely to become a habitual smoker. Gestalt-field theorists deny that this is the case. Doing a thing once or may times will affect subsequent behaviour only in the degree to which doing it gives the doer a feeling for the act or insight into the consequences of its performance. It is the thought process, not the action, which is crucial. For this reason, Gestalt-field psychologists emphasize experience rather than behaviour, with experience defined as *an interactive event in which a person comes to see and feel the consequences of a given course of action, through acting and seeing what happens.*

The emphasis of S-R associationists upon overt behaviour has led to school practices designed to produce a desired kind of behaviour and to methods of evaluation which measures overt behaviour—and nothing else. Teachers, or other school authorities, decide which specific behaviours they want students to display. They then stimulate the students in such way as to evoke the desired behaviours. The success of the process is judged by how dependably the behaviour can be invoked in the future (usually on tests). Field psychologists protest this approach to education; they argue that a student may learn little more from it than the insights he gains about teachers and schools and about how to play the memory-work game successfully.

WHAT IS THE RELATION BETWEEN LEARNING AND THINKING?

Much is said about the importance of "teaching students to think". This is one objective of education on which people of all shades of opinion *seem* to agree. Agreement ceases when "thinking" must be defined and the methods for promoting thinking specified.

Should students be required to think as part of their activity in school? One group of educators seems to feel that school should prepare students to think, but that during the period of preparation thinking is not necessary. These people usually argue that the purpose of education is to give students background—the factual equipment with which to think at some later time. Proponents of this position often do not make themselves clear as to when thinking should start. Apparently some of them feel that thinking should not begin before the age of 21.

There are others who seem to feel that it is good for students to think part of the time while in school but not all of the time. They often associate thinking with certain courses, like higher mathematics. People of this persuasion may classify courses into two categories: background "fact courses" and courses in which students need to think. The former are usually considered just as important as the latter.

Probably most people who feel that learning may consist of the thoughtless acquisition of facts or skills are oriented in the direction either of mental disciplines or of S-R associationism.

Gestalt-field psychologists feel that learning and thought are closely allied; one does not occur without the other. Change of insight is invariably accompanied by thought of some kind; and thought of any kind invariably produces some change of insight, however small. Since thought occupies a crucial place in the learning theory of Gestalt-field psychologists, we treat this subject in considerable detail.

What is Thinking?

Broadly defined, thinking is verbalized or unverbalized behaviour which is related in some way to the pursuit of goals. But there is a level of conscious behaviour which can scarcely be called thinking. This is reverie—fanciful musing or daydreaming. It is a more or less undirected association of ideas. Whenever a problem arises, reverie is supplanted by directed or pointed thinking.

Thinking, in its usual sense, is goal-related problem solving. It is an attempt to work through an obstacle in order to find the means to achieve an end. For purposes of analysis, we may distinguish two levels of problem solving. Any line drawn between them is necessarily arbitrary. One level may be termed *simple problem solving*. Simple problem solving does not involve weighty decisions. Examples of problems on this level are expressed in the following questions: Shall I wear a red or green tie today? Shall I have eggs or cereal for breakfast? Shall I drive or walk to work? Shall I spend the evening reading a book or watching a motion picture? We usually solve these problems without lengthy deliberation. Our anxiety level remains low. Once we have made a decision, we are unlikely to worry about it later.

The other level of thinking may be termed *complex problem solving*. It is on this level that we face a problem which is not so easy to settle—that is, unless we decide to ignore it. Complex problem solving usually requires more effort and time and is accompanied by a higher anxiety level. Such problem solving requires us to develop major new insights, or, in layman's language, to undergo a "change of mind". The distinguishing characteristic of this level of problem solving is that each problem presents us with something new. Although many elements of the problem may be familiar, some will be unfamiliar. Each act of complex problem solving requires some degree of originality or creativity. Examples of problems on this level are suggested by questions such as: Shall I encourage my son to go to college? Shall I seek a divorce? Shall I change my registration from Democrat to Republican? Shall I switch my church affiliation? Of course, not all complex problem solving involves questions as weighty as these. Deciding which insecticide to use or which service station to patronize might also require complex problem solving.

What Forms Does Problem Solving Take?

Since simple problem solving pretty well takes care of itself, we shall concern ourselves here with the more complex variety. Problem solving, whether simple or complex, takes various forms. There is more than one route by which we may secure answers to our questions. Not all routes are equally effective, and some which work—in the sense that they lead to answers—are undesirable because their answers are not dependable. Let us consider first some of the roads to truth which often produce unreliable results.

Deductive Reason

The terms *reason* and *thinking* often are used interchangeably. Historically, reason has meant something other than reflection, as we now commonly define reflection. Reasoning has been defined as the process of deducing conclusions from given premises. It involves logic alone. In contrast, reflection includes not only logical processes but also the gathering of evidence—empirical or factual data. Reflection combines deduction and induction, whereas deductive reason confines itself to the former.

What is wrong with deductive reason? A conclusion based on reasoning alone can never be any better than the premises from which the reasoning began. If the premises are false, the conclusion will be false—unless through invalid reasoning one reaches a right conclusion from wrong premises. Historically, those who have placed heavy reliance upon reason usually have disdained the careful experimentation and observation which would have been necessary to test the truth of their premises.

The formal use of reason as a road to truth dates back to early Greek civilization. Aristotle originated the classical laws of logic and invented the syllogism as a purported reasoning device. A number of modern writers feel that many of the problems which beset Western civilization are a result of the Aristotelian tradition. Central to this tradition are these propositions:

1. A is A.
2. Everything but A is non-A.
3. Nothing is both A and non-A.

Reasoning which starts from these "laws" has an either-or quality. Either-or reasoning (sometimes called two-valued orientation) occurs when we are able to see only two choices in a complex situation. It causes us to see the world and ourselves only in terms of black and white. One may wonder, for example, if his life has been a success. He can always find some evidence that it has and some evidence that it has not. Either-or reasoning is likely to keep him from seeing that his life has been both a success and a failure. Instead, he is compelled to conclude that it has been *either* a success or a failure.

Common Sense

As we use the term here, *Common-sense* thinking is based purely upon sensory data, particularly of a superficial or limited sort. It stops short of seeking deep and complex relationships and confines itself to the way things appear upon cursory examination. It is common sense, for example, to believe that the earth is flat and that the sun revolves around the earth. This is the way it *looks* upon mere inspection.

Common-sense thinking often reflects the fallacy of *post hoc, ergo proper hoc* ("after this, therefore on account of it"). Events are given a cause-effect interpretation simply because they are consecutive. For example, a swimming pool is opened to all races. A riot takes place. It would be common sense to conclude that the second event was caused by the first. But this conclusion is not dependable because there may have been present some other causal factor not evident upon casual observation.

It would require many volumes to catalogue all the mistaken beliefs of the past which have seemed a matter of common sense to those who held them. The early common-sense beliefs is alchemy, magic and witchcraft may seem crude and indefensible today, but many of our present-day common-sense beliefs are probably based on just as little evidence.

Intuition

For answers to some problems it has been recommended that we rely upon intuition. Women are supposed to have a well-developed capacity for intuition and men are supposed to be frequent victims of it. What people mean by intuition is not always clear. In this book an intuitive judgment refers to a hypothesis based upon personal convictions; any evidence which supports it is hidden and vague even to the person who states the hypothesis.

What is wrong with intuition? One thing wrong is that no one can describe in objective terms what happens during an act of intuition and there is no way to verify its reliability. Intuitive thought does not make use of publicly verifiable data, runs no tests on its hypotheses, and totally ignores the fact that its assumptions may be false (or debatable). A common feature of intuitive thinking is that the claim that one has been intuitive often occurs *after* the event about which intuitive judgement was rendered. A man who breaks his leg one afternoon may report the next day that on the morning before the accident he had had a premonition of impending disaster. It may be that intuitive judgements which turn out to be true are merely good guesses; the bad guesses are conveniently forgotten.

In spite of the difficulties which intuition presents, we should not rule it out of court summarily. A hunch without any evident basis may be a highly productive starting point. Intuition may be, as Stuart Chase suggests, a "loose term for a half-conscious blend of many minute observations." These "half-conscious observations" may be very good observations, even though not susceptible to verbalization. Intuitive thinking may be a worthwhile source of hypotheses. Our only mistake is in taking them authoritatively as if they were established truth.

Appeal to Authority

We appeal to authority when, rather than thinking a matter through ourselves, we accept without question an answer supplied by someone else. Reliance on authority is legitimate and necessary provided the authorities on whose opinions we rely have themselves used dependable methods in arriving at their opinions. If there is reason to suspect that an authority has used any of the more questionable roads to truth described herein, we should take his word with several grains of salt. In any case, it is always well to be critical of conclusions which we take ready-made from others.

The most common source of authority in public school is, of course, textbooks. Many students regard the utterances of textbook writers as ultimate truth, which is hardly surprising in view of our tendency to elevate textbooks to a central position in our educational system. Second to textbooks, students often consider their teachers authorities and take at face value most of what teachers say.

Often an appeal to authority attempts to uncover the dictates of natural law or some divine or supernatural power which exists above and beyond human experience. An excellent example of how a decision of major importance may stem from this kind of reliance on authority comes from the administration of President William McKinley. Of McKinley's method of solving the problem of whether to seize the Philippines, Charles and Mary Beard say:

> The intellectual and moral methods by which he resolved his perplexity the President later explained............."I walked the floor of the White House night after night," he said, "and I am not ashamed to tell you, gentlemen, that I went down on my knees and prayed Almighty God for light and guidance

> more than one night. And one night late it come to me in this way—I don't know how it was, but it came—.......There was nothing left for us to do but take them all, and to educate the Filipinos, and uplift and civilize and Christianize them...."

Rationalization

Rationalization is the attempt to defend a cherished belief by a largely unrecognized slanting of evidence. Rationalization may make use of well-established facts, but it neglects some of the facts which are both available and pertinent. Rationalization is inventing "good reasons" for what we are already determined to believe. As we shall soon see, scientific reflection differs fundamentally from rationalization. But teachers who say they want their students to think often mean rationalize rather than reflect. Many teachers prize thinking only if there is some advance guarantee that thinkers will not reach unorthodox conclusions about touchy issues.

We find much rationalization in textbooks. Nor is this limited to the United States. Walworth has produced conclusive evidence that history books used in the secondary schools of Mexico, Spain, Germany, Great Britain, Canada, and the United States differ greatly in what the "true facts" are considered to be.

For example, a book written by Toro for the education of Mexican students treats the annexation of Texas as follows: ".......The partisans of the South looked toward us to increase their territory, make new slave states out of it, and strengthen their domination; and they resolutely determined to acquire Texas, counting upon the aid of President Jackson, an unscrupulous man who, as a proprietor of slaves, was personally interested in the matter and resorted to every sort of means, even the most immoral, to accomplish his ends. ....." High school students of the United States may read the more "enlightening" pages of Faulkner and Kepner and learn that "It was hardly to be expected that these aggressive Anglo-Saxon frontiersmen could long dwell in peace under the control of a people representing a very different civilization, and under a weak and inefficient government continually changing as one revolution succeeded another."

No doubt teachers in Mexico, like teachers in the United States, feel that they are teaching the facts and that learning these facts will help students think about their problems. Yet both textbooks cannot be completely right, and both may be largely wrong. The statement that Jackson was *unscrupulous* is as nonfactual as the statement that government in Mexico was *weak and inefficient.*

WHAT IS THE REFLECTIVE METHOD?

There is no essential difference between reflection, as we use it in this book, and scientific process, broadly defined. The term *scientific* does carry a connotation which is less suited to our purposes than does the term *reflective.* In the thinking of many persons *science* implies white-gowned technicians, microscopes and telescopes, chemical tables, and cyclotrons. It suggests precise measurement, use of mathematics, a large amount of rather esoteric wizardry, and neglect of moral values. But *scientific* in its broadest sense covers not only a special kind of gadgetry and techniques but also a unique outlook, attitude, and method of inquiry.

Reflection refers to the essential but non-gadgetlike features of scientific method—to an attitude of mind and a generalized set of operations with which we may approach all problems, whether physical, social, or psychological. John Dewey gave us a classic definition of reflection when he called it the "active, persistent, and careful consideration of any belief or supposed form of knowledge in the light of the grounds that support it and the further conclusions to which it tends......." Dewey conceived of reflection as the kind of thought which embodies the scientific method, defined in its broadest sense. To him, all thinking which is worth while is reflection, as we have defined it. Reflection leads to generalization of a kind which is understood by learners and which has maximum transfer value to new situations.

It is possible to describe reflection as psychological movement through a series of steps. Such movement results in a progressive development of insight about a problem. These steps are as follows :

1. Recognition and definition of a problem. This occurs when we become aware of a goal and an intervening

obstacle. Often a problem consists of a newly sensed discrepancy in known data.

2. Formulation of hypotheses. Hypotheses are possible answers. They are invented generalizations which to be used most successfully must be verified by human experience. In a relativistic sense, all scientific generalizations are hypotheses in which greater or lesser degrees of assurance can be placed. They range from hunches based on minimum data to laws which reflect a very high degree of factual verification.
3. Elaboration of logical implications of hypotheses. This includes deducing observations which have already been made—so that hypotheses may be checked against present knowledge; and deducing observations which have not yet been made—so that hypotheses may be tested through experiments yet to be designed.
4. Testing of hypotheses. This involves attempts to verify consequences deduced under step 3 above, in terms of both the data of previous experience and data procured in experimental tests.
5. Drawing conclusions. This consists of acceptance, modification, or rejection of hypotheses, or concluding that as of now the available pertinent evidence does not warrant taking any stand at all.

Although the foregoing steps are present in each completed act of reflection, no one should suppose that a person goes through them in the consecutive, orderly fashion in which they may be listed on paper. Reflection normally is characterized by confusion, hesitation, backtracking, and "going around in circles." In many cases it appears to a thinker that he will never reach a solution at all. And once reached, a conclusion often must be abandoned and the process started all over again. Reflection is seldom easy; at best it is exhilarating and exciting, and at worst it is painfully hard work beset with many frustrating moments.

There is a great deal more to understanding the reflective process than merely listing the steps. Experience of the past few centuries has led to certain conventions concerning how a reflective or scientific process is to be pursued. We use the term *conventions* because there is nothing absolutistic about the rules which govern testing of hypotheses. Pragmatically, the rules accepted at present have been shown to lead to more productive results than any alternative rules which have yet been devised. But there is no reason to suppose that the rules of reflection will not continue to evolve as mankind gains more experience. We list some of the more important of these rules together with some needed qualifications.

1. Whenever one insight or conclusion is accepted in preference to another, it is presumed that *reasons exist for its acceptance.* The grounds for acceptance may be scant, but as long as they are better than the grounds any competing insight can offer, they justify its tentative acceptance. What we regard as true does not need to be proved in any final sense; it requires only some supporting evidence.

2. Insights are always *provisional.* That is, all knowledge is assumed to be a product of human experience and hence subject to change. No question is closed to re-examination provided a reason to re-examine it develops. This does not mean that one may not establish principles or laws which are assumed to be valid for a very long period of time. Such principles or laws are not absolutes so long as people remain willing to re-examine them at any time questions arise involving them.

3. Insights are consistent with each other. *We assume that two contradictory insights can never be true at the same time, for the same purpose, and under the same conditions.* This does not mean that one may not switch from one idea to another which is incompatible with it. Changing one's mind is not an example of inconsistency; in fact, a reflective person is known for his flexibility. A person is inconsistent only when he holds two opposites at once and under the same assumed conditions. This rule is apparently the same as what Ernest Bayles calls the "principle of harmony." He states it thus: "....The process of testing hypothesis by the use of data is one asking whether the data agree with the hypothesis. Which hypothesis, if any, causes the data to fall into a thoroughly harmonious pattern? A problem can be considered solved *beyond reasonable doubt* when and only when (1) one proposed solution presents a pattern which harmonizes all the data which have been obtained......... and (2) there are no data which are incompatible with that proposal."

4. All pertinent, available evidence is examined before

conclusions are drawn. An investigator looks at all facts then available, no matter how unpalatable some of them may seem. There is never a slanting, ignoring, or distorting of data to prove a point. Taboos and ungovernable prejudices do not mix with a reflective approach. Dr. Bayles refers to this principle as the principle of "adequacy"—the data must be adequate, i.e., as complete as possible. The crucial datum, of course, is the actual predicated functioning of a hypothesis in new situations. If it "works" in this manner, this is the best thing which can be said for it.

5. The ultimate authority for any scientific conclusion is to be found in perceivable phenomena, as suggested through observation and experiment. This statement can easily be misconstrued and needs considerable qualification. Human beings seem capable of an unlimited range of experience, including what we commonly call mystical. Mystical experiences may be hallucinations (which are common to man) or they may represent some kind of contact or involvement with an "otherworldly" realm accessible at present only to a small proportion of persons. A person who is relativistically oriented does not like arbitrarily to rule out any kind of evidence. He prefers, rather, the idea of an "open universe"—in which anything is possible. On the other hand, without better evidence than is now available, those who use a reflective approach remain highly skeptical of evidence which purportedly is derived from a world other than the "here and now."

6. Closely related to the problems stemming from number 5 above is the rule that all operations in a reflective act must be performed openly and in a fashion that will enable other competent persons to repeat them. Each act of reflection must be able to supply its own recipe, so to speak; or, stated in another way, it must be subject to operational description. A mechanic overhauling a carburetor can describe each step along the way, and, if I am bright enough, I can repeat it. So can you, or anyone else. We are saying that scientific reflection is a *public* rather than a private road to truth. This is not the same as saying that there are no private roads: in fact, there may be a great many.

Although the foregoing rules have been described separately, it should be obvious that they are closely interrelated. Each hinges to some degree upon the others. Nor is there any implication that this is a complete "listing" of rules governing the reflective method.

The purpose of rules associated with a reflective approach is to make for "good thinking," which, in the final test, may be judged *only against its results.* The presumed purpose of any act of thought is to provide a person with tested insights which are worth more than the insights formerly held. Prior to the above discussion of reflection, we described several supposedly spurious or incomplete methods of thought; these were judged inadequate solely on the ground that they lead to less reliable or less usable insights than does reflection.

To summarize the chapter, we have suggested that, although animal experimentation has led to conflicting conclusions about learning, apparently it has been demonstrated that all members of the animal kingdom, under the right circumstances, can learn insightfully. Next, we contrasted the two major descriptions of learning: conditioning and development of insight. Finally, we suggested that a Gestalt-field psychologist equates development of insight with thinking, and that there are various kinds of "thinking," the most productive of which is scientific reflection.

3

Skinner's Theory of Learning

The psychology which would support the emphasis on teaching machines for Dale's education has been developed by a professor at Harvard, B. F. Skinner (1904—). Skinner has found *operant conditioning* highly effective in training animals and he is confident that it promises equal success when used with children and youth. In operant conditioning, teachers are considered architects and builders of students' behaviour. Learning objectives are divided in a large number of very small tasks and reinforced one by one. Operants—sets of acts—are reinforced—strengthened—so as to increase the probability of their recurrence in the future. In this process it is of prime importance that teachers employ properly timed and spaced schedules of reinforcement.

Professor Skinner considers it the purpose of psychology to predict and control *behaviour* of individual organisms. He insists upon limiting psychological study to observable behaviour of organisms; his only data are those acquired by sensory observation. He opposes the use by psychologists or teachers of such terms as *will power, sensation, image, drive,* or *instinct;* these refer to supposedly nonphysical events. *Behaviour* is ".....the movement of an organism or of its parts in a frame of reference provided by the organism itself or by various external objects or fields of force."

Skinner's psychology is a strictly engineering type of science which supposedly is devoid of theory of any kind. He insists that psychology is a science of overt behaviour and only overt behaviour. He defines learning as a change in probability of response. In most cases this change is brought about by operant conditioning.

Operant conditioning is the learning process whereby a response is made more probable or more frequent; an *operant is* strengthened—reinforced. Reinforcement is explained in Chapter 2. An operant is a set of acts which constitutes an organism's doing something—raising its head, pushing a lever, saying "horse". In the process of operant conditioning operant responses are modified or changed. Reinforcement means that the probability of the repetition of certain responses is increased.

Skinner thinks that nearly all human behaviour is a product of operant reinforcement. In everyday life, in various fields including education, people constantly change the probabilities of responses of others by arranging reinforcing consequences. Operant reinforcement improves the efficiency of behaviour. Through it we learn to keep our balance, walk, play games, and handle tools and instruments; we perform a set of motions, reinforcement occurs, and the likelihood of our repeating the motions is increased.

Whenever something reinforces a particular form of behaviour, the chances are better that behaviour will be repeated. The task of psychologists is to gain more understanding of conditions under which reinforcement works best. To the many "natural" reinforcers of behaviour a host of artificial reinforcers may be added. "Any list of values is a list of reinforcers—conditioned or otherwise. We are so constituted that under certain circumstances food, water, sexual contact, and so on, will make any behaviour which produces them more likely to occur again. other things may acquire this power.....An organism can be reinforced by—can be made to 'choose'—almost any given state of affairs."

HOW HAS SKINNER USED ANIMALS TO STUDY OPERANT REINFORCEMENT?

In general, experimental psychologists have not related their laws and theories to instances of learning in real life. However, Professor Skinner and his associates have experienced remarkable success in training animals. It is probable that even professional animal trainers, through study of the procedures used in operant conditioning, could improve their techniques. In one college class period, by presenting food to a hungry pigeon at the right time, Skinner has implanted in the bird three or four well-defined responses such as turning around, pacing the floor in a figure-eight pattern, stretching the neck, and stamping the foot.

Skinner's basic thesis is that, since an organism tends in the future to do what it was doing at the time of reinforcement, one can, by baiting each step of the way, lead it to do very much what the experimenter wishes it to do. Using this thesis as a basis for his procedure, he has taught rats to use a marble to obtain food from a vending machine, pigeons to play a modified game of tennis, and dogs to operate the pedal of a refuse can so as to retrieve a bone.

Skinner has centered his study on lower animals because their behaviour is simpler, conditions surrounding them may be controlled better, basic processes are revealed more readily and can be recorded over longer periods of time, and observations are not complicated by social relations between subjects and the psychologist.

The "Skinner box" is a simple box which was made to contain a rat, a lever, and a device for delivering a pellet of food each time the rat pressed the lever. Recording devices are set outside the box so that the experimenter can go home at night and see in the morning what the rat has been doing. There also are Skinner boxes for the study of pigeons and other animals. A rat or pigeon learns rapidly in a Skinner box because in the box there is little else for him to do. Skinner says, "The barest possible statement of the process is this : we make a given consequence contingent [dependent] upon certain physical properties of behaviour (the upward movement of the head), and the behaviour is then observed to increase in frequency."

A pigeon's behaviour can be reinforced in such a way that neck stretching will become habitual. The pigeon is placed in a cage so that the experimenter can sight across its head at a scale pinned on the far wall of the cage. The height at which the head is normally held is established on the scale; then some line, which is reached only infrequently, is selected. The experimenter, keeping his eye on the scale, quickly opens the food tray whenever the bird's head rises above the established line. As a result, learning occurs; ...."we observe an immediate change in the frequency with which the head crosses the line. We also observe, and this is of some importance theoretically, that higher lines are now being crossed. We may advance almost immediately to a higher line in determining when food is to be presented. In a minute or two, the bird's posture has changed so that the top of the head seldom falls below the line which we first chose."

By training two pigeons separately to do their parts in a total performance, Skinner has constructed a social scene within which competition is exemplified by two pigeons playing a modified game of ping-pong. He accomplished the training through operant reinforcement. First, the pigeons were reinforced when they merely pushed the ball. Then when the ball got by one pigeon the other was reinforced. He also has trained pigeons to coordinate their behaviour in dancing in a cooperative manner which rivals the skills of most able human dancers.

Reinforcement procedures may vary according to intervals of time and the number of responses between reinforcements. A schedule of reinforcement is a pattern of "rewarding" behaviour based upon a fixed time interval and a fixed number of responses between "rewards". In a laboratory, Skinner and Ferster have obtained performances appropriate to each of nine different ratio-interval schedules. When a stimulus is presented the pigeon executes the performance appropriate to its reinforcement schedule. Then when another stimulus is presented, the pigeon executes the performance appropriate to its specific schedule. Skinner thinks that this achievement makes more plausible the extension of laboratory results to daily life. To him, learning, in the everyday life of people, is more complicated but nevertheless of the same basic nature as an animal's learning through operant conditioning.

In operant conditioning experiments, the species of organism studied has made surprisingly little difference. "Comparable results have been obtained with pigeons, rats, dogs, monkeys, human children, and most recently,........human psychotic subjects. In spite of great phylogenetic differences, all these organisms show amazingly similar properties of the learning process."

WHAT PSYCHOLOGICAL THEORY UNDERLINES SKINNER'S TEACHING PROCEDURES?

Throughout his study and writings, Professor Skinner has adhered rigorously to a basic conviction that psychologists should restrict their study to the correlations between stimuli and responses and not meddle with any "make-believe" psychology which constructs intervening physiological or mental links between stimuli and responses. Adherents of Skinner's position consider study of these intervening variables "........a dummy physiology doing duty for truth when facts are missing."

In a sense Skinner's psychology, operant behaviourism, is a modern extension of the earlier stimulus-response psychologies—connectionism as developed by Thorndike and behaviourism as developed by Watson. Thorndike dealt with both physical and mental elements but was always mechanistic in his study of man. Watson, too, was mechanistic; however, he limited his study to the behaviour of biological organisms. Skinner, like both Thorndike and Watson, assumes that man is neutral and passive and that all behaviour can be described in mechanistic terms. In his study of man and animals, he constantly is mechanistic, elementistic, and associationistic; to him, psychology is *the science of behaviour.*

What is the Meaning of "the Science of Behaviour"?

Skinner sees a great and crucial future for a science of behaviour. In his view, since a science of behaviour is concerned with domonstrating the consequences of cultural practices, there is reason to believe that presence of such a science will be an essential mark of the culture or cultures which will survive in the future, and that the culture most likely to survive is the one in which the methods of science are most effectively applied to the problems of human behaviour. Consequently, throughout his work he has striven constantly to be scientific to the nth degree. He sees *science* as " .... more than a set of attitudes. It is a search for order, for uniformities, for lawful relations among the events in nature. It begins, as we all begin, by observing single episodes, but it quickly passes on to the general rule, to scientific law." Thus, he places himself in line as a contemporary representative of inductive, atomistic science following the earlier pattern of Francis Bacon and John Stuart Mill. One can get the "flavour" of Skinner's work only through reading his books and papers. His frequent usage of the definite article *the* as contrasted with his infrequent usage of the indefinite articles *a* or *an* is quickly apparent. Like other "realistic" scientists, he assumes that this practice adds to objectivity and makes reports of studies more "scientific."

A "Realistic" Definition of Science

Skinner works on the basic assumption that there is order in nature, including human behaviour, and that it is the function of science to *discover* the order; this is the commitment of a *realistic,* as opposed to a *relativistic,* scientist. Within Skinner's realistic outlook, science is concerned with discovery of pre-existent laws which govern the world about us. Knowledge of these laws enhances predictability, and thereby control, of the variables which cause events to occur. This supposedly is as true in psychology as in physics or chemistry. Thus, man, through discovery of laws and organization of them into systems, enables himself to deal effectively with aspects of the naturalistic world.

Skinner recognizes that "....... it is time to insist that science does not progress by carefully designed steps called 'experiments' each of which has a well-defined beginning and end. Science is a continuous and often a disorderly and accidental process." Nevertheless he leaves unrecognized the relativistic principle that *reality* consist of that which we make of what comes to us and is "...... definable as something which might, should, or does make a difference to someone or something."

Man, a Subject of Science

According to Skinner, it is not to be assumed that human

behaviour has nay peculiar properties which require a unique method or special kind of knowledge. The variables of psychology, like the variables of any other science, must be described in physical terms. In Skinner's psychology, the dependent variable in a situation is the behaviour of an individual organism. The independent variable consists of external conditions of which the behaviour is a function. This means that behaviour operates upon the environment to generate consequences; *it* behaves.

The laws of the science of psychology are as definite as those of any other science. Skinner says, "It is decidedly not true that a horse may be led to water but cannot be made to drink". He thinks that, through applying the laws of psychology and arranging a history of severe deprivation, it could be made absolutely sure that drinking would occur; likewise, a desired behaviour can be caused in a human being.

Skinner's goal in psychology is to achieve the degree of prediction and control in regard to human behaviour that has been achieved by the physical sciences. The scientist of behaviour evaluates probability of behaviour and explores conditions that determine it. Through gathering data in regard to the frequencies of responses which have already occurred, he is able to make accurate statements about the likelihood of occurrence of a single future response of the same kind; frequency of response indicates probability of response. "We are concerned, then, with the causes of human behaviour. We want to know why men behave as they do . Any condition or event which can be shown to have an effect upon behaviour must be taken into account. By discovering and analyzing these causes, we can predict behaviour; to the extent that we can manipulate them, we can control behaviour."

The problem of predicting whether a man will commit suicide is of the same nature as the problem of predicting the probability of explosion of the first atomic bomb. The basic datum in scientific analysis of behaviour is probability. However, the actual observed dependent variable is frequency of response. Since much important human behaviour occurs only once, it cannot be studied in terms of frequencies. A man may marry only once, he may engage in a business deal only once—he will commit suicide only once. So, like the probability of the first atomic bomb explosion, some behaviour cannot be stated in terms of frequency. Nevertheless, it can be evaluated in terms of probabilities of many of the component events which can be based upon data in the form of frequencies, and any behaviour may be studied in terms of its component parts.

How is the Science of Behaviour Related to Determinism?

Skinner's psychology implies a strictly naturalistic determinism. He notes that a scientific conception of human behaviour dictates one practice and a philosophy of personal freedom another; and that a scientific conception of human behaviour entails the acceptance of an assumption of determinism. Determinism means that behaviour is caused, and that the behaviour which appears is the only kind which could have appeared. Skinner emphasizes that the same type of determinism which is commonly accepted as applying to machines applies equally to human beings. As machines have become more lifelike, living organisms have been found to be more like machines. Today, many machines are deliberately designed to operate in ways which resemble "human behaviour." "Man has, in short, created the machine in his own image." Since mechanical calculators now solve equations too difficult or too time consuming even for human mathematicians, human beings have lost much of their uniqueness.

Determinism carries with it the implication that environment determines an individual even when he alters his own environment. "It does not matter that the individual may take it upon himself to control the variables of which his own behaviour is a function or, in a broad sense, to engage in the design of his own culture. He does this only because he is the product of a culture which generates self-control or cultural design as a mode of behaviour."

Skinner says, "The scientist, like any organism, is the product of a unique history." He considers science of major importance in human affairs but recognizes that even scientists and science are not free. Science, too, is a part of the course of events and it cannot interfere with that course. Thus, science and scientists must be explained in any adequate account which science gives of human behaviour in general. Science supplies an account of processes of which it itself is an example.

HOW IS OPERANT CONDITIONING NONPHYSIOLOGICAL AND NONPHENOMENOLOGICAL?

A system of operant conditioning has no place for study of either physiological or phenomenological psychology. *Physiological psychology* is devoted to study of physiological, neurological, and biological functions within an organism. *Phenomenological psychology* centers upon what events mean to the persons involved. In a sense it is similar to physiological psychology in that it, too, is centered upon what takes place within a person. However, it differs sharply from physiological psychology in that major emphasis is placed upon the process of experiencing. Because Skinner rejects both physiological and phenomenological psychology, his friends sometimes speak of his dealing with the "empty organism."

Nonphysiological Psychology

Skinner is convinced that the practice of looking inside an organism for an explanation of behaviour has tended to obscure the variables which lie outside the organism and are immediately available for scientific analysis. These variables outside the organism are in its environmental history and its immediate environment. Their study permits behaviour to be explained scientifically just as behaviour of nonliving objects is explained scientifically by physicists. These independent variables are of many sorts and their relation to behaviour is often subtle and complex; nevertheless, according to Skinner, it is only through analyzing them that we may hope to reach an adequate account of behaviour.

Since not all statements about the nervous system are expressed in the same terms and cannot be confirmed by the same method of observation as the facts for which they are supposed to account, they are theories. Thus, Skinner feels that they can make little contribution to a scientific psychology. In the present stage of science a neurological explanation of behaviour is impossible. However, this fact in no way implies that a scientific psychology of learning cannot be established separate from any neurological theory.

Nonphenomenological Psychology

Statements about mental events, like neurological statements, also are theoretical. Thus, Skinner belittles attempts of psychologists to infer what a physical situation *means* to an organism or to distinguish between the physical world and the psychological world of experience. He constantly emphasizes that events affecting an organism must be capable of being described in the language of physical science. To him, the "free inner man" who is held responsible for the behaviour of the external biological organism is only a prescientific substitute for the kinds of external causes of behaviour which are susceptible to scientific analysis. Hence there is no place in scientific psychology for study of the personal experience of a man.

Skinner sees the practice of some scientists, who indicate that they are describing only half the universe and that there is another half—a world of self, mind, or consciousness—as a part of the cultural heritage from which science has emerged but which now stands in the way of a unified scientific account of nature. Even in discussing the higher human function, thinking, Skinner sees little need for the concept *self.* He recognizes that behaviour is a function of the environment, that environment, then, presumably means any event in the universe capable of affecting the organism, and that a very small part of this universe is private, i.e., it is enclosed within the organism's own skin. Thus, some independent variables, for example, an aching tooth, may be related to behaviour in a unique way. However, he sees no reason to suppose that the stimulating effect of an inflamed tooth is essentially different from that of a hot stove.

Since the self is not identical with the physical organism, such a concept is not essential in any analysis of behaviour. The concept may have had an early advantage in representing a relatively coherent response system, but it is hazardous in that it may lead us to expect consistencies and functional integrities which do not exist. "The alternative to the use of the concept [self] is simply to deal with demonstrated covariations in the strength of responses."

In opposing the "inner man" concept of human behaviour Skinner notes the similarity of the inner man concept to a "God within" which does not occupy space and thus may be multiplied at will, as is done in the Freudian pattern. He points out that as more and more of the behaviour of organisms has come to be explained in terms of stimuli, at each stage of scientific development of psychology, some part of the control of the organism has passed from a hypothetical inner entity to the external environment. "The 'will' has retreated up the spinal cord, through the lower and then the higher parts of the brain, and finally, with the conditioned reflex, has escaped through the front of the head."

In Skinner's system there is no place for the statement that behaviour is under the control of an incentive or goal. A scientific psychology, as Skinner defines it, replaces statements which might use such words as *incentive, goal,* or *purpose* with statements about conditioning. Instead of saying that a man behaves because of the consequences which are to follow his behaviour, we simply state that he bahaves thus and so because of the consequences which have followed similar behaviour in the past. When one is "looking for something" he is emitting responses which in the past produced something as a consequence. When one says, "I am looking for my glasses," what he really means is ".... ' I have lost my glasses' 'I shall stop what I am doing when I find my glasses,' or 'When I have done this in the past, I have found my glasses.' "

Since the terms *pleasant and satisfying* do not refer to any physical property of reinforcing events, and physical sciences use neither of these terms nor their equivalents, they, too, should be deleted from the language of a science of psychology. Furthermore, since behaviour is always the behaviour of an individual, a science of behaviour which concerns only the behaviour of groups is not likely to be of help in understanding particular cases. Thus, "A 'social force' is no more useful in manipulating behaviour than an inner state of hunger, anxiety, or skepticism."

WHAT IS THE NATURE OF OPERANT CONDITIONING OR REINFORCEMENT?

In the pigeon experiment, the process of *operant conditioning* is the change in frequency with which the head is lifted to a given height, the *reinforcer* is food, and the *reinforcement* is food presentation when the response is emitted. The *operant* is the behaviour upon which the reinforcement is contingent—the height to which the head must be raised.

In operant conditioning, the important stimulus is the one immediately following the response, not the one preceding it. Any emitted response which leads to reinforcement is thereby strengthened. It is not the specific S-R tendency that is strengthened, but rather the *general tendency* to make the response. A rat presses a lever and gets food. Because of this, the rat will be more likely to press the lever again. "What is changed is the future probability of response in the same *class*." The operant as a class of behaviour, rather than the response as a particular instance, is reinforced. Since each reinforcement builds up a reserve of responses, a pigeon may continue to raise its head or a rat to press the lever several, or even many, times after food has ceased to appear.

The law of operant conditioning is that, if the occurrence of an operant is followed by presentation of a reinforcing stimulus, the strength—probability—is increased. What is strengthened is not a stimulus-response connection; the operant requires no specific eliciting stimulus. Insofar as the organism is concerned, the only important property of the operant contingency is time; the reinforcer follows the response. How this is brought about does not matter. The process of operant conditioning may be described adequately without any mention of a stimulus which acts before the response is made. In reinforcing a pigeon's neck stretching it is necessary only for one to wait for neck stretching to occur. It is not necessary for the experimenter to elicit it.

In operant conditioning, the subject's seeing a connection is in no way essential. Skinner considers Thorndike's expression "trial and error learning" to be superfluous and out of place. As he has observed the behaviour of pigeons and other animals, he has seen no reason to call the movements being taught "trials" and any movements which did not achieve a specified consequence "errors." "The statement that the bird 'learns that it will get food by stretching its neck' is an inaccurate report of what has happened." A Gestalt-field explanation of how the bird learns, of course, would be just this.

Skinner observes that the behaviour which is more likely to be reinforced is the more likely to occur. Presence of a cat is the occasion upon which the response "cat" is likely to be reinforced. However, a stimulus eliciting "cat" is in no way an essential part of the operant conditioning process. Operant reinforcement of a behaviour is contingent—dependent—upon a response, not the stimulus which gave rise to that response. The response *c-a-t* is reinforced after it is uttered. The stimulus involved here is a discriminative, not an eliciting, one. "The discriminative stimulus does not elicit a response, it simply alters a probability of occurrence." It is not correct to say that an operant reinforcement strengthened the response which preceded it; the response has already occurred and cannot be changed. What has been changed is that the probability that that class of responses will occur in the future has been increased.

Skinner revised Thorndike's law of effect. "Instead of saying that a man behaves because of the consequences which *are* to follow his behaviour we simply say that he behaves because of the consequences which *have* followed similar behaviour in the past. This is, of course, the Law of Effect or operant conditioning." The law of effect exemplified in operant conditioning simply specifies a procedure for altering the probability of a chosen response. By progressively changing the *contingencies of reinforcement* in the direction of the desired behaviour, one can see learning occur.

What are Contingencies of Reinforcement?

A contingency of reinforcement is a sequence in which a response is followed by a reinforcing stimulus. The basic three-term contingency of operant conditioning is response, stimulus, and reinforcement in that order. In a contingency the occurrence of an operant—response—is *followed by* presentation of a reinforcing stimulus, and the strength—probability—of recurrence of the operant is increased. The three-term contingency of operant reinforcement occurs when a child is taught to read; a given response is reinforced with "Right" or "Wrong" according to how the student responds to the appropriate visual stimulus—word or sentence.

The key to successful teaching or training is to analyze the effect of reinforcement and design techniques which manipulate the process with considerable precision—to set up specific reinforcing contingencies. In this way the behaviour of an individual organism may be brought under precise control. Implicit in operant behaviourism is the conviction that "When all relevant variables have been arranged, an organism will or will not respond. If it does not, it cannot. If it can, it will."

How Does Operant Differ from Respondent or Reflexive Conditioning?

Reflexive learning involves such situations as are described in the Pavlovian dog studies. Essentially it is a process of stimulus substitution. An organism supposedly responds reflexively to a natural or unconditioned stimulus. A new stimulus is presented along with the original stimulus and the organism comes to respond to the new stimulus in the same way it formerly did to the original one. The new stimulus becomes a conditioned stimulus; the organism has learned. In reflexive or respondent conditioning the key stimulus is the one which precedes the response. Whereas reflexive learning is an S-R process, operant learning is an R-S process.

In operant learning, the significant stimulus is that which immediately follows the response. Any modification of the environment is a stimulus. Operant behaviour is that behaviour which operates upon the environment to generate consequences. Notice that in this process not the person or the environment but it—behaviour—behaves; behaviour is a phenomenon of nature. Just as wind blows, behaviour behaves.

Although Skinner acknowledges two kinds of learning—operant and reflexive—he places far greater emphasis upon operant learning, which is under the control of its consequences. He sees most human behaviour and consequently nearly all human conditioning or learning as operant. He feels that, if all the behaviour which falls into the pattern of simple reflexes were assembled, it would represent only very small fraction of the total behaviour of an organism. He is convinced that early investigators over-worked the principle of reflexive conditioning and made exaggerated claims for it. However, he warns that the area of reflex behaviour should not be overlooked. To ignore completely the principle of the conditioned reflex would be unwarranted. But "It is neither plausible nor expedient to conceive of the organism as a complicated jack-in-the-box with a long list of tricks, each of which may be evoked by pressing the proper button. The greater part of the behaviour of the intact organism is not under this primitive sort of stimulus control. The environment affects the organism in many ways which are not conveniently classed as 'stimuli,' and even in the field of stimulation only a small part of the forces acting upon the organism elicit responses in the invariable manner of reflex action." The environment is so constructed that certain things tend to happen together. Respondent conditioning is the effect of this phenomenon upon behaviour. When certain events like the color and taste of ripe fruit occur together, an organism responds in the same manner to either stimulus, color or taste. It has learned this through respondent conditioning. However, the importance of this kind of learning has been emphasized far too much. Behaviour such as eating a meal or driving a car shows but little respondent character; most of it is operant in nature.

WHAT ARE THE PROCESSES OF OPERANT REINFORCEMENT AND EXTINCTION?

In operant conditioning, an operant is strengthened through its *reinforcement* or weakened through its *extinction*. The psychologist's task is simply to account for probability of responses in terms of a history of reinforcement and extinction. The effect of *reinforcement* always is to increase the probability of response. Extinction is the reverse of reinforcement. When a reinforcing stimulus no longer occurs following a response, the response becomes less and less frequent; this is operant *extinction*. "Conditioning builds up a predisposition to respond—a 'reserve'—which extinction exhausts."

What are the Two Kinds of Reinforcers?

Any stimulus whose presentation or removal increase the probability of a response is a reinforcer. Consequently, there are two kinds of reinforcers or reinforcing events—positive and negative. A positive reinforcer is any stimulus the *presentation* of which strengthens the behaviour upon which it is made contingent; a negative reinforcer is any stimulus the *withdrawal* of which strengthens that behaviour. Since in both cases responses are strengthened, reinforcement is taking place. A positive reinforcement consists of presenting a stimulus, of adding something—food, water or a teacher's smile—to an organism's environment. A negative reinforcement consists of removing something—a loud noise, an electric shock, or a teacher's frown—from the situation. In both of these cases the probability that the response will recur is increased.

Although in lay usage both positive and negative reinforcers are "rewards," Skinner warns against defining a positive reinforcer as pleasant or satisfying and a negative reinforcer as annoying. "It would be as difficult to show that the reinforcing power of an aversion stimulus is due to its unpleasantness as to show that the reinforcing power of a positive reinforcer is due to its pleasantness." When a person reports that an event is pleasant, this simply means that the event is of such kind that it reinforces him. Physical science uses no such terms as *pleasant* and *unpleasant* or their equivalents. The terms in no way refer to physical properties of reinforcing agents.

Is Punishment Reinforcement?

Punishment is a basically different process from reinforcement. Whereas reinforcement involves presentation of a positive reinforcer or removal of a netative one, punishment consists of presentation of a negative stimulus or removal of a positive one. Again, whereas reinforcement is defined in terms of strengthening of response, punishment supposedly is a process which weakens a response. Putting it succinctly, when a stimulus is involved in strengthening a response there is reinforcement; when a stimulus is presented or withdrawn in an attempt to weaken a response, there is punishment.

Results of experiments indicate that punishment does not permanently reduce a tendency to respond. Thorndike's experiments with human subjects indicated that a reward strengthened the behaviour which preceded it but that punishment did not weaken it. Through reward, behaviour may be stamped in; but the converse, that through punishment it can be stamped out, does not hold. Whereas reinforcement can be controlled to good advantage, in the long run punishment works to the disadvantage of both the punished organism and the punishing agency. Its results are neither predictable nor dependable. Extinction—permitting a behaviour to die out by not reinforcing it—and not punishment is the appropriate process for breaking habits.

What are the Types of Operant Reinforcement?

There are two rather distinct types of operant reinforcement—stimulus discrimination and response differentiation. Nearly all human learning can be classified under these two. However, the process of respondent (reflexive) conditioning must not be completely ignored.

Through operant reinforcement a relatively complete new unit of behaviour may be learned or an existing unit of behaviour may be refined. In general, reinforcement which leads to behaviour acquirement is a process of discrimination of stimuli, whereas behaviour refinement or skill development is a process of differentiation of response.

Discrimination of Stimuli

Operant discrimination is a change in behaviour as the result of changes in the environment—stimuli—of the organism. A pigeon can be made to be more likely to respond by stretching its neck at times when a light is on. This probability is increased by discrimination. Imitative behaviour is an example of the result of discriminative operant reinforcement. Such behaviour does not arise because of any inherent reflex mechanism but develops in the history of the individual as a result of discriminative reinforcements. The visual stimulation of someone waving a hand is the occasion upon which waving a hand probably received reinforcement. The reinforcement, not the stimulation from the other person's waving his hand, is the cause of future hand waving in similar situations. Because objects in shop windows into which other people are looking are likely to reinforce looking into such windows, when a person sees other people looking into a shop window he too is likely to look. Taking an interest or attending are only some other expressions that are commonly used to describe the consequence of discriminative operant reinforcement . "Attention is a controlling *relation*—the relation between a response and a discriminative stimulus. When someone is paying attention he is under special control of a stimulus."

Differentiation of Response

Skills are improved through differences in reinforcements of varying responses. Many differentiation reinforcements may be supplied automatically by mechanical exigencies of the environment of an organism. To throw a ball skilfully, a person must release it at the proper moment; instances in which release comes before or after the proper moment are not reinforced. However, in more complex skill learning, reinforcement must be supplied by a teacher. In this process, reinforcement which develops skill must be immediate. "By reinforcing a series of successive approximations, we bring a rare response to a very high probability in a short time."

Through the procedure of operant conditioning, within which differentiation of response is reinforced, a hungry pigeon well adapted to the experimental situation and the food tray usually can be brought to respond by pecking a specific spot in two or three minutes. To get the pigeon to peck a specific spot as quickly as possible, the bird is given food when it turns slightly in the direction of the spot. This increases the frequency of turning toward the spot. Reinforcement is then withheld until the bird makes a slight movement toward the spot. Then positions which are successively closer to the spot are reinforced. Then reinforcement is given only when the head is moved slightly forward, and finally only when the beak actually makes contact with the spot.

In target practice a rifleman needs a report of the accuracy of the shot from time to time to maintain the reinforcing power of feedback. However, after some practice he eventually knows before the target is hit whether the shot was good or bad. His own behaviour generates a stimulating feedback. Hits and misses generate different forms of this feedback. Likewise, good form in bowling is reinforced by feedback from the bowler's body.

What is Extinction?

We know that, in general, when we engage in behaviour which no longer "pays off," we find ourselves less inclined to behave in that way again. If we get no answers to telephone calls, we eventually stop telephoning. In operant behaviourism this phenomenon would be described by saying that when reinforcement is no longer forthcoming , a response becomes less and less frequent. This is the process of operant extinction.

Operant extinction takes place much more slowly than does operant reinforcement. However, as an organism responds less and less, a uniform process of extinction may be detected Since behaviour during extinction is a result of the conditioning which had preceded it, extinction occurs quickly when only a few of given response have been reinforced and is greatly protracted when there has been a long history of reinforcement.

The extinction process includes the interesting phenomenon of spontaneous recovery. Even after prolonged extinction, an organism, at the beginning of another session of an activity in which it had been trained but now is no longer being reinforced, often will respond at a higher rate for at least a few moments.

Sometimes an extinction curve is disturbed by an emotional effect. Failure of a response to be reinforced not only leads to operant extinction but also may be accompanied by a reaction commonly called frustration or rage. A pigeon that has failed to receive reinforcement flaps its wings and engages in other emotional behaviour. A mechanic, who is in the habit of having bolts unscrew when he turns his wrench, vents his spleen when one breaks off instead. However, after exercising his vocabulary he turns back to the next bolt. Likewise a pigeon or rat will turn again to the operating key of the box when the emotional response has subsided. Extinction curves often show cyclic oscillation as the emotional response builds up, disappears, and builds up again.

Whereas the mere passage of time after reinforcement has surprisingly little effect upon loss of the act or habit, extinction is an effective way of removing an operant from the repertoire of an organism. When unaccompanied by extinction, forgetting takes place very slowly if at all. Note the key difference here: Whereas mere forgetting is the losing of a habit through the passage of time, extinction requires that the response be emitted without reinforcement. "In human behaviour skilled responses generated by relatively precise contingencies frequently survive unused for as much as half a lifetime." The commonly heard assertion that early experiences of a child determine the personality of the mature person implies that the effect of operant reinforcement is very durable and that in human beings operant extinction is unlikely to occur on a large scale.

The resistance to extinction generated by intermittent reinforcement of a response is much greater than that achieved by the same number of reinforcements given for consecutive responses. If we only occasionally reinforce a child's good behaviour, the behaviour survives after reinforcement is discontinued much longer than if we had reinforced every instance up to the same total number of reinforcements. Since intermittent reinforcement generates longer extinction curves than does continuous reinforcement, there is no simple relation between the number of reinforcements and the number of unreinforced responses necessary for extinction.

HOW MAY OPERANT CONDITIONING BE APPLIED TO SCHOOLROOM PRACTICES?

Skinner is convinced that operant conditioning, so fruitful when applied to animal training, promises equal success when used in schools. He feels that the most efficient control of human learning requires instrumental aid. He is appalled at the present inefficient practices in schools and recommends a procedure whereby they can be corrected. He recognizes the *first* task of teachers to be to shape proper responses, to get children to pronounce and write responses properly. But he sees their *principal* task as bringing proper behaviour under many sorts of stimulus control. "Teaching spelling is mainly a process of shaping complex forms of behaviour. In other subjects—for example, arithmetic—responses must be brought under the control of appropriate stimuli."

What are the Shortcomings of Current Educational Practice?

Skinner believes that it is in bringing correct responses under stimulus control that the greatest inefficiency of current teaching procedures occurs. "In education we design and re-design our curricula in a desperate attempt to provide a liberal education while steadfastly refusing to employ available engineering techniques which would efficiently build the interests and instill the knowledge which are the goals of education."

Skinner notes some current weaknesses in educational practices:

(1) Behaviour is dominated by aversion (escape) stimulation;
(2) too great a lapse of time exists between behaviour and its reinforcement;
(3) a skilful programme of reinforcement which moves forward through a series of progressive approximations to the final complex behaviour desired is lacking; and
(4) reinforcement of desired behaviour occurs much too infrequently.

Behaviour Dominated by Aversion Stimulation

Although the type of threatened displeasure or pain has been changed in the past fifty years, behaviour in the lower grades is still dominated by aversive stimulation—a child is trying to escape or keep away from something. Fifty years ago a child read numbers, copied numbers, and memorized tables to escape the birch rod or cane, i.e., as far as the child was concerned, he did these things to avoid or escape punishment. Today a school child behaves the way he does primarily to escape the threat of a series of minor distasteful events—the teacher's displeasure, criticism or ridicule by his classmates, a poor showing in competition, low marks, or a trip to the principal's office. When children are dominated by this atmosphere, getting the right answer is in itself a rather insignificant event. Thus, the emphasis in teaching and learning is not centered where it should be—in operant conditioning.

Excessive Time Lapse between Behaviour and Reinforcement

Unless explicit mediating behaviour has been set up, the lapse of only a few seconds between a response and its reinforcement destroys most of the effect. A grade on a test taken near the end of the week is too far away from the behaviours the students emitted—sent out—in studying the subject matter earlier in the week. Reinforcing stimuli should follow the response immediately.

Through use of the generalized reinforcer—approval—schools and society reinforce acquisition of the type of behaviour learned in school. This is done by awarding grades, promotions, keys diplomas, degrees, and medals. Skinner notes that these reinforcers do reinforce going to school and gaining a diploma or degree; their shortcoming is that they seldom if ever reinforce the subject matter elements themselves.

Absence of a Programme of Serial Reinforcement

A carefully planned programme of teaching supposedly should move forward step by step by reinforcing a series of progressive approximations to the final behaviour which is desired. To bring a human organism into possession of mathematical behaviour most efficiently, a long series of reinforcement contingencies is necessary. Since a teacher has only so much time, he cannot deal with a pupil's responses one at a time and it is usually necessary for him to reinforce the desired behaviour only in blocks of responses.

Infrequency of Reinforcement

Perhaps the most serious criticism of current classroom procedures is the relative infrequency of reinforcement of the desired acts of students. It is just not humanly possible for one teacher to provide an adequate number of reinforcement *contingencies* for a class of 30 or 40 children. Skinner estimates that, although adequate efficient mathematical behaviour at the level of the first four grades usually requires somewhere between 25,000 and 50,000 reinforcement contingencies, a teacher at best could provide only a few thousand. Thus, even our best schools may be criticized for their inefficiency in teaching drill subjects such as arithmetic. Advances recently made in the control of the learning process, Skinner believes, suggest that classroom practices should be thoroughly revised.

What are the Relevant Considerations in Conditioning—Teaching—a Child?

In order to plan a procedure for inculcating certain desired behaviour in a child, certain specific questions need to be answered:

(1) What behaviour is to be established?
(2) What reinforcers are available?
(3) What responses are available?
(4) How can reinforcements be most efficiently scheduled?

Behaviour to be Established

To teach efficiently the first job of a teacher is to determine carefully just what it is he plans to teach at a specific time. A teacher is the architect and builder of behaviours. He must decide what he wants to teach, then teach it. His objectives are specific, and they are defined in terms of desired behaviours. Thus, in determining achievement of objectives of a school, operant behaviourism requires a teacher-centred classroom.

Reinforcers Available

What does a school have in its possession which will reinforce a child? Since the sheer control of nature in itself is reinforcing, the material to be learned may provide considerable automatic reinforcement. Children play for hours with mechanical toys, paints, and puzzles. These feed back significant changes in the environment and are reasonably free of aversive properties. Automatic reinforcement from manipulation of the environment is probably rather mild. However, in teaching, the net amount of reinforcement in each contingency is of little significance. When properly and carefully used, a series of very slight reinforcements may be tremendously effective in controlling behaviour.

In addition to automatic reinforcement arising from manipulation of the environment, some other reinforcers are available and often used. A child behaves in a certain way and the behaviour is reinforced by its immediate consequences. Reinforcement may follow from a child's excelling others. However, when he is competitively "rewarded," the reinforcement of this child is, of necessity, aversive—"punishing"—to others. The good will and affection of the teacher also may be reinforcing. A positive "reward" or "consequence" (stimulus) strengthens the behaviour that is part of the contingency including that stimulus; it supposedly has nothing to do with organismic purpose.

Responses Available

In planning a programme of progressive approximations that will lead to the desired final form of behaviour a teacher must have an inventory of responses which are available throughout the conditioning process.

Most Efficient Scheduling of Reinforcements

To schedule reinforcements efficiently means to make them contingent upon the desired behaviour. Here two considerations are involved: gradual elaboration of extremely complex patterns of behaviour and maintenance of the behaviour in strength at each stage. "The whole process of becoming competent in any field must be divided into a very large number of very small steps, and reinforcement must be contingent upon the accomplishment of each step......By making each successive step as small as possible, the frequency of reinforcement can be raised to a maximum, while the possibly aversive consequences of being wrong are reduced to a minimum."

Skinner contends that the necessary requirements for adequate reinforcement are not excessive but they probably are incompatible with current realities of present-day classrooms. Experimental studies of learning have indicated that, in order to arrange the contingencies of reinforcement which are most efficient in controlling learning in an organism, mechanical and electrical devices must be used. As a mere reinforcing mechanism, a teacher is out of date—and would be even if he devoted all his time to a single child. Only through mechanical devices can the necessarily large number of contingencies be provided. "We have every reason to expect, therefore, that the most effective control of human learning will require instrumental aid."

How do Teaching Machines Work?

In Skinner's view, education must become more efficient to a degree that cannot be accomplished merely by our building more schools and preparing more teachers; adequate systems of labour-saving capital equipment, i.e., teaching machines, must be developed. He is critical, too, of traditional education which makes students more and more the passive receivers of instruction. Teaching machines, he feels, encourage students to take an "active" role in the instructional process. They must develop the answers before they are reinforced.

Requirements of an Appropriate Teaching Machine

Skinner thinks that, in light of modern psychological knowledge, an appropriate teaching machine has two basic requirements: First, a student must compose his response rather than select it from a set of alternatives. Second, in acquiring complex behaviour, a student must pass through a carefully designed sequence of steps; each step must be so small that it always can be taken, yet in taking it the student must move somewhat closer to fully competent behaviour, and the machine must operate so as to make sure that steps are taken in a carefully prescribed order.

Operation of a Teaching Machine

Skinner anticipates no particular difficulty in producing workable teaching machines. The necessary contingencies may be arranged either mechanically or electrically. Let's see how he describes a teaching device:

> The device consists of a box about the size of a small record player. On the top surface is a glazed window through which a question or problem printed on a paper tape may

be seen. The child answers the question by moving one or more sliders upon which the digits 0 through 9 are printed. The answer appears in square holes punched in the paper upon which the question is printed. When the answer has been set, the child turns a knob. The operation is as simple as adjusting a television set. If the answer is right, the knob turns freely and can be made to ring a bell or provide some other conditioned reinforcement. If the answer is wrong, the knob will not turn. A counter may be added to tally wrong answers. The knob must then be reversed slightly and a second attempt at a right answer made. (Unlike the flash card, the device reports a wrong answer without giving the right answer). When the answer is right, a further turn of the knob engages a clutch which moves the next problem into place in the window. This movement cannot be completed, however, until the sliders have been returned to zero.

What are the Advantages of the Use of Mechanical Teaching Devices?

Skinner claims a long list of advantages available through use of mechanical teaching devices in present-day classrooms.

(1) Reinforcement for the right answer is immediate.
(2) Provided traces of earlier aversive control can be erased, more manipulation of the device probably will be reinforcing enough to keep an average pupil at work for a suitable period each day.
(3) All at one time, a teacher may supervise an entire class at work on such devices; yet each child may complete as many problems as possible in the class period and progress at his own rate.
(4) Any child who is forced to leave school for a period may return at any time and continue from where he left off.
(5) Each child may advance at his own rate and when he gets too far ahead of the class may be assigned to other tasks.
(6) Through carefully designing materials, teachers may

arrange problems in a serial order in the direction of an immensely complex repertoire.

(7) Since the machines record the number of mistakes, tapes can be modified to enhance their effectiveness.

(8) Knowing just what each student has done, a teacher can apply necessary supplementary reinforcement at the greatest vantage point.

Can Machines Teach a Child to Think?

Skinner emphasizes that thinking or originality is not absence of lawfulness and it should never be considered a spontaneous process. He points out that as long as thinking is identified with spontaneity or lawlessness it is a hopeless task to attempt systematically to influence a child's thinking in any way. Thinking, like the rest of the behaviour of an organism, is a lawful process. Thus, verbal behaviour, in terms of which human thinking eventually must be defined, should be treated in its own right as a substantial goal of education. In inculcating this behaviour, learning devices can teach verbal thinking, i.e., establish the large and important repertoire of verbal relationships encountered in science and logic.

Skinner thinks it is of critical importance for us to realize that, in operant behaviourism, thought is not some mysterious process which is the cause of behaviour, but the behaviour itself. Man thinking is man behaving, and human thought is operant, not reflexive, behaviour. "Shakespeare's thought was his behaviour *with respect to his extremely complex environment.*" "In the broadest possible sense, the thought of Julius Caesar was simply the sum total of his responses to the complex world in which he lived."

Skinner observes that study of what traditionally has been called the human mind is more appropriately a study of concepts and methods which have emerged from an analysis of behaviour. Thinking behaviour is verbal or nonverbal, overt or covert. It is primarily the verbal behaviour of men which has survived in recorded form, but from this and other records we can know something about their nonverbal behaviour. When we say that Caesar thought Brutus could be trusted we do not necessarily mean that he ever said as much. Rather he behaved verbally and otherwise as if Brutus could be trusted. The rest of his behaviour, his nonverbal plans and achievements, were also part of his thoughts.

Although in earlier behaviouristic analyses thinking was identified with subaudible talking, Skinner feels that nothing is gained by so doing. There are difficulties in assuming that covert behaviour is always executed by the muscular apparatus responsible for the overt form. Furthermore, the data which give rise to the notion of covert speech can be treated, as such, with a high degree of rigor. Rather than identifying thinking with *talking*, a better case can be made for identifying it with a special kind of *behaving*, that which automatically affects behaviour and is reinforcing because it does.

Thinking is more productive when verbal responses lead to specific consequences and are reinforced because they do so. Just as a musician plays or composes what reinforces him audibly or an artist paints what reinforces him visually, a speaker or writer, engaged in verbal fantasy, says that which is reinforced by hearing it, or writes that which is reinforced by reading it. However, it must be recognized that in any case the solution to a problem is simply a response which alters the situation so that another strong response can be emitted. "Reinforcing contingencies shape the behaviour of the individual, and novel contingencies generate novel forms of behaviour." Thus, man's present better control of the world could be described and expressed just as well by saying that the environment now is in better control of man.

The key to effective teaching of thinking, as well as any other behaviour, is immediate feedback. To teach thinking, we should "......analyze the behaviour called 'thinking' and produce it according to specifications. A programme specifically concerned with such behaviour could be composed of material already available in logic, mathematics, scientific method, and psychology."

4

The Cognitive-Field Theory of Learning

The cognitive-field theory represents a relativistic, as opposed to an absolutistic (mechanistic), way of viewing man and the learning process. Readers are warned that should they attempt to understand its concepts mechanistically, they will not grasp this theory. A mechanist attempts to explain all the fullness and variety of a universe in terms of machine-like objects and movements. Thus, a mechanist in psychology reduces all human activities to movements, usually in terms of stimuli and responses. He considers a person an organism which is a product of its unique history of stimulus-response patterns. Just as an automobile is built by workmen who assemble its respective parts, a person is educated by teachers who feed into his physiological make-up the various aspects of environment which supposedly make him what mechanistic teachers want him to be.

The basic principle of *relativism* is that nothing is perceivable or conceivable as a thing-in-itself. Rather, everything is perceived or conceived in relation to other things. That is, a thing is perceived as a figure against a background, experienced from a given angle or direction of envisionment. Consequently, relativism means that psychological reality is defined, not in "objective," physical terms, but in psychological, perceptual terms. So defined, reality consists of what one makes of that which comes to him through his senses or otherwise.

See if you can get the point of this story. What is the significance of the third umpire's statement? What makes a ball a ball and a strike a strike? "The story concerns three baseball umpires who were discussing the problems of their profession. The first umpire said, 'Some's balls and some's strikes and I calls 'em as they is.' The second umpire said, 'Some's balls and some's strikes and I call 'em as I sees 'em.' While the third umpire said, [I sees 'em comin' across and] 'some's balls and some's strikes but they ain't nothin' till I calls 'em.' "

The cognitive-field theory of learning is closely related to, and derived from, *cognitive and field* psychological theories. *Cognitive* is derived from the Latin verb *cognoscere*, which means "to know." Cognitive theory deals with the problem of how people gain an understanding of themselves and their environments and how, using their cognitions, they act in relation to their environments. Field theory centers on the idea that all psychological activity of a person occurs in a field; it is a part of a totality of coexisting factors which are mutually interdependent.

A field consists of the concurrent interrelationships in any one situation. A field situation is perceived in such a way that any change in the field depends upon the field at that time. An astronomer uses "field" to describe the universe and predict the orbit of stars. A biologist relates the function of cells to their location in a growth "field." A physicist uses "field" in his study of the structure of an atom. To a psychologist "field" means the total psychological world in which a person lives *at a certain time.* It includes matters past, present and future, concrete and abstract, actual and imaginary—all interpreted as simultaneous aspects of a situation.

A cognitive-field theory of learning often is called merely *field theory.* However, since it describes how a person gains understanding of himself and his world in a situation where his self and his environment compose a totality of mutually interdependent, coexisting facts, *cognitive-field* is more truly descriptive of the learning process. Within cognitive-field theory, learning, briefly defined, is a relativistic process by which a learner develops new insights or changes old ones. In no sense is learning a mechanistic, atomistic process of connecting stimuli and responses within a biological organism.

Insight, concisely defined, is a basic sense of, or feeling for, relationships. Although there is nothing about the term *insight* which requires it to be *right* in any absolutistic sense, it is a grasp of a thing which often does go deeper than words. Thus, it is a realizing sense of a matter. Insight into a matter is its meaning. Meaning, so used, denotes that to which a matter or idea points or what it signifies. The insights of a person are not equated with his consciousness or awareness of his ability to describe them verbally; their essence is a sense of, or feeling for, pattern in a life situation.

Development of insight means getting the feel of a matter, grasping the idea, catching on to or seeing through a situation. An insight is acquired through doing something and seeing what happens. The focus of the learning is on the seeing, not, as has been assumed by S-R associationists, on the doing. Seeing, here, is broadly defined to mean catching the point or getting the idea. Any or all of the senses may be involved. The sensory action may be so rudimentary that the person involved may not realize it is going on at all; he may think he is learning through the "mind's eye."

During World War II, one of the authors watched a group of "noncoms" teaching recruits in basic training to fire Army rifles (the author was one of these "rookies"). Army rifles have a powerful recoil or kick. A soldier is supposed to "squeeze" the trigger gradually and smoothly until the rifle fires. Recruits usually anticipate the recoil and jump before the shell explodes; thus, their aim is completely spoiled. The problem for a noncom was to teach his "pupil" not to make the anticipatory jump. Recruits were convinced that they really did not jump until after the explosion and thus hours of blankety-blankety-blanks had little, if any, effect. Corporal Jones helped his "pupil" gain an insight. He "scolded" him several times for jumping, with no avail. Then while his pupil's attention was diverted to a fellow sufferer, the corporal slipped a fired cartridge into the firing chamber. The recruit aimed, started to squeeze, and again jumped out of his skin. He had gained an insight. He was jumping before his rifle fired and thus ruining his aim. His jumping before the rifle had fired then ceased.

Cognitive-field psychology explains development of insight as change in cognitive structure of a life space. To think of learning as development of insight and apply the thinking to school situations most advantageously, we need a psychological structure upon which to build our thinking. This is provided by cognitive-field psychology. A person's *insights* collectively constitute the *cognitive structure* of his life space. *Cognitive structure* means the way a person perceives the psychological aspects of the personal, physical, and social world. Such a world includes a person and all of his facts, concepts, beliefs, and expectations. Consequently, the cognitive structure of life spaces figures in development of language, emotions, actions, and social interrelations.

WHAT IS COGNITIVE-FIELD PSYCHOLOGY?

The development of cognitive-field psychology is attributed largely to Kurt Lewin and his associates and students. Lewin (1890-1947), a native of Germany, received his doctorate at the University of Berlin, where he was later professor of psychology and philosophy. In 1932 he came to the United States. He taught at Stanford, Cornell, and Iowa, and in 1944 became director of the Research Center for Group Dynamics at the Massachusetts Institute of Technology. His students now are working at the Research Center for Group Dynamics, University of Michigan, Duke, Kansas Universities, and other institutions.

Lewin considered psychology a science closely related to everyday life. He wanted most of all to study the various problems of the social sciences involving minority groups, political organizations, and international and intercultural relations. In the course of applying his psychological theory to problems in these areas he became interested in "teaching" and "learning". In keeping with his interests, he developed some new problems for psychology and was highly creative in his methods for solving them. As a leader in development of methods of group dynamics and action research, he thought that actual experiments with groups could be performed under precisely controlled conditions. His study of the effects of various social climates on youth is an example of an experiment in group dynamics. This study was conducted with groups of boys in a boys' club. By means of the relationship of a leader to his respective group, anarchic, autocratic, and democratic social climates were experimentally developed. Careful note was made of the behaviours of the boys in each social climate. The process required to change the social climate of a group from one form to another also was studied. In many circles, action research has become an accepted method of scientific procedure; group studies are so performed that key individuals in the social situation being investigated, through serving as recorders, observers, and analyzers, actively participate in conducting the study. Through this method teachers may systematically study the student-teacher relationships which exist in their own school.

The center of Lewin's psychological interest was in the motivating conditions of person-environment situations. Furthermore, he was extremely interested in democratic principles and practices. It is no accident that his psychological system provides a foundation for a psychology of learning germane to American democratic society. Although field theory is applicable to all fields of psychology, it is particularly useful in social, personality, and educational psychology.

Lewin thought that during its development psychology somehow had missed much of what was at the heart of scientific modes of thought. He was convinced that the various S-R associationisms represented an inadequate approach to the study of psychology. Thus, he developed his "field psychology" in such way as to make it fundamentally different from the various S-R associationisms. Whereas S-R associationisms study psychology as a series of events, the very term *field* of field psychology implies that, psychologically interpreted, everything happens at once. Within field psychology, behaviour has a unique meaning; it is described, not in physical terms, but in terms of what exists for the person being studied.

Lewin's goal was to make the concepts of field psychology of sufficient scope to be applicable to all kinds of behaviour and yet specific enough to permit representation of a definite person in a concrete situation. He observed that conventional laws of S-R associationistic psychology are based on statistical predictions, and that statistical predictions may apply to the average of children or to the typical behaviour of an age group, but they do not anticipate what a given person will do in a specific situation. He thought that objectivity in psychology demanded representing the field adequately and accurately as it exists for an individual at a particular time. Consequently, to be objective in psychology one must be subjective; one must observe situations as the person being studied views them.

What is the Method of Cognitive-Field Psychology?

Lewin's *field* psychology more precisely is called *topological and vector* psychology. In developing his psychology he borrowed ideas and concepts from other disciplines, namely, geometry and physics. Key concepts which he borrowed were "topology" from geometry and "vector" from physics. In using these and related concepts, he did not adhere rigidly to the definitions of their mother sciences but construed them in a manner most useful to his system of psychology.

Some scientists have criticized Lewin for giving these terms a somewhat different meaning from what they have in other areas of knowledge. Lewin has answered their criticism by stating that scientists in any area should use any concept in the ways that lend themselves most effectually to pursuit of their problems. Relativists encourage cooperation among all scientific endeavours, but they do not insist that any area of science be restricted by the specific laws, principles, concepts, and definitions of a sister science.

Through use of topological and vector concepts, Lewin pictured psychological reality in terms of field relationships of a person and his environment. In so doing he applied the method of field theory as it had been developed in the physical sciences. However, since concepts of the physical sciences did not lend themselves to a science of psychology, he did not use the same concepts and facts as did field theorists in sister sciences.

What is the Role of Theories and Laws in Cognitive-Field Psychology?

In contrast to the professed practice of most S-R associationists, including Skinner, Lewin made much use of hypotheses and theories. To him, scientific method included not only the processes of observation and classification of data, but also formulating and testing hypotheses. Letting the facts speak for themselves was not enough. He wanted to develop considered hunches and see whether they would check out. Consequently, collection and classification of behavioural facts was deemed an inadequate process for answering questions involving conditions and causes of events. Lewin agreed with S-R associationists that research should begin with careful observation. However, since he emphasized the importance of inferring the motives of people being studied, his observation was done in a different way and for a different purpose.

> Only with the help of theories can one determine casual interrelationships. A science without theory is blind because it lacks that element which alone is able to organize facts and to give direction to research. Even from a practical point of view the mere gathering of facts has limited value. It cannot give an answer to the question that is most important for practical purposes—namely, what must one do to obtain a desired effect in given concrete cases? To answer this question it is necessary to have a theory, but a theory which is empirical and not speculative. This means that theory and fact must be closely related to each other.

Lewin's purpose was to formulate laws—relationships—predictive of behaviour of individual persons in their specific life spaces. He was convinced that in order to understand and predict behaviour, one must consider a person and his environment a pattern of interdependent facts or functions. Furthermore, he regarded as lawful all events which occur in a person's life space, even those occurring only once. Thus, instead of placing emphasis on a mathematical average of as many different cases as possible, he centered attention on careful, full descriptions of particular person-environmental situations. "The general laws of psychology are statements of the empirical relations between these constructive elements or certain properties of them. It is possible to construct an infinite number of constellations [life spaces] in line with these laws; each of these constellations corresponds to an individual case at a given time."

What are Some Essential Features of Cognitive-Field Psychology?

There are some features of field psychology which make it distinctly different from any of the mechanistic psychologies. The foremost of these features is its unique approach to the study of perception and reality. Other important characteristics are interpretation of intelligent behaviour as purposive, emphasis upon psychological functions rather than objects, a situational as opposed to a historical point of view, and stress upon the principle of contemporaneity. We expand each of these points in the following sections.

1. *Perception and Reality Defined Relativistically:* The field, i.e., life space, which influences an individual is described, not in "objective," physical terms, but in the way it exists for that person at that time. Thus, there is no attempt to relate behaviour to a biological organism and its physical or geographical environment as such. In field psychology, the psychological concept *person* is much broader than is the biological concept *organism*. A life space or field consists of the content of an individual's perception. Neither the organism nor the environment alone is the one main factor. Rather, a person and his environment are simultaneously interacting and participating in perception; they constitute an SMI (simultaneous mutual interaction).

Perception, here, is interpreted in its broadest possible sense. It does not mean mere consciousness. There is evidence from observation of human and animal behaviour that one cannot use consciousness as the sole criterion of what is a part of a life space. A child playing in his yard behaves differently when his mother is home and when she is out, yet he probably at no time verbalizes—is specially conscious—of her being home or away. Children in a schoolroom with teacher A conduct themselves quite differently from when they are with teacher B. Yet they may at no time consciously formulate the two patterns of behaviour. Likewise dogs and other animals size up situations and do the best they can for themselves; however, there is little if any evidence that in so doing they carry on a conscious process. Perception, then, must be construed to cover all the different ways one has of getting to know his environment.

In *apparently* the same situation, a person at different times may perceive quite different aspects of a situation and behave accordingly. Furthermore, provision of opportunity for one to perceive certain aspects of a physical or social environment in a certain way by no means guarantees that that particular perception will occur or that the perception which does occur will have anything like a one-to-one relationship to the objective environment as it appears to someone else. Drs. Adelbert Ames, E. Engel, and Hadley Cantril have performed experiments at the Institute of Associated Research, Hanover, New Hampshire, which show that in perception nothing is absolutely fixed. Rather, one interprets everything in terms of the situation as a whole. What one perceives—his reality—consists of what he makes of what seems to be himself and his environment. Depending on the habits—insights or understandings—he brings to a particular occasion, he seems to give meaning and order to things in terms of his own needs, abilities, and purposes.

A description of two experiments performed at the Hanover Institute will give some idea of the nature and significance of these studies. Dr. Engel was curious to see what would happen when a person viewed two different pictures through a stereoscope. One set of his "stereograms" consisted of pairs of small photographs of football players, one to be viewed by the right eye, the other by the left. There was enough similarity in the pairs of pictures for a subject to get binocular fusion. However, when a person looked into the stereoscope and described the face he saw it was neither of the faces represented by the photographs. Instead, he described a new and different face, usually made up of the dominant features of both faces he was viewing with separate eyes.

Dr. Cantril reports experiments with a pair of stereograms. Each stereogram was a photograph of a statue in the Louvre; one the Madonna with Child, the other a lovely young female nude. A typical viewing of the pair of stereograms proceeded as follows: The subject first saw only a Madonna with Child, then a few seconds later exclaimed, "but my—she is undressing." She had somehow lost the baby she was holding and her robe had slipped from her shoulders. "Then in a few more seconds she lost her robe completely and became a young nude." Sometimes the process is reversed. Other people never see the nude and others never see the Madonna. Apparently, what a person "sees" in a situation depends upon his needs, abilities, purposes, and insights as well as upon what is "out there."

Since reality, relativistically defined , consists of what one makes of what comes to him through his senses or otherwise, one's person is what he makes of himself, and his environment consists of what he makes of that which surrounds him. In keeping with his relativistic outlook, a field psychologist shuns the use of concepts implying fixed traits or rigid habits of personalities. He recognizes the difficulty of man's ever getting outside himself sufficiently to make final statements about what is absolutely real or true. Since he regards truth as tentative and instrumental (not final), he shies away from making dogmatic statements about the nature of man and the universe. Rather, a statement is considered true because of its accuracy in prediction and the consensus of people competent in its area in regard to the possible consequences of acting on it—its usefulness. It should be emphasized here that a relativistic definition of truth in no way discounts the value of truths. Rather, it supposedly defines truth in a more discerning manner.

2. *Purposiveness of Behaviour:* Within cognitive-field psychology *purposive* is nearly a synonym for *intelligent.* A unique characteristic of human beings is their capacity to pursue long-sighted, as well as short-sighted, self-interests. Field psychologists recognize the significance of this fact. When a child is behaving purposively, he is pursuing his goals in light of the insights he has available; he is behaving intelligently. The goal or goals toward which a child strives psychologically exist in his present life space. The phenomenon of goal is such that expectation—not actual realization—is its essence. Although the content of a gaol may be in the future or may not occur at all, this gal as a psychological fact necessarily lies in the present life space. A student's goal to become a teacher is a goal toward teaching as he now sees it. This goal may be a far cry from teaching as it eventually is experienced.

The *purposiveness* of cognitive-field psychology is *immanent,* not *transcendental,* to the world of experience; it prevails in workaday life situations. That is, careful study of children, as well as of other animate beings, in life situations indicates that if they are active at all they are trying to do something, and that, through our anticipating what they are trying to do, we can predict most accurately what they are going to do. Whether there is transcendental—supernatural—purpose in the universe is another problem which is related only indirectly to the concept *purposive* as developed in field psychology. Relativistic purposiveness is immanent.

3. *Emphasis Upon Psychological Function:* A third important feature of cognitive-field psychology is its emphasis upon psychological functions or events as contrasted with objects or movements. A fallacy of S-R associationists, noted by relativistic field theorists, has been their tendency to describe the character of an activity by its physical aspects only and to neglect the great effect of the psychological setting. For example, experiments on satiation clearly indicate that fatigue often is largely a matter of psychological boredom, not physical tiredness. Moving one's arm in an identical way while making certain lines may have different psychological and physiological effects, according to the meaning of this activity to him. The act of repeatedly making a pattern of four lines may have become disintegrated and the arm fatigued as a result of oversatiation. Then a change of the same movements of making a different pattern of lines or a picture from these lines suffices to bring a reorganization of the activity and erase the bodily symptoms of fatigue. If the meaning of an activity is changed by imbedding it in a different context, bodily symptoms of fatigue tend to disappear.

Psychological is understood to mean in accordance with the logic of a growing mind or intelligence. To be psychological in his pursuits, a field psychologist must look at the world through the eyes of a learner. To describe a situation psychologically, one must describe the situation which confronts an individual. Such a situation is viewed as a pattern of person-environmental relationships which provide and limit opportunity. Once the person-environmental structure is established, the problem is to use constructs and methods adequate to deal with the underlying dynamics of behaviour and to do this in a scientifically sound manner.

A construct is an invented idea. It is a generalized concept not directly observed but formed from data that are observed. Its purpose is to correlate a broad range of data which have some basic functional similarly, despite marked superficial differences. Need, psychologically defined, is an example of a construct. It has no length, breadth, thickness, or mass, yet it is a crucial, functional concept in studying human activity. Lewinians speak of observable data as *phenotypes* and unobservable, constructual representations as *genotypes.*

A functional definition of psychological behaviour opens the way for extensive use of systematic constructs. Whereas an S-R associationist supposedly restricts his generalizations to those based on the use of "objective" data, a relativistic field psychologist knowingly uses constructs which go beyond the observable data. Constructs provide a means of bridging the gap between general laws which cannot be observed and the functions of individual persons which can be gathered as data. Thus, through the use of a few constructs the essence of an individual case can be adequately represented.

4. *Situational Emphasis:* A fourth definitive characteristic of cognitive-field psychology is that a study always begins with a description of a situation as a whole—the field—and proceeds to specific and detailed analysis of various aspects of the situation. At no time are aspects of a field viewed as isolated elements. In the study of a life space with its various constructs, the idea constantly is kept to the forefront that no two constructs or concepts are mutually exclusive, but that everything to some degree and in some sense is dependent upon everything else. Readers again are cautioned that, should they slip into giving the constructs independent physical or biological existence, they will be attempting to understand a relativistic psychology in mechanistic fashion.

5. *Principle of Contemporaneity:* The fifth essential feature of cognitive-field psychology is the one most often misunderstood. Contemporaneity literally means all at one time. A psychological field or life space is a construct of such nature that it contains everything psychological which is taking place in relation to a specific person at a given time. The unit of time, microscopically viewed, is a moment; however, macroscopically considered, it may cover hours or even weeks. Whatever the length of time, evrything is going on at once—that is the meaning of *field*. Readers are urged neither to reject the concept of contemporaneity summarily nor to give it an oversimplified interpretation.

Use of the concept *psychological field* implies that everything which affects behaviour at a given time should be represented in the field existing at that time, and that only those facts can affect behaviour which exists at a given time contains, as well as the environment of the present, the views of that individual about his future and his past. It should be emphasized that any psychological past or psychological future is a simultaneous part of a psychological field existing at a given time. Psychologically, there is no past or future except as it enters into the present. "Since neither the [physical] past nor the [physical] future exists at the present moment it cannot have effect at the present."

An individual's views about the past, as about the rest of the physical and social world, are often incorrect; nevertheless they constitute a significant psychological past in his own life space. Furthermore, the goals of an individual as a psychological fact lie in the present and they too constitute an essential part of his life space. The content of the goals may lie in the future and they may never occur. The nature of an expectation is not dependent upon the event's coming to pass. If an Indian warrior were brave so that in the future he would go to the happy hunting ground, whether or not there actually existed a future happy hunting ground would have no bearning on his being brave. His happy hunting ground is a part—a goal region—of his contemporaneous life space.

The principle of contemporaneity means that psychological events are determined by conditions at the time behaviour occurs. One cannot derive behaviour from either the future or the past as such. Both S-R associationists and field psychologists see little basis for future cause of events. However, field psychologists differ sharply from S-R assciationists in their insistence that derivation of behaviour from the past is equally metaphysical—beyond the realm of science. Since past events do not now exist, they, as such, can have no effect on the present. Thus, influence of a future can be only anticipatory, and effects of a past can be only indirect. However, through continuity of life spaces, past psychological fields do have their "trace"—residue—in a present field which influences a person's behaviour. *Trace* is a region or condition of a present life space which has *similarity* to a characteristic of earlier life spaces. In other words, *trace* means that there is some similarity of regions of succeeding life spaces. When a person uses an earlier acquired insight in solving a current problem, the insight is an example of trace.

The principle of contemporaneity has definite implications for education. When through continuity the past enters into the present, knowledge of the past and its heritage is of great value and significance. However, the mistake of making records and remains of the past *in themselves* the central materials of education is that it cuts the vital connection of present and past. Thus, it tends ot make the past a rival of the present and the present a more or less futile imitation of a past which can never be known in its absolutely exact form. Lewin's principal construct to represent a contemporaneous situation is *life space.*

WHAT IS A LIFE SPACE?

Life space is a scientific formulation developed for the purpose of expressing what is possible and impossible in the life of a person and anticipating what is likely to occur. It represents the total pattern of factors or influences which affect behaviour at a certain moment. Behaviour means any change in a life space which is psychological—in accordance with a growing intelligence. A person's life space represents the total world in which the person lives. This may include his precepts, knowledge, and beliefs; his forward and backward time perspective; and abstract ideas as well as concrete objects. Man's universe has become largely symbolic in nature. Thus, a life space includes not only physical reality but also language, myth, art, and religion.

Lewin's basic formula is $B = f(P, E)$. Behaviour, B, is the f, function; P, psychological person; and E, psychological environment. A psychological person and his psychological environment, so formulated constitute a life space. A life space or psychological field is not defined in terms of mere consciousness or awareness; neither is it an organism in an environment. Rather, it is a dynamic whole of such nature that a change in any part affects other parts, and every change depends upon the whole; it is a totality of coexisting facts. Psychological person and psychological environment are not mutually exclusive; however, they may be considered to function as subwholes of a psychological field or life space. A life space is surrounded by a foreign hull—the aspects of the physical and social environment which to that person at that moment are not psychological. The

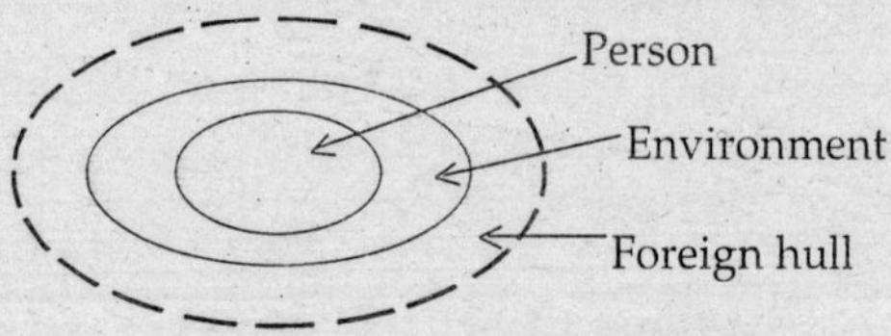

Fig 4.1 : A Life Space.

foreign hull of a life space consists of all the potential perceptions as contrasted with the functional perceptions of a person's unique field.

In a life space, a person and his environment are in simultaneous mutual interaction (SMI) and are mutually interdependent. Each depends upon the other for its nature and functions; it is impossible to treat one adequately without also treating the other. One's person is definitive of one's environment and likewise one's environment is definitive of oneself. A person, his environment, and the foreign hull of his life space may be represented by concentric figures. A person is within his environment and both are within the foreign hull as shown in Fig. 4.1.

What is a Person?

A psychological self or person is a crucial aspect of a life space. Under no circumstances is a person considered identical with an organism. Thus, a person is not limited to a mind or body; neither is it a mind and body. Rather, a person is a *consciously behaving self.* It is the center of abilities and needs; it is what a child means when he says "I" or "me". The concepts *self* and *person* are used interchangeably and may be considered synonyms. Teachers more often think if Billy Smith and Sally Anderson as persons. However, Billy and Sally, when thinking of themselves, are more likely to use the term *self.* A person is in no sense an abstract ego or self which can be experienced apart from any social context. It is within the social living of an individual that a self emerges and continues to change throughout life. It may be said that the basic human need is for preservation and enhancement of this emergent self or person. One even owns a "loyal" dog in order to enhance and give constancy to his psychological self or person.

A person may be represented as a differentiated region of a life space. The field of a newborn baby is something like "one big blooming buzzing confusion." Then as one lives his life, although he may not think of it in these specific terms, his total situation is structured as his *self*—person—and his *environment*. Some aspects of experience involve the central core of a person; they are very near and dear to him. Others are of a less vital, peripheral sort. We may think of a person as structured in outer

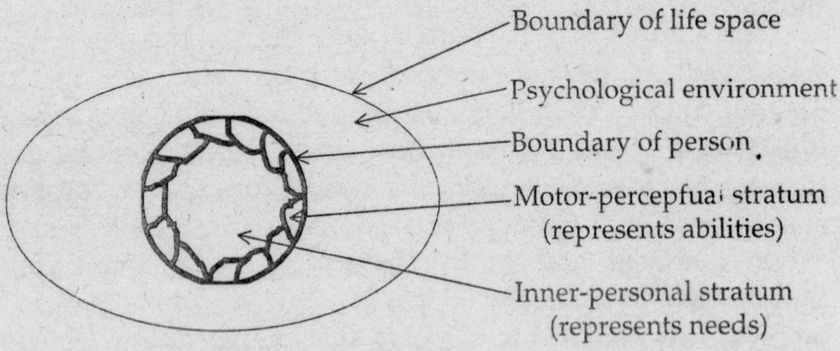

Fig. 4.2 : A Structured Person in a Life space.

and inner layers. Some experiences involve only the more peripheral areas, whereas others embrace the most central regions of a psychological person.

Psychologically, a person is composed of (1) a motor-perceptual stratum (region) and (2) an inner-personal stratum (region). The motor-perceptual stratum has the position of a boundary zone between the inner-personal region and the environment. It represents the knowing and manipulative abilities of a person. *Motor-perceptual system* denotes the phenomenon which a mechanist would see simply as body or organism. A mechanist, that is, would set his pattern of thinking in a physiological rather than a psychological frame of reference. In a sense, the motor-perceptual system is the tool of the inner-personal system. Like regions of the environment, it provides opportunity and limits opportunity. However, it is more closely identified with the self than is the environment. Whereas abilities are centered in the motor-perceptual system, needs are centered in the inner-personal system. Since the motor-perceptual region is between the inner-personal region and the environment, it performs functions of both person and environment. This means that a person acts in relation to his environment and simultaneously realizes the consequences of so doing.

The form which the development of selfhood takes depends upon the interaction of a person and his environment. An organism, in a sense, is an aspect of each—person and environment. Furthermore, whether something belongs to the self or to the environment depends, among other things, upon present needs and other factors of the inner-personal region. "Needs or other states of the inner-personal regions can influence the environment only by way of a bodily expression or a bodily action, that is, by way of a region which one can call the motor region."

What is a Psychological Environment?

The psychological environment of a life space consists of everything psychologically outside an individual person which means anything to him. It is made up of everything in which, toward which, or away from which a person can change his psychological position. "Environment is understood psychologically sometimes to mean the *momentary situation* of the child, at other times to mean the *milieu*, in the sense of the chief characteristics of the permanent situation."

What is a Foreign Hull?

A foreign hull is composed of those aspects of an organism's environment which are observably by the one studying the particular person but which at that moment have no significance for the person being studied. Thus, it is the complex of all nonpsychological factors surrounding a life space. It is made up of physical and social factors which, at the time being considered, are not subject to a person's psychological conceptualization, but which may at any time become parts of his psychological field. Thus, it is that part of his physical and social environment which, at the moment under consideration, is not included in his psychological environment. The physical and social conditions of the foreign hull limit the variety of possible life spaces. Anything which appears to be in a child's physical environment, but of which he is completely oblivious, is in the foreign hull of his life space. However, if he reacts to that thing in any way, either positively or negatively, it is no longer in his foreign hull but in his life space proper. Should Billy have only contempt for Miss Smith, she is in his life space just as much as if he loves and respects her.

Nonpsychological factors observed only by an outsider can at the next moment become psychological for the person being studied. A characteristic of the parts of a life space and their regions is permeability. There can be movement both ways through the boundary of a person or a life space or through any of their regions. For an aspect of the physical world to influence the intelligent behaviour of a person, it must be moved from a foreign hull into his life space through his interaction with it.

Continuity of Life Spaces

A life space is of a moment's duration. One moves through a series of life spaces. In dynamic human beings, we would not expect consecutive life spaces to be identical. However, we can anticipate some degree of similarity and continuity of life spaces as the experiences of one moment shade into those of the next. For practical schoolroom procedures, depending upon the purposes being pursued, we assume a fixity of life spaces for longer periods than a moment—perhaps a class period, a week, or a month.

Within a series of overlapping life spaces, a person's life is a continuity of psychological tensions, locomotions, and new equilibriums. When there is an increase of tension in one part of a life space relative to the rest of the system, disequilibrium occurs. When a person finds himself in a state of disequilibrium and attempts to return to equilibrium, psychic energy is expended; he engages in psychological locomotion. Should tension throughout the system become completely equalized, output of energy would cease; the total system would come to rest.

Of course, throughout a life span this absolute balance is never achieved. Since a person is intelligent and purposive, he expands and restructures his life space and consequently new disequilibriums emerge. This process gives a dynamic nature to human living which makes it immensely interesting and challenging.

HOW IS LEARNING DEFINED IN COGNITIVE-FIELD THEORY?

Kurt Lewin was interested primarily in a study of human motivation. Thus, his field theory was not developed as a theory of learning, but more as a theory of motivation and perception. However, he was concerned with the application of his theory to learning situations and he did some writing in this vein. To develop a cognitive-field theory of learning, one must, while borrowing heavily from the ideas and constructs of Lewin, to some degree deviate from his usages in order to center thinking upon a psychology of learning.

Whereas S-R associationists tend to consider learning a separate psychological process, field theorists see it as one of the several interdependent functions within the framework of life spaces. Since, in field psychology, learning and development are nearly synonymous concepts, there is much in common between this section on cognitive-field theory of learning which treats development within a relativistic frame of reference.

Field psychological is a purposive psychology; it assumes that intellectual processes are deeply affected by an individual's goals and that learning activity, including habit formation, is goal directed. Goal or purpose, therefore, is central to cognitive-field learning theory. This contrasts sharply with S-R associationisms, which either ignore goal or purpose completely or make it only peripheral and incidental. Associationists have tended to consider any concept of goal direction or purposiveness *teleological.* To them, *teleological* means deriving present behaviour from the future and consequently sounds mystical and superstitious. Thus, associationists have placed emphasis upon past events as the cause of present behaviour. Since field psychology is goal centered, cognitive-field theorists inveigh against use of such mechanistic terms as *reflex arc, connectionism, conditioning, associationism,* and *reinforcement.*

Cognitive-field theory involves the kind of generalizations about learning which may be applied to actual persons in school situations. It is associated with the knowing and understanding functions which give meaning to a situation. It is built around the purposes underlying behaviour, the goals involved in behaviour, and persons' means and processes of understanding themselves as they function in relation to their goals. Factors of a life space acquire meaning as a person formulates his goals and develops insights into ways of achieving them. Thus, this is a "goal-insight" theory of learning.

Why is Cognitive-Field Theory Contrasted with S-R Associationisms?

Cognitive-field theory is so developed as to contrast rather sharply with the various associationistic or stimulus-response theories. Advocates of this theory do not deny existence of neural couplings but they do challenge the importance of the concept; they assert that it is inadequate to explain the learning process. Their position continues to be supported by research. In 1958 K. S. Lashley (1890-1958), who had devoted a lifetime to study of nervous function, stated: "I cannot pretend to have formulated a complete and satisfactory account of how the brain thinks. I recognize gaps and inconsistencies in my formulation of the problems, and the hypotheses and I have suggested will probably collapse under the weight of additional evidence."

Lewin performed his early research with associative learning. He discovered that for terms or ideas to be associated—to have a connection formed between them—they had to belong to the same tension system. He found no force within mere association of items which leads to their reproduction; reproduction of acts or thoughts must be motivated. Thus, he contended that items are linked together in "memory" no through connections or associations but by the way they fit into the field organization or the task as a whole—by their configuration.

Since cognitive-field theorists are convinced that psychological activity depends upon energy related to psychological tension systems, to them no mere coupling principle can adequately explain psychic activity. They challenge forcefully the principle of adhesion, the attachment of one thing to another so that revival of the first brings forth the second. Consequently, they think that "reward" and "punishment" do not stamp in and stamp out associations. Rather, they bring changes in the valences—values—of parts of the psychological environment and in the tension systems of the person in relation to his environment.

Perception of situations, not physical events as such, is the immediate cause of behaviour. A psychological tension system exists whenever a psychological need or intention appears. As a need or intention is fulfilled, tension is released. The strength of a need correlates with a psychological force. Such a force has two basic results. It leads either to psychological movement of the person in the direction of the force or to a change of his cognitive structure corresponding to such a locomotion. This means that release of tension may be achieved either through reaching a goal or through restructuring one's life space, i.e., through learning to "see things differently."

A high school girl has a driving ambition to become a movie star; thus in her life space there is a pressing tension between herself and stardom. Assuming that, like most girls, she does not have "the stuff" to become a movie star, tension must be relieved through some other course. She might reconstruct her life space so as to substitute a reachable goal for her earlier unattainable one. Or she might achieve a more drastic reconstruction and change her goals so that there is nothing left of stardom or any substitute. Such reconstruction of a life space is the essence of the learning process. Learning, so construed, is a change in the cognitive structure of, or insights in regard to, one's life space, which consists of a person and his environment.

How is Learning a Change in Insight or in Cognitive Structure?

Insights may be verbal, preverbal, or nonverbal. One may gain an insight before he has words to express it, one may have a complete and exact verbalization involving no or little insight, or the insight and the verbalization may be achieved simultaneously. There is evidence that even nonverbal animals solve mazes by formulating a series of cognitive structures and testing them, and that they solve their problems through gaining insight into their situations. By being given food, a dog is taught to "sit". Later he wants a toy which he sees on a table. He goes to the table, assumes his "sitting" position, and barks.

It is an insightful process when a ball player gets a feel for the correct swing of his bat, when a little child discovers how to dress himself, when a boy or girl learns to drive an automobile, when a child gets the ideas of multiplication, perhaps through addition, or when a college student learns how to "read" Shakespeare.

It is in connection with goal-directed behaviour that insightful learning occurs. One's direction or purposeful activity in his life space is dependent upon its cognitive structure. Remember that a life space contains a person (self) as well as his environment, and that through gaining and changing insights he cognitively structures both. A completely new situation would be cognitively unstructured; a person would have no knowledge of what would lead or point to what. Thus, at that moment his behaviour would be completely random. (This is the position of an animal when it is first placed in a "problem box.") However, rarely, if ever, does a person function in a completely unstructured situation. More often we find students in situations which are inadequately or inharmoniously structured. This means that they have problems and need to extend their learning—change cognitive structures.

A person's behaviour in a relatively unstructured situation would appear exploratory, vacillating, and contradictory. An adolescent, for example, vacillates between a child's and an adult's world, neither of which to him is well structured. Newly acquired adult regions of his life space will not fit into a child's world, and some of the child's regions to which he clings will not fit in the adult world he is, at times, attempting to enter.

A child's behaviour, to a very large degree, depends upon the cognitive structure of his life space. Learning results in building psychological traces which contribute to the structure and dynamics of future life spaces and thus affect future performance. Memory processes refer to cognitively structured similarities between an individual's life spaces which exist at different times. It is because of the continuity of life spaces and their cognitive structures that learning is of value to a person.

Good insight into a present life space or situation tends to provide excellent foresight into the cognitive structure of future life spaces. Suppose a college student wishes to understand and appreciate principles of human development and learning and to prepare himself to apply them in future teaching situations. An excellent procedure would be for him to acquire a deep understanding of himself, his environment, and their relationships in his current series of life spaces.

Learning is a process whereby, through active experience, insights are changed so as to become more serviceable for future guidance. Human beings, when behaving intelligently, are assumed to be purposive and their learning is related to their purposiveness. According to cognitive-field psychology, a child in a learning situation is not unfolding according to nature; neither is he being passively conditioned always to respond in a desired manner. Rather, at his level of maturity and comprehension, he is differentiating and restructuring himself and his environment; he is gaining or changing insights.

Learning is a dynamic process; a constantly expanding world of understanding is reaching out to encompass a constantly expanding psychological world. At birth, a child's world is very small. But on his level he is trying to understand that small world. He is trying to understand how to get food. Soon he will be seeking warmth. Later he will seek means of getting attention. When he is an adult, in order more adequately to influence his own adult destiny, he will seek insights into his world as it affects him. Hence, to one with a cognitive-field approach, learning means development of a sense of direction or bearing which can be used, when occasion offers and if found desirable, as a guide for conduct. This all means that learning is enhancement of intelligence.

Lewin considered learning to consist of four types of change, namely, change in cognitive structure, change in motivation, change in group belongingness or ideology, and gain in voluntary control of musculature or learning skills. He distinguished between the first two rather sharply. Thus, he tended to separate cognitive and motivational problems. To him, change in cognitive structure meant development of perceptual knowledge. It was centered in the topological—structural—aspects of a situation. Change in motivation, in contrast, meant learning to like or dislike certain areas—aspects of a life space. However, he recognized that even changes in motivation arise from changes in cognitive structure; to change the valence of an activity for a child, one must change the cognitive structure of that child's life space in regard to it.

Growing into a culture through one's change in group belongingness and ideology and his development of skills also involves primarily perceptions of oneself and the people and objects around him. Thus, these two types of change, too, are principally a process of change in the cognitive structure. Consequently, in treating learning, Lewin's pivotal concept was change in cognitive structure. In 1945 he wrote, "A change in action ideology, a real acceptance of a changed set of facts and values, a change in the perceived social world—all three are but different expressions of the same process."

The cognitive structure of a life space corresponds to the meaningful knowledge of a person, knowledge being defined in the broadest sense possible. A change of cognitive structure may occur in any part of a person's life space, including the psychological past, present, or future. By defining all learning as essentially a process of developing cognitive structure or insights, we escape the dangers of forming a dichotomy—split—of knowledge and motivation. The formation of this dichotomy has led in the past to a rather sharp distinction between learning of facts and development of personality, character, and attitudes. Ideas involving emotional, motivational, and imaginative functions ultimately are as necessary in "factual" mathematical, scientific, and historical pursuits as they are in literature and the fine arts.

Differentiation and Generalization

Changes in cognitive structure are of three types: differentiation and its complement—generalization—and restructurization. Differentiation is the process in which regions are subdivided into smaller regions. An example of differentiation in early life is a child's distinguishing parts of his body—arms, legs, head, and trunk. In differentiation of unstructured areas, previously vague and unstructured areas of a life space become cognitively structured and thus more specific. A person makes more sense of what, to him, was previously a "blooming, buzzing confusion." As a child grows he differentiates himself—his person—from his environment, different aspects of his person and environment from each other, and an irreality level from the reality level of his life space. When he realizes that there is no Santa Claus but continues to talk about him, he is differentiating irreality from reality. In contrast, a very young child does not make this distinction; everything is "real". In this way a child distinguishes and identifies significant features of himself and his environment. Also, during a person's psychological development, through differentiation his time perspective enlarges. He differentiates past and future time regions of a present life space and thereby brings a more and more distant past and future to affect present behaviour.

One generalizes when he forms a concept which includes previously differentiated aspects of himself or his environment. Generalization arises through categorization of subregions into a unified region of one's life space. When a child learns that cats, dogs, horses, and birds are animals or a student learns that his hopes, dreams, beliefs, and anticipations are all subregions of a "future" region in his contemporaneous life space, he is generalizing.

Restructurization

A person not only differentiates and generalizes his life space into new regions but simultaneously changes the meanings of respective regions in relationship to himself and to one another. Restructurization means that one defines or redefines directions in his life space; he learns what actions will lead to what results. He does this through perception of significant, relationships of different functional regions of his life space. Consequently, restructurization consists of separating certain regions which have been connected and connecting certain regions which have been separated. (Remember that regions are defined as functionally distinguishable parts of a life space.)

When we were quite young, most of us differentiated people from their environments. Later we differentiated people into various races, classes, and groups. Perhaps about the same time we generalized them into Republicans and Democrats or

Christians and non-Christians. As a person learns, he continues to differentiate and generalize himself and his environment, but he also restructures the differentiated and generalized regions of his life space so as to give them new meanings.

What is Habit?

Habit is assumed to be goal directed. It is fluid, effective, efficient action arising through a person's operating on the basis of the insights he possesses. Habit is not a fixed sequence of acts which can be explained adequately as a system of preformed pathways in the nervous system. (Of course, some sort of concomitant neural action is not denied.) When one operates in terms of the insights or cognitive structure he has, habit is manifested. Change in cognitive structure through differentiation, generalization, and restructurization means a change in meaning. When an event has meaning its psychological position and direction are determined; one knows what actions will lead to what results. This is the basis of habit. The habits of a person at a given time constitute a significant function of his life space. Habit enables one to behave intelligently without thinking. Often there is not time to think; indeed, thinking then might be disastrous. What happens when your car is closely following a large truck going 70 miles per hour and the truck stops abruptly?

What is Intelligence?

Cognitive-field psychologists define intelligence as ability to respond in present situations on the basis of anticipation of future possible consequences and with a view to controlling the consequences which ensue. One's intelligence so defined consists of the number and quality of his insights. Within this frame of reference, successful behaviour rightfully may be called intelligent only when a person might have done otherwise and his actions were premised upon his envisioning what he was doing and why. Learning is enhancement of one's intelligence. This means that all of its forms—development of logical organization, social insight, appreciation, information, and skills—have a common element. They all involve a change in the experiential situation of a person which gives him a basis for a greater predictability and control in relation to his behaviour; they enhance his intelligence.

Whereas S-R associationists are prone to think of intelligence as something substantive—nounlike—with which a child is born and which can be changed little if at all, cognitive-field psychologists place greater emphasis upon the adjective *intelligent* or the adverb *intelligently.* Behaviourists and connectionists consider children, in their essential nature, passive pieces of protoplasm, more or less sensitive to external and internal stimulation. The ones with the highest number of receptors and the most sensitive receptors are deemed most intelligent; they react the quickest and most accurately when their "triggers" are pulled.

As an adjective *intelligent* is descriptive of effectual behaviour. An innate specific intelligence is not necessarily postulated at all. The intelligence that any intelligence test measures consists of a person's insights and his ability to use them in situations. These insights are in no way innate but are acquired as a dynamic person interacts with his psychological environment. These is little psychological basis for the assertion that IQ is innately constant. The organism which plays its part as a person develops insights has genetic qualities, but these are biological, not psychological, traits.

How does Intelligent Behaviour Differ from Nonintelligent Behaviour?

Cognitive-field psychologists view an intelligently behaving person as one who acts as if he is pursuing a purpose and has some foresight as to how it is to achieved. Nonintelligent behaviour arises when a person is pushed or pulled about as an inert, nonliving object, just as a stone dislodged from a place of support falls to a lower lodgement. Let us picture a man straddling a pole and attempting to raise it from among a pile of similar poles. He is behaving intelligently. As the poles are moved, their position changes and suddenly a group of poles falls on the far end of the pole he is lifting; another group in the center serves as a fulcrum and the poles raise him into the air. When he is raised into the air, he displays non-intelligent behaviour. He is behaving—moving—but there is no connection between this specific movement and his foresight of consequences. In intelligent behaviour, an activity is carried forward to a goal through a process by which one constantly searches out the conditions for the next step all along the way. Intelligence, then, is largely a matter of foresight.

What is Thinking?

Thinking involves time and a series of life spaces. It is a process whereby an individual remakes old habits and forms new ones. It includes finding, elaborating, and testing hypotheses. Whereas is S-R associationisms creative thinking and imagination really are not "creative" (they represent formulation of new relationships of old materials), in congnitive-field psychology progress in thinking is considered a truly creative event. In this event there is psychological locomotion. A person is oriented toward a goal and there is structuring or restructuring of the field. Thus, thinking arises in a situation where a person feels a need—has a goal. In place of a clear path to that goal he encounters a forked road or no road; the problem presents itself as an unclear, unstructured region. In thinking, then, there is a transformation or restructurization of the total field arising through perception of the total situation. We think our way into a system of living. Progress in thinking means that one is fortunate enough to approach a solution by a new, more productive path. Through thinking one achieves fruitful changes in the cognitive structure of his life space—he gains new insights and he changes old ones.

WHAT IS THE MEANING OF COGNITIVE-FIELD PSYCHOLOGY FOR A SCHOOL SITUATION?

Advocates of cognitive-field psychology think that a teacher should teach, not baby-sit or dictate. A baby-sitter usually performs a custodial function but teaches children little, if anything. A dictator imposes the "right" answers. A teacher, in contrast with both, should perform his democratic teaching role in a process of student-teacher mutual inquiry.

The role of a teacher should be similar to that of a head scientist in a scientific laboratory; he should lead children such manner that he helps them formulate and solve problems. To accomplish this, he should have a rich, extensive background of varied knowledge; he should be alert to the habitual attitudes and outlooks students are developing; and his ideal should be to promote an atmosphere which fosters maximum insightful growth. This means that he should be able to judge which attitudes or insights are conducive to continued growth and which are detrimental. He also should have sympathetic understanding of students as persons and should develop an accurate idea of what actually is going on in the minds—life spaces—of those whom he is teaching.

Topology of a life space shows the various possibilities for psychological movement or action; *vectors* show the moving forces within the topological structure. To understand the behaviour of a child, one must determine the psychological position of the child's person in reference to the goal regions of his life space. This entails knowing the child's social position within and outside various groups, his position in relation to various ideas and activities, and the role of physical objects in his life space. The relative region of a life space in which a child is located determines the qualities of his immediate surroundings. It sets the possibilities for the child's next step in his psychological life—his topology. It also determines his *vectors*—what step or event means action toward and what step means action away from his goals.

A student's life space on a given evening, topologically, may contain a TV set, a book, and a movie. Vectorially, each object and activity has some degree of valence—alluring or repelling power. Should he go to the movie, this means that movie valence is greatest of all. When one behaves intelligently, he does what he wants most to do; if he does not want *to do* it more than he wants *not to do* it, he does not do it.

In a cognitive-field approach to the study of a school situation, a teacher and his students each is considered as a person and his life space. The goal of a teacher should be to have a common intersection of these life spaces. The way to peripheral regions of a person is quite accessible in ordinary conversation. However, it is more difficult to reach more central region, i.e., those needs near and dear to him. To gain an understanding of each child and his cognitive world, a teacher has to develop a sort of disciplined naivete. In order adequately to see Tom through he must see through Tom. He must see Tom's person and environment as Tom sees it. When a teacher gains rapport with a child—when he gains his confidence—his influence can extend to the child's central regions and he is in a position to speak of the child's needs. What a child needs depends primarily upon how he sizes up himself and his material and social environment.

For a teacher to analyze a psychological situation, he should describe the structure of a person and his environment and ascertain their dynamic properties—what they have to do with the child's behaviour. A teacher must see the relationships between the various regions or parts of the child's life space. He must establish the nature of the respective factors residing within, at, and outside the boundary. Factors outside the boundary of a life space, the foreign hull, are those which may be perceived by others but at the moment have no place in the perceptual world of the person being studied. Knowing these facts helps a teacher determine what is possible and what is not, and what might happen and what might not. Then, to understand and accurately predict behaviour, a teacher, in addition to understanding the structure of the child's field, i.e., the interpositional relationships between the parts in his life space, must also ascertain the dynamic properties of the child's life space—the valences of his goals and the barriers to his goals.

Now what does all this mean in a school situation? Let us see an example on schoolroom. "Alice is so absorbed with her teacher and school work that she is oblivious to everything else about her including the other children." The teacher is central in Alice's life space. Alice's school work also is far within the border of her life space. The other children and everything else in the room that is not part of Alice's school work are in the foreign hull of her life space. "Helen is a social butterfly; she wants the attention of most of the children in the classroom. She does give attention to the teacher from time to time, but right now she is concerned with other things." The other children are in Halen's life space; the teacher is at the margin, sometimes in and sometimes out. "John's body is in the classroom but 'psychologically' John is riding a shiny new tractor which is being operated in the field adjoining the school." John's school environment and his psychological environment have little in common. Whereas nothing within the room is in his life space, the tractor is as central as it can be and its valence is very high.

WHAT ARE THE KEY CONCEPTS OF FIELD OR TOPOLOGICAL AND VECTOR PSYCHOLOGY?

Readers will find this section, which explains why field psychology is more specifically named "topological and vector psychology," somewhat technical and perhaps difficult. However, should they seek sharper insights into the deeper implications of field theory, this section will greatly enhance their understanding.

Lewin said, "Topological and vectorial concepts combine power of analysis, conceptual precision, usefulness for derivation and fitness for the total range of psychological problems in a way which, in my opinion, make them superior to any other known conceptual tool in psychology. He felt that topological and vector, or field psychology was characterized by a set of concepts or constructs which permitted representation of psychological reality in a highly adequate fashion. He wanted concepts broad enough to be applicable to all kinds of behaviour and at the same time specific enough to represent a definite person in a concrete situation. This system implements a person's being represented as separated from and yet enclosed within a larger totality—his life space. Thus, it enables one to represent adequately a psychological situation which includes a person, his environment, his needs, his goals and their dynamic interrelations.

For one to grasp fully the ideas of a relativistic, field psychology, it is essential that its key concepts be defined precisely as they are used in this frame of reference. In studying these concepts, readers should keep in mind the essential idea of field psychology: the meanings of all its constructs are mutually interdependent. Each depends for its meaning upon the meanings of all the others.

Furthermore, it should be remembered that a diagram of a life space is figurative. It is difficult, perhaps impossible, to show everything at once. A complete and accurate image of a life space would show all of the psychological facts and constructs in a momentary situation represented by a differentiated person and a differentiated environment. A differentiated person or environment is one structured or functionally divided into various aspects as perceived by the one being studied. Some differentiated aspects of a person are friends, ambitions, self-aggrandizement, and needs and abilities to know about various matters and to carry out activities of different kinds. A differentiated environment contains everything perceived by the person at the time under study.

Lastly we should guard against reifying or making physical things of the psychological constructs whose purpose is to symbolize relationships primarily functional in nature. For example, we should at no time think of a psychological person as synonymous with a biological organism or of a psychological and a physical environment as the same concept.

What are the Three Pivotal Concepts of Field Psychology?

The three pivotal concepts of congnitive-field psychology are life space, topology, and vector. Whereas *life space* is treated in some detail on pages 110-111 of this chapter the concepts *topology and vector* have heretofore been only briefly defined. In this section *life space* is summarized, then *topology* and *vector* are explained in greater detail.

Life Space

Life space contains the whole of one's psychological reality—what one makes of what comes to him. It includes everything that one needs to know about a person in order to understand his concrete behaviour in a specific psychological environment at a certain time. The psychological environment and the person constitute the situation as perceived by that person. Emergence of the properties of a life space depends partly upon the state of the individual as a product of a continuity of life spaces and partly upon his interaction with his physical and social surroundings.

Topology

Topology is a nonmetrical geometry which encompasses concepts such as inside, outside, and boundary but has no dealings with length, breadth, or thickness. No distances are defined.

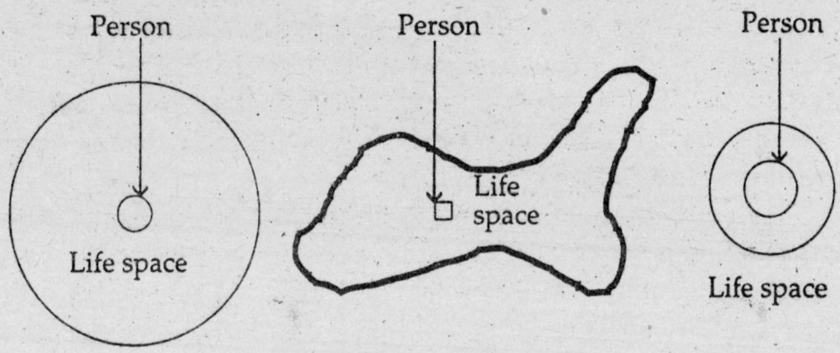

Fig. 4.3 : Topology of Life Space—Three Equal Figures.

Rather topology is concerned with the relative position of the geometric figures being considered. "Topologically there is no difference between a circle, an ellipse, a regular or irregular polygon with any number of sides.... A drop of water and the earth are, from a topological point of view, fully equivalent."

Two basic concepts which topological space denotes are connectedness and part-whole relationships. Topologically, things may be next to, inside, or outside one another. Size or shape has no significance in a topological figure. The life spaces in Fig. 4.3 are topologically equal. Each is a completely bounded area within a larger bounded area.

Topological concepts are used to represent the structure of a life space, to define the range of possible perceptions and actions. This is accomplished by showing the arrangement of the functional parts of a life space. The parts are shown as various regions and their boundaries.

In addition to the person whose life space is being studied, regions represent activities like eating, going to the movies, and making decisions; more passive incidents like being fired or being rewarded; and social entities such as family, church, school, and gang. If the region "going to the movies" is located in a person's life space, the person is either engaging in or thinking about engaging in that activity. If "being fired" is in his life space, he is perceiving that incident and its consequences. "Church" in a life space involves what one makes out of what "church" means to him.

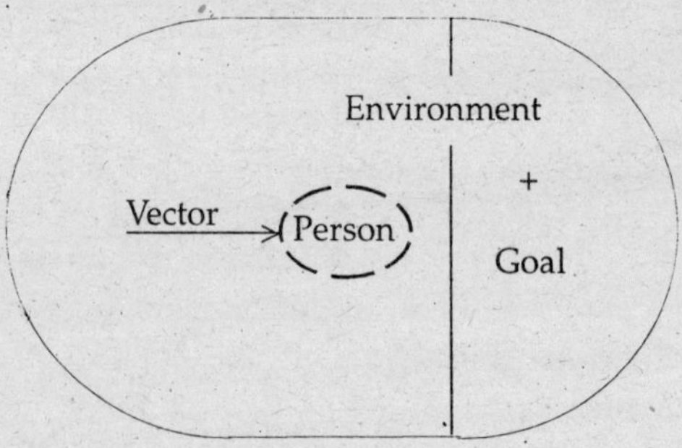

Fig. 4.4 : A Vactor.

Vector

The concept *vector* is borrowed from a system used in mechanics to represent direction and strength as two of the three properties of a force. The third property is its point of application. In psychology a vector represents a force which is influencing movement toward or away from a goal. A force is a tendency to act in a certain way or direction. A vector is a concept equivalent to, and descriptive of, a psychological force. If there is only one vector—force—there is locomotion in the direction toward which the vector points. However, if two or more vectors are pointing in several different ways, movement is in the direction of the resultant force.

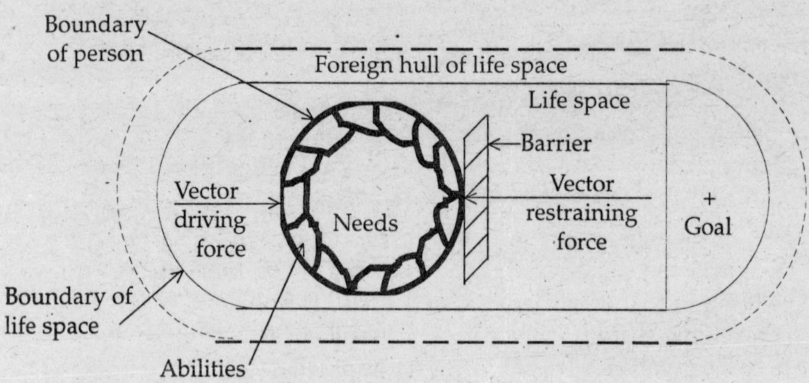

Fig. 4.5 : Life space of an Individual.

Whereas topological concepts are used to illustrate structurally what is possible, vectorial concepts describe the dynamics of a situation—what is happening or is likely to happen. Thus, vectors deal with the tendencies of a life space to change or resist change. In an illustration of what is happening or likely to happen, a vector may represent either a driving or a restraining force. A driving force is a tendency to change or move. A restraining force is a barrier or obstacle to psychological locomotion, which opposes some driving force. Both driving and restraining forces may arise from the needs and abilities of the person being studied, from actions of another person, or from the impersonal aspects of a situation.

What are the Auxiliary Concepts of Field Psychology?

The pivotal concepts—life space, topology, and vector—and ideas auxiliary to the basic formula—$B = f(P, E)$—are illustrated in Fig. 4.5. The latter are described in the following glossary of key auxiliary concepts of field psychology. These elements of construction represent ideas, not "objective" self-evident phenomena.

An analysis of the structure and dynamics of the life space of a child in school will reveal numerous interdependent aspects of the situation such as the child's relationships with his teacher and other students, the social pressures arising from his family, and even the consequences of his family's relations with other families. All of these various factors of a situation may be expressed through the use of the key pivotal and auxiliary concepts of field psychology.

Key Auxiliary Concepts of Field Psychology

Person : A consciously behaving self. Center of abilities and needs. That which a child means when he says "I" or "me."

Person-Centered Constructs

Needs : States of a person which, if they exist in relation to a goal, have a part in determining behaviour toward that goal. Correspond to a tension system of the inner-personal region of a person.

Abilities : Cognitive—capacity to know environment. Executive—capacity to manipulate environment.

Environment : Everything in which, toward which, or away from which a person can make psychological movement—do anything about. Person and environment are mutually dependent upon one another.

Foreign hull of life space : Complex of all nonpsychological facts which surround a life space. That part of a person's physical environment which, at a particular moment, is not included in his psychological environment. Physical and social raw materials. Foreign hull limits behavioural possibilities.

Cognitive structure : An environment, including a person, as known by the person. Synonyms are *insight* or *understanding*. Has one dimension—clarity.

Valences : Positive or negative imperative environmental facts. Properties which regions of a life space have if an individual is drawn toward them or away from them. A region which possesses a positive valence is one of such nature that forces correlated with the valence of that region tend to move the person in the direction of that region. A negative valence means that forces tend to move the person away from that region.

Tension : Very closely related to, and descriptive of, psychological needs. The state of one system relative to the state of surrounding systems. Either created as a result of opposed forces or induced by internal physiological changes or external stimuli. An inner-personal region may come into equilibrium in a state of tension. Release of tension may be achieved either through reaching a goal or through restructuring the life space.

Goal : A region of valence. A common region toward which forces within a life space point. Region of life space to which a person is psychologically attracted.

Barrier : Dynamic part of an environment which resists motion through it. That which stands in the way of a person's reaching his goal.

Force : Immediate determinant of the locomotions of a person. The tendency to act in a certain direction. Its properties are strength, direction, and point of application. It is represented by a vector. The strength of a force is related to, but not identical with, the strength of a valence. The combination of forces acting at the same point at a given time is a resultant force. Force is analogous, but not identical with, *drive* or *excitatory tendency* as used in S-R associationisms. (*Drive*, behaviouristically defined, is a strong, persistent stimulus which demands an adjustive response.)

What is Behaviour?

In cognitive-field psychology *behaviour*, when used, is defined quite differently from the way S-R associationists define it. The latter, in harmony with their interpretation of psychology as a study of the relationships of biological organisms and their physical and social environments, think of behaviour as some kind and degree of observable muscular or glandular movement. The movement may be only incipient or covert or it may be overt; nevertheless, its being behaviour means that it is physical movement. Were adequate devices available, it supposedly could be observed and measured. Cognitive-field psychologists do not accept this definition of behaviour.

In speaking of behaviour, cognitive-field psychologists imply psychological locomotion but not necessarily any sort of physiological movement. One may "come closer" to another person, yet exhibit no physical evidence of locomotion. Behaviour takes place in a life space, rather than in observable space. Psychological behaviour is more or less conscious—verbal or symbolic—and may be equated with experience. Every specific instance of behaviour must be viewed as the result of interaction of several pertinent features of a concrete situation. Broadly defined, then, behaviour means any change in a life space which is subject to psychological laws. Thus behaviour may be a change of the relative location of a person and his environment, a cognitive reorganization of his environment, or a restructuring of his person; it includes any change in valence of any part of his life space.

Psychological behaviour and *locomotion* are analogous concepts. *Behaviour* describes the simultaneous functions within a life space of an individual. *Locomotion* refers to the relative positions of respective regions of a person's *temporally continuous* life spaces. When we concentrate study upon a person and his current environmental situation, *behaviour* adequately denotes changes which occur in a life space. However, when we consider a time element, a person appears to occupy a series of overlapping life spaces. The life spaces usually manifest a continuity; they are similar but not identical. Change in subsequent life spaces is locomotion. Consequently, depending upon whether we are centering our study upon the person-environment interactivity or the psychological continuity of a person's life spaces, we may represent any psychological phenomenon in terms of either behaviour or locomotion; behaviour centers upon how one sizes things up, locomotion on what one does about it as he moves into new life spaces.

5

How Do People Differ from Each Other?

In addition to understanding some of the common aspects of man's psychological, biological, and sociological nature, it is important for teachers to understand the ways individuals differ from each other. For differ they do, and tremendously. After saying this, we must remember that if everyone were completely unique in every aspect it would be most difficult for people to work together in groups or for teachers to teach groups of children and youth. Human beings of a given culture are more alike than they are different and, there appear to be forces at work in the American culture which induce ever greater similarity among individuals. In spite of our similarities, we must take individual differences seriously into account.

In the United States they attempt to educate all the children of all the people through the twelfth grade. For social reasons, they try to keep children moving along through school so that most of those of a given age will be concentrated at a single grade level, e.g., most 8-year-olds will be in the third grade. Whether this is the best possible practice may be debatable, but nevertheless we do it and must prepare teachers as best we can to cope with the situation.

Because of their practice of promoting pupils according to age rather than achievement or ability, a teacher can expect to find a wide range of difference among students in his classroom. A typical four-year comprehensive high school will enroll freshmen with measured IQs from 60 to 125 or higher, reading levels from the third to beyond the twelfth grade, and arithmetic levels from fourth to fourteenth grade. Although spreads of personality, interests, and attitudes cannot be stated so readily, we can assume that the span of differences here is equally great. In a large unselected population there is a continuous variation from a very low to a very high manifestation of traits. However, the wider the deviation from the average of any trait, the fewer are the individuals in which that degree of the trait is manifested.

Before we examine current concepts regarding individual differences, we may profitably survey some of the ideas which have appeared historically. As in the other areas we have explored, in our ideas concerning individual differences past influences are always with us.

WHAT ATTITUDES HAVE BEEN HELD HISTORICALLY CONCERNING INDIVIDUAL DIFFERENCES?

Attitudes in regard to individual differences date back to and before the time of the ancient Greek philosophers. Aristotle tended to divide people into two kinds: those with and those without "deliberative faculty." He taught that men who lack the deliberative faculty are by nature slaves. He thought that inferior persons have enough ability to follow directions given by others but not enough to direct their own lives. They differ from lower animals in that, rather then being driven by instinct, they do engage in reason, but only passively. Thus, Aristotle believed that, although natural slaves are men and not brutes, they differ in kind, not merely degree, from those men who are naturally free. Consequently, he considered use of slaves similar to use of domesticated animals.

Ancient aristocrats, represented by Aristotle, denied anything like natural equality of men and justified the institution of slavery in terms of natural inequality. As free men were distinguished from slaves, so education was distinguished from training. It apparently never occurred to an ancient aristocratic thinker that a manual worker of any kind should, for any reason, study subjects such as poetry and music. Workers were trained to master a specific job and their education stopped. Adler and Mayer state the role of education in the ancient world, as conceived by the aristocratic class: "Education, liberal in purpose and character, is for free men, for citizenship, leisure, and lofty pursuits. Slaves, serfs, manual workers, and even skilled artisans are trained, much as animals are trained."

The idea of a natural aristocracy, that is, a group superior because of its biological inheritance, continued to be accepted without much question down to the eighteenth century. In fact, in colonial America the sharp class structure reflected the widespread belief that people differ naturally, ranging all the way from those who are fit only to rule to those who are fit only to serve. Certainly such colonial leaders as Alexander Hamilton and the Adamses believed in a natural aristocracy. Although Thomas Jefferson personally may have believed that all men are born potentially equal, as his statement in the Declaration of Independence seems to imply, he was clearly aware of the social fact of inequality. In a letter written in 1814 he stated, "The mass of our citizens may be divided into two classes—the laboring and the learned. ... At the discharging of the pupils from the elementary schools the two classes separate—those destined for labor will engage in the business of agriculture, or enter into apprenticeship to such handicraft art as may be their choice; their companions, destined to the pursuits of science, will proceed to the College."

Growing Ideas of Natural Equality

If readers will recall the various theories of man's psychological nature, they will realize that, well before the eighteenth century ended, lines of thought running counter to the idea of natural inequality had appeared. In a large sense Western religions—Judaism and Christianity—contained a strong element of equalitarianism. If all men are equal in the sight of God, then may it not also be true that under the right social conditions they would be equal in the sight of man?

John Locke's seventeenth-century *tabula rasa* theory supported the idea of natural equality. If mind at birth is a clean slate, environment evidently plays a crucial role. Although one might assume that some clean slates are better then others, one can just as easily assume that a slate is a slate and all that is important is the writing on it. This is precisely what John B. Watson, a twentieth-century follower of the *tabula rasa* idea, did.

Faculty psychology was explicitly developed by Christian Wolff in the eighteenth century. It emphasized that individual differences are developed and that people are born virtually equal. The central thesis of faculty psychology is that each person has a single unitary mind; this mind has several specific faculties, such as memory, will, and reason; and the strengths of these faculties depend upon the degree to which they are exercised. Within this pattern of thinking individual differences might be construed as the result of different amounts of exercise of the various faculties of the mind.

A curious pseudo science, designed for the purpose of measuring individual differences, arose in connection with faculty psychology. This was phrenology. Phrenologists felt it reasonable to assume a relationship between the development of one's faculties and the contour of one's skull. Early in the nineteenth century, E.G. Gall listed 27 powers of the mind. He then attempted to link them with 27 regions of the brain. He assumed that development of a specific function depends on development of the corresponding brain area. Such cerebral development was thought to exert pressure on the skull, pressing it outward in the form of bumps.

Phrenologists thus thought they could measure the relative development of a person's faculties by feeling his skull. "Bump feeling" was taken very seriously by some of our most prominent early American educators. Horace Mann, secretary of the Massachusetts State Board of Education from 1837 to 1848 and a leading figure in American education, was enthusiastic over the "science" of phrenology. Even now the modern testing movement, with its tendency to think of each personality as consisting of a mosaic of abilities, talents, and traits, sometimes is referred to as "bump feeling gone statistical."

In spite of such developments as phrenology, professional psychologists of the nineteenth century were little concerned with individual differences. The introspectionist Wilhelm M. Wundt (1832-1920), who established the world's first experimental psychology laboratory at Leipzig in 1879, was not interested in particular human beings. He arrived at his generalized man in a manner fairly satisfactory to himself, but the process gave him little, if any, insight into what a particular person would do in a specific situation. Science, as he saw it, was concerned with abstract generalizations, not with specific cases. To him individual differences were but exceptions which proved the rule. Any particular person, because of his special constitution, might not fit exactly the conditions prescribed by the general rule. However, he was confident that generalized men, like gravity of any other generic concept, when completely formulated, would account for each individual case. Hence, he saw little purpose in studying the unique nature of individuals.

Growing Interest in Individuals

Some educators of Wundt's period or slightly earlier were transitional figures in that they were beginning to show an interest in individual children as such. These pioneering thinkers used "the individual" sometimes to mean human nature in general, other times to mean an individual child or youth. They began to observe individual children and youth, but usually continued to think of them as representatives of children and youth in general. Yet their growing interest in individual children and youth eventually led toward study of individual differences.

The scientific movement in child study and education in the early 1900s specifically focused attention on individual differences among school children and youth. Edward L. Thorndike in 1906 stated, "The practical consequence of the fact of individual differences is that every general law of teaching has to be applied with consideration of the particular person in question. Every stimulus must be given not to men or to children in general, but to a particular individual or group characterized by certain peculiarities."

At about the same time, John B. Watson was writing about human behaviour and learning in such a way as to imply that all healthy normal people are essentially equal *at birth*. However, like Thorndike, he was aware of great differences among them and attributed these to differences in environment. In recent years so much emphasis has been placed on individual differences that many people tend to assume that each child, in every respect, is completely unique. This represents as great an extreme on the side of individualism as is represented on the side of "sameness" by those who regard all persons as essentially alike.

WHAT ARE THE SOURCES AND NATURE OF INDIVIDUAL DIFFERENCES?

Traditionally, the two basic sources of individual differences have been considered to be heredity and environment. Although it is true that heredity and environment do influence human traits, they also influence each other and human traits cannot be separated into those which depend entirely upon heredity and those which depend completely upon environment. For any individual, presence or absence of a certain type of hereditary structure can provide or limit opportunity for development, but it cannot insure that a certain kind of behaviour will or will not be manifested. A person's genes help provide and limit opportunity but do not determine what will be made of that opportunity.

Although all traits manifested by human beings are to some degree a product of interaction of genetic and environmental factors, for all practical purposes certain physical characteristics, such as blood type, may be attributed to heredity, and certain behavioural traits, such as customs and language, to environment. Other traits, stature and skin color, for example, are strongly affected by both genetic and environmental factors.

Genetic endowment is probably more similar among the races of man than most biologists and psychologists thought two or three decades ago. It is interesting to know, however, that, except for identical twins, every human being on earth is probably genetically unique. The number of possible gene combinations is such that a single human pair can produce 20 different types of children—more than the total number of human beings who have ever existed. Nevertheless, what we must remember is that, among people considered normal, the *range* of genetic variation is not very great.

Environmental influences begin interacting with hereditary factors even before a child is born. Congenital influences (those entering the picture during the gestation period) should be differentiated from genetic influences (those exercised by the nature of a germ plasm). Since an embryo or fetus, through osmosis, receives nourishment from the blood stream of its mother, any conditions which alter the chemical composition of the mother's blood may have some effect upon development of the fetus or embryo. When embryos have suffered drastic changes in physical environment, including changes in temperature and nutrition, they sometimes have grown into monstrosities. Many psychologists are convinced that the very event of birth has at least some influence upon the characteristics of an individual. Birth also brings with it a sudden and drastic change in environment. There is a marked change in posture and external temperature. New functions such as breathing and eating must be established.

Some factors of postnatal environment which influence development of a child are the economic and social status of his family, the attitudes he senses in his parents and other adults, his position in the family, and his relationships with his siblings. School environment, too, is important, particularly during a child's early years. Each child, on his level of comprehension, sizes up his environment so as to contribute to his frame of mind and attitude toward learning. Pupil-teacher and pupil-pupil relationships have much to do with the structure of the personalities involved in a school situation.

As we continue our exploration we should bear in mind that differences, particularly those which result largely from environmental influence, remain relative to one's situation throughout his lifetime. Although there is a high degree of continuity in the traits of a given person, they do change. No child carries within him a rigidly fixed degree of introversion, temper, generosity, mechanical interest, musical ability, or any other characteristic.

Differences Imposed by Specific Cultural Forces

The impact of family and peer group is probably of greatest importance. A child or youth may appear as a deviate to teachers because he is in some respects very much like his parents or friends. For example, if he steals school property, it is possible that this kind of thievery is a culture trait of his peer group or family, or both.

Several of the more conspicuous kinds of individual differences are related to social-class membership. Achievement in school, particularly in academic areas, tends to correlate closely with social-class membership; middle-class children or youth tend to outperform lower-class children or youth. The same is true of achievement on intelligence tests and other tests of academic aptitude. This should not be taken to mean that the genetic endowment of lower-class persons necessarily decrees inferior performance. There is little question that most of the tests used to measure academic aptitude reflect a "culture bias," i.e., they discriminate unfairly against lower-class children.

Kenneth Eells, a well-known contemporary psychologist, found that by changing tests so that verbal skills played a less important role in determining ability, and by changing problems to insure their beings familiar to lower-class children, he could greatly reduce the differences in test scores between middle- and lower-class children. However, many psychologists do not agree with Eells' position. His conclusion that the chief difference in performance between children of various social strata results from differences in verbal skills has been challenged by other experts, including F. T. Tyler.

If, as Eells suggests, differences in test performance and achievement in school between lower- and middle-class children are largely attributable to differences in verbal skill, then genetic endowment may have little to do with differences in performance. A middle-class child usually has vastly greater opportunity to learn verbal skills than does a lower-class child.

Race, nationality, and ethnic-group membership also help furnish an explanation for some of the individual differences which teachers observe in children. With respect to academic achievement, children from an ethnic group which has a tradition of scholarship will, on the average, achieve at a higher level than others. Personality differences may also be tied to ethnic-group membership.

Race may contribute to individual differences in the sense that a particular race may be culturally different from other races.

This cultural difference may be a result of national origin, or differences in educational opportunity, or other factors. In any case, a teacher sometimes finds that those of his students who are members of minority races are different in significant ways from the rest.

Some major difficulties are encountered when we attempt to measure and explain racial and nationality differences. First, with such admixtures of peoples as now exist it is virtually impossible to isolate representatives of pure races. Second, because of prejudices within some cultures, people who are labeled as members of a minority race often have not experienced the environmental situations common to the majority. Generally, discriminatory practices of a majority group tend to limit opportunities of a minority group. Third, psychological tests usually have been standardized on specific populations of the nation where they are developed and their scores are thus relatively meaningless when the tests are given to other racial or national groups.

Careful study of individual differences in relation to race and nationality discloses wide variation in specific traits within any "race" or "nationality," overlapping of racial and nationality groups measuring similarly on any trait, and lack of any one pattern of traits characteristic of a racial or nationality group. Although societies commonly attribute certain stereotyped psychological traits to each racial and nationality group, careful scientific study of differences does not support these generalizations.

After discussing the foregoing hereditary and cultural factors which produce individual differences, we must make clear that probably no single factor can be isolated as the determiner of any specific aspect of personality. Personality traits appear to be products of a totality of interacting personal and environmental influences.

Sexual Differences

On a variety of types of tests, boys and girls show significant differences from each other. For example, boys are superior in reaction time, speed of tapping, muscular strength, dexterity with tools, skill with numbers, and comprehension of spatial relations.

Girls excel in speed of word association, quick adaptations, shift of attention, finger dexterity, color discrimination, and verbal memory. These differences appear early in life and tend to increase with age. (Why are little girls in the first and second grades generally considered to be "ahead" of boys of the same age?) On Bearnreuter's Personality Inventory, boys indicate more extraversion, dominance, and self-sufficiency, and fewer evidences of neurotic inclinations than do girls. On the Allport-Vernon Study of Values, men register higher in verbal commitment to theoretical, economic, and political values and women to aesthetic, social, and religious values.

The value of some of these tests is open to question, chiefly for the reason that they might seem to suggest "instinctive" differences between sexes. Anthropological research has shown that, if one looks at the human race as a whole, no such differences can be proved or disproved. Even if it could be proved that "instinctive" differences, such as are indicated in the foregoing studies, exist, such differences would not be of major importance to teachers.

What is of great importance to a teacher is an understanding of the sex roles which our culture and its major subcultures create. Most members of each sex from a rather early age try to follow the roles specified for them. Some do not succeed, and as a result we have "tomboys" and "sissies". But most do succeed fairly well.

What are some of the more important aspects of these roles? Any attempt to describe male and female roles in our culture is complicated by the fact that they have changed rather drastically within the past one-third of a century. Some of the historical features of male-female roles are so deeply seated, however, that they remain highly influential even if not consistently practiced.

Boys are supposed to be boys, which has meant rough and tough, aggressive, bold, inquisitive, and uninhibited. The plea of adults to little boys is "Act like men," which usually means "Don't cry when you get hurt," "Don't run away from a fight," "Be independent". Girls are supposed to be girls, which means dainty, gentle, obedient, cautious, and circumspect. When we enjoin girls to "act like ladies" we mean such things as "Keep clean and neat," "Don't think or talk about sex," "Don't cause adults any trouble."

Change has been in the direction of confusing and even reversing the traditional sex roles. We no longer expect women to be as retiring, obedient, and modest as we once did. We no longer expect men to be as stalwart, unemotional, and independent as we once did.

Teachers need to realize that changing sex roles confuse children and youth, as well as adults. Boys often no longer know what to expect from girls and girls no longer know what to expect from boys. Both are likely to feel conflict. Teachers can be of real service by helping boys and girls understand what is happening. Frequently a person who feels conflict is helped if he can see how cultural change tends to produce conflict in individuals.

HOW ARE INDIVIDUAL DIFFERENCES MEASURED?

Individual differences of students are customarily measured by use of copyrighted standardized psychological tests. Such tests are designed to gain a comprehensive picture of some aspect of students. Thus, they are quite different in purpose and structure from teacher-made tests. Tests have been devised to measure various kinds of differences. However, intelligence or ability tests continue to hold a prominent position in most comprehensive testing programmes.

A psychological test is an instrument so constructed as to achieve an objective and standardized measure of a sample of a person's behaviour. When a psychologist or psychometrist sets out to measure the vocabulary of a child or youth, he observes that person's performance with only a limited number of words. He carefully selects these words with the goal of having them typify the total vocabulary of the child. Thus, testing discovers in short order what less systematic observation of a child's daily life can unearth only in a much longer period of time. Tests are a quick and relatively objective method of systematically observing a child in a variety of situations. Since standardized tests judge all children by the same standards and hence supposedly eliminate the influence of personal biases, these tests appear to be more "scientific" than are personal observations and interviews.

What will Standardized Tests Not Do?

Teachers use systematic testing to the best advantage when they are acquainted with tests to the point of knowing what and what not to expect of them. Thus, it is essential that the purposes and limitations of each test be known. A teacher who realizes that standardized tests are possibly—but not necessarily—the most accurate method yet devised of estimating the nature of certain human characteristics will be able to benefit his students and himself through the use of standardized test scores. On the other hand, one who blindly becomes a test enthusiast probably will do more harm than good with tests. Although some tests are valuable for more than one purpose, each type of test has its unique function. A test which is very good for one purpose may provide useless or even misleading information when used for a purpose for which it was not devised.

Below are listed some limitations of standardized tests which should be recognized.

1. Tests do not reveal universal human abilities the natures of which are sharply defined and well understood.
2. Results of one standardized test, regardless of its excellence, do not alone provide a sound basis for counselling and guidance.
3. Intelligence tests do not measure a faculty which, although differing in degree, is essentially the same in all human beings.
4. Intelligence tests which measure academic aptitude do not necessarily measure capacity for intelligent behaviour in life.
5. Although bright students usually remain bright adults and dull students usually remain dull, a person will not necessarily continue to score at a certain level merely because he did so on one occasion.
6. Tests never have been devised which exactly measure any general ability, capacity, aptitude, or other trait.

What Knowledge of Statistics Must a Teacher Have?

A psychological test is usually accompanied by a formula for deriving its score. To score a multiple-choice test accurately the formula often specifies that the grader count the number of items right and subtract some fraction of the number wrong. The fraction of the number wrong to be subtracted is the reciprocal of a number one less than the number of choices on each question. (The reciprocal of 3 is 1/3.) A true-false test with two possible answers for each question should be scored by taking the number right less the number wrong. A selection test with four possible answers for each question should be scored by taking the number right less one-third the number wrong. Statistically, when this procedure is followed those students who know no correct answers probably will score zero. A student will receive a positive score to the degree that he has accurate hunches or insights into the correct answers for the questions.

Some knowledge of statistics seems necessary in order to interpret test scores accurately. A few fundamental statistical concepts are described below.

Average

The average, or arithmetic mean, is the score most representative of an entire group tested. It is found by dividing the sum of all the scores by the number of scores. If four students measure IQs of 70, 90, 95, and 113, the mean is 92. This is found by adding the scores and dividing their sum by 4. An average score provides a means of comparing an individual child's score with that of members of his group. It also may be used in comparing scores of various groups.

Standard Deviation

Some measure other than average must be used to determine just how far above or below the average the score of a child or youth falls. Two groups may show the same averages on the same test and yet have a great difference in variability. Variability means the extent to which scores are spread or scattered. The measure of variability most commonly used and encountered is standard deviation, indicated by the symbol SD or σ (sigma).

Let us assume two hypothetical groups of 35 children each. Each group measures a mean or average IQ of 100, but the groups

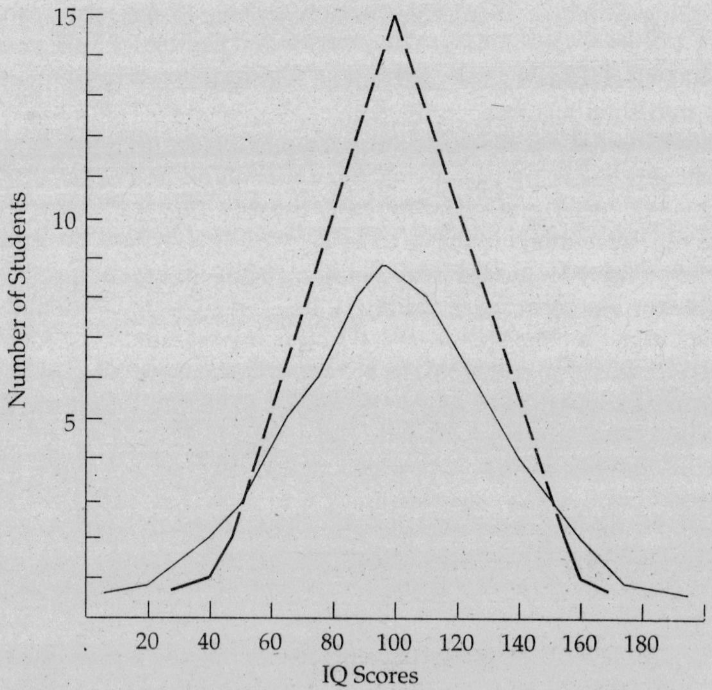

Fig. 5.1: Variability of Two Groups.

are so composed that there is a great difference in their variability. The variability of the two groups is shown in Fig. 5.1. Respective sigmas are 15+ and 30+.

Here we see that it is the comparative σ scores or standard deviations which indicate the relative variability of the groups. A standard deviation is obtained by taking the square root of the average of the squared deviations. Steps in this process are:

1. Find the deviation of each person's score from the mean.
2. Square each of these deviations.
3. Find the sum of these squared deviations.
4. Divide this sum by the number of scores in the group.
5. Find the square root of this average. This is σ or SD.

If the scores on a test constitute a normal distribution, about two-thirds (68 %) of the scores will fall within one SD above and below the mean, 95 per cent of the scores will fall within two SDs above and below the mean, and three SDs above and below the mean will include almost all of the scores. Fig. 5.3 shows a normal distribution curve.

The use of standard deviation is valuable in that it enables the measure of a particular trait to be divided into approximately six equal parts. The spread in the trait being measured is about the same from the mean to one SD above or below the mean as it is from 2 SD to 3 SD above or below the mean. Note that standard deviations equate the degrees of the trait being measured, not the number of people scoring any particular score. On a normal curve as we move farther away from the average, or mean, the amount of change in each succeeding given numerical fraction of the group becomes greater.

Percentile

A percentile is that point in a distribution below which a given percentage of the cases occurs. When we divide the scores made by a large group of children on a given test into 100 equal parts, each part is called a percentile. When a student scores at the 85th percentile, his score is achieved superior to 85 per cent of those taking the test. The amounts of ability represented by each percentile are not equal; in fact, when the distribution of scores is normal there is about the same amount of difference in the measured trait between the 98th and 99th percentile as between the 50th and 60th.

What Kinds of Traits May Be Measured with Psychological Tests?

The physiques, personalities, interests, intelligence, aptitudes, and achievements of children may be measured with varying degrees of accuracy. Organic traits are measured quite readily. The other kinds of traits are less tangible and consequently more difficult to evaluate mathematically.

Personality is especially hard to measure because in this area attitudes and behaviour tend to vary with the situation. For example, a child may be introverted in a classroom but extraverted at a ball game. Hartshorne and May, in their studies of deceit, found honesty to be specific to certain situations. Even without such studies, any student of culture would know that most Americans learn to turn such personality traits as honesty, truthfulness, and charity on and off as convenient, like water from a faucet. Even so, there is enough continuity of personality traits in most persons to give the tests some predictive value. Several standardized tests in this field have been used extensively with useful results.

Personality tests are controversial in the sense that they measure adjustment and the test writers, some critics feel, assume that adjustment is conformity to the cultural *status quo*. If this is true, then a conformist should do much better on such tests than a nonconformist. Since these tests are widely used in screening applicants for jobs in corporations, one critic of such tests included in his book a section entitled "How to Cheat on Personality Tests".

Such tests may be valuable in spotting personality deviations of such serious nature that special counselling or psychiatric referral is desirable. But one should guard against using scores of these tests as a weapon to suppress the creativity of "odd balls," who may sometime produce great works of art or achieve spectacular breakthroughs in science.

As in the case of personality traits, interests of a given individual vary according to time and place and great caution must be observed in interpreting interest tests. Without further evidence, a test score showing high interest in one area and low interest in another probably should not be given too great weight in vocational counselling. Many persons have found great contentment in a vocation which at one time in their life had no appeal.

Intelligence and aptitude are closely related. Both are measured through sampling achievement in certain areas. Intelligence is ability to learn or capacity to form insights. It is measured by finding out how much a person knows and can do. Thus, intelligence tests are designed to find how much a person knows about certain matters and how well he can solve certain types of problems. On the basis of a person's performance, we infer his "mental age," from which an IQ score can be derived.

Aptitude is ability to learn in specific areas, such as music, mechanics, clerical tasks, and relatively abstract academic subjects. It is usually measured by how well a person can perform certain tasks directly or indirectly related to high performance in the area. Relatively high ability to succeed in the tasks required by the test is assumed to indicate relatively high aptitude in the area to which the task is relevant.

Achievement tests are designed, as a rule, to measure how much a student has learned in one or more of the standard school subjects—reading, composition, arithmetic, social studies, science, foreign language, and the like. One of the authors recently undertook the study of a large number of achievement tests in widespread use. He found the available tests to be very spotty in character, with weaknesses of the following nature.

1. English mechanics tests stress too heavily pure mechanics, such as comma placement, in contrast to ability to recognize whether a sentence or paragraph is, in the main, a good sentence or paragraph.
2. Reading tests properly include tests of comprehension, but almost never do they include items which would reveal the most important comprehension skill of all—"ability to read between the lines".
3. Arithmetic tests focus almost exclusively on mechanics, and but rarely attempt to reveal a student's understanding of mathematical concepts or number theory.
4. Tests in social studies focus on fact learning—the names of people, dates, and places. For the most part the items deal with trivial matters. The tests, with rare exceptions, do not attempt to discover a student's understanding of critical issues confronting twentieth-century civilization.
5. Literature tests ignore important works of fiction, drama, and poetry of the past 20 years, and some ignore all works of the twentieth century.
6. Science tests are frequently obsolete, and in addition emphasize terminology far too much. Virtually without exception, science tests appear to ignore completely the question of what the scientific outlook is.

Children deviate the farthest from the average in specialized abilities and traits as contrasted with their more general abilities. Thorndike noted that variability is greater in traits peculiar to man than in those peculiar to animals and in acquired traits as contrasted with original traits. Binet observed that the higher (the greater degree of abstraction required) and more complex the process, the more it varies from individual to individual.

Studies of abnormal persons provide examples of how extreme variation of traits may be found in a single individual. People have been observed who were so deficient in general intelligence that it was necessary to confine them in institutions for the feeble-minded, but who, at the same time, were strikingly gifted in some specific trait such as artistic ability, mechanical aptitude, arithmetic ability, ability to memorize, or musical talent. These often are spoken of as idiot-savants. On a less extreme level, often people who are mediocre in most respects are phenomenally good in one area of activity.

Verbal or linguistic ability is the one area in which people are not found highly proficient when they measure below average in general intelligence. In our culture verbal ability and general intelligence correlate highly. In fact, one of the best measures of academic or school aptitude is a vocabulary test. The *coefficient of correlation* of verbal ability or vocabulary and academic aptitude or intelligence is about. 50. This means that there is a fair degree of correspondence between the two sets of measures—verbal scores and intelligence scores.

Coefficients of correlation vary from a perfect positive (+1.00) through 0.00 to a perfect negative (—1.00). Numerical description of a correlation enables one to realize the degree of relationship that exists. The degree or size of a correlation refers not to positiveness as opposed to negativeness but to the distance from zero (whether positive or negative). A positive correlation between verbal aptitude and intelligence means that persons who tend to score high in verbal aptitude also tend to score high in intelligence. A negative correlation would exist if persons who scored high on one scored low on the other.

A zero correlation signifies that there is no relationship between the scores different persons get on the two tests which are being evaluated against each other. A correlation of .50 means that there is a fairly strong, but only a fairly strong, positive relationship between scores. Actually it means that scores on one test can be predicted from scores on the other test 13 per cent better than they could if there were no correlation at all, that is, if prediction had to be used upon pure chance. The formula for finding *efficiency of prediction* in percentage is 100 $(1-\sqrt{1-r^2})$ where r represents the coefficient of correlation.

WHAT IS INTELLIGENCE?

Considerable controversy and confusion have surrounded the use of the term *intelligence.* Our purpose in this section is to cut through some of the uncertainty by describing, in comparative fashion, the major positions which have been taken with respect to a number of the issues surrounding intelligence.

Nature of Intelligence

In the literature relating to intelligence, we find implied a distinction between the *nature* of intelligence and the *origin* of intelligence. The nature of intelligence is how intelligence works in situations calling for it. It is the process, working itself out. For purposes of analysis issues relating to the process can be discussed independently of issues relating to the origin of intelligence, although obviously the two cannot be regarded as unrelated.

Intelligence as Capacity to Learn

Psychologists have advanced numerous competing theories of the nature of intelligence. Alfred Binet (1857-1911), a French psychologist who in 1905 designed the first widely used test of mental ability, gave little attention to a theoretical definition of intelligence. To him, intelligence was unitary in the sense that each person had a certain amount which could be used for any purpose; it was a general ability to learn. If a person did better in one field of activity than in another, it was due, not to any fundamental variation in intelligence relative to the two fields, but to factors such as learning, interest, and motivation. To illustrate: a person who learns to play a musical instrument brilliantly does not have a different kind of intelligence from that of a brilliant engineer, chef, actor, or seamstress. Rather, he chooses to direct his talents toward music because a combination of environmental factors impels him in this direction.

Although their formulations were different, most other early twentieth-century psychologists likewise held the view that intelligence is a general capacity or potential for learning and can be directed along any line which interest dictates. Lewis Terman (1877-1956), an American psychologist, saw intelligence as ability to do abstract thinking, an ability which can be directed toward repairing an automobile motor just as well as toward solving a problem in quantum mechanics. William Stern (1871-1938), a German professor, regarded intelligence as adaptability to new problems and conditions of life. To him, solving a problem involving marital discord was as good an example of the functioning of intelligence as devising original algebraic formulations.

The concept of intelligence, as unitary or general, finally came under considerable criticism. Charles E. Spearman (1863-1945), an English psychologist, thought that two factors contributed to every intelligent act: *g*, a general factor operative in all situations, and *s*, a specific factor operative only in situations where that specific factor is involved. Thus, he thought that a person's capacity to act in any situation depends both upon his general capacity and upon the special capacity involved in that particular act. To illustrate: a person might have a fairly mediocre general intelligence but a very high order of special capacity in, say, music.

To split intelligence still further, the American psychologist Edward L. Thorndike (1874-1949) divided intelligence into three kinds, mechanical, social, and abstract. He thought that each kind of intelligence is manifested by the quality of response which a person can make to stimuli in whichever of the three areas is involved. A person might have a high order of mechanical intelligence without a corresponding level of social or abstract intelligence. In this case he would be highly competent in working with, say, motors but might be ineffective in working with other persons or solving problems in higher mathematics. Similarly, a person might be extremely adept in persuading others, in which case he might perform brilliantly as a salesman; but he might be incapable of changing a tire or passing first-year economics.

All of these early definitions of the nature of intelligence assumed that, whether intelligence is unitary or composed of two, three, or more somewhat independent factors, it is basically a capacity—a learning potential. This capacity, whatever its origin, was assumed by early twentieth-century psychologists to be relatively fixed once a person reached adulthood. Further, virtually all of the early workers in the area of intelligence were adherents to some degree of a stimulus-response (mechanistic, reflex-are) psychology. This means that they construed the nature of intelligence as capacity to form new response to stimuli in rapid and accurate manner in situations which so permit.

Intelligence as Ability to Act with Foresight

When we think of intelligence as the ability to act with foresight, we are not contradicting the notion that intelligence is a capacity; we are making different assumptions about the nature of this capacity. When one acts with foresight, he "looks ahead"; he tries to anticipate the consequences of acting in a particular way. He makes forecasts regarding the outcome of alternative lines of action. These forecasts are based upon experience. They are made possible by the fact that experience has equipped the person with a number of functional generalizations (rules or principles), which are invoked as needed to predict the consequences of present action. For example, if experience has taught that although rattle-snake bites are not usually fatal they do make one very ill, a person will behave very cautiously in rattle-snake country so as to avoid getting bitten.

When intelligence is defined in such manner, the quality or level of intelligence hinges in part on the number and accuracy of rules which a person has learned and also on his ability to invoke these rules, flexibly and imaginatively, in situations which call for them. Seldom does a rule learned from past experience fit a new situation precisely. Thus, ability to recognize what is appropriate to a situation and to take proper action is, from the point of view here stated, an indication of intelligence. We cannot divorce intelligence from what we usually call originality or creativity.

When two situations seems alike superficially, then, intelligent persons characteristically discern differences that would escape the less intelligent. They do not slur over fine distinctions whenever such distinctions are relevant to solving to problem at hand. They are able to test their hunches and hypotheses intellectually so that in their overt behaviour they appear to do a minimum of fumbling in difficult situations; they choose the correct act almost instantly. (But not in every kind of situation—Einstein required many years to develop and perfect the theory of relativity.)

The foregoing view of intelligence rejects the notion that intelligence is fixed. With an increase in age and experience, a person may show increased flexibility of behaviour and imagination. Furthermore, a person's gain in intelligence may not be equated with a gain in age: it may be much faster in rate, or much slower; and adults may continue to gain in intelligence as long as they live. On the other hand, for certain individuals intelligence may appear to be relatively fixed—these are persons who, for various reasons, cease growing intellectually. The point is, we cannot say such persons cease growing because of innate limitations.

Advocates of the view that intelligence is capacity to act with accurate foresight are not likely to take a stand with respect to the old argument of whether intelligence is unitary or a composite of special capacities. Evidence which would settle this issue does not seem to exist. Furthermore, as time goes on, the issue seems increasingly unimportant. A view consistent with organismic biology and field psychology would be that, whether intelligence is characterized either by generalized or specialized capacities, these capacities are interdependent and interact continuously.

Whereas this second over-all position concerning the nature of intelligence harmonizes well with a relativistic, field psychology, it does not harmonize with the notion that intelligence is based upon the capacity to form and retain new connections in the nervous system. Although this second position does assume that intelligence is related to capacity to learn, it defines learning in a very different manner.

Sources of Intelligence

We now turn to a second category of issues. Where does intelligence come from? What causes one person to act with high intelligence and another with low? Again, we present three positions which may be taken on this matter.

Intelligence as Genetic Endowment

According to this position, intelligence bears a one-to-one relation to the quality of genes which determine the structure and functioning of the organic-neural-endocrine system. Intelligence is a function of the way an organism is put together. In other words, intelligence hinges on physical structure. From this point of view, intelligence is relatively fixed in each individual; a person can function only to a certain point of efficiency in the neural connections he can form—he can do no more. To expect additional achievement would be like expecting the runner of a 4-minute mile to increase his speed so that he was running the mile in, respectively, 3½ minutes, 3 minutes, 2½ minutes, etc. The limits of an organism permit only so much of a given kind of achievement and no more.

Obviously, this outlook harmonizes well a psychology which emphasizes physiology as a determiner of what can be achieved. In American psychology, connectionism and behaviourism are most in tune with this view of intelligence. A brief survey of the history of the intelligence testing movement bears this statement out. During the early 1900s, psychologists tended to define intelligence mechanistically as the capacity to establish new S-R bonds, form new connections in the nervous system, or form new habits. These psychologists assumed intelligence to be dependent upon the number and variety of potential neural pathways and the speed with which these pathways could be activated.

The two traits crucial to intelligence—complexity and modifiability of the nervous system—supposedly were transmitted from parents to offspring. Thus, connectionistic psychologists reasoned that intelligence, like other physical traits, is determined by physical inheritance and that its level is constant for each individual just as the color of his eyes and skin is constant. Even though most professional psychologists have abandoned this point of view, it persists in the thinking of many public school teachers, counsellors, and administrators.

Intelligence as a Product of Learning

An opposite point of view holds that all people except those who are obviously defective have the same potential at birth. The intelligence they achieve stems from opportunities for learning which they have had. Since the potential of each person is very high, few persons ever come close to reaching maximum biological potential.

Every environmentalist necessarily—if he is consistent—accepts the notion that intelligence is, at least in large measure, learned. This is a comforting belief for persons who are required to work with seemingly retarded people. It provides a source of never ending optimism. To a considerable extent welfare workers, sociologists, and some public school teachers find the extreme environmentalist point of view satisfying.

Some of the studies of changes of IQ in individuals give support to the hypothesis that intelligence is learned rather than inborn. A number of these studies are cited in a following section. However, other research rather strongly supports the notion that one's potential intelligence is a matter of genetic endowment and is therefore relatively fixed. Actually, research provides us with no conclusive data to back either of the extreme positions we have just described.

Intelligence as a Function of Interaction

A third position concerning the origin of intelligence harmonizes well with a relativistic, field psychology and also with the data provided so far by test results. This position assumes that intelligence is capacity to act with foresight, i.e., to assess accurately the consequences of a proposed action, and then goes on to by-pass completely the issue of whether intelligence is inherited or learned. This third position considers the latter argument to be as fruitless as arguments over any other aspect of the nature-nurture controversy.

Intelligence, in this view, is a product of the interaction of a human self and its perceived environment. That is, in assessing the basis of intelligence one assumes that both poles—person or self and psychological environment—are important *but that it is impossible to assess the relative importance of either pole.* Further, in the interactive process the *quality of perception* is of crucial importance. A person may have a physical organism of excellent quality, but his perceptions (interpretations of environment) may, because of previous learnings, be extremely faulty. Conversely, a person may have a mediocre physical organism, but, because of previous learnings, his perceptions may be first rate. Since there is no known way at present of determining the relative importance of physical structure or learning as a source of intelligence, we may relegate this argument to the same limbo as the argument over how many angels can dance on the head of a pin.

One qualification is necessary: perception hinges in part on the efficiency of sensory organs and other physical structures. If the goal is to pounce on a field mouse, then a high-flying eagle can behave more intelligently than a man; not only does his position *vis-a-vis* the mouse confer an advantage, but he can *see* more acutely. Obviously, poor eyesight, deafness, "taste blindness," and other sensory defects reduce the capacity for dependable perception. On the other hand, man as well as other creatures can often go far in compensating for impaired sensory capacity, e.g., consider Helen Keller.

This interactionist position appears similar to that taken by Combs. After pointing out that certain physical conditions, such as mongolism, microcephalia, cretinism, etc., as well as certain injury- or disease-induced defects of the central nervous system or sensory organs, may reduce the capacity to make accurate perceptions, Combs goes on to say that in most persons the quality of perception hinges on the kinds of experiences one has had. He cites factors such as opportunity for exposure to a rich environment, the length of time a person has had to improve perceptions, a person's goals and values, the cultural milieu in which he is placed, his concept of self, and his felling of threat.

The two latter points need to be enlarged upon. A person is unlikely to behave any more intelligently than he thinks he can. If I am convinced that I am stupid with respect to certain tasks, my conviction will limit my capacity for perception in connection with these tasks. All teachers have known students who had persuaded themselves that they could not learn arithmetic, the parts of speech, or spelling. Once convinced, they found it quite impossible to learn these things. On the other hand, overconfidence as to what one can learn can lead to equally serious inaccuracies of perception.

A sense of threat also limits capacity for accurate perception. People are inclined, when they feel threat, to restrict their perception to the source of threat; they become aware of nothing else. For example, a man may reach a state where he can think of nothing but a disliked employer. Obviously, his capacity to think in balanced fashion is greatly reduced. In addition to the "tunnel vision" effect mentioned above, threat tends to make persons defensive and rigid concerning their present pattern of attitudes, values, and beliefs. That is, threat produces "closed-mindedness." In either case, capacity for intelligent action is reduced.

To summarize and restate the position, intelligence is a product of the *interaction of a person and his perceived, i.e., psychological, environment.* We can attribute no particular portion of intelligence to heredity and no particular portion to environment.

WHAT IS THE INTELLIGENCE TESTING MOVEMENT?

We have touched upon some of the figures prominent earlier in the century in the study of intelligence. Binet will be long remembered as the pioneer. He developed his first tests as a means of identifying academically promising children in the schools of Paris. The few tests available at that time measured only special aptitudes; Binet wanted tests that would survey broadly a child's capacity for academic learning. He developed thirty tests of tasks which he deemed related to academic success or failure.

The use of intelligence tests received its first big impetus during World War I. In the interests of efficiency, group tests, the famous Army Alpha and Beta, were developed. (The Binet test is administered by a trained practitioner to one person at a time.)

Persons who scored extremely low on the tests were rejected from the service and those who were retained were, if lucky, assigned duties in accordance with test scores.

During the 1920s some of the shortcomings of early intelligence tests were brought to light. The constancy of the IQ was seriously challenged and standardized tests were found to overemphasize verbal skills and to confer an unfair advantage on persons with middle-class language skills and thought habits. Consequently, although World War II provided another major stimulus to the testing movement, the term *intelligence* tended to be taboo in military circles. Military general classification tests (not recognized as intelligence tests) and tests of special abilities and aptitudes were designed to give quick measures of abilities and aptitudes. There was little concern for the *source* of these traits. Note that a distinction was made between ability and aptitude. An ability was defined as capacity to do something, such as fly an airplane. Abilities are already achieved. An aptitude was defined as capacity to learn—one's potential in a particular field. For example, a person may not know how to fly yet, but he may indicate, through test results, a high aptitude for flight instruction. No assumptions were made in these tests as to whether aptitudes are primarily a matter of inheritance or of learning.

There are now on the market a number of group intelligence tests designed to be administered to entire classroom of youngsters at one time. These can be scored by a teacher or, if machine scoring is available, by machine. As we discuss the inadequacies of intelligence tests in a later section, remember that group tests are more subject to criticism than are individual tests, although both types can be criticized—as much on the basis of how they are used as on the basis of inherent defects in the tests.

The two best-known and most widely used individual tests today are the Wechsler Intelligence Scale for Children (WISC) and the Stanford-Binet Intelligence Test (SBIT). The latter is a revision, performed at Stanford University, of the earlier Binet scales. The Stanford-Binet seeks to find the general intelligence of a child by means of a many-sided survey of his mentality. Some of the tests are nonverbal, which makes it possible to administer them to any person who can understand spoken directions.

HOW IS INTELLIGENCE MEASURED?

There is evidence that tests available at present measure something that, under certain circumstances, is useful in predicting certain future behaviours. In order to make any use at all of these tests, teachers must understand some concepts employed by the test makers.

The Concept of Mental Age

Intelligence is measured in terms of either mental age (MA), intelligence quotient (IQ), or percentile. Mental age, introduced by Binet in 1908, is a year-month notation which supposedly represents an absolute level of capacity. *Absolute,* as used here, is an antonym of *relative.* It means that a mental age is not determined by a relationship of other units. Rather than stating a relationship—as the IQ and the percentile do—MA states a maximum level of achievement. A scored MA of 9 years, 6 months, means that the person being measured can perform a group of tasks which can be performed by an average 9½- year-old.

Mental age has no relationship to chronological age (CA). It is determined entirely by a subject's performance on a test and by a table of norms found by testing a large number of children of each age. An MA of 10 means the same regardless of the chronological age of a subject. Even though a 4-year-old with an MA of 6 probably does not act the same way in a given situation as a 6-year-old with an MA of 6, test scores would not indicate any difference between them.

The Concept of Intelligence Quotient

Intelligence quotient represents the relationship of mental age to chronological age. The use of mental age implemented placement of pupils in grade levels adapted to them, but it gave no help in anticipating the level upon which children would be learning three or four years later. Four students, at present measuring the same mental age, might be far apart in their school work four years from now. Suppose that student A is 6 years old, B is 8, C is 10, and D is 12, and all four measure a mental age of 8 years and so are placed in the same class. Four years hence, provided their motivation and opportunity remained constant, A's mental age would be 13.3, B's would be 12, C's would be 11.2, and D's would be 10.7.

For the testing process to be serviceable something new was necessary. This was the intelligence quotient—IQ. By definition, IQ equals mental age divided by chronological age and multiplied by 100—IQ = MA/CA × 100. Then, through transposing, one may derive the formula MA = CA × IQ/100. Teachers have greater use for the latter formula. Its application indicates that a 12-year-old with an IQ of 80 is capable of working at approximately a 9½-year level; his MA is 9.6.

The principal advantage of the use of IQ as contrasted with a statement of a retardation or acceleration of so many months in mental age is that it makes it possible to compare relative degrees of measured intelligence of children and youth of deference ages. An IQ of 100 means normal or average capacity for performance regardless of a child's age. IQs of 90 or 110, for children of any age, indicate comparable degrees of retardation or acceleration.

Wechsler recently has developed the concept *deviation IQ*, which is slightly different, but perhaps more functional, than the earlier meaning of IQ. Within Wechsler's system, each person tested is assigned an IQ which, at his age, represents his intelligence rating as related to the abilities of other people his own age. IQs obtained by successive retests with the WISC automatically give the subject's relative position in the chronological age group to which he belongs at each time of testing.

Deviation IQ is the amount by which a subject deviates above or below the average performance of individual of his own age group. An IQ of 100 on the WISC is set as the mean score for each age, and the standard deviation is set equal to 15 IQ points. When any standardized IQ test is given to a cross section of a large number of children, it can be assumed that the mean IQ will be approximately 100 and the standard deviation of the IQ will be approximately 15 or 16. Wechsler, however, has developed his tests and norms in such a way that the SD is definitely 15.

When the intelligence of a large number of children representing a cross section of Americans is measured by means of the WISC, certain general results may be anticipated. The middle 68 per cent (one σ each side of the mean) will measure IQs between 85 and 115; 95 per cent (between —2σ and +2σ) will score IQs between 70 and 130. Practically all children (between —3σ and +3σ) will score IQs between 55 and 145 (see Fig. 5.2).

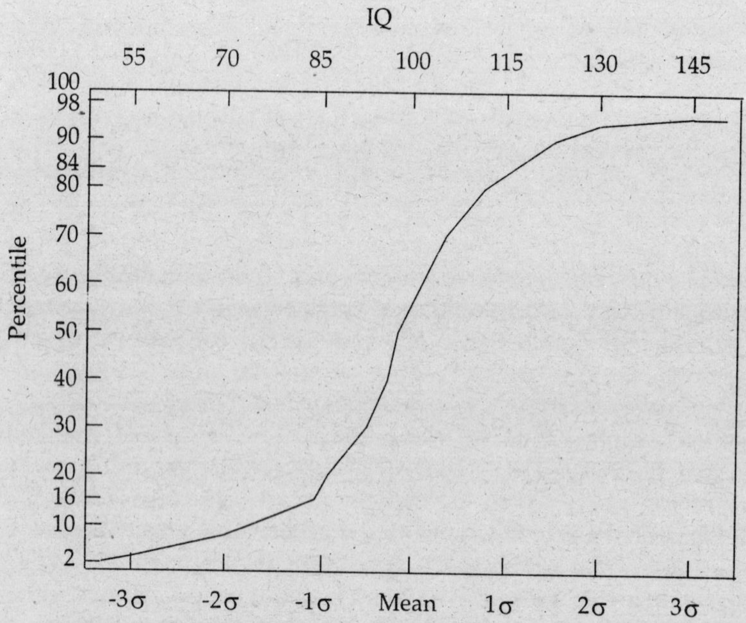

Fig. 5.2 : Relation of WISC IQs and SDs with Percentile Ranks.

The Concept of Percentile

A *percentile* means the percentage of people whose scores fall below that point on a curve. Thus, when a person scores in the 90th percentile on a test, it means that 90 per cent of the people being tested have scores below that score. Hence percentile scores are in terms of people, not test items. Table 5.1 means that 90 per cent of people measure an IQ of below 119 on the WISC.

Table 5.1.
Relations of IQ on WISC to Percentile Rank

Percentile Rank	*Equivalent IQ*
99	135+
97	128
95	125
90	119
80	113
75	110
70	108
60	104
50	100
40	96
30	92
20	87
10	81
5	75
3	72
1	65

Some Facts About the Distribution of IQs

When an IQ test, is given to a large number of children representing a cross section of a population, the scores will tend to fall into a normal distribution or bell curve. It will be recalled that about 68 per cent will lie within one standard deviation above and below 100, 95 per cent will lie within two standard deviations above and below the mean, and three standard deviations above and below the mean will include almost all of the scores.

A normal distribution curve indicates that, although there are some extremes in measured intelligence, most children are pretty much alike. However, our growing tendency to have an increased number of children in school for an increased number of years has meant greater spread in IQ of students in most classes. Schools now contain virtually the whole child population representing the entire range of human differences as measured

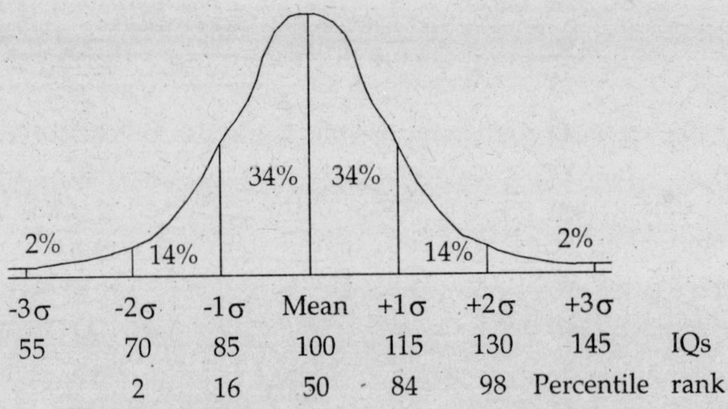

Fig. 5.3 : Normal Distribution Curve with Standard Deviations, WISC IQs, and Percentile Ranks.

by IQ tests. In a typical school class, the mental ages of children cover a range of about six years. The upper 50 per cent of pupils in a grade are capable of about the same quality of learning as are the lower 50 per cent of those in the next higher grade.

HOW USEFUL ARE INTELLIGENCE TESTS?

If we understand clearly what can and cannot be done with intelligence test scores, they can serve as a useful adjunct to other kinds of information about individual differences.

Probably the greatest fault of present test results lies in the more or less confused assumptions of both test makers and test users as to the nature and source of intelligence. We have already indicated that intelligence testing gained its impetus in a period when connectionistic psychology was in vogue. Intelligence was defined as capacity to make new responses and this capacity was regarded as rooted in the physiological make-up of the organism and hence as largely hereditary. This conception of intelligence seems virtually impossible to prove and can be judged only on the basis of the long-range consequences of accepting it. Enough studies have been completed which show marked variability of

IQ in a single individual to force even connectionists to modify their thinking—if not about the nature and origin of intelligence, at least about what available tests can measure.

Some qualifications have been introduced during the past 25 years or so:

(1) It is perhaps impossible to devise a test which will separate what is innate in capacity from what is learned. However, this qualification usually leads to the supposition that further refinement of tests will reduce the learning component that appears in results, thus making tests approach ever more closely the ideal of measuring "pure intelligence."

(2) Tests commonly used in schools tend to measure, more than anything else, capacity for an academic kind of learning, closely associated with middle-class values and verbal skills. Here again, attempts at refinement lead to reducing the extent to which test performance hinges on middle-class verbosity; but the supposition remains that there is an innate, relatively fixed, capacity of the human organism which, ideally, is measurable.

(3) Test results vary because of inaccuracies in the tests and because of changes in the mental or physical state of subjects over a period of time. This criticism leads to attempts to refine tests in the direction of greater validity and to control better the conditions under which tests are given. Again, the assumption is the mental capacity of a relatively innate and fixed nature exists.

None of these qualifications markedly reduces confusion over the use of intelligence tests. The modifications in thinking about tests still fail to cut loose from the assumption that intelligence is a given quantity, which, if only we could learn how, could be measured in its "pure" of "absolute" state. In contrast, such modern *tabula rasa* theorists as still exist would perhaps deny the validity of intelligence test results altogether except as a possible measure of pure learning.

If one accepts the interpretation of intelligence preferred by relativistic field psychologists, he is forced at once to abandon all attempts to measure either innate capacity per se or learning per se. A person with this psychological orientation will cease being concerned with the sources of intelligent behaviour as such. Instead he will focus on trying to measure how effectively people engage in the process of intelligent behaviour—or, simply stated, how well people can test ideas so as to achieve desired consequences. Such a change in emphasis might lead teachers to consider student achievement on certain types of teacher-made tests, intelligent student behaviour, and discerning student statements during discussions possibly as valid measures of intelligence as existing IQ tests.

In order to show the basis for certain persistent criticisms of the all-too-common assumption that intelligence tests measure a fixed, innate capacity, we review some of the studies which show how, in some instances measured IQ fluctuates.

The Variability of IQ Scores

In 1935 a study was conducted to see how a group of children would perform on various intelligence tests. During a period of one month, 14 different intelligence tests were administered to 149 children in the high sixth and low seventh grades. There was found to be no correlation between the order of taking the tests and the results obtained. No child showed an IQ variation of fewer than 21 points. The average variation was about 42 points; i.e., the average child scored 42 points lower in IQ on one test than he did on some other tests in the 14. One child showed a spread of 84 points between his lowest and his highest IQ scores.

Other studies have been made to determine how specific children would score on the same or similar IQ tests over a period of time within which their psychological environments were significantly changed. These studies seem to indicate that, whatever it is that an IQ test measures, it can be raised, or lowered, through a marked change in environment. We shall give one example of each of three different kinds of studies which have contributed to a knowledge of the effects of changes in environment upon IQ scores.

1. *A study of identical twins reared in different kinds of environments:* Newman, Freeman, and Holzinger in 1937 reported a complete case study of 19 pairs of identical twins reared apart. They found that, whereas the average IQ difference of the identical twins reared together was 5.9 points, it was 8.2 for the twins reared apart.

2. *A Study of two groups that, on the average, had different hereditary potentialities but similar environmental influences :* Burks

in California studied a group of adopted children placed in foster homes during the first year of their lives and a control group of "own children" matched with the adopted children in regard to age and sex of children and locality and occupational level of homes. She estimated the average IQ of the adopted children at the time of adoption to be approximately 100. When tested from ages 5 to 14 they averaged IQs of 107.4. However, the mean IQ of the control group of "own children" was 115.1. This seems to be evidence that a "superior" home can promote a considerable increase in a child's tested intelligence quotient.

3. *A study of a group of children measured before and after experiencing a decidedly changed environment:* Several studies were pursued in the child study laboratory of the University of Iowa during the late 1930s which are pertinent to the problem of constancy of IQs. Wellman has reported these studies. One was an investigation of the effect on IQ of a child's attending the University of Iowa Nursery School; 228 children with an average age of 40 months and a mean IQ of 117.3 in the fall measured a mean IQ of 124.3 in the spring. The following fall they measured a mean IQ of 123.9; this grew to a mean IQ of 127.7 in the spring. Thus, in a 20-month period, average measured IQs were raised 104 points.

Experiments with twins, siblings, and children in foster homes seem to indicate that children living in privileged environments test higher in intelligence than do children in less privileged environments. Children moved from unfavourable to more favourable environments tend to measure higher in intelligence than their twins who remain in the more unfavourable environments. Stoddard in 1943 wrote: "It can be predicted with some confidence that when homes and schools give the child what he truly need, at all ages from the first year upward, there will be a radical revision in the norms and standards of mental tests."

An article published in 1961 reported data on intelligence score variability as dramatic as any the authors have seen. Mr. Mayer begins by reviewing studies demonstrating what is commonly called the "culture bias" of intelligence tests used at present. For example, in large American metropolitan areas the average IQ of school children in a wealthy suburb is about 120, while school children in the worst slums average about 85. New

York City, among others, is making a determined effort to "build a fire" under slum youngsters in order to improve academic performance and increase the proportion who graduate and go on to college.

In Manhattanville Junior High School 43, a few spectacular results have been observed. One boy leaped from a measured IQ of 97 on entrance to 139 before high school graduation. Another who started with an IQ of 74 ended with a scholarship to New York University. Another started with an IQ of 99 and finished in the top 15 per cent on the College Entrance Board's examination and with a full scholarship to Amherst.

How Can We Make the Best Use of Intelligence Test Scores?

In the authors' judgment, we are on the safest ground by beginning with the assumptions implicit in a relativistic, field psychology. We begin by assuming that *no available "intelligence" tests measure completely satisfactorily what a field psychologist means by intelligence.* Opinions may vary as to what present IQ tests measure, but the burden of evidence suggests that they measure a certain kind of academic capacity—that which we commonly associate with success in a college preparatory curriculum in a school dominated by traditional middle-class culture. Further, the scholastic potential which these tests do measure is highly unlikely to "stay put" and, in some cases, will vary over a wide range. By establishing the right sort of learning environment, it seems well established that IQ scores for given individuals can be raised markedly. Since a capacity is itself regarded as a function of person-environment interaction, we cease thinking of anyone as having a fixed capacity, or potential, along academic lines or any other.

6

Race and Intelligence

The previous article states that one explanation advanced to account for the current inequality in educational outcomes has to do with the possibility of genetic differences between the races. There is little disagreement over the statement that whites score higher than blacks on intelligence tests. On the average, blacks score about fifteen IQ points below whites. According to the classification system accepted by the American Association of Mental Deficiency, the average black youth would be considered a slow learner. Blacks have fared no better on the so-called "culture-fair" tests. While no one seems to question the finding that blacks score lower on conventional intelligence tests, there is considerable debate as to the causes of their lower average scores. The explanations advanced run the gamut from genetic selection factors to inadequate schools.

Since the 1920s, social scientists have favoured cultural explanations in accounting for racial differences in measured intelligence. More recently, however, an increasing number of psychologists have been impressed with evidence supporting the notion of ethnic or racial superiority or inferiority. Foremost among the new hereditarians has been Arthur Jensen, this nation's most controversial educational psychologist, whose two published papers—"Social Class, Race, and Genetics" (portions of which are reprinted herein), and "How Much Can We Boost IQ and Scholastic Achievement?"—have caused as much or more public and private debate among educators and psychologists than any other two articles in recent history. In the opening selection, Jensen presents his case with respect to racial differences is mental ability. In the following article, Frank Morris Challenges many of Jensen's major findings on scientific grounds and raises the question of objectivity in social science research.

Thought Questions

Are differences between the races reduced or eliminated when environmental opportunities are equalized?

Is it reasonable to assume that the human brain is exempt from racial variation in light of the evidence the almost all other anatomical and physiological attributes are so affected?

How do environmentalists explain the fact that the American Indian, who according to available indices of environmental disadvantage is the most deprived group, fares better on IQ and achievement tests than blacks?

How do proponents of a genetic viewpoint explain the fact that persons having the same genes are distributed over an IQ range of more than twenty-five points? Is this area of racial variation in IQ one that should be researched further, or would it be better for society if this issue were left alone?

READING 2

Social Class, Race and Genetics : Implications for Education

Arthur R. Jensen

RACIAL DIFFERENCES

Racial differences in mental abilities, whatever their sources, must be taken into account if programs are to be developed to make schooling more beneficial for more of our population. This, of course, is the intention of large-scale programs such as Project Head Start.

One may ask, why bring race into the picture? Are not all differences in mental test scores and school performance due to environmental and social-class differences? If we cannot define "race" with perfect precision, have we any business using it as a variable in our psychological or educational research? My answer to these questions, as an educational psychologist, is wholly operational and pragmatic. I assume that one legitimate aim of research is to discover the sources of individual differences in educationally relevant variables such as IQ and school performance. Now, if we have a multiple regression equation made up of a host of socioeconomic and other environmental variables that predict educationally important criteria, and if the prediction is substantially improved by adding the variable called race to the prediction equation, I maintain that race is by definition a relevant and valid variable. For this purpose no more precise definition or criterion for classification by race is needed than the teacher's judgment. In the studies I have reviewed which used this multiple regression approach, the addition of race along with environmental variables has always substantially boosted the total variance accounted for. For example, in a study by Alan B. Wilson, the dichotomy "Negro-non-Negro", when included among eleven other variables, made the largest independent contribution to the prediction of intelligence test scores of 6th grade students in Berkeley schools (Wilson, Jensen, and Elliott, 1966). Whether we are investigating the environmental or genetic aspects of the total variance is another matter entirely. To the extent that Negro-white differences are due to environmental influences, this method can tell us whether or not we had succeeded in identifying these influences. We only have to hypothesize what they are, measure them, and include them in the multiple-regression equation. If our hypotheses are correct, the variance contributed by "race" would be absorbed by the hypothesized environmental variables. Many of these environmental variables, I believe, are important and as yet unidentified. Research of this kind is presently going on in various parts of the country, typified, for example, by the work of Martin Deutsch of New York University and Robert Hess of the University of Chicago (*e.g.*, Deutsch, 1966; Hess and Shipman, 1965). One aim of these researchers has been to go beyond crude socioeconomic variables to find the truly causal environmental influences on educability which are now thought to lie in more subtle psychological aspects of intra-family and inter-personal interactions during the child's development. Our hope is that if such environmental effects can be clearly identified it might be possible through some kind of early educational intervention to boost the child's chances of doing well in school.

There is no question about the large average difference between Negroes and whites in performance on standard intelligence tests and in school performance. The differences, whatever their cause, are so large as to be a major concern to educators. For example, of a national sample of 10 million men between the ages of 18 and 26 tested on the Armed Forces Qualification Test, 68 per cent of Negroes as compared with 19 per cent of whites failed the test (*U.S. News and World Report*, Oct. 17, 1966). The failure cut-off score that yields these percentages

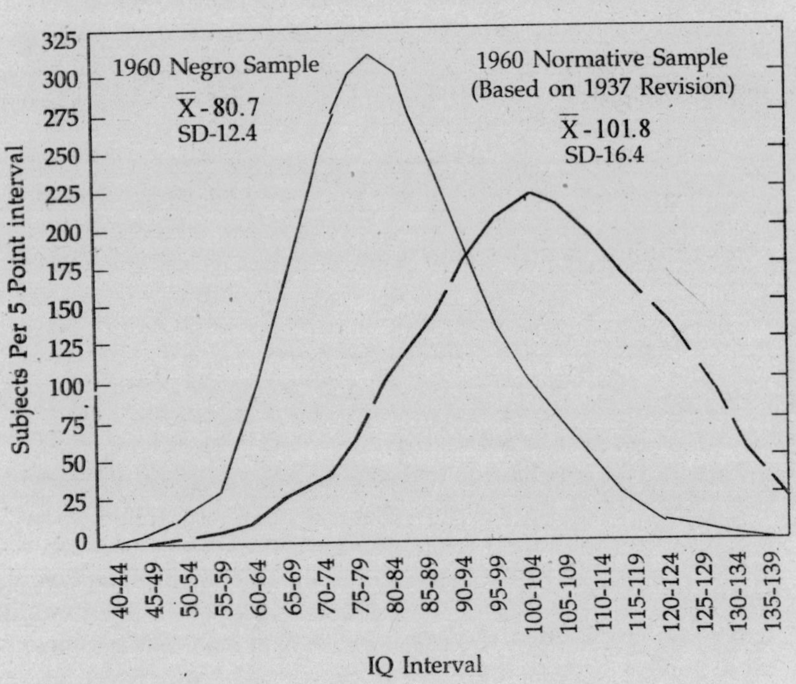

Fig. 6.1: Stanford-Binet IQ distribution of Negro children in five Southeastern states (solid line) and of white children in the 1960 normative sample. (Kennedy, Van de Riet, and White, 1963.)

is equivalent to a Stanford-Binet IQ of 86. Figure 6.1 shows the results of the best normative study we have of Negroes on the Stanford-Binet, based on 1800 children (Kennedy, Van de Riet, and White, 1963). Since these norms are based on a sample of the population of five Southeastern states, they cannot be regarded as an unbiased representation of the Negro population of the United States. The median Negro-white overlap is only 7 per cent in this figure, as compared with 8 per cent in the Armed Forces Qualification Test on a national sample of the male population between ages 18 and 26. But since there is a significant sex difference among Negroes in IQ—almost certainly a cultural phenomenon—the addition of female scores to the distribution would cause the overlap to be a good deal higher. A fair estimate would be about 12 per cent Negro-white overlap for the total U.S. population. Merely to point out that the Stanford-Binet or the Armed Forces Qualification Test may be culturally biased, which they no doubt are, does not in itself solve the major problem, since the tests do, in fact, predict educational and occupational performance.

Let us now look a bit further into these data to see if what is revealed by the distributions of total IQ might be concealing some important complexities in the situation. Figure 6.2 shows a comparison of Negro and white children on two of the Stanford-Binet subtests : Vocabulary and Diget Span. The degree to which other subtests differentiate between Negro and white children falls between these extremes. Intuitively, we would say that digit span is less culturally biased than vocabulary. You may be surprised, in view of this fact, that past attempts to develop so-called culture-fair or culture-free intelligence tests have not used the digit span technique. The tests that were hopefully devised to be culture-fair, like the now defunct Davis-Eells Games, showed almost as large Negro-white and social-class differences as tests like the Standford-Binet and even group-administered paper-and-pencil tests. Why has digit span been neglected as a potentially valuable method of assessing intellectual ability among persons across a wide range of environmental variation? Much of the reason, I believe, is that the low reliability of the meager digit span tests in standard batteries has made them appear inferior to other tests. For example, corrected for attenuation the digit-span test in the Weschler Adult Intelligence Scale correlates .75

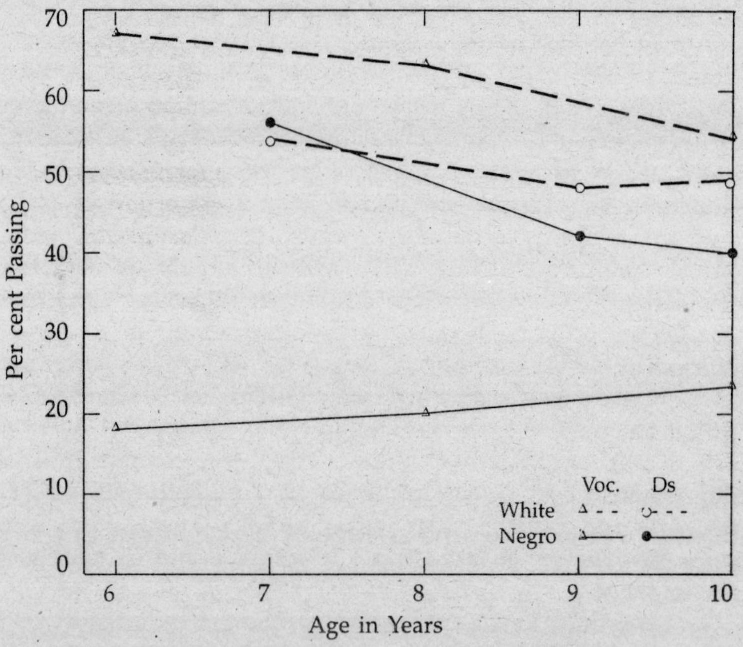

Fig. 6.2: Percentage of Negro and white children passing the Vocabulary and Digit Span tests of the Stanford-Binet at various ages. (Data from Kennedy, Van de Riet, and White, 1963; Terman and Merrill, 1960.)

with total IQ (minus digit-span) and has a loading of .80 on the general factor common to all the subtests (Wechsler, 1958). The ability to repeat two digits at age 2½ correlates .62 with Stanford-Binet IQ—uncorrected for attenuation (Terman and Merrill, 1960). We have been able to devise memory-span tests administered under laboratory conditions which have reliabilities comparable to those for height and weight. By manipulating procedural variables, such as stimulus modality (auditory or visual), by varying the interval between presentation and recall, and by several other more complex variations of the digit-span paradigm, it is possible to obtain a profile of factorially independent scores for each subject. These factors derived from laboratory measures of short-term memory are not psychologically trivial. In a sample of 50 University of California undergraduates these factors had a multiple correlation of .76 (.68 after correction for shrinkage) with college grade-point average (Jensen, 1965b).

One of the conclusions I draw from the large discrepancies between various subtest scores on standard intelligence tests administered to Negroes is that we probably will not advance our understanding of group differences markedly by collecting more data with global, omnibus tests of general intelligence. Practically all the evidence of Negro-white intellectual differences based on such tests has been reviewed by Shuey (1966). While this mass of evidence shows great consistency and leaves no doubt concerning the presence of mean differences in measures of the phenotype, I find little information about the extent to which Negro-white differences have a genetic basis. Racial variations have been identified in just about every anatomical or physiological characteristic anyone has chosen to study, and it would be surprising indeed if the brain alone were exempt from this generalization. But the relevance of physiological differences to behavior will have to be proved in the psychological realm by psychological techniques. As far as I can tell from my search of the relevant literature, research on racial differences does not even begin to permit one to sort out the hereditary and environmental components of the demonstrated phenotypic differences in mental abilities. Therefore, statements concerning the relative importance of genetic and environmental factors in racial differences can at present be nothing but conjecture and surmise. The only answer, I submit, is to transmute conjecture into scientifically testable hypothesis and then do the necessary research. It is good scientific strategy to begin with the simplest possible hypothesis, that is, the one that adds the fewest assumptions to what is already established. Stated in the simplest form, the hypothesis is that the difference between the means of Negroes and whites in tested intelligence is caused by the same factors, operating in the same degrees, that cause differences in intelligence between individuals within either group. I can find no evidence to date in the published literature which would permit rejection of this hypothesis. Nor do I believe that appropriate data for a direct test of the hypothesis have yet been obtained . But the question arises whether there has been an official decision to create the impression that such hypothesis have already been scientifically tested with conclusive results. A recent publication of the U.S.

Office of Education states : "It is a demonstrable fact that the talent pool in any one ethnic group is substantially the same as that in any other ethnic group" (U.S. Office of Education, 1966). A Department of Labor report on the Negro family says: "Intelligence potential is distributed among Negro infants in the same proportion and pattern as among Icelanders or Chinese, or any other group" (Department of Labor, 1965). Such statements entirely lack a factual basis and uncritical acceptance of them may unwittingly harm many Negro children born and unborn.

Future research in this area will contribute little more to our understanding of human differences and will have only meagre educational implications if the emphasis is placed solely on differences in global intelligence tests scores, which reflect only an undifferentiated composite of abilities having of the fear that such research will turn out scientifically valid instances which would reinforce fears of limited black capabilities or basically black racial inferiority. This impression is completely wrong. Black people do not fear research into this area : they only fear research into this area that is inaccurate, incomplete, invalid, and sometimes blatantly racist. Black fears of incomplete and racist research in this area are based on the following : beliefs, assumptions, and, most important, black experiences.

First, white researchers—especially white researchers with racist view-points—can usually get exceptionally wide exposure (press, mass media, as well as academic journals). Researchers with a nonracist or black perspective often cannot get similar exposure or similar availability of research funding . Because of limited white understanding of how truly vicious racism has made the environment for most black people (and cumulative effects of a racist environment over the years), there is a tendency for white researchers to either overcompensate or overemphasize the negative effects of environment (à la Moynihan) or to either minimize the negative effects of environment, which in effect supports a basically racist viewpoint (à la Jensen). A true understanding of the environment-heredity-genetic interaction requires an understanding of the political, historical, and economic forces, as well as the psychological forces that have created the environment of black people in this country. This is clearly an area where scholars and scientists differ in determining which facts and which evidence are crucial, and in the influences that sometimes flow from conflicting evidence.

The question of racially influenced genetic differences in mental abilities cuts across a number of social and biological sciences. To fully integrate valid interdisciplinary findings requires both a basic social science theory *and* a great deal of selectivity. It is in the selectivity of data for a comprehensive theory that the perspective of a scholar's values rises to the forefront.

Here is the basic dilemma. In discussing environmental variance, we are faced with not only knowing the current environmental-genetic interaction of blacks, but we must also have an idea of cumulative or noncumulative interaction effects over time. Because these cumulative, negative environmental effects upon black people are especially difficult to measure with the tools of current social science analysis, there appears to be tendency to underestimate these affects because they cannot be adequately and precisely substantiated with specified statistical degrees of confidence. Too often, it is not recognized that this weakness in analysis lies to a considerable extent with the state of the available social science tools. For the social scientist who extensively relies upon and has used these tools, however, there is quite a tendency to underestimate and possibly ignore academic facts not easily ascertainable or tested within the limitations of our current techniques. The end result is that the work of every scholar who ignores the present over time and cumulative effects of black Americans surviving and adapting to an inequitable (compared with whites), undercapitalized, and racist environment is clearly biased toward favoring whites in any comparison with blacks. It is important to remember that this likelihood of underestimating these difficult-to-measure, negative environmental effects is not only a disadvantage to the black people in the United States, but also tends to reflect unfavourably on poor and oppressed people throughout the world in comparison with middle-class North American or European Whites.

The other end of the dilemma is to recognise that when many white scholars attempt to discuss the historical, political, economic, or psychological effects of negative environments upon black people, any manipulation of the evidence is susceptible to being criticized as vulnerable to personal, racial, or cultural bias in interpretation. This is in addition to the problem of the likely overemphasis of either the negative environment (Moynihan) or its underemphasis (Jensen). One of the major advantages of sensitive black scholars in dealing with this subject is that there is a greater probability of avoiding the Moynihan-Jensen distortions (although, of course, all black scholars are not sensitive black scholars).

THE WHITE AND THE BLACK PERSPECTIVES

The Jensen article clearly reflected the white perspective. It is important that I be quite clean in what I mean by perspective. I define a scholar's perspective as a blindness over certain unquestioned assumptions and inferences that support or reinforce the value preferences, clientele, sponsoring group, race, religion, creed, nation, or dogma in which a scholar may feel threatened if attacked or questioned. Every social scientist who ignores, underestimates, or deprecates the tragic effect upon black Americans of living in an environment where major adaptations were required to survive American racism is guilty of using the white perspective and abusing scholarly responsibility.

Black scholars, for a variety of reasons, have not articulated a black perspective with the attendant publicity that a white perspective piece like Jensen's can command. If black scholars were as readily able to get their perspective across, the entire black community would feel less threatened by articles such as Jensen's. A true black perspective should not be threatened at all by articles such as Jensen's. A true black perspective could come to the same conclusion as Jensen; specifically, that mental ability and other phenotypes are in all probability more greatly influenced by heredity than by environment. This same perspective could argue that generations of white inbreeding had left a large proportion of the white population (in contrast to the black population) incapable of feeling, expressing, or understanding certain humanistic emotions, sensitivities, and empathies. Black scholars could then define intelligence using the dimensions that I indicated above. They may even start to develop tests for these qualities. If black scholars had, in fact, been pursuing intelligence-testing from this perspective, then Jensen would not have appeared nearly so threatening.

It is obvious that we could develop black IQ tests as culturally biased as white IQ tests. For example, suppose white adolescents or adults had reading comprehension tests based on paragraphs such as the following :

> Last week I decided to "make it" to the "City". We headed straight Uptown and "Fell by" this "blind pig". This place was really "together". The hostess was a "stone fox" who made sure everything was "everything". The owner was a really "down" dude who kept the "jive" elements out and didn't let any "block-boys", "gorilla" their way past him. The food was *laid* from "wrinkled steak" and "greens" right down to "Georgia Hams" and the "Ripple" flowed "for days". As for "sounds" — "Hot Buttered Soul" and "Movement" hung in. I knew there wouldn't be any "busts", so I just *laid* in and "grooved". [The purpose of this brief example is to simply show that what is defined as legitimate to constitute intelligence is greatly influenced by one's values].

In addition to asking questions about what one comprehended from the above paragraph, one could develop a series of objective analogies. One such analogy could be the following :

"Wrinkled steak" is to

(*a*) filet mignon
(*b*) barbecued spareribs
(*c*) chitterlings
(*d*) fried chicken

as "Ripple" is to

(*a*) C.C.
(*b*) Thunderbird
(*c*) J & B
(*d*) Beer

The correct answer is that "wrinkled steak" is to chitterlings as "Ripple" is to Thunderbird (wine).

The point to be made from the above is that to test the IQs of whites by instruments heavily weighted in the black subculture is as equally invalid as testing the IQs of blacks with instruments heavily weighted in the dominant white culture.

THE JENSEN PERSPECTIVE

Much of what is wrong in the evaluation of black peo[illegible] social scientists viewed the black cultural experience through the white perspective. Often at the root of the problem has been an ignorance of black culture, and the result has been a distortion in the interpretation of the black experience.

> The total denial of Negro culture is consonant with the melting pot mythology and it stems from a very narrow conceptionization of culture by non-anthropologists. Social science has refused to look beyond the surface similarities between Negro and white behavior and, therefore, has dismissed the idea of subtle yet enduring differences. In the absence of an ethnohistorical perspective, when differences appear in behavior, intelligence or cognition, they are explained as evidence of genetic defects or as evidence of the negative effects of slavery, discrimination and poverty. Thus the social scientist interprets differences in behavior as genetic pathology or the alleged pathology of the environment; he therefore fails to understand the distortion of the Negro culture that his ethnocentric assumptions and measuring devices have created. The picture that emerges from such an interpretive schema may be seen as culturally biased and as a distortion of the Negro experience [Stephen and Baratz, 1970 : 32].

It is sometimes lost in the emotionalism that revolves around the Jensen article that the major criticisms against it do not arise because he raised the issue of genetically influenced racial differences in mental abilities. Black people do not have to fear the following statement, which should have been Jensen's (1969: 80) major contribution :

> Any groups which have been geographically and socially isolated from one another for many generations are practically certain to differ in their gene pools, and consequently to show differences in any phenotypic traits involving high heritability..... Races are said to be "breeding populations", which is to say that matings within the group have a much higher probability than matings outside the group. Races are more technically viewed by geneticists as populations having different distributions of gene frequencies. These genetic differences are manifested in

> virtually every anatomical, physiological, and biological comparison one can make between representative samples of identifiable racial groups. There is no reason to assume that the brain should be exempt from this generalization. There seems to be little question that racial differences in genetically conditioned behavioral characteristics, such as mental abilities should exist just as physical differences [sic]. The real questions are not whether there are or are not genetic racial differences that affect behavior because there undoubtably are. The proper questions to ask from a scientific standpoint are : What is the direction of the difference? And what is the significance of the difference—medically, socially or economically.

Other scholars than Jensen have documented ethnic and probable race-related differences in patterns of learning. They, unlike Jensen, did not engage in provocative extrapolations beyond their data. The problem with the Jensen article was simple, because he raised the question of genetically based differences in mental ability among different racial populations; the same amount of controversy that accompanied his article should have also happened to the Stodolsky and Lesser articles which preceded his in the same journal by more than a year. Similar to Jensen, this article noted racial differences in tests of mental abilities. Note their conclusions (Stodolsky and Lesser 1967) :

> Our main point is that the study of mental abilities suggests that there may be patterns of attributes (cognitive, personality, motivational, and so forth) which are related in some way of ethnic group membership..... We know ethnic groups differ in patterns of ability no matter what the social class level within the ethnic group, and our educational problem now becomes that of providing equal educational opportunity to all ethnic groups in maximize their development, even at the expense of magnifying differences among the groups.

The fact that the kinds of criticisms and inferences that accompanied the Jensen article did not accompany the Stodolsky and Lesser suggests two things. First, it suggests that the latter article did not make the unsupported inferences of the former.

Second, it suggests that the question of genetic or racially related differences in mental abilities is not too sensitive to be scientifically debated if the debate is truly scientific and fair.

I will document from the Jensen article and from his interview in the *New York Times Magazine* statements which show that Jensen was neither scientific nor fair in the inferences and conclusions he drew from his data. In many cases, these inferences were value-laden and consistently reflected a bias towards a racist hypothesis. It is because of such nonscientific comparisons, inferences, and omissions which follow that caused Jensen and the article to come under such attack.

One of the most unscientific aspects about the Jensen article was to imply that his was a deterministic model instead of one that is really quite stochastic. There are high degrees of uncertainty about Jensen's parameters; the limits of inferences about the nature of the environmental variable. I have spelled out elsewhere the numerous uncertainties and stochastic inferences in greater detail (Morris, 1971). The point I want to make here is that Jensen either did not realize or did not care that by not making it clear that he was writing about a stochastic model, many readers, especially nonprofessional readers, would get the clear impression that he was writing about a deterministic model. If he did not realize this, then he was simply greatly influenced by the "white perspective". If he did realize it, then it is a matter of either gross insensitivity or of racism.

> When the advancement of a hypothesis by a scholar with standing is bound to have a great impact on the resolution of current social and political issues of enormous magnitude, I am suggesting that scholarly responsibility dictates care in advancing them with the full panoply of scientific validation when they do not in fact have a sufficient degree of firmness [Hyman, 1969].

Another example of less than optimal scientific candor was Jensen's focusing upon the concept of "g" as if it were the only or the universally accepted theory of intelligence. Actually, it represents only one of a number of theories, several of which are based upon more recent data and are more widely accepted than "g" (Deutsch, 1969). It is important to note that the "g" theory is probably the most culture bound and the one which magnifies black-white differences. Modern approaches to the nature of intelligence, which, by the way, also use factor analysis in many cases, do not agree with Jensen on the importance of "g". The work of Guilford (1967), for example, paints a multifactoral, multifaceted picture of intelligence which he believes is more reflective of the actual complexity of human beings. The point I am stressing is that by neither acknowledging these other theories nor by addressing them, Jensen reinforced a certainty that was not warranted from the data.

> None of these theories of intelligence has been "proven"; incontrovertible data have not been gathered to confirm any of them. However each [a number] of theories mentioned is as valid and prominent as 'g'. Jensen's entire argument appears to be inextricably linked with the concept of 'g'. Questioning 'g' throws Jensen's whole line of reasoning into doubt [Deutsch, 1969 : 83].

Jensen's academic nonobjectivity is probably most apparent when he is interpreting data he presents in his article. A number of times he does not relate how the data he presents can support an environmental emphasis hypothesis. For example, in discussing the effect of birth weight differences on intelligence, he writes (Jensen, 1969 : 71) :

> Prematurity and low birth weight have markedly higher incidence among Negroes than among whites. That birth weight difference *per se* are not [sic] a predominant factor in Negro-white IQ differences as suggested by the findings of a study which compared Negro and white children matched for birth weight. The Negro children in all weight groups performed significantly less well on mental tests at three and five years of age than the white children of comparable birth weight.

Jensen's main conclusion from these data by Hardy is that birth weight is not the *predominant* factor in the black-white difference. Jensen ignores the obvious fact (to me at least) that the environments of representative samples of black babies differ considerably from the environments of a representative sample of white babies between birth and ages three through five. To ignore environmental differences or to assume black-white environmental comparability in the United States is deeply resented by blacks and is considered the height of scholarly irresponsibility.

The most blatant example of scholarly blindness is the fact that Jensen does not see how persuasive a case he has made for an environmental emphasis explanation for a great deal, if not all, of the black-white IQ differential. Jensen first notes (1969 : 81) that the black-white IQ difference is approximately fifteen points or one standard deviation. He then notes (1969 : 100) that Stanford-Binet gains of approximately eight to ten points could be attributed to the dynamics of the testing situation for "disadvantaged" children. He then notes that gains in IQ from five to ten points (of course, the gain can be from twenty to thirty points or more in some cases) could in some cases be attributed to compensatory and nursery school training. Jensen is finally willing to concede that different environments can account for approximately five points of the difference. When added together (although it does not mean that all environmental variables are additive in every case), these IQ points, which Jensen concedes are greatly environmentally influenced or controlled, could more than account for the black-white difference in IQ scores.

Jensen's personal biases were quite apparent in the way he discussed the reliability and validity of the methodology of various studies that he referred to in his article. Jensen vigorously attacked the methodology of the Rosenthal and Jacobson (1968) study. The conclusion of this study, namely that children's IQ scores may be greatly influenced by teacher expectations, does not fit too well with the Jensen hypothesis. In contrast to the way he analyzed the Rosenthal and Jacobson book, he was impressed with the Coleman study. In fact, he considered the Coleman Report one of the few studies that was "methodologically adequate" in collecting data (Jensen, 1969 : 84). Jensen exclusively relied upon the Coleman Report (1966) for his data in comparing black-Indian IQ scores and environments.

A number of scholars have pointed out many methodological weaknesses with the Coleman Report (for greater detail about methodological weaknesses of the Coleman Report, *see* Nichols, 1966; Dyer, 1968; Bowles, 1968). It seems inconceivable to me that Jensen could have been as thoroughly aware of the methodological strengths and weaknesses of that report. I can only conclude that there is either an academic or personal bias in the data analysis. This bias worked against any interpretation of the data which placed the burden of the differences in the IQ scores on other than the black children themselves.

Jensen's nonobjectivity toward black America came to the forefront in numerous ways. It is possible that his veiwpoints on black America are so deeply woven into his belief system that he can make invidious comparisons without actually realizing it. In the following passage, Jensen (1969 : 76) is paraphrasing the geneticist Theodosius Dobzhansky :

> Some minimum level of ability is required for learning most skills. But while you can teach almost any one to play chess or the piano, or to conduct an orchestra, or to write prose, you cannot teach everyone to be a Capablanca, a Paderewski, a Toscanini, or a Bernard Shaw.

The verbatim quotation (Dobzhansky, 1968 : 554) reads as follows:

> Almost everybody could of become [sic], if properly brought up and properly trained, a fairly competent farmer, or a craftman of some sort, or a soldier, a sailor, tradesman, teacher or priest, certain ones would be more easily trainable to be soldiers and others to be teachers. It is even more probable that only a relatively few individuals would have the genetic wherewithal for certain highly specialized professions, such as musician, or singer, or poet, or high achievement in sports or wisdom or leadership.

I find the emphasis and, more importantly, the basic meaning of Dobzhansky's quote changed significantly by Jensen's paraphrase. I particularly resent the racial implications of Jensen's selectivity and omissions. Black Americans have made significant contributions in all areas mentioned by Dobzhansky. Jensen's paraphrase represents a very subtle personal bias. First, all the specific men mentioned represent a particular middle-class preference. Music encompasses much more than the style of a Capablanca or a Toscanini. Bernard Shaw represents one style of prose. Dobzhansky's statement would include a Duke Ellington, Nina Simone, LeRoi Jones (Imamu Ameer Baraka), Martin Luther King, Jr., Willie Mays, and Malcom X. Jensen's paraphrase would not. Now I ask the reader to judge : is this objective, unbiased scholarship? Is it correct scholarship? Is it fair and accurate scholarship?

Jensen's culture-bound white racism is nowhere more apparent than in his August 31, 1969, interview in the *New York Times Magazine.* In a letter to the *Times* later, he referred to this interview as one of the most accurate reflections of his views.

He contends that the number of intelligence genes seems to be lower, overall in the black population, than in the white. If one believes this, he is left with a problem, since there are few if any true blacks in the United States. Jensen has a "scientific" answer for this problem : "As to the effect of racial mixing, nobody has yet performed experiments that reveal its relative effect on IQ. If the racial mixture were not there, it is possible that the IQ differences between whites and blacks would be even greater" (Edson, 1969 : 10).

Jensen followed these inferences with a third knockout punch. He guessed that a possible explanation of the black-white IQ differences could be because the Negroes brought to the United States as slaves "were selected for their strength and docility rather than for mental ability" (Edson, 1969 : 43).

Jensen cannot prove any of the above. It is not clear that he has any data that would lead one to believe there is a higher probability the above inferences are more likely true than false. I notice that all three inferences assume the worst as far as black America is concerned. There are no inferences here about the effect upon white IQs of the selection processes that led to different white migrations. The white Europeans who migrated were less successful than those who did not leave. Where is the inference that they were less intelligent? Where are the inferences about the many whites who came as indentured servants? Jensen implies that without racial mixing the IQ gap could be greater. What scientific data lead him to his inference? What keeps him from seeing the possibility of a reduction in the IQ gap or even blacks being ahead of whites if there were no interracial mixing?

Jensen displays his ignorance of contemporary research on slavery (by both U.S. and African scholars) by not realizing that black slaves were not chosen for their strength but rather because they were less desirable to the chief; because the slave possessed a rebellious nature, because the person was already a slave, because the person had committed criminal acts, or, finally, because the person had fallen into disfavor.

All of the above should make Jensen's basic biases clear. It is one thing to say that there are racial differences from the genetic interaction of different breeding populations. It is quite another things, however, to make relative IQ comparisons which, among other things, make assumptions that stress relative comparable environments between blacks and whites and which ignore the cumulative effects of past environmental difficulties including those difficulties that could result in disadvantageous reproductive factors. It is racism at its worst to attribute a pejorative difference in black-white IQ scores to genetic differences, when environmental influences upon blacks and whites in the United States are so far from being comparable.

CONCLUSION

White social scientist such as Jensen should be especially careful of making inferences or drawing conclusions that depend upon a crucial assumption of black-white environmental comparability or on assumptions that we are able to measure degrees of interracial environmental differences with any specified statistical degrees of confidence. When inferences are made about black mental abilities in which the negative effects of living and adapting to racist environmental pressures are ignored or underemphasized, then these inferences are not only likely to be scientifically invalid, but they also are clearly aimed at supporting racism.

7

Intelligence and Attainment

Psychologists studying cognitive development are interested in the *processes* of intellectual growth. A rather different tradition has been the 'psychometric' one. Here psychologists have devised tests to measure a person's *aptitude or attainment*. Generally, the emphasis has been on comparing individuals for their performance, in a quantified way.

Aptitude or ability tests are designed to predict what a person can accomplish, given further training. The most well-known aptitude tests are intelligence tests. 'Intelligence' is usually taken as the ability to cope with one's environment (we discuss the definition of intelligence in more detail later), and intelligence tests are meant to measure this general kind of aptitude. In practice, however, intelligence tests have been used to predict educational ability and, later, achievement. There can also be more specific aptitude tests, for example, for musical ability or for pilot training.

Attainment tests, by contrast, measure what a person has achieved after training. Conventional examinations are attainment tests, as would be, to use the previous examples, an examination in music or a test of competence after completing a course of training as a pilot. The UK Education Reform Act (1988) specifies attainment targets for three core subjects—English, Mathematics and Science. Here a single assessment system is used to inform schools and teachers in planning the progress of their pupils, to report individual achievements to parents and other teachers, and to contribute to published statistics for local and national use. The Task Group on Assessment and Testing (TGAT) in the context of the National Curriculum explicitly makes a distinction between the assessment of *ability* and the assessment of *attainment*:

> Ability tests.... provide a general impression of which children are more or less successful. Such norm-referenced assessment has the advantage that overall performance can be reported as a single letter or number and that each child's performance can be compared with that of other children. Yet any aim to increase 'ability' is probably too general a concept to guide teaching. TGAT proposed that teachers should assess only that which is observable. Teaching decisions.... should always be based on an assessment, no matter how informal, of the children's responses to the current activity. (School Examination and Assessment Council, 1990).

In this chapter we shall first discuss the nature of intelligence tests and their history. Then we will consider the educational needs of both gifted children and children with special needs. We move on to examine other methods of assessment used in the educational system and finally more recent theories of the structure of intellect.

The Early History of Intelligence Tests

Galton, in the 1880s was one of the first to attempt the scientific measurement of intelligence with a series of tests of reaction time and memory acuity. His view that intelligence, like physical variables of height and weight , was disturbed systematically in the general population was an influential one, but his tests turned out to have little predictive value with regard to adult success or school performance, and were abandoned.

Early in the twentieth century, two French psychologists, Binet and Simon (1905), published tests which, they claimed, could identify children who were failing to make progress within the normal school system. Their aim was to give these children the special education which the overcrowded Paris schools were unable to provide. The battery of tests which Binet and Simon had devised represented the kinds of abilities which, in their view, children typically used during the school years, and included word definitions, comprehension, tests of reasoning and knowledge of numbers. Their assumption was that children who could not perform these tasks were unlikely to be able to cope with the normal level of school work. Binet and Simon had a very practical assignment—to differentiate between those who were failing at school and those who were successful; their intention was not to measure an abstract cognitive quality.

When they published their definition of intelligence in 1916 the emphasis was still on adaptation to real life situations; they called it 'judgement' :

> It seem to us that in intelligence there is a fundamental faculty, the impairment or the lack of which is of the utmost importance for practical life. This faculty is *judgement,* otherwise called good sense, practical sense, initiative, the faculty of adapting oneself to circumstances. To judge well, to reason well, these are the essential activities of intelligence. (Binet and Simon, 1916).

Binet and Simon developed age scales of mental ability by selecting items characteristic of what children of different ages could begin to succeed at. For example, a younger child might be able to repeat three numbers; an older child might not only be able to do this but also repeat five numbers in reverse order. Any particular child would then attempt test items of increasing difficulty until he/she consistently failed them, at which point the tester could calculate the child's 'mental age'. The avarage 5-year-old, for example, would complete test items at the 5-year-old level; a retarded 5-year-old might fail to solve test problems beyond the 4-year-old level, and would then have a mental age of 4. Later, these age scores were expressed as a ratio of mental age (MA) to chronological age (CA) and this formed the basis for the 'Intelligence Quotient' (IQ) :

$$\frac{\text{Mental age}}{\text{Chronological age}} \times 100 = \text{IQ}$$

The average child's IQ by this calculation would be 100 and

the IQs of children above or below the average could be calculated accordingly. The numerical scores of the IQ were less cumbersome than the original age scores and made it possible to compare the relative intellectual capability of individuals, even at different ages. The IQ assessment also made it easier to calculate correlations between intelligence and a whole range of variables.

The Stanford-Binet Intelligence Scale

After Binet and Simon had produced their scale of items for measuring mental age, it was adopted by Terman at Stanford University, California, for use in the USA. Terman increased the original 54 tests to 90, and age graded the items on 1,000 children and 400 adults. This process of age grading items on a large representative sample is called *standardizing*. The scale, published in 1916, was called the First Revision of the Stanford-Binet. It produced mental age scores, like the original Binet test, and IQ was calculated as the ratio of MA to CA.

There were two main types of test item—verbal and non-verbal. Verbal tests relied on language abilities, *e.g.*, general knowledge, comprehension, understanding similarities between things, vocabulary. Non-verbal or performance tests aimed to measure the child's perceptual skills and non-verbal reasoning, such as the ability to arrange picture in a logical sequence to make a coherent story, to copy designs using a set of coloured blocks, or assemble pieces of a jigsaw-type puzzle into the right arrangement as quickly as possible.

In 1937, Terman and a colleague, Merrill, produced a substantial extension and revision of the scale. This Second Revision was made up of two similar but separate scales, each comprising 192 tests; these were called the L and M scales, and could be used as alternate forms of the test. The Second Revision was standardized on nearly 3,200 persons and, as before, was used to calculate mental age and from that, IQ.

In 1960 a Third Revision was published. This revision was necessary because some of the earlier items were clearly becoming dated or inappropriate for certain groups of subjects. The two separate L and M scales were recombined into a single L-M scale, taking the best from each and dropping some items. The test was standardized on nearly 4,500 persons.

Another change in the 1960 revision was in the calculation of IQ. The formula using mental age had two important drawbacks. First, it had been assumed that mental age did not increase after age 16—an arbitrary assumption since found to be false. Secondly, the variation in IQ across individuals was different, depending on age level. Therefore, it was decided to calculate IQ in terms of the deviation or *standard score* of the subject from others of his or her own age. The final test was designed so that at each age level from 2 years to 18 years, the mean score was 100, but the standard deviation was 16. Thus someone with an IQ of 100 is at the mean for his or her age level; an IQ of 116 means a score one standard deviation above the mean, and so on.

The Reliability of the Scale

If a test is said to be *reliable,* this means it can be used consistently to measure something. One way of assessing whether a scale is reliable is to give it twice to the same persons within a short time interval and see if the same result is achieved. Unfortunately, there is some familiarity or practice effect if the time gap is very short. An alternative is to use two versions of the same test. This was available in the L and M scales of the 1937 revision and when these were given within a week of each other, correlations ranging from 0.83 to 0.98 were obtained (depending on the age and intelligence of subjects). This remains the best evidence of reliability, even for the 1960 scale.

The Validity of the Scale

If a test is *valid,* then it should be measuring what it is designed to measure, in this case, intelligence. How do we know that the Stanford-Binet scale is doing this?

Three sources of validity are cited in the manual (Terman and Merrill, 1960) :

1. The items are based on the 1937 scale, in turn based on the 1916 scale, in turn based on Binet's items.
2. The items were such that performance on them improved with age.

3. Performance on individual items agreed well with performance on the total scale. Those items with poor correlations were dropped. The average item correlation with the total scale was increased from 0.61 in the 1937 scale to 0.66 in the 1960 scale.

As can be seen, the evidence for validity is limited. The evidence that the scale comprises a large number of subtests which correlate reasonably together (3, above), and the performance improves with age (2, above), does not tell us much. These criteria could hold for a test of physical dexterity or social confidence, as much as intelligence. Thus, a lot hinges on the nature of the items, being traced back to the earlier scales (1, above), and thus to the strengths and limitations of the beliefs of the first investigators—Binet, Simon and, later, Terman.

Binet devised his test for educational purposes, and other researchers have generally found that intelligence test scores do give a reasonable prediction of academic achievement. This is another possible source of validity. It does not prove that the tests measure 'intelligence' in a very general sense, but it does suggest they provide some measure of conventional academic ability, or ability to profit by the conventional educational system. This was the basis of the later use of the tests to select children for different kinds of educational provision.

Later Uses of Intelligence Tests

The Binet test was initially used simply to differentiate between 'normal' children and those with learning difficulties; an IQ of 70 was taken as the cut-off point below which the child needed special education. However, in the UK Cyril Burt went on from there to argue that in any group of normal children, the variations in mental ability would be so wide as to make it impossible to teach them all at the same level. Since he had observed that the gap between the bright and dull children became even wider at the secondary school, he recommended the organization of classes on the basis of mental ability rather than chronological age. It was this view that the individual should be assigned a place in society according to his or her intellectual ability which was to have far-reaching effects on the educational system in Britain.

During the First World War, when large numbers of people were being assigned into categories to meet the requirements of different work roles, there was a proliferation of group intelligence and aptitude tests. After the war, the large industrial companies also demanded batteries of selection tests which could measure specific aptitudes in skills such as engineering, typing, dressmaking. This type of selection procedure, it was claimed, provided an effective means of assigning individual to occupations appropriate to their abilities. Burt was one of the first psychologists in the newly formed National Institute of Industrial Psychology, and with his strong commitment to the idea that intelligence was innate, static throughout life and measurable, he proposed that intelligence tests also be used in schools with the aim of providing all children with an education appropriate to their level of mental ability. In his day Burt was highly respected as an educational psychologist, although he is now discredited because of his fraudulent research into the heritability of intelligence.

With hindsight it is easy to see that the hierarchical concept of intelligence presented by these pioneers in the field of psychometrics reflected the hierarchical structure of society, and so was readily accepted as a means of assigning individuals to 'suitable' roles in that society. At that time, however, it was believed that intelligence tests were objective and accurate means of assessing mental ability. The tests, in fact appeared to offer a fairer measure of the potential ability of children from differing backgrounds than did conventional examinations and school reports; for example, they were thought to be less susceptible to social biases which might affect teachers' evaluations. Unfortunately, insufficient weight was given to the effects of a child's environment on test performance, due to Burt's unfounded assumption that the tests measured 'innate ability'.

What then were the implications of the psychometric approach for educational practice? If, as Burt and many psychometrists believed, intelligence is an innate, stable factor, then it would follow logically that once suitable measures had been devised, children could be grouped according to ability levels for educational purposes. In the years following the First World War, when the Hadow Report (1926) recommended the establishment of secondary education for all children after 11, current psychological thinking had a very strong influence. Previously the majority of children had remained at the same elementary school until they were old enough to leave; only those bright enough to win a scholarship at 11 went on to 'grammar schools'. The Hadow Report suggested that for all children there should be a definite change of school at the age of 11 and that there should be a range of post-primary schools available—technical, selective and non-selective modern schools as well as traditional grammar schools.

In order to assign each child to the appropriate school, some form of assessment would have to take place; by implication, the classification of children through some form of grading or streaming was to begin during the primary school years. This official approval of selection and streaming was extended in the Hadow Report on Primary Education (1931) and the Handbook of Suggestions far Teachers (1937). The Spens Report (1938), also strongly influenced by psychometric thinking, advocated three-track streaming in primary schools and a selective tripartite system for the secondary years of schooling. (In practice, the number of technical schools was very few so the system was a *bipartite* one of allocating children to either a 'grammar' or 'secondary modern' school at the age of 11.)

Thus, by the late 1930s it was standard practice to select children at 11+ on the basis of attainment in English and arithmetic, and performance on an intelligence tests. Furthermore, it was widely believed that children could be accurately categorized into different groups, each with particular educational needs (*see* Table 7.1). Thus, children were not only selected at 11, but, once in the secondary schools, were further streamed into even narrower ability groups, the A, B and C streams. A hierarchical attitude to the curriculum grew up, with children in the A stream following academic courses, while C stream children studied practical subjects like domestic science, art, crafts etc.

By the end of the Second World War, attitudes were changing again. A Labour government came to power with a large majority and popular support for an attack on inequality in society. IQ tests themselves were coming to be seen as a less objective measure of mental ability than the psychologists claimed. There was also greater awareness of the detrimental effects which selection and streaming had on children, and the way in which the selective system discriminated against children from under-privileged backgrounds. However, despite the reaction against streaming in schools, the 11+ and the tripartite system, the Labour government failed to make the establishment of a comprehensive system of secondary education a high priority. The 1944 Education Act aimed to provide equality of opportunity for all children 'according to age, aptitude and ability', but it left the implementation of this policy to the local education authorities. Official sanction had been given to egalitarianism, but so firmly entrenched was the selective system that the changeover to a comprehensive system of secondary education was a very gradual one.

Table 7.1

The Categorization of Children on the Basis of *IQ*, as Envisaged during the 1930s

IQ	*Educational category*	*% of population*
50	Ineducable idiots : occupation Centres	0.2
50-70	Mentally defective : special schools	2.0
70-85	Dull and backward : 'C' classes in schools	10.0
85-115	Normal pupils : 'B' and 'A' classes in senior Schools	76.0
115-30	Bright pupils : selective central schools	10.0
130-50	Scholarship pupils : secondary schools	2.0
150+	Scholarship pupils : ultimately university honours	0.2

Source : Adapted from Evans and Waites, 1981

Burt and his colleagues continued to support the use of tests in the selective system and to defend the psychometric position against the hostile political climate of the post-war years. Although the 11+ as a selection procedure had, by the 1970s, been abolished in most parts of Britain, many of the arguments concerning selection, streaming, equality of opportunity and maintenance of standards continue in educational debate today; the controversies have not been resolved. Even this brief review of intelligence testing indicates the enormous influence the psychometric movement has had on educational thinking in this century.

The use of IQ tests may, however, still have application to some areas of educational psychology. In particular, the tests may be used as part of the assessment process in considering children at the extremes of the normal educational distribution—children with learning difficulties and gifted children.

The Child with Special Needs

Children with special needs are usually considered as those who are failing within the normal educational system or who are, in some way, performing below the avarage which can be expected of children from their age group. In the past these children were categorized according to their handicaps, *e.g.* as educationally subnormal (ESN) pupils with IQs below 85, maladjusted pupils, on physically handicapped pupils (Ministry of Education, 1959); three to four children in every 1,000, labelled 'the mentally handicapped', were considered to be 'ineducable' and either remained at home or were placed in training centres or hospitals. In 1970 the Education (Handicapped Children) Act allowed the mentally handicapped to be educated in separate schools or institutions. At this point, the terms ESN(M) (where M stood for 'moderate') and ESN(S) (were S stood for 'severe') came into use; an IQ of 50 marked the dividing line between the two. More recently, the Warnock Report (1978) has suggested a radical change in procedure by recommending that 'statutory categorization of pupils should be abolished' and that educational provision should arise from a detailed description of the special needs of each child.

The Education Reform Act (1988) explicity states that the National curriculum should be broad enough to cover 'the substantial majority of the ability spectrum' at each level. Furthermore, the Act requires local education authorities to ensure that pupils with special educational needs have their statements amended, if necessary, to take account of the national Curriculum. The aim is that each pupil should be 'stretched' to reach his or her potential.

How has this change in perspective come about? At the extremes, there is usually little disagreement about the meaning of a label attached to a particular child but there is also a large area in which it is difficult to know where the cut-off point between 'normal' and 'abnormal' behaviour or attainment occurs. When can it be said that a child's behaviour is so disturbed that he or she can be labelled 'maladjusted'? How far below the norm for his or her class does a child have to fall to be called 'a slow learner'? How do we take into account the variety of factors that may contribute to educational failure?

Some learning difficulties have been ascribed to general intellectual impairment. Others, however, may be due to an unstimulating or stressful home background, to emotional disturbance, to a physical condition, to poor diet, or to a combination of factors. For example, Down's syndrome ('mongolism') results from a chromosomal abnormality and can be labelled as a distinct category of disability, yet for the individual so classified there can be a wide range of social, emotional and educational possibilities, and the attitudes of those who interact with him or her may be crucial factors. Similarly, Galloway (1979) pointed out an even wider range of abilities encompassed in the category ESN(M) :

> assessment as ESN(M) may meant that a child is very backward in all areas of development and needs specialized teaching of a sort that no ordinary school can be expected to provide; or that he is seriously retarded educationally due to prolonged illness; or that his educatinal retardation is due to learning difficulties associated with some specific perceptual problem; or that he comes from a problem family and is performing at the same level that one should expect of any child in similar circumstances.

Particular concern arose over the observations that ethnic minority children were disproportionately over-represented in the ESN category, and the use of intelligence tests as an accurate means of selection came under heavy criticism.

Intelligence tests are not now used routinely as they were in the past to assess low-attaining children. Educational psychologists try instead to assess children in the context of their home background, medical history of life events and in relation to the problems which the children, their parents or their teachers are experiencing. For example, if a child has had prolonged periods of illness or a traumatic event such as the loss of a parent, then these circumstances are taken into account when assessing present levels of attainment.

Methods of assessment are chosen which best answer the questions raised and which are linked to intervention procedures, such as specialist tuition. These methods may include IQ tests, but many other measures are also used. For example, naturalistic observation of the child's behaviour systematically recorded by parents and teachers can lead to a greater understanding of language capacity, performance on cognitive tasks and attention span. This approach can bypass formal testing and provide useful baselines for future progress. Educational tests can also give measures of attainment in specific areas, such as mathematics and reading. Diagnostic tests can help unravel reasons for a child's poor performance (for example, reading disabilities). Social assessment can be helpful, especially when linked with training programmes. These can cover self-help, communication and social skills, emotional adjustment and health.

The method of provision for the educational needs of these children remains a controversial one. If children with special needs continue within the normal school system, they have the advantages of sports facilities, laboratories, library and other school resources, as well as the possibility of choice from the full range of school subjects; there are also opportunities to mix with ordinary children and to learn the social skills they will need for survival in adult life. The task of educating the child with special needs can stimulate teachers to develop more creative and flexible methods. Additionally, the presence of these children in the ordinary setting gives staff and other pupils the opportunity to develop positive attitudes towards disability, based on familiarity and understanding rather than prejudice and ignorance.

There are also disadvantages. Lessons may not always be designed to cater for these children's needs. There may be a frequent sense of failure and inadequacy, and other children may not always be tolerant. Resentment may arise from the extra time and tuition which children with special needs require. To some educationalists there remain strong arguments in favour of special schools staffed by people trained to meet the social, emotional, physical and educational needs of these children. Even the Warnock Report (1978) recognized that there are some very severely disabled individuals for whom special schools are a necessity.

However, the main recommendations of the Warnock Report were that most children with special needs should not be segregated into special schools or classes. The 1981 Education Act has required in Britain that local authorities integrate children with special needs into mainstream education. The implementation of the Act is taking time, with wide variations from region to region but the Education Reform Act (1988), while acknowledging that a statement of special educational needs may specify some modification in the ranges of levels appropriate at different key stages for the individual child, requires that 'any departure from the National Curriculum be decided in the light of educational, medical, psychological and other evidence about the pupil including the views of the pupil's parents' (DES, 1989, paragraph 56). However, the present concern with accountability in school performance may discourage teachers from devoting their energies to children who have extreme learning difficulties. Clearly there is a great need for training and support for teachers in this task and such major changes cannot take place without considerable financial outlay; integration cannot happen overnight, and it is necessary to create a climate in which acceptance of the child with special needs can take place.

The Gifted Child

Gifted children also have special needs. A child may be described as 'gifted' who is outstanding in either a general domain (such as exceptional performance on an intelligence test), or a more specific area of ability, such as music, or sport. Some researchers have attempted to identify the characteristics of gifted children at an early age, drawing up checklists such as the two shown in Table 7.2. Such checklists are of limited value : they void the issue of whether general or specific abilities are the criteria for giftedness. In practice, most research studies of giftedness are concerned with the high IQ child, and these offer the most cohesive group of investigations.

Even if we identify criteria of giftedness, we still have the problem of where to set, the borderline between gifted children and others. Terman (1925) defined the gifted child as one who had an IQ of over 140; Ogilvie (1973) set the borderline at 130. DeHaan and Havighurst (1960) set it at 120. The figures shown in Table 7.3 indicate the approximate numbers cut off by different borderlines on a standard intelligence tests such as the Stanford-Binet or the Wechsler (WISC-R) test (*see* below). These figures refer to a total school population and will very considerably from one neighbourhood to another as well as from chance fluctuations. Thus, while the average school class should contain one child with an IQ of 130 or over, the number might fluctuate from none in many classes to say six in a few.

Table 7.2

Signs of Giftedness according to Bridges, and Tempest

Bridge (1969)	Tempest (1974)
1. They read as early as 3 years old	1. Exceptionally good reader
2. High powers of abstraction	2. Ability to deal with abstract problems
3. High qualitative level of questioning	3. High level of curiosity expressed through perceptive questions
4. Speed of thought	4. Quickness of response
5. Do not want to write as this breaks up oral communication	5. Ability to work quickly, although sometimes inaccurately
6. Withdraw to work on their own	6. Work on their own
7. Enormous energy	7. Likely to be physically superior
	8. Likely to be highly competitive
	9. More selective in interests

The most famous study of giftedness is Terman's (1925-59) *Genetic Studies of Genius.* This embodies a longitudinal study which has not yet been completed even though Terman himself is dead and the participants are now in their 70s and 80s. At the beginning of the study the participants ranged in age from 6 to 12 years and represented roughly the brightest 1 per cent of children in the State of California at that time. Almost all had IQs of 140 and over as measured by the Stanford-Binet and the average score was 151. They excelled in reading, language and general information. Physical health and growth were superior from birth on. According to mothers' reports, they walked and talked early. Teachers' reports on maladjustment indicated that only 13 per cent of the gifted were 'nervous' as compared to 16 per cent of controls; thus common sense views that gifted children were likely to be more disturbed than other children were not confirmed in Terman's sample.

A follow-up in 1947 when the mean age was 35 indicated that the initial level of intelligence had been maintained. Health statistics were superior; death rate was low and only 5 per cent admitted serious maladjustment. Sixty-eight per cent had graduated from college. Many had been outstanding in their professions; for example, they had produced a large number of publications and patents.

Table 7.3

Percentage of Gifted Children at Different cut-off Points

IQ	*Approx. numbers*
150 and over	0.1 (1 in 1000)
140 and over	0.5 (1 in 200)
130	2.5 (1 in 40)
120 and over	10 (1 in 10)

In 1959 another follow-up indicated that they had continued to maintain their high achievements in occupational level; 71 per cent were in professional, semiprofessional or managerial positions compared with 14 per cent of the Californian population as a whole, and their average income was higher than that of the average college graduate.

Most of the subjects in Terman's sample appeared to be exceptionally well-integrated, healthy and well-adjusted individuals. Unfortunately, as Terman's selection procedure was partly based on teachers' ratings, home background factors may have confounded his criterion of high intelligence. For example, working class and ethnic minority children might well have been under-represented from the start of the study. Certainly, social environment and home upbringing played an important part in the success of Terman's sample, even though, true to the psychometric tradition, he initially emphasized genetic influences.

Some of the literature on giftedness stresses problems and difficulties which gifted children experience, or that giftedness, especially where it is not recognized, can become a handicap. Hitchfield (1973) found that teachers were not good at identifying the gifted child. Sixty per cent of the children with an IQ of 140 + were *not* rated by teachers as being in the top 5 per cent in areas such as use of books, mathematical ability, general knowledge and oral ability; 45 per cent were not rated as being exceptionally good in any of these areas.

Torrance, writing of highly creative children, argued that 'society in general is downright savage towards creative thinkers' (1970) and accused teachers of misunderstanding gifted children's unusual questions and answers. He argued that 'when teachers fail to understand highly creative children, refusal to learn, delinquency or withdrawal may be a consequence'. Joan Freeman tackled the question of whether this is an accurate picture of gifted children in her study, described in box 13.1.

There have been fears that the educational needs of children of high ability cannot be met by lessons pitched at the level of the middle range of ability. Ogilvie (1973), in the Schools Council Report on gifted children in primary schools, suggested that many local education authorities were not making any provision for gifted children. We can distinguish three broad categories of method which have been used in practice :

1. *Acceleration* : the bright child is promoted to a higher class or admitted to school at a younger age than usual. Ultimately, this can mean admission to university at a very young age. Many teachers are against this, as, they claim, the child may be *intellectually* at a level of older children but not sufficiently mature *socially or emotionally* to adjust well.

2. *Segregation* : the brighter children are selected for particular schools on the basis of their ability, and the curriculum adjusted accordingly. Opinions are divided on the effectiveness of this method. Some point to the academic success of selective schools; some argue, too, that special abilities such as musical or dance talents are best catered for in specialized schools, such as the Menuhin School or the Royal Ballet School. Others argue that segregation is unfair, socially divisive and hard to implement.

3. *Enrichment* : an enriched education is provided for gifted children within the normal classroom. There are a number of ways in which this method can be implemented. Extra-curricular activities can give interesting opportunities to brighter children, especially if these are organized by specialist, enthusiastic teachers and provide opportunities for such children to spend time with others of similar ability. Withdrawal from the normal class can also give the gifted child the stimulus to work independently. Finally, individualized learning programmes offer another approach. Enrichment could avoid the negative aspects of the previous two methods and have the advantage that it can also be made available to moderate-ability children if they are interested.

Different Methods of Assessing Intelligence

In this section, we describe in more detail the techniques psychologists have devised to measure intelligence and attainment. We saw earlier that the first intelligence test to be used widely was the Stanford-Binet Intelligence Scale. Table 7.4 shows the type of test items used in the scale. (The examples are similar but not identical to the original tests items.) From the child's responses to age-standardized items of these types, the psychologist can obtain an overall IQ score.

The revisions of the Stanford-Binet scale tried to take account of cultural and educational changes in children's experiences, but the tests is quite heavily loaded with verbal items, especially for older age groups. Verbal tests may under-estimate the intellectual capacity of children who speak a different dialect, or for whom the language of the test is not their mother tongue; furthermore, some backgrounds do not stress the language skills measured by intelligence tests. Thus, children who have language difficulties or who come from another cultural background may be at a disadvantage when taking the test.

However, many educational psychologists treat the Stanford-Binet test as a clinical interview in which they can gain insights into the child's personality, self image, attention-span and motivation as well as level of intelligence. Thus, in the hands of an experienced clinician, it can be of diagnostic value. From this point of view, it is as well to remember Binet's original brief, which was to assess scholarship attainment in normal and retarded children and not to assess an abstract intellectual quality.

Another series of widely used intelligence tests was devised by Wechsler. In contrast to the Stanford-Binet, the Wechsler tests give a verbal IQ and a performance IQ as well as a full-scale IQ. As in the 1960 revisions of the Stanford-Binet, Wechsler did not estimate intelligence from mental age as Binet did, but related a child's score to the distribution of scores for other children of the same age. Raw scores are changed into standard scores within the subject's age group; subtest scores are then added and converted into an IQ with a mean of 100 and a standard deviation of 15. The correlation between full-scale Wechsler IQ scores and Stanford-Binet IQ scores of the same children is high, at around 0.80.

Table 7.4

Items Similar to those Used in the Stanford-Binet Intelligence Scale

Vocabulary :	the child is asked to give the meaning of words; these increase difficulty—'What is an apple?'; 'What is harmony?'
Verbal analogies :	the child is asked is to explain differences and similarities between things—' a rabbit is timid, a lion is ....?'; 'in what way are spring and autumn alike?'
Arithmetic :	the child is given a series of arithmetical problems to solve
Memory :	the child may be asked to repeat a series of numbers : 4-7-3-8-5-9; the child copies a bead chain from memory
General information :	the child is asked questions on topics of general knowledge; 'What is the capital of France?'; 'How many pennies are in a pound?'; 'Who wrote *Macbeth*?'
Absurdities :	The child is asked to say what is silly about a picture in which the characters are doing something silly like sunbathing in the rain; older children are asked to say what is silly about an absurd sentence
Missing parts picture :	the child is asked to say what is missing in a

	picture : a door without a handle, a table without a leg
Spatial problems :	the child traces a path through a maze
Comprehension :	the child is asked questions that test adaptiveness and practical judgment; 'What is the thing to do if you are lost in a strange city?'; 'What should you do if a child younger than you hits you?'

The main Wechsler test is the Wechsler Intelligence Scale for Children (WISC-R) designed for children from 6 to 16 years. In addition, there are tests for the preschool and early school years—the Wechsler Preschool and Primary Scale of Intelligence (WPPSI)—and also for adults of 16 and over—the Wechsler Adult Intelligence Scale (WAIS). Examples of items from the verbal and the performance subscales of the WISC-R are given in Table 7.5. (Again, the examples are similar to but not identical to the actual test items.) Although the performance scale places very little emphasis on verbal skills, there is, in fact, a high correlation between the verbal and performance scales of the test.

The Stanford-Binet and the Wechsler tests are individually administrated. However, for reasons of speed and efficiency, psychologists have devised tests that can be given to groups of people. While individual tests are mainly used in clinical settings for help in the diagnosis of learning difficulties, group tests are used largely for selection purposes in education (as the 11+ test was), or at work. Correlations between individual and group tests are fairly high and it is felt that they are each measuring the same kinds of ability. However, the group test has certain disadvantages. The examiner may not notice signs of anxiety in the testee which would be more obvious in a one-to-one testing situation; furthermore, once the test has begun there is no opportunity for the psychologist to reassure the candidate. People with language difficulties or people for whom English is a second language are at a disadvantage since they may find it hard to read the instructions for each item. This criticism applies, for example, to the AH-6 test, a group test designed to discriminate among highly intelligent adults; the instructions for items are deliberately complex and require a good command of the English language.

One example of a non-verbal group test is Raven's Progressive Matrices. This is a test for adults and children which requires testees to complete matrices in which every square but one has been filled in according to a certain pattern (Figure 7.1). When the testee has worked out the principle, he or she can then select the missing part of the design from a number of possible alternatives. Raven designed the test as a measure of Spearman's 'g' factor (*see* below), that is, the ability to understand relations among abstract items. The most commonly used version is in black and white but a brightly coloured version is also available to make the test more interesting to younger children and to testees who are not accustomed to test situations (for example, in cross-cultural research). For people of above average intelligence, there is a more difficult version, the Advanced Progressive Matrices; there is also a tactile version for the visually impaired. Although it is a non-verbal test, it has not been found to be completely culture-free, but it is less influenced than many verbal tests by the subject's social and educational background.

Table 7.5

Items Similar to those Used in the WISC-R Intelligence Scale

Verbal scale items	
Information :	the child is asked a series of general knowledge questions
Comprehension :	the child explains why certain courses of action are appropriate : 'What should you do if you break a friend's toy by mistake?'
Digit span :	the child is asked to repeat a series of numbers which increase in length, either in the same order or backwards
Similarities :	the child is asked to say in what way two things are alike, *e.g.* a pear and a plum
Arithmetic :	the child answers a series of arithmetical problems
Vocabulary :	the child is asked to define words of increasing difficulty
Performance scale items	
Picture arrangement :	the child is shown a series of cartoon pictures which are out of order and asked to arrange

	them correctly
Picture completion :	the child is asked to say which part is missing in a picture; a dog with one ear, a cup with no handle
Block design :	the child is shown blocks which have some sides all white, some all red and some half white and half red; the child is asked to reproduce a series of designs using first four blocks and later nine
Object assembly :	the child has to assemble a jigsaw of parts into a whole shape; *e.g.* a dog, a human foot
Coding :	the child matches symbols with numbers according to a given code
Mazes :	the child traces a route on a series of mazes

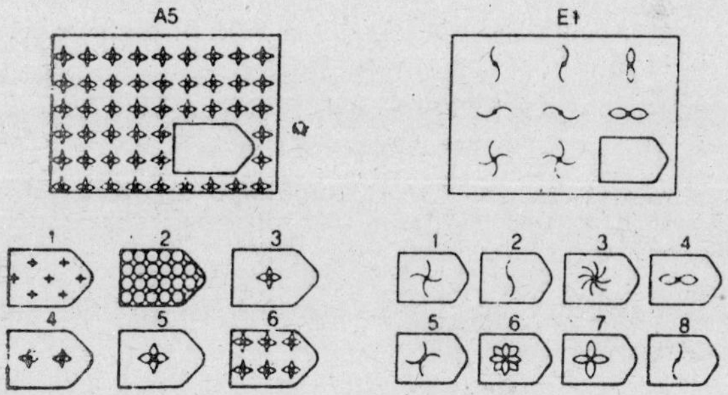

Fig. 7.1: Sample items from the Progressive matrices (from Raven, 1958)

'Culture-free' and 'Culture-fair' Tests

The test described so far have often been criticized on the grounds that they discriminate against individuals from minority cultures. Within our society, children who do not speak English at home, or whose cultural background is different, or who speak non-standard English, tend to score less highly than children from the dominant culture. Cross-cultural studies of intelligence also indicate that tests that have been standardized in one culture are not necessarily appropriate in another. Even the non-verbal items in traditional intelligence tests may be culturally loaded. Several attempts have been made to device tests that are 'culture-free' but they have been largely unsuccessful; it is difficult to evaluate their validity, and anyway a realistic concept of intelligence must be based in a cultural context.

'Culture-specific' tests represent one attempt to design tests that measure the abilities of people from minority cultures. One example is the Black Intelligence Test of Cultural Homogeneity (BITCH), which uses non-standard English and slang expressions. Items in the test (Williams, 1973) include :

1. *Nose opened* means (A) flirting; (B) teed off; (C) deeply in love; (D) very angry.
2. *Blood* means (A) a vampire; (B) a dependent individual; (C) an injured person; (D) a brother of colour.
3. *Mother's day* means (A) black independence day; (B) a day when mothers are honoured; (C) a day the welfare cheques come in; (D) every first Sunday in church.

Black children more often than not get the right answers (1, C; 2, D; 3, C) than white children, but although they score more highly on BITCH than on standard tests of intelligence, the BITCH tests does not predict academic attainment in the way that standard intelligence tests do.

Mercer (*see* Rice, 1979) has devised an alternative method for testing children from minority cultures by adjusting the norms from standard tests. Her System of Multicultural Pluralistic Assessment (SOMPA) is a battery of tests especially developed for ethnic minority children aged from 5 to 11. These include : the WISC as an assessment of the child's performance in the school environment; an interview with parents covering health, family background and the child's social competence in his or her own cultural environment; and a medical examination to check whether physical, perceptual or dietary factors might be impairing the child's performance in school. The aim of this battery of tests is to measure potential ability and to recognize the social competence which the child already has, even if this is not usually acknowledge in standard intelligence tests.

Assessment of Attainment

Very commonly *attainment* tests are used in schools as a means of measuring performance in a particular subject, or in the basic skills of reading, comprehension and numeracy. This kind of test aims to give both teachers and student feedback about the effectiveness of a particular course of instruction and acts as a check on how much has actually been learned. The form which tests of attainment take varies widely from informal observation to standardized tests.

Examinations

The examination can be test devised by the class teacher or a public examination produced by one of the official Boards of Examiners, for example, the General Certificate of Secondary Education (GCSE). At the time of writing, all syllabuses and examinations which the UK Examining Boards produce have to meet general and subject-specific *national criteria* which have been approved by the Secretary of State for Education. At present formal selection takes place for the majority of pupils at 16+. Just as the 11+ examination was used to predict a child's potential for particular types of secondary education, so formal examination results often form the basis for judgements about an individual's potential for a particular career or for entry into further and higher education. Public examinations also serve the function of maintaining and monitoring national standards of performance.

There are a number of drawbacks, however, to this type of selection procedure. First, how *reliable* are examination results? Research into standards of marking indicate that wide fluctuations in allocation of marks can occur, particularly in the marking of essay-type answers. The public Boards of Examiners have attempted to overcome such unreliability by adopting marking schemes and devising systems of checking and re-checking scripts so that greater consistency among examiners is achieved. Furthermore, the national criteria (*see* above) for GCSE require an element of teacher involvement in assessment (*e.g.* in coursework and project work). But in less formal examinations there is greater possibility of bias and subjectivity in marking.

Another area of concern is *validity*. The examination should represent a valid selection of topics from the syllabus which candidates have followed, and should test the extent to which they have realized the aims of particular course of study. However, the conventional three-hour examination may not be the most appropriate means of evaluating a candidate's understanding and achievement in a subject area. Furthermore, individuals vary in the extent to which they do themselves justice in examination settings. Anxiety, stress, lack of motivation, language or reading difficulties may hamper candidates in their capacity to express what they know. Attempts to overcome this problem, *e.g.* through the required use in GCSE examination of orals, project work and continuous assessment, are now much more common than they were in the past, but the emphasis continues to be largely on written work.

How far do examinations succeed in predicting future performance? Their *predictive validity* is highly valued by colleges, universities and employers; but there are reasons to be cautious in placing so much weight on examination results. The success of the Open University in Britain, which requires no entry qualifications, indicates a large pool of people who have the capacity to benefit from higher education despite having failed to obtain conventionally required examination grades at school. Furthermore, many occupations require skills, aptitudes and personal qualities which are not measured by conventional examinations.

Standardized Tests of Attainment

Standardized attainment tests, which are published commercially and restricted in their availability to registered users, are different from examinations. The National Foundation for Educational Research (NFER) supplies a wide range of tests to measure attainment in reading, verbal reasoning, English, numeracy and comprehension. Attainment tests have been pre-tested on large numbers of children in order to eliminate badly worded questions or items that fail to discriminate among candidates. The instructions for administering the tests are usually standard so that candidates will all have taken the test under broadly similar conditions. This enable the teacher to make a meaningful assessment of an individual's performance in comparison with others of the same age.

Performance may be expressed in terms of an age; children at primary school, for example, are often given a reading age which helps parents and teachers evaluate the child's progress. Alternatively, attainment may be expressed as a quotient : a child may be given a Verbal Reasoning Quotient or an English Attainment Quotient. The child's performance can then be easily compared with the norm. Hence, these are sometimes called *norm-referenced* tests. Since the school curriculum is always changing, these tests must be kept up to date; the norms, too, need to be recent ones since norms for one generation may be inappropriate for another.

May attainment tests correlate quite highly with IQ, but their primary function is to measure achievement within a particular subject area rather than general intelligence. They are of use to the teacher for assessing pupil progress in basic skills and they have the advantage over informal class examination results that they have been properly standardized on large representative samples. Thus they play a useful part in the on-going record of children's progress throughout the school years.

Criterion-referenced Tests

In recent years there has been a move away from norm-referenced standardized tests towards criterion-referenced tests which set definite levels of performance to be achieved by pupils. In this system the person passes or fails a test regardless of the percentage of individuals of the same age who perform at that level. Criterion-referenced tests focus on a form of assessment which is closer to the school-based learning process since the emphasis is on what pupils 'know, understand and can do' (DES, 1985). From this standpoint they may be viewed as tests which take into account aspects of attainment which are less easily assessed by conventional 3-hour examinations. Furthermore, criterion-referenced tests are currently associated with curriculum-reform, especially in the growing concern with oral and practical work.

The tester decides on criteria which it is expected that the individual should have achieved. For example, a teacher might want to know whether a pupil understood how to do long division. The criterion would be reached if the child successfully solved 20 long division problems. The criteria need not be based on age norms, although frequently educators *do* have expectations about what a child should be able to do by a particular age. Rather, the teacher is using absolute criteria in assessing a skill. An example would be whether or not you pass the driving test. You either pass or not; the test is the same whatever your age. The Associated Board of the Royal School of Music sets standards of attainment in musical performance; this system of Grades is another example of a criterion-referenced test.

The British Abilities Scale is a criterion-referenced intelligence test designed by Elliot and his colleagues (1979) for use with subjects between the ages of 2 and 17. The subtests measure, for example, reasoning, spatial imagery, short-term memory, problem-solving; there is also a test for measuring social reasoning. The test can be used in a flexible way by educational psychologists not only to calculate IQ, but also to measure *changes* in particular abilities and to examine an individual's profile of abilities.

It has been claimed (ILEA, 1982) that the use of criterion-referenced tests in school is highly motivating to students at all levels of ability since they are able to see progress and achieve success at their own pace. In principle, all pupils could pass a criterion-referenced tests if they could demonstrate that they had met the objectives of the particular course of study in question. The *principle of readiness* refers to the strategy of only entering pupils for such tests when they are likely to succeed. In practice, however, most children are still taught in mixed-ability, same-age classes and this places constraints on the organization of testing each pupil when he or she is 'ready': The fact that criterion-referenced tests involve competition against targets rather than against peers may play a part in creating a cooperative classroom atmosphere. They also have the advantage that objectives are clearly stated so that pupils are aware of what is expected of them.

National Standards of Attainment

A wider function of attainment tests is their role in the evaluation of *national* standards. The Assessment of Performance

Unit (APU) was set up by the Department of Education and Science (DES) in 1975 with the general objective of promoting 'the development of methods of assessing and monitoring the achievement of children at school, and to seek to identify the incidence of underachievement in the areas of Language, Mathematics, Science as well as personal, aesthetic and physical development at primary and secondary levels'. Critics point to the narrowly quantitative nature of the research results and argue that much of the quality of learning is missed in such large-scale surveys. In addition, there are fears that this type of monitoring procedure may impose constraints on the curriculum and hinder imaginative teaching, which does not lend itself to quantitative evaluation. An example of an APU study is given in box 13.2.

Educators have also expressed concern about the role of nationally prescribed tests done by all pupils at the ages of 7, 11, 14 and 16 as required in the National Curriculum in the UK. (*See* Table 7.6.)

All National Curriculum subjects have Attainment Targets, or goals showing what children should know or do at each stage. Pupils are measured on a 10-point scale with an average child reaching Level 2 by age 7, Level 4 by age 11, Level 5 or 6 by age 14, and Level 6 or 7 by age 16. Children are assessed by a series of national tests (or Standard Assessment Tasks) given at four key stages, at ages 7, 11, 14 and 16. In Table 7.6 you can see examples of attainment targets in maths (using and applying maths) at Levels 3, 6, 8 and 10.

Alternative Approaches to Assessment

There has been a radical shift on the part of psychologists and educators away from standardized tests towords more flexible types of assessment which are directly related to the individual's needs in a particular context. More weight is being given to teacher-assessment and self-assessment; personal and social qualities are being taken into account. Significantly, it has been recommended that records of achievement be used as a means of recording progress and attainment within the National Curriculum assessment system.

Several factors account for this change. First, we have seen how educational psychologists have become more sceptical about

Tabel 7.6
Testing at the Four Key Stages in Mathematics in the National Curriculum

Level	*Statements of attainment*	*Example*
3	Pupils should:	
(Keystage I)	—select the materials and the mathematics to use for a task; check results and consider whether they are sensible	Estimate the distance around the school hall; select appropriate method for measuring and units to be used; measure and compare the results
	—explain work being done and record findings systematically	Sketch a plan of the school hall and enter measurements made
	—make and test predictions	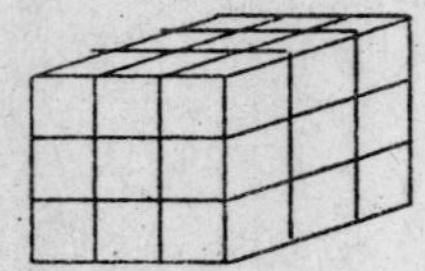 Predict the number of cubes needed to construct this figure and test the prediction
6 (Keystage 2)	—design a task and select appropriate mathematics and resources; check there is sufficient information and obtain any that is missing; use 'trial and improvement' methods	Design and make a device to measure accurately a given period of time, *e.g.* two minutes

	—use oral, written or visual forms to record and present findings	Plot Cartesian coordinates to represent simple function mappings : x—>2x+3, (or y=2x+3).
	—make and text generalizations and simple hypotheses; define and reason in simple contexts with some precision	Explore the pattern :  State 1 1 square 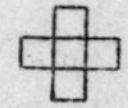 Stage 2 5 squares 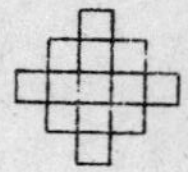 Stage 3 13 squares 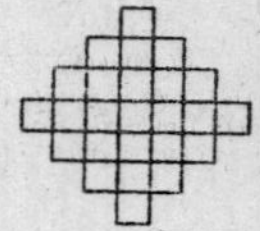 Stage 4 25 squares Use the difference method to extend the pattern; determine a rule for the sequence and test the rule
8 (Keystage 3)	—devise a mathematical task and make detailed plan of the work; work methodically, checking information for completeness; consider whether the results are of the right order	Decide where to put a telephone box in the locality.

(Contd.)

	Statements of attainment	Example
	—make statments of conjecture using 'if ..... then ....'; define, reason, prove and disprove	In exploring decimals and fractions with a calculator or microcomputer make statements of the type. 'If the denominator has prime factors other than 2 or 5, then the decimal will recur'; offer justifications, explanations and proofs of such statements
ʒe 4)	—design, plan and carry through a mathematical task to a successful conclusion; present-alternative solutions and justify selected route	Investigate and design traffic light and l-way systems for a city centre, given the street plan and traffic flows; present an analysis of the effects of the systems and suggest a best solution
	—give definitions which are sufficient or minimal; use symbolization with confidence; construct a proof including proof by contradiction	Rearrange the equation $x^3 -5x +3 =0$ to obtain the iterative formula $x_{n+1}=\frac{(x_n^3+3)}{5}$ and test whether it converges or diverges for different initial values of x

Source : DES, 1990.

the practical usefulness of the concept of IQ. With regard to learning failure, for example, the present-day psychologist is more likely to focus on specific areas of difficulty with a view to diagnosis and remedial education than on an overall intelligence test score. Secondly, the cultural bias in standardized tests and and in test situations seems to be a major obstacle which stands in the way of accurate assessments of a child's level of performance. Rigidity in the scoring and administration of tests can too easily result in the under-rating of the child's ability. Thirdly, the narrow range of abilities measured by traditional intelligence tests often fails to do justice to the complex nature of a child's cognitive development, and there is the danger of concluding that an aptitude that cannot be quantified in some way is not worth considering. Although careful use of intelligence tests may still have some part to play in assessment, it should be part of a wider assessment of the individual's specific achievements, needs and strengths, home environments, relationship with peers and teachers, motivation, interests, imagination, sensitivity to others and intellectual independence.

One recently-adopted procedure is *profiling* or *records of achievement* in which teachers and pupils collaborate to produce a profile of individual achievements, interests and social skills. In prevocational courses, *e.g.* in Youth Training Schemes (YTS), the Certificate of Pre-Vocational Education (CPVE) and the Technical and Vocational Education Initiative (TVEI), which cover a broad range of work experience, profiling is felt to be the only means of assessing perfarmance. Murphy and Torrance (1988) give a useful evaluation of profiling as an alternative to traditional tests of achievement, but note the difficulties which face teachers as they attempt to develop a policy for profiling in schools and colleges. They recommend certain conditions as being essential for promoting the change which the DES recommends :

— a review of school aims and curricular intentions;
— a review of existing assessment, recording and reporting practices;
— the establishment of a school assessment policy;
— appropriate training for testers;
— more flexible teaching methods, such as small group work;

— more flexible timetabling to facilitate the integration of teaching, observation, assessment and discussion.

(Murphy and Torrance, 1988)

A key feature is the process of negotiation and regular dialogue between pupil and teacher. Clearly this can be difficult to achieve when teachers are working with large numbers of pupils, and there is a real danger of bias in such assessments even when there is a framework, such as checklists, systematic observation and personal self-assessment information. This flexible method of gathering information about individuals must also be judged on its capacity to deal with issues concerning the competence of assessors and bias in the measures.

Concepts of Intelligence and Ability

Our review of methods of assessment leads back to a basic question—what do tests, be they of intelligence or attainment, measure? Binet, it will be remembered, had devised his intelligence tests in order to identify those childen who would be unsuccessful in school, and investigations have shown that intelligence tests correlate fairly well with academic attainments. But a difficulty which has persisted throughout the history of intelligence testing has been a lack of agreement as to the definition of intelligence itself. A famous symposium in 1921 produced 13 different definitions by psychologists and the concept remains controversial to this day.

The Psychometric Approach

Spearman (1927) proposed that there was a common factor—which he called 'g' —of general intelligence, to be found in a wide variety of mental skills. He distinguished 'g' from those abilities specific to a particular skill. Thus a person's score on an arithmetic test would result from general mental as well as a specific numerical ability. The more intellectually demanding the task, the more it involved the grasping and application of relationships, and the more it depended on the 'g' factor.

By contrast, Thurstone (1938) claimed to have identified eight primary factors of intelligence. These were : verbal;

numerical; spatial; rote memory; perceptual speed; world fluency; inductive reasoning and deductive reasoning. His eight factors have been criticized for their narrowness and for the fact that they are to some extent determined by the particular tests which he chose. He later conceded that a 'second-order factor', a form of 'g', ran through the eight primary abilities.

More recently, many psychologists have become dissatisfied with the psychometric model on the grounds that it focuses too much on individual abilities without taking enough account of the testing situation or, at a wider level, the social and educational context within which the assessment takes place. In the following sections we look at attempts by psychologist to break free from the straitjacket of the psychometric tradition of intelligence testing by acknowledging a wider range of cognitive abilities in the individual and by taking into the social context as an integral part of the child's development as a thinker.

Cognitive Style

Some psychologists have chosen to look at the 'cognitive style' of the individual, *i.e.*, the characteristic way in which he or she approaches the world. Cognitive style is often viewed along one dimensions, such as convergence/divergence, or field-dependence/field-independence (*see* below). Guilford (1967) distinguished *convergent* and *divergent* thinking. The converger, he suggested, is good at dealing with problems that require one correct answer and will tend not to go beyond the information given; the converger, therefore, can cope well with the kinds of tasks that are commonly presented in intelligence tests. *Divergers*, by contrast, are in their element with the open-ended situations that call for a variety of responses involving fluency, flexibility, originality and elaboration of ideas. Since these two approaches to tasks seem to represent two distinct cognitive styles, educators have been interested in implications of research in this area. For example, Hudson (1966) showed that convergent and divergent tests were able to discriminate between science and arts specialists.

A whole battery of tests of divergent thinking were devised (Torrance 1972); one example is 'uses of objects' ; a child is asked to thinks of as many alternative uses of common objects as possible (*e.g.* uses of a brick, a paper clip, a cardboard box). Responses

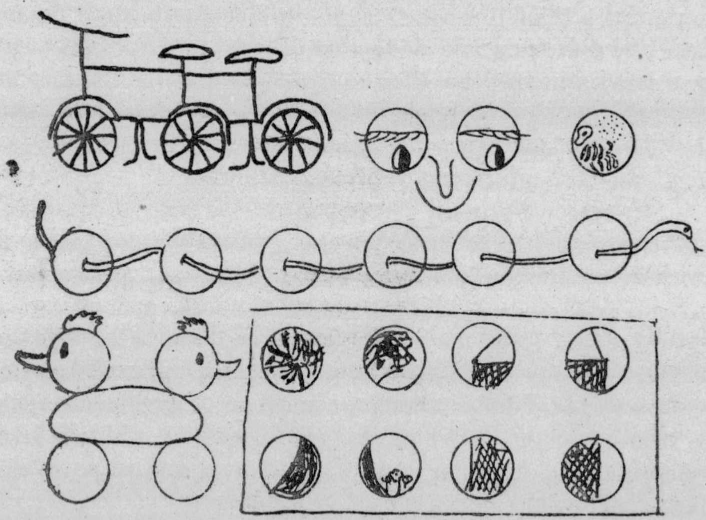

Fig. 7.2: Circles test : chrldren are given a page of circles and asked . to add to them in any way they like, Responses are scored for fluency, flexibility and originality. Some children treat each circle separately others combine the circles into larger pictures

are scored for fluency and originality. Another example is the 'circles' test, shown in figure 7.2. The tests have, however, been criticized for subjectivity in their scoring and lack of agreement concerning what actually is an original response. The very nature of divergent thinking abilities makes them unsuited to formal timed test situations (Wallach and Kogan, 1965).

There have been other attempts to characterize important ways in which individuals differ in cognitive style. Witkin *et al.* (1962), for example, differentiated between *field-independence* and *field-dependence* in an individual's responses to perceptual patterns. Witkin's Embedded Figure Test, which is designed to differentiate the two types of person, requires a child to outline simpler figures in more complex design.

Some people concentrate on the whole picture and are uninfluenced by the 'field' or surrounding context. These field-independent persons are better at logical, rational tasks and are less likely to be influenced by their social surroundings. Filed-dependent persons, by contrast, focus on details of a figure, are less analytical, and more affected by external factors and social influences.

Witkin argues that these characteristic responses to a perceptual field are also reflected in an individual's approach to cognitive tasks. Field-independent people are better at tasks that require a logical solution, at mathematics and science and at spatial tasks; they are also more independent in the social sense and less likely to be swayed in their judgement by other people than are field-dependent subjects. Witkin found high correlations (0.66) between field-independence are certain subtests of the WISC (block design, picture completion and object assembly). He has argued that the Embedded Figures Test can identify spatial abilities which verbal tests overlook. Boys are on average more field-independent than girls. Parallels can also be drawn with work on *brain lateralization theory*, which suggests that each hemisphere of the brain has primary responsibility for certain mental abilities—the left for logical, verbal activities, the right for intuitive, emotional and spatial abilities. The observed differences in cognitive style between males and females may be in part due to differences in hemispheric dominance. Girl talk earlier than boys and tend to score better on language tests (left-hemisphere lateralization); boys tend to perform better than girls on visual-spatial tasks (right-hemisphere lateralization).

The investigation of cognitive style is an exciting field of inquiry which could have considerable implications for education. So far, the difficulty seems to lie in identifying which styles are important and in producing adequate assessment procedures.

Gardner's Multiple Intelligences

In what may be considered a variant of the cognitive style approach, Gardner (1983) has proposed a theory of 'multiple intelligences' in a book called *Frames of Mind*. He suggests that there are six distinct kinds of intelligence—linguistic, logical-mathematical, spatial, musical, body-kinesthetic and personal. The first three are already familiar from the psychometric tradition, but the last three constitute more of a radical departure.

Musical intelligence refers to the abilities to comprehend and play or compose music. Bodily-kinesthetic intelligence refers to bodily control and grace of movement as shown, for example, in athletics, dance or skating. Personal intelligence refer to the abilities to understand one's own behaviour and that of others; this is clearly related to social and interpersonal skills and to role-taking ability.

Gardner used a number of criteria to select these particular intelligences. These were :

1. Selective impairment of particular kinds of intelligence by brain damage.
2. The existence of individuals with exceptional talent in particular kinds of intelligence.
3. A distinctive developmental history for each kind of intelligence.
4. An evolutionary history demonstrating the adaptive value of each kind of intelligence.
5. A set of core operations or procedures which characterize each kind of intelligence.
6. Experimental evidence that different kinds of intelligence are relatively independent (this is the traditional psychometric method).
7. The connection of each kind of intelligence to some kind of symbolic system (such as words, pictures, musical notation).

Each distinctive intelligence should satisfy most, if not all, of these criteria. Essentially Gardner is criticizing the use of conventional intelligence tests beyond their original purposes which were, as we have seen, to predict academic skills, and which led to an emphasis on verbal and reasoning skills. Gardner focuses instead on the diversity of abilities which human beings can have.

Intelligence in a Social-cultural Context

The psychometric approach focuses largely on the internal cognitive processes of individuals but tells us little about the social context within which intelligent behaviour occurs. Wechsler (1975), in fact recognized this aspect of intelligent functioning when he wrote that the assessment of intelligence is inevitably a value judgement. However, despite Wechsler's apparent admission that intelligent behaviour must be meaningful within a particular social setting , this is scarcely reflected in the design of traditional intelligence tests, such as the WISC-R and the Stanford-Binet. These have only been designed and validated in the context of Western educational systems.

In recent years there has been a growing interest in a broader *contextualist* approach to intelligence. Contextualists take the view that intelligence must be defined within a particular cultural context and that comparisons across cultures can only be made with caution. Berry (1984) argues that it is important to define intelligence in terms of 'cognitive competence' which is needed in a particular culture, and that psychologists should take local or folk conceptions of intelligence into account when they construct tests (Figure 7.3). For example, the ability to shoot with

Fig. 7.3: Intelligence needs to be seen in its cultural context (from Current Contents, 1981)

a bow and arrow is irrelevant for most people in our society, but skill in the construction and use of the bow and arrow may well be of prime importance among hunter-gatherers. Tests that have been validated in the technologically advanced society would not assess this skill, yet it could not be concluded that the hunter-gatherers were less intelligent.

Sternberg (1984a), as strong defender of the contextualist approach, defines intelligence as 'consisting of purposive selection and shaping of and adaptation to real-world environments relevant to one's life'. From this perspective we can only understand intelligence within the framework of real life situations. He argues that it is far more useful to see intelligence as being embedded in a particular context than as a static quality possessed by an individual; but he does not, however suggest that *everything* is relative and that no comparison is possible across cultures or among groups within the society. More important is the relative emphasis that different cultures place upon certain skills at different historical times. For example, skills needed for reading are present in individuals from pre-literate societies but are not, developed and are thus not important until literacy becomes widespread. Within modern Western society, in the past decades or so, children are gaining familiarity with electronic toys and home computers; these depend more on visual, auditory and manual aspects of intelligence —skills that are not so readily measured by traditional intelligence tests. The contextualist view presents a malleable concept of intelligence which can accommodate to such changes over space and time.

Is it possible then, to measure intelligence from the contextualist stance? Sternberg suggests that one obvious way of finding out what constitutes intelligence within a particular context is to ask members of the culture. For example, his research in the USA has revealed some overlap between lay-persons' concepts of intelligence and psychologists' views, but the lay-person is more likely to mention *social* competence as an important factor in intelligent functioning. Sternberg identified three broad constellations of behaviour which his American interviewees perceived as being intelligent :

1. *Practical problem-solving ability* : 'Keeps an open mind'; 'responds thoughtfully to others' ideas'.

2. *Verbal ability* : 'speaks clearly and articulately', 'is knowledgeable about a field'.
3. *Social competence* : 'admits mistakes'; 'displays interest in the world at large'; 'thinks before speaking and doing'.

Clearly the constructs of intelligence would vary across cultures, but Sternberg argues that the method could be used to discover what *is* intelligent in different social contexts. There is thus a tension between what Berry (1984) calls 'locally sensitive' or culturally relative concepts of intelligence and the wider aim of arriving at a 'pan-cultural' or universal understanding of cognitive processes. Psychologists are not yet ready to agree that the evidence supports only one position. As Berry writes of the assessment of intelligence within and across cultures :

> If ...... consistent and invariant factors emerge, then a position of general intelligence may be supportable (but it is likely to be a general intelligence construct which differs from our present culture-bound construct). If, however, factors emerge which appear to be culturally relative (that is, patterns exist, but vary according to cultural context), then the cognitive style approach may be supportable (but, again, the styles may be quite different from those identified at the present time). And if no factors emerge, if cognitive abilities are unrelated to each other, then the specific abilities approach will be supported (1984).

Sternberg's Triarchic Theory of Human Intelligence

Sternberg (1984b) has proposed a 'triarchic' theory of intelligence which embodies the contextualist approach together with an attempt to suggest two universal aspects of human intelligence which can be considered across cultures. These universal aspects cannot be specific *tasks,* since tasks are relative to each culture. Rather, Sternberg considers the *processes* by which tasks are coped with, in line with his definition of intelligence already given.

One of these universal aspects is considered to be a 'two-facet subtheory' approach to task demands, which contrasts the novelty or familiarity of the task. At one extreme a task can measure the ability to automatize information processing. Reading skills might provide an example. For the infant school child reading tasks are largely assessing the ability to deal with novel demands; many words, and even the process of reading itself, are fairly new. For most adults, reading has become a rapid automatized process. Differences in reading skill are then a matter of ability to automatize information processing.

The 'two-facet' theory is compatible with the contextualist approach. It makes it clear that what is apparently the same task can put quite different demands on an individual from different contexts or with different prior experiences. Obviously, a verbal test item imposes different demands, depending on the degree of literacy of the person, and the community he or she is from.

The other universal aspect of Sternberg's triarchic theory is what he calls 'componential analysis'. This involves analysing the actual cognitive processes involved in coping with any task. He considers three main kinds of component : *Knowledge acquisition*—processes involved in gaining knowledge necessary to deal with a task; *performance components*—encoding symbols and making comparisons, for example; *metacomponents*—executive functions which plan the overall approach to the task, monitor success or failure, and respond to external feedback.

Consider the task of doing a crossword for example. Knowledge acquisition components might include knowing how to use dictionaries or a thesaurus to help solve certain clues. Performance components might include interpreting the clue, and making comparisons of possible solutions with the clue. Metacomponents might include overall strategic decisions such as which clue to tackle first, when to consult a dictionary, or realizing that one word already filled in might be wrong as it does not fit with another one. Again, this kind of analysis of task components could be compatible with the contextualist view.

Sternberg's theory is a relatively new one and has attracted much attention. It is too soon to judge how successful it will be, but this approach and other recent developments (such as the general contextualist approach, and Gardner's theory of multiple intelligences) do seem to herald a major shift in the way psychologists will use the term 'intelligence' in the future.

Further Reading

A readable view of different approaches to the study of intelligence, including Piagetian theory and information processing approaches as well as the psychometric approach, is R. Kail and J. W. Pellegrino 1985 : *Human intelligence : Perspective and Prospects.* New York : Freeman. An authoritative sourcebook is A. Anastasi 1982 : *Psychological Testing,* 5th ed. New York : Macmillan. Some recent developments are described in H. Gardner 1983 : *Frames of Mind.* New York, Basic Books, and R. J. Sternberg, 1985 : *Beyond IQ : A Triarchic Theory of Human Intelligence.* Cambridge University Press.

A critical review of the social uses of IQ testing is presented in B. Evans and B. Waites 1981 : *IQ and Mental Testing : an Unnatural Science and its History.* London, Macmillan. If you want to find out more about the changes which are taking place in the philosophy and practice of educational assessment in Britain, read R. Murphy and H. Torrance 1988 : *The Changing Face of Educational Assessment.* Milton Keynes : Open University Press. A comprehensive guide to the theory and practice of integration is the book by S. Hegarty and K. Pocklington 1981 : *Educating Pupils with Special Needs in the Primary School.* Windsor : NFER. See also Alan Goddard 1988 : 'Processes in special education', in G. Blenkin and A.V. Kelly (eds), *The Primary Curriculum in Action,* London : Paul Chapman.

For an overview of research on gifted children, see J. Freeman (ed.) 1985 : *The Psychology of Gifted Children.* Chichester : Wiley.

Discussion Points

1. What different abilities or process underlie intelligent action?
2. Does intelligence mean the same thing in different societies?
3. How valuable are selective procedures in the educational system?
4. How do the psychometric methods of assessing-intellectual development compare with those of Piaget?
5. In what ways can the needs of exceptional children be met within the ordinary school system?

Practical Exercises

1. Ask people from a variety of backgrounds to say what they mean by 'intelligence', or to describe someone they think of as highly intelligent. Sort their answers into categories. Compare with the categories used by Sternberg. Which factors, *e.g.* age, cultural background, level of educational attainment, might contribute towards your interviewee's concept of intelligence?
2. Collaborate with three or four other students to design a test of general information. Each of you contribute five questions that measure knowledge of a particular field (such as music, politics, sport, the peace movement) with which *you* are familiar. Administer the test to other students or to people from different backgrounds and note their reactions. Score the tests and look at the distribution of total scores. How would you assess *(a)* the reliability of your test and *(b)* its validity as a test of general information?
3. Design a way in which children's story writing abilities could be assessed. You will need to considered (*a*) under what conditions the stories should be written; (*b*) instructions about form and content, if any; (*c*) what criteria you would use in judging the standard of the stories, and whether qualitative or quantitative methods would be used in assessment. You could try out your method with a small sample of stories obtained from children in say the 8-11 age range at a local school.

Box 7.1

Giftedness in a Social Context

The definition of giftedness varies across cultures and throughout history and thus cannot be viewed apart from its social context. Thus argued Joan Freeman in the introduction to the Gulbenkian

---

Based on material in J. Freeman 1980 : in R. Povey (ed). *Educating the Gifted Child,* London : Harper and Row.

Research Project on gifted children which she directed. Her aim was to discover whether the experience of being labelled as 'gifted' had any behavioural effects on children. She was also interested in the part played by parents and teachers in the emotional development of high-ability children. Specifically, she was concerned to test a prevailing view that gifted children may be emotionally disturbed at home or at school because their intellectual maturity makes them out of tune with the others in the environment. Accordingly, she asked three research questions:

1. Are children identified by parents as 'gifted' different from other children not so identified?
2. Are the home backgrounds of these children identified as gifted by their parents different from those not so identified?
3. Do gifted children suffer from emotional problems when receiving non-specialist education?

Freeman's sample consisted of three groups with 70 children in each, ranging in age from 5 to 16 years. The Target Group (T) was a sample of children selected from the records of the National Association for Gifted Children (NAGC), *i.e.* children whose parents had identified them as begin of exceptionally high ability. Control Group 1 (C1) was a sample of children who were matched with the above children for ability (as measured by the Raven's Progressive Matrices), age, sex and school. The essential difference was that these children were not in the NAGC. Control Group 2 (C2) was a sample of children of normal ability matched with C1 for age, sex and school class so that they differed only in ability. In this way, each target child was matched with two control children in different ways—one for high ability but not in the NAGC (C1) and one of normal ability (C2).

The children were given a battery of tests covering intelligence (Stanford-Binet), and social adjustment (Bristol Social Adjustment Guides); interviews were carried out with parents (at home) and teachers (at school) about the children's behaviour, their own attitudes to education and views on how educational aims are achieved; in addition, the home background of the children was assessed.

With regard to intelligence, there were significant differences between the target group and control groups C1 and C2. The T and C1 children had been accurately matched for intelligence on the Raven's Matrices Test but when Stanford-Binet scores were compared, they were found to be significantly different (*see* box Table 7.1.1). Freeman explained these differences as follows. The Raven's Matrices Test is non-verbal and so more 'culture-free' than a verbal test; furthermore, it does not discriminate finely amongst children at upper levels of ability. The Stanford-Binet test, by contrast, does give a more precise assessment at higher levels of intelligence and measures many learned abilities which would put children from privileged, educationally stimulating homes at an advantage. Thus the differences shown in box Table 7.1.1 may indicate that the target group had been identified and recognized by their parents as being of exceptional ability.

Box Table 7.1.1

Raven's Matrices Scores and Stanford-Binet IQs of Target (T) and Control (C) Children

	IQ	*T*	*C1*	*C2*
Raven's	mean	34.5	34.6	28.8
matrices	s.d.	12.9	11.5	11.6
Stanford-	mean	147.1	134.3	119.2
Binet	s.d.	17.4	17.1	16.1

Interviews with the parents suggested behaviour differences between the T group and groups C1 and C2. The target children were rated as more 'difficult', 'sensitive', 'emotional' and as having 'few friends'. Parents described them as 'very emotional' five times as often as controls and as 'feeling different' 17 times as often as controls. Similarly, teachers' ratings on individual items on the Bristol Social Adjustment Guides indicated that the target children had more problems in making friends and were more likely to be either withdrawn or aggressive in the classroom (*see* box Table 7.1.2).

Box Table 7.1.2

Percentage of Children in Each Group Getting High Scores from Teachers' Ratings on Items from the Bristol Social Adjustment Guide

	T	*C1*	*C2*	*Significance level*
Peer maladaptiveness (problems in making friends)	29	14	9	$p < 0.01$
Withdrawal (being socially withdrawn)	23	10	10	$p < 0.01$
Hostility (aggressive and over-reaching)	39	17	13	$p < 0.01$

From home interviews, Freeman observed that the target children were more likely to have unusual backgrounds, *e.g.* were adopted, came from families where the parents were divorced or separated, or from single-parent families. (One-parent families, for example, were found seven times as often in T as in C groups.) Their mothers were more frequently well-educated but were also discontented about their own achievements. This was surprising since many of these mothers had successful professional or managerial careers (53 per cent as opposed to 33 per cent in C1 and C2). The homes of the target children were very stimulating, parents encouraged their children's education and attainment. However, this involvement at times took the form of an 'intense pursuit of culture' which in the view of Freeman put some pressure on the children.

What might cause the adjustment problems of the target group of children? In order to find out whether the emotional difficulties were due to intelligence or to other factors. Freeman compared the highest IQ children from the *whole* sample (*i.e.* children with IQs of 141+ from both target and control groups) with the rest. The features which had distinguished the target groups from the controls were rarely those which distinguished high IQ children from the rest. In fact, Freeman found no evidence to suggest that problems arose simply from being highly intelligent but rather from the way in which giftedness was handled. For example, signs of unhappiness, such as finding it difficult to make friends, did not feature in the list of behaviours that could be identified with high IQ. Although T group parents frequently reported that their children were difficult because they were gifted. Freeman's results did not support such a viewpoint.

Freeman suggested that the T group parents had joined the NAGC not only because their children were gifted but because they were difficult. The problems, she suggested stemmed from parental expectations and handling of these bright children. The parents of the target children were more likely to be dissatisfied with school, but this Freeman saw as being related to the parents' ambitions for their children rather than the children's giftedness by itself. Her overall conclusion was that she could see no good reason for segregating gifted children from normal children. Those gifted children who did have problems were also found to have a number of disturbing environmental factors, such as intense parental pressure, which seemed to be more responsible for the difficulties than giftedness by itself.

This is a challenging study which is unfortunately weakened by the IQ differences between T and C1 children. Freeman's view that the act of labelling a bright child as 'gifted' can have negative effects on the child's behaviour remains controversial.

Box 7.2

The Assessment of Pupils' Writing

This report by the Assessment of Performance Unit (APU) was the second in a series aiming to present a national picture of the language performance of 11-year-old pupils in England. Wales and Northern Ireland. Here we consider one part of the survey concerned specifically with writing ability.

The research team was concerned to devise methods of assessment which would reflect the complex nature o' the writing process. Thus their aim was to assess not only basic skills, such as spelling and punctuation, but also higher-order skills such as the ability to organize thought, the expression of feeling and sensitivity to the needs of the reader.

In May 1980, 9850 pupils in 691 schools participated in the

[Based on material in Assessment or Performance Unit 1982: Primary Survey Report no. 2, London; HMSO.]

survey; of these around 3,400 completed tests of writing. A series of ten writing booklets were designed containing four writing tasks to be completed by each pupil :

1. An accurate description of something the pupil had observed. All pupils completed this task.
2. A longer writing task, *e.g.* an autobiographical anecdote, a letter to a public figure, a personal response to a poem, an explanation of a personal preference. The purpose of this writing was to assess a range of writing skills including narrating, expressing feeling, explaining a point of view, making a request. There were ten of these tasks, distributed among the schools participating in the survey, of which each pupil did one.
3. A text-based exercise such as editing a piece of writing or making notes.
4. Several short questions about pupils ' attitudes towards writing in general, their feelings about the tasks in the APU booklet and their preference for writing at home or at school.

The APU team were aware that if the writing tasks were seen as tests the pupils might produce unnatural, stilted writing. To avoid this, the team encouraged teachers to introduce the writing tasks as they would in normal lessons and to allow time for discussion before the children began to write. In this way, they hoped to move away from the model of the pupil writing for the teacher-as-examiner towards the model of the pupil writing in an authentic way for a sensitive and interested reader. However, the writing was still done under test conditions where it could not be assumed that the children would be in the right frame of mind to produce their best writing, and the team admit that the actual contexts in which the children wrote did not provide genuine audiences.

Two forms of assessment were used, *impression marking* and *analytic marking*. Impression marking involved rapid reading of a script and the allocation of a single mark awarded on a seven-point scale; a score of one indicated that the marker considered the pupil to be a very poor writer for an 11-year-old and a mark of seven corresponded to the marker's judgement that the pupil was a very able writer for this age-group. Each script was double-marked by two members of the team to check on the reliability of this method. Analytic marking was carried out on a random subsample of 10 per cent of the scripts selected from across the whole range of booklets. This involved assessing the pupil writers on a five-point scale with reference to the following set of criteria: relevance of content and coherence of organization in the essay; appropriateness and style, *e.g.* extent to which vocabulary and form of words were appropriate to the topic; knowledge of grammatical conventions, *e.g.* punctuation, sentence structure; and knowledge of orthographic conventions, *i.e.* handwriting and spelling.

Box Figure 7.2.1 shows the distribution of marks based on impression marking. In the examiners' opinion, 3.8 per cent of pupils produced work which was extremely poor ; 1.8 per cent of pupils produced written work of outstanding quality. Impression marking scores were correlated with each of the analytic criteria and the highest inter-correlation was found between impression marking and the first analytic category of *content and organization* (r = 0.70). This result, argue the APU team, indicates that markers of essays written by children are responding to general qualities in the writing rather than specific aspects. The result also indicated that some individual markers 'were inclined to award higher or lower marks than the majority'.

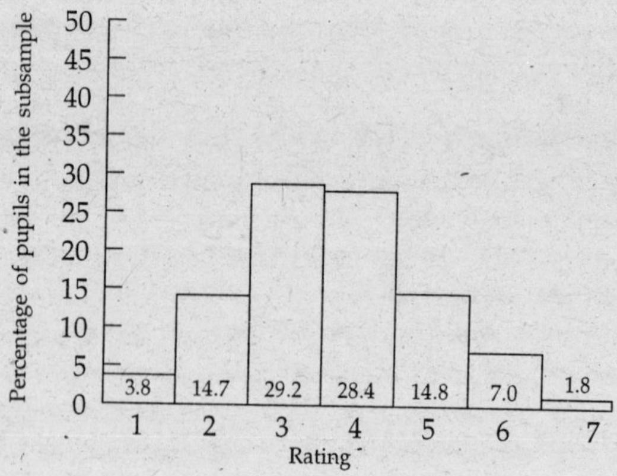

Box Fig. 7.2.1: Distribution of ratings in the APU report : general impression marking

With regard to analytic marking, the results are summarized as follows :

> 96 per cent of pupils obtained sufficient control of writing to be understood at first reading.
> 95 per cent had some knowledge of how sentences are separated or related.
> 15 per cent had numerous errors—*i.e.* one spelling mistake in each line and one grammatical mistakes in each three lines.
> 15 per cent were well in command of spelling and grammar conventions

Pupils answers to questions on their attitudes towards writing indicated the following factors :

> For many 11-year-olds the most enjoyable writing experience is the creation of an exciting story.
> Eleven-year-olds do not enjoy writing 'exercises' (*e.g.* exercises to improve punctuation) or copying from books.
> Girls are more likely than boys to become involved in writing long pieces or in writing for their own enjoyment at home.
> Many 11-year-olds' perceptions of writing relates only to one or two uses of the written language, and there is scope for much greater development, *e.g.* writing for different types of audience.

The APU team expressed the intention of assessing complex cognitive and affective processes involved in writing. However, the general experience of reading the report of the APU is a disappointing one. Many of the results seem rather obvious, including the approximately normal distribution obtained in box Figure 7.2.1. Also, little of the children's writing experience comes through. For example, when the team looks at the children's use of dialogue in stories they do not consider the ways in which children use dialogue to express feelings or to show their awareness of psychological states in their characters. Instead, the team limits itself to an analysis of punctuation. This is one example among many of the failures of the team to interpret anything that could not be quantified. In a critique of the study, Rosen (1982) wrote that 'though we may see the team locked in an heroic struggle with the tiger of assessment, we must also see that they should not have ventured on the jungle safari in the first place...... There is an alternative; it is the active participation of teachers in assessment, teachers who are close to the children being assessed. It is such critiques of purely quantitative measures from large-scale surveys which have encouraged the development of teacher-based assessment.

8

Individual Differences and Intelligence

INTRODUCTION

For the teacher who is preparing for tomorrow's class it would be comforting to know that every cherubic first-grader is as able as every other cherubic first-grader. But most teachers, if they think about it at all, do not believe that students are very much alike. The teacher, however, frequently must behave in the classroom as if they were. And forgetting individual differences may arouse less anxiety than continual thought about ways of adjusting the instruction to meet the needs of each student. Whether or not we do anything about them, any one hour in the classroom shows us that wide differences do exist. We are forcibly reminded of the distinctive qualities of physical appearance. Differences in ability (even if we cannot quite define "ability") are sometimes just as striking. For example, we may admire Johnny's adroitness in grasping new ideas, the fluency of Mary's paraphrasing, and the keenness of Elmer's inductive thinking. Nor can we avoid observing, sometimes with furrowed brow, Tony's halting perusal of a simple sentence, Stella's difficulty in understanding basic addition, and Jerry's slow progress after tackling new materials.

Individual differences in ability do exist. Symonds has demonstrated this by using Table 8.1.

Table 8.1

Mental Age	*Number of Children Age 6*	*Number of Children Age 9*
13		1
12		4
11		11
10		21
9	1	25
8	7	21
7	24	11
6	36	4
5	24	1
4	7	
3	1	
	100	99

We shall assume that the 100 six-year-olds are in the first grade. What do these data show? If mental age is a figure that shows how intelligent these children are (at least as measured by an intelligence test), we see that about one third (36 per cent) are as intelligent as we would expect; they have a mental age of six. However—much to the surprise of many parents—64 per cent of the six-year-olds are either above or below the average mental age for their own group. Assuming that the work required only the mental ability of the average six-year-old, about one third (1% + 7% + 24%) might find the first grade too easy (we do not know that they do). Similarly, about one third might find it too difficult. The situation is about the same for the nine-year-olds, except that there is a greater spread of mental age here. One nine-year-old is an average thirteen-year-old, while another is only as intelligent as the average five-year-old—an eight year range in mental age for the group. The range for the six-year-olds is six years. About 8 per cent of the six-year-olds could be doing third or fourth-grade work, while 37 per cent of the fourth-graders are finding fourth-grade work difficult to do.

To summarize, these figures illustrate the following :

(1) there can be a wide range of ability in any one grade or class;
(2) the academic demands made in one grade may be suitable for only one third of the students;
(3) that there is a sizable overlap in the ability of children of different ages and grades, especially the least able of the older with the most able of the younger; and
(4) the range of individual differences becomes greater as we move up the grades.

Recently, both the general American public and the individual educator have been concerned especially with the third of the students who find the work at their grade level too easy. This is phrased as the problem of educating the "gifted." In the first article which follows, Vernon discusses this problem and points out the difficulties in identifying them, predicting their future academic success, and finding ways within present-day school practices and democratic ideology to promote their learning. Graphic evidence of these difficulties is furnished by Frankel in his study of high-ability students in the Bronx High School of Science.

Differences in ability is only one aspect of the problem, although probably the most important one. There are differences in physique, previous learning, family background, personality traits, sex, social class, race, and even culture. A school located in almost any large American city may have to carry on its educational activities while coping with this entire array of differences. The readings which follow deal with social-class and personality differences as they relate to ability and intellectual pursuits.

What can the schools and teachers do about the wide range and array of differences? This is the question which Vernon carefully considers for both American and English schools. As a general social and educational problem the question was raised by Burt in his discussion on the meaning and measurement of intelligence and its possible genetic determination. The social and cultural context within which education must find solutions to problems caused by variations in student ability was discussed by Vernon. Vernon has more to say about this. Skinner states that teaching machines can have the effect of reducing individual differences and sensitively adjusting instruction for individual students. Differences in the effects of frustration were also referred to in a study by Waterhouse and Child. Taken together, the readings should point out the many aspects of the problem as it confronts the schools and at the same time indicate some broad criteria any solution must satisfy.

RELATIONSHIP OF READINGS

The key article in this chapter is the one by Vernon. The author combines a sound knowledge of the psychology of individual differences with a knowledge of the many practical problems faced in the schools. It is an excellent illustration of the translation of theory into practice. The report by Frankel, an attempt to discover what besides high ability makes for success in school, furnishes evidence to support Vernon's conclusions. The article by Schatzman and Strauss shows that linguistic differences, important in school achievement, are related to social-class differences.

EDUCATION AND THE PSYCHOLOGY OF INDIVIDUAL DIFFERENCES

This article, written by an eminent English educational psychologist, is another outstanding example of how psychological theory can be translated into educational practice. However, there may be some disappointment that the author is not more prescriptive about what should be done in the schools to solve this problem. On the basis of theory, Vernon recommends only a general framework within which workable solutions may be found. The student can compare Vernon's translation of theory into practice with the opinions expressed by Kendler. The student can see how the use of theory to shape practice is often complicated by such extra-psychological factors as, in the words of Vernon, social prejudice and traditions, financial shortages, increasing birthrates and other factors. This state of affairs often is an frustrating for the educational psychologist as for the teacher.

Vernon focuses his discussion on differences in ability. He uses Hebb's distinction between Intelligence A, or potential intelligence, and Intelligence B, or observable and test intelligence. This can be compared with the distinctions Burt has made, especially the one he attributes to Plato—the distinction between cybernetic and dynamic intelligence. Vernon believes that there is moderate constancy and that there may be over-all consolidation of the child's particular level of ability by the time he enters the first grade. Vernon's explanation of this is in terms of the stimulation present or lacking in the home environment. Vernon's suggestion that the educational environment keep "just sufficiently ahead of each pupil's capacity to stretch his mind to the utmost" also recalls the discussions of motivation, particularly Bugelski's comments on the role of anxiety in learning and the report by Waterhouse and Child on frustration. This view, however, seems opposed to that of Skinner, who would try to keep learning well within the capacity of the student.

In discussing the question of developing special courses of study as a way of adjusting the curriculum to individual differences in both ability and interest, Vernon raises the question of intelligence as being a bundle of group factors—a theory endorsed by Guilford. Vernon makes a distinction between group factors and "special factors" (as defined by Spearman) and shows how conventional classroom assignments and grouping can perhaps best adjust to such differences. It may be that the teaching machine and programmed learning may be most helpful in adjusting instruction to such special factors.

A central issue in this discussion is the question of discovering the academically able and predicting academic success. In connection with this the student should answer the following questions:

(1) Why may admitting only students with high IQ's to college be a mistake?
(2) Why must we often trust to luck in discovering the future genius?
(3) Why must our predictions of future ability and academic success be short-term and flexible?

One of the most urgent and most controversial questions in education today is what kind of organization will encourage the fullest development of the varied mental capacities and inclinations of students. There are certain fundamental psychological principles, and some advances in recent years in the field of mental testing, which may help to guide our views on educational policies. Although the present system of allocating students to suitable courses of study in England is about as different as it could be from the system in America, and although I possess little direct knowledge of the American educational system, it would seem worth while to pool our experiences and the results of the tremendous amount of research that has been done, in an attempt, perhaps, to see our way a little more clearly.

One of the chief advocates of educational acceleration and scholarships for the gifted has been Professor S. L. Pressey of Ohio State University. Let us take as our starting point three of the main arguments that he puts forward. First, the education of the most talented is unnecessarily lengthy, and, since adults tend to reach the peak of achievement in most fields in their thirties or earlier, we are wasting much of their productive life. Second, acceleration does not involve hurrying or strain, but represents rather the natural pace for the more able. Wherever it has been tried it has worked successfully, and there is no need for it to lead to any social or emotional maladjustment. Nevertheless objections of this kind are continually being put forward, when the real reasons for doing nothing are the economic and financial consequences, or pure inertia or prejudice. Third, a vast range of differences in abilities and interests exists among students who have had similar educational opportunities.

Now the problem is even wider than this. In general, pupils and students are so heterogeneous in their characteristics and potentialities that it might seem desirable to plan for each one an education uniquely suited to himself. However this is neither possible, nor desirable, for education implies not only individual development but also the training of different individuals to conform to society's patterns of intellectual and social norms. Thus there are positive advantages in educating diverse individuals in groups. Nevertheless, there must be some restriction of their heterogeneity, otherwise the educational process becomes inefficient and frustrating to the students as well as to the teacher. It would be absurd, for example, to try to train imbecile children and university students of atomic physics in the same group. To take a less extreme example: the tiny country school where one teacher copes with a very wide age and ability range performs many valuable functions: but there is no doubt, in England at least, that its educational efficiency tends to be below average.

Given, then, that there must be some reduction in heterogeneity, the psychologist would surely urge the following stipulations. Any grouping should be based on some characteristic which: first, is stable and enduring; second, can be accurately assessed; third, has a major influence on educational progress; and fourth, is acceptable to society. Difficulties arise because few characteristics, apart from age and physical handicap, meet these requirements. Age does largely, though of course far from completely, determine intellectual, emotional, and sensory-motor maturity; there are no difficulties of assessment, and it wins general acceptance. There is general agreement, also, that the deaf, the blind and partially sighted, and certain other physically handicapped groups should be segregated for special schooling under specially qualified teachers, though doubts arise in deciding what degree of defect requires such treatment. All other types of homogeneity seem to arouse intense controversy. Differentiation on the basis of sex, for example is rejected by most psychological opinion; yet it occurs in many European and a few American schools and colleges and is strongly supported by many parents and alumni. The explosive topic of race will not be considered, and religion will be omitted as having relatively little relation to educational capabilities. Socio-economic class deserves some consideration.

Social class is fairly stable and assessable. We know that it is so closely associated with cultural level and with attitudes toward education that it has a marked effect on educational progress. In England, for example, where children are graded according to their suitability for advanced secondary education at eleven to twelve years of age by means of objective tests of intelligence and achievement, about three times as large a proportion of children of the white-collar classes pass the tests as do children of manual workers. Furthermore, social class gives one of the best indications of future achievement and adjustment in school. Havighurst and his colleagues have shown that, despite the greater social mobility in America, the social class of an American student's parents largely determines the stage he reaches in the educational ladder, and the kinds of courses he selects in high school. Thus there is some justification for the practice, common in Europe and not unknown in the United States, of having separate secondary schools for the middle and upper classes, entry to which is mainly by parental income. This system, however, is repugnant to the temper of the age in all democratic countries. Unfortunately, class is so pervasive that almost any form of selection or grouping is likely to be affected by it. Thus, selection by ability has become a source of acute political dissension in England between the more conservative who wish to retain it and the socialist or working class who wish to abolish it and substitute something more like the American common, or comprehensive, school.

Yet another, apparently sensible, criterion for the grouping of pupils—namely, a common linguistic background, usually breaks down because it too is associated with racial or with social class differences. One important reason why upper class parents tend to segregate their children, though they would seldom openly admit it, is that they do not want them to talk like children in the industrial slums. The psychologist may deplore these sociological and political influence on education, but he cannot afford to neglect them.

Let us turn then to ability grouping. In the early 1920's, when group intelligence tests became widespread, it was all very simple. We were taught that the tests measured innate intelligence, unaffected by social background, and that this was the main determiner of educability. Thus if pupils could be put into groups which were homogeneous with respect to intelligence, each group could progress at its own rate and the teacher's burden would be very much lightened. Moreover, the IQ was supposed to give a reliable indication of a child's ultimate educational powers; whether he was bright enough, or too dull, ever to manage work of college level, or to tackle advanced topics like mathematics. To a large extent this advice given by psychologists was put into practice in England. Age grouping gave way to ability grouping, though it was soon realised that too wide an age range of bright youngsters and old dullards in a single class is socially unhealthy.

The usual practice, then, came to be the classification of children within an age grade in any large school into three or more streams or tracks on the basis of intelligence, previous achievement, or a combination of the two. Also, as mentioned earlier, the brighter children were segregated from the average and duller ones at eleven years for accelerated schooling.

Nowadays views on intelligence have been greatly modified. Indeed the term has been largely discarded by many American psychologists, as too liable to misinterpretation. Nevertheless, the distinction between intelligence and attainments still has limited value, despite their close overlapping. Intelligence can be defined as the more general thinking capacities: capacities for reasoning, for grasping relations, for comprehension, for new learning, and for concept development. That is, capacities which are not so much specifically taught as picked up by children in the course of their interaction with the home, school and wider environments. Whereas attainments refer rather to concepts and skills which depend more on direct instruction and on the child's interest and industriousness in the particular subjects studied. Such a distinction is one of degree rather than of kind, and it is entirely false to think of intelligence as causing, or making possible, attainments. It is at least as arguable that, through the acquisition of attainments at home and at school, the child is enabled to build up his intelligence.

Both depend to a considerable extent on innate potentialities or maturation—on what the Canadian psychologist Hebb calls Intelligence A—some characteristic of the central nervous system which enables certain children to develop mentally, to form percepts and concepts, habits and ideas, to build up complex intellectual skills more readily than other children. Intelligence A is the capacity to acquire Intelligence B—that is, the intelligence which we actually observe in everyday life or at school, and which our tests sample fairly effectively. Intelligence B, as Jean Piaget also shows in his post-war books, is built up gradually; it does not depend solely on the child's genes, but also on the stimulation of the child by the world in which he is reared and which gets him to exercise his potentialities. How far specific attainments involve different genes from those underlying general intelligence seems to me a moot point; one could certainly make a good case for it in the field of music and possibly other talents.

But, like most heredity-environment controversies, this seems an unprofitable argument, since we can never in fact observe or measure Intelligence A or other potentialities directly; they are purely hypothetical constructs.

We can no longer regard intelligence as setting a fixed rate of mental growth, or as having a definite termination. The early pioneers of mental testing seem to have regarded the IQ as a fairly constant characteristic of each individual because there was good agreement or correlation between two applications of the Stanford-Binet test a week or a month apart. But this tells us little about the fluctuations in ability to be expected during five or more years of schooling. On surveying the many investigations that have been made into this problem recently, a number of technical snags were found. Most of the published results were more or less distorted by such factors as abnormal standard deviation of the IQs, extreme similarity or dissimilarity of the tests employed, above average intelligence level of the tested group, frequency of retesting, etc. However, allowing for these it appeared safe to conclude that either over the six to ten or the eleven to eighteen year period, the correlation between two similar (though not identical) intelligence tests does not drop below a coefficient of 0.70. This implies that the typical individual would vary only 7 IQ points up or down. Although the majority do not fluctuate very widely, as many as 17 per cent might alter considerably, that is, anywhere from 15 points (or 1 standard deviation) up to about 40 points.

All-round educational attainments seem to be at least as stable. Certainly it is a mistake to think of the IQ as something fixed, and attainments as varying widely with the teaching received and other environmental causes. I would suggest that both show moderate constancy, partly because both are based on genetic potentiality—Hebb's Intelligence A—but also because their growth is essentially cumulative. By the time the child reaches school at five or six years, the interaction of potentiality and home stimulus have consolidated in him a certain level of ability which will closely determine his rate of progress for the next few years. Good or poor teaching, or other marked environmental irregularities and changes in personality adjustment, motivation, and interests, will result in considerable alterations only among a small minority. Again by eleven or twelve years the consolidated level gives fairly close predictions of the rate of progress over the next six years, as we have been able to show by our follow-up studies of the English secondary school examinations. The correlations of intelligence tests, of English and Arithmetic tests, and of teachers' estimates of ability with successful secondary school performance over two, and even up to five years average close to 0.80, when suitably corrected for homogeneity. By combining these three sources of information the coefficient can be raised to about 0.86. This, of course, refers to a whole age group . The figure may sound surprising to American educational psychologists, because they normally do their resting within pre-selected groups such as students seeking college admission. But if they likewise calculated the efficiency of their aptitude and achievement tests and school grades in separating, say, the top 20 per cent of high school students who are most suitable for college courses from the bottom 80 per cent, there is no doubt that they would reach at least a good predictions.

Yet even a correlation of, say, 0.85 allows of a considerable degree of error. Suppose we did send 100 unselected eighteen- to nineteen-year-olds to college and found which twenty were the most successful, in fact only fourteen of the twenty would have been correctly indicated by our tests and high school grades. In other words, using the best criteria available, about one-quarter to one-third of those we should select for college are likely to be unsuitable. They would have been equalled or surpassed by some 7½ per cent of those thought unsuitable, had the latter been given the opportunity. We can represent the situation as Table 8.2 shows.

Table 8.2

	Successful in College	*Unsuccessful in College*	*Total*
Selected on the basis of tests and previous grades	14	6	20
Rejected on the basis of tests and previous grades	6	74	80
Total	20	80	100

This is precisely the situation that obtains in English selection for advanced schooling in what we call grammar schools. A very high statistical level of accuracy is reached, and yet many pupils admitted to grammar school are unsuitable, and some who are rejected turn out to be so-called late developers who have to be transferred later on, or otherwise show outstanding ability. The psychologist, however, would naturally expect such fluctuations in abilities during adolescence and young adulthood; as students progress to more advanced courses, their interests and adjustment often change and they develop unsuspected capacities, or drop below their previous promise. Whatever kind of system of selection or acceleration was adopted in America, really accurate prediction would likewise be found impossible.

Frequently one hears the argument that far too large a proportion of our talented youth fails to get to college; there are many millions with high IQs who are being wasted. This argument is no more impressive than the statement: since college students are above average in height, we should ensure that all six-footers reach college. While IQ may be somewhat more relevant, its correlation with success in college for a representative sample would not exceed 0.75, and this means that 40 per cent of students picked merely by high IQ would turn out unsuitable. Even if we raised our standards and insisted, say, that all students with IQs of 125 and above, the best 5 per cent only, should be accelerated in high school, or sent to college, nearly one-quarter of our choices would let us down. At the opposite extreme, even if we went as low as an IQ of 90 and included the top three-quarters of the population, we would still find that 2 per cent of those excluded might have made the grade. In order to catch all or nearly all those capable of benefiting from a more advanced or accelerated educational course, we should need to go so far down in the scale of ability that many students would be brought in who would not benefit or who might have been more appropriately allocated to some quite different course, say of vocational training.

No definite conclusions or recommendations will be arrived at in this paper; but the main educational implication so far would seem to be that any predictions we make about students, or any selection, should be short-term and flexible. Such procedures should take into account not merely abilities but also interests and values—whether, for example, the student and his family are keen for him to take college preparatory courses or to go to college. While all assessments are likely to have a considerable margin of error, they will certainly be less inaccurate when based on the way the student is shaping and progressing in work of a similar nature to that which he will undertake. Clearly, too, caution should be exercised regarding any statements which imply that a considerable proportion of the population is always going to be intellectually incapable of absorbing the higher reaches of education. There is still a lot of truth in this, but the trouble is in determining *which* members of the population fall into this category. The limitation is at least as much a matter of defective intellectual interests and defective attitudes to education in the environment from which the weaker students come as it is to these students' innate intellectual inferiority.

Another deduction may be drawn from the work of Hebb, Piaget, and others on intellectual growth: such work suggests the desirability of the educational environment keeping just sufficiently ahead of each pupil's capacity to stretch his mind to the utmost. Hebb found that dogs or rats brought up in the restricted environment of a cage were less able, as adults, to perform new learning and problem solving tasks than those brought up in a richer and freer environment. Similarly with children, inadequate educational stimulation may mean not only that they learn less than they should, but that they also become less able to acquire further thinking skills. Experimental evidence can be provided on this point.

Recently, some 800 boys in a large English city who had been tested and allocated to fourteen very diverse secondary schools at age eleven were retested at fourteen. After allowing for initial level and regression effects, there were differences between the different school groups amounting to 12 IQ points. The pupils in the average selective or grammar school had gained 7 points (nearly half a standard deviation) over those in the non-selective schools. All this difference cannot be attributed to the effectiveness of schooling as such. Grammar school boys mostly came from better homes where they received more encouragement and help with their work, while the non-selective school boys lived in culturally and materially poorer homes, where there was often active opposition to education. Nevertheless, a rank correlation of 0.85 was found between the city administrator's assessment of the degree of stimulation likely to be provided by the fourteen schools, and the actual order of average gains among the pupils in these schools. Clearly, much more transfer had occurred than Thorndike found in his classic experiment on different high school courses.

This finding recalls Lorge's work on the intelligence level of thirty-four-year-old adults who had varying amounts of secondary and tertiary education after they were tested at fourteen years; and also a recent study by Husen of several thousand Swedish boys at nine and nineteen years. Husen found that those who had full education throughout the period gained the equivalent of some 12 IQ points over those who had left school at fourteen to fifteen and received no further education.

During World War II, under the auspices of the British Navy, the Raven Matrices scores (a non-verbal reasoning test) of 90,000 men recruited at various ages from seventeen to forty were compared and a general tendency to decline with age was noted. Clearly, however, those who had been in unskilled and labouring occupations, where they had made little use of their brains, declined earlier and more rapidly than those from skilled trades and clerical work, which had presumably done more to exercise them.

Now according to the older views, intelligence was said to grow steadily in childhood, then to slow down and reach a constant maximum at around fourteen to fifteen years of age. No one ever explained how, if this were so, high school and college students could continue to increase their scores on suitable tests in the late 'teens. But these results are quite reconcilable if we remember that, around the time of the World War I, probably the majority of average and duller individuals were leaving school by the age of fifteen; their intellectual capacities not only ceased to develop but began to stagnate, whereas the brighter, who either stayed on at school or entered more stimulating jobs, continued to improve. Thus the combination of a rising group and a declining group produced the apparently constant average level in the adolescent and young adult population.

The objection may be raised, as it was raised to Lorge's findings, that intelligence tests depend greatly on vocabularly and reading comprehension, capacities which are naturally much affected by length and quality of schooling. The objection rests, of course, on the old confusion between intelligence as a hypothetical innate potentiality (Intelligence A) and intelligence as directly manifested (Intelligence B). Actually, further work by Lovell, indicates that it is not mere verbal skills which are most affected by the stimulating or depressing qualities of adolescent environment, but rather the flexibility aspect of intelligence, or the capacity to form and apply new concepts. A more serious weakness is that we know so little, as yet, regarding the kinds of educational process that have greatest transfer value, or do most to stimulate the growth of ability.

Now the implications of such findings for educational organisation would seem clear. They definitely support some system like the English one of grouping pupils by ability, and pushing forward the brighter ones more rapidly in selective schools or classes. And they suggest that there is considerable substance in the complaint made by many American parents that the American system of public education seriously retards the bright child who is willing and able to tackle more difficult courses. On the other hand, there is the danger that average of duller students, if they are less pushed, will tend to fall more and more behind. Thus, it becomes even more difficult for those whose capacity happens to improve later to get back into the stream that would be appropriate. In other words, homogeneous grouping by ability tends to stereotype those who were less able initially and freeze them at a lower level.

This is a very real problem in English elementary schools, where pupils may be classified by teachers as early as seven years old into those thought likely to pass or fail the eleven year examinations. Such classification, being based mainly on early progress in reading and number-work, naturally gives a great advantage to children from middle-class families who are more likely to be helped and encouraged at home. Thus, a rather rigid system of selection may mean that the initially slow learners drop so far behind that they are, in effect, being condemned very early to an inferior schooling and a manual occupation for life. However, evidence indicates that such rigidity is the exception rather than the rule; perhaps owing to the influence of psychological teaching, most primary schools now do retain a fair degree of flexibility of transfer from one stream to another, and a sufficient degree of overlapping between the curricula of the several streams.

A similar danger arises at the bottom end of the ability range, where, in many educational systems, the very backward pupils may be classified as mentally defective and sent to special schools. It may be that their abilities too become stereotyped at this level, although they might have been capable of returning to ordinary school classes later. Miss Bernardine Schmidt's famous research at Chicago definitely supports this view, although her claims are by now pretty thoroughly discredited. In England, at least, most mental defectives receive a type of education far better suited to their lowly intellectual level and their weak emotional adjustment than they would get in ordinary schools. Yet they usually stay as backward as ever or even decline. No one who has observed such children vegetating hopelessly in an ordinary school, and then busy and interested at a special school could doubt the desirability of some type of homogeneous grouping. Nevertheless, I agree that here too irreversible segregation is to be avoided, and that injustices do occur.

One other consideration that I wish to raise in respect to ability grouping is that—as educationists well know—any scheme for grading of students has a "backwash" effect on education, by acting as an incentive to the teachers, the students and their parents. The eleven year selection examinations in England provide a terrible object-lesson; many, though by no means all, primary schools concentrate so exclusively on cramming their fifth and sixth grade pupils for objective tests that any other educational activity, however valuable it might be to children's general growth, tends to get crowded out. Much ill-feeling is engendered among snobbish parents; often they coach children themselves from published manuals of intelligence and other tests; or they communicate their anxieties to their off-spring and sometimes induce serious strain. Actually the effects on young children's mental health are apt to be greatly exaggerated by the sensational press. A careful survey of child guidance clinic cases has been made and no tendency for an increase in referrals was found around the time of the examination. In only one child in about 500 does the examination appear to contribute to maladjustment, and then only in children who were already prone to anxiety through earlier upbringing or constitutional weakness.

Probably other competitive examinations, such as those at the end of a secondary course, are associated with mental breakdown at least as frequently. Nevertheless, the existence of unnecessary stress even in a small minority, and distortion of the educational process among the majority, are the most serious defects of the English system, and have to be weighed very carefully against possible advantages in intellectual acceleration.

Now although sound psychological reasons for expecting intellectual benefits through grouping can be given, it is very difficult to prove. Furthermore, such limited experimental comparisons as have been carried out seem to have yielded negative results. It is doubtful whether such studies have been adequately designed to answer the important questions. International comparisons, again, yield no sure evidence. It is commonly stated that the products of English grammar schools, when they enter college, are two years ahead of American students of the same age. Even if this generalization were true it proves nothing, since only some 3 to 4 per cent ever reach the university in England. Also, it may well be that superiority in academic achievement is counterbalanced by poorer development in social and other more subtle qualities. It would seem, and some day it may be shown empirically, that the English system of grouping and selection does produce improvement in achievement at the top end, whereas the common school system is better for the average or dull, and also obviates many of the difficulties that arise through fluctuations in, or stereotyping of, mental growth. If this were so, it would be a matter for society rather than psychologists to decide which outcome it prefers.

No doubt it will be suggested that, instead of grouping by general intelligence and previous all-round achievement, we should consider type of ability and interests along special lines. This might be called the multi-dimensional as opposed to the uni-dimensional approach. British and American psychologists have always differed on this, just as have their educational systems. The British, following Spearman, have tended to stress the importance of general ability: children who are above average in one school subject are likely to be above average in all others. Only to a limited extent, as Burt demonstrated in 1917, do we get more specialised types of ability showing in the primary school—for example, some children being generally poorer at number work than at English subjects, or better at all practical and manual activities. In contrast, Thurstone in 1938, from his analysis of tests given to college students, claimed that abilities are largely independent—attributable to a series of separate factors; verbal, number, reasoning, spatial, etc. When he extended his testing downwards to eighth grade and younger children, who were less highly selected, he in fact found much overlapping among these factors. So that, while his statistical approach was quite different, his results confirmed Burt's in showing that something like 50 per cent of the variance in children's abilities, at least in abilities that are relevant to educational progress, could be accounted for by a general factor. This means then that it is extraordinarily difficult to differentiate secondary school pupils by type of ability into even such broad categories as linguistic or academic on the one hand, and scientific or technical-mechanical, on the other. For the most part, those who are best at one course would also be above average at the other, and *vice versa*.

If we confine our attention to a narrow ability range, say the top 20 per cent as in England, then we find it possible, with our present verbal and spatial tests, to differentiate the extremes. Of course there are no distinct types of children any more than there are tall and short types in height. We can pick out roughly one-sixth who are relatively superior on the linguistic to the technical side, and one-sixth who are more suited to the other type of course. There remain two-thirds who are likely to do equally well or badly at either. Roughly the same is true of American college students. The efficiency of prediction of overall level of achievement by means of tests is much greater than the efficiency for classifying according to, say, engineering or arts, and this is only the broadest and most obvious dichotomy. If we tried to go further and split off, say, foreign linguists, social studies students, mathematicians, biologists, physicists, engineers, commercial students, art students and agriculturalists, we should certainly be far less successful still. Probably the linguists, mathematicians and physicists would be distinguishable from the artists and agriculturalists more readily by their generally higher intelligence and previous attainment than by such specialised tests as we have available at present.

Some psychologists would claim that abilities differentiate with age, so that suitability for different lines of study or type of curriculum would become more clear-cut near the end of secondary schooling or during college years. No satisfactory evidence for this claim can be found except in so far as groups of older students are usually more highly selected in respect to general ability. In the independent college, the scientist might make a hash of French, or the good historian fail in engineering, because in such a population practically all cases fall within the top 10 per cent as regards general ability. There would be much less differentiation in the state universities, where students range roughly over the top 30 to 40 per cent of the scale.

However, the outlook for guidance or selection into types of courses is not quite so dim if we take account of interests, since interests have the tremendous advantage, for classification purposes, of showing quite low, sometimes even negative, correlations with one another. The good scientist and the good business man, for example, may differ little in such abilities as we are able to test. They would however loathe one another's jobs, and would likely be thoroughly bored by any education or training designed to prepare them for the other's technical career. In England we find that we can differentiate nearly two-thirds of the more able pupils into the academically and the technically-minded at eleven as against the one-third mentioned earlier, by taking, account of *interests* as well as *abilities.* One difficulty with interests, though, is that they cannot develop without experience. There must be many adults who fail to get much satisfaction from their vocational and avocational pursuits because their education has not provided sufficient opportunities for them to experience, say, painting, farming, or mechanical work. The American system of offering a wide choice of secondary school subjects, while often criticised by educators for its fragmentariness, is sounder in this respect than the English which gives less variety and indeed tends to stereotype the more able pupils either in an Arts or a Science field from about the age of fourteen, and to discourage less academic inclinations. The shortage of technologists and high-grade technicians in England is at least as serious as that in America. Clearly one of the reasons is the high social prestige of academic courses of study which hinders the provision of experience that might stimulate the development of more practical interests.

Another obvious difficulty arises from the variability of interests during adolescence. Among many students interests may not be sufficiently stable nor assessable to allow firm and satisfactory educational or vocational specialisation until the end of secondary schooling or even later. Nevertheless, one investigation at London University of adult technologist and Arts men did suggest that some differentiation of interests would have been apparent in the great majority as early as twelve years. This is a field where psychologically trained counsellors can already help in making earlier diagnoses, and where current work on personality gives promise of improved tests.

How about the problem of discovering the brilliantly talented individual—the occasional future genius? Clearly, neither our tests of abilities nor of interests are going to be much use here, and we must continue to trust mainly to luck, to the perceptiveness of the school or college teacher who encourages him, and to the individual's own drive, which enables him to break through the barriers of the educational system. Admirable as Terman's follow-up studies of children with high IQs are, some harm has been done by labelling them studies of "genius."

One other point of psychological theory: although it has been shown that the group factors underlying particular types of curriculum are disappointingly small and difficult to diagnose, this does not dispose of what Spearman called specific factors. Individual pupils show great variations with respect to specific topics within any course, depending on their particular past experience and interests, and on their emotional responses to the teacher and other members of the class. Thus, even when they are satisfactorily grouped for, say, oral reading, they will show considerable heterogeneity in silent reading or spelling, let alone in non-related subjects. For such reasons, many educational psychologists currently look more to individual assignments and small-group work within classes to cope with most of the problems of individual differences than to overall grouping into separate classes. With this goes the notion of enrichment of courses among the brighter students. The adequacy of such solutions is doubtful since they clearly imply increasing the degree of heterogeneity within the class and thus run counter to the thesis of this paper.

What conclusions can we come to then? No evaluation of the various mechanisms of acceleration that have been, or are being, tried out in America such as grade-skipping, advanced standing, and the shortening of courses through enriched programmes will be made here. But the evidence does seem to point to the desirability of some form of grouping, such as indeed already exists in many American high schools. Nevertheless, we have seen that there are many dangers in introducing anything that implies competitive selection or stereotyping of ability levels. It is, therefore, preferable to keep to grouping by age, and later by interest, as far as possible. Up until about nine years of age or the fourth grade, there would seem to be no good case for any ability grouping other than segregation of the lower-grade feebleminded, the physically handicapped, and, perhaps, temporary remedial classes for the higher-grade defectives and the very backward. However, by the age of about thirteen or the eighth grade, the range and complexity of abilities *appears* to have become much wider. It is still doubtful how satisfactorily we can measure range of ability in any absolute sense even at this age. But everybody can't go on studying everything, and, in the interests of professional and vocational objectives, some specialisation should begin to be introduced. Hence, some degree of grouping by general ability, and to an increasing extent by interest, would seem legitimate. While it is true that many thinkers strongly deprecate early specialisation, surely its dangers should be balanced against the waste of productive years which results at present from the late postponement of any specialisation. Between the fourth and eighth grades one can only suggest that the curriculum be largely of an exploratory or diagnostic character, designed not merely to provide essential skills, but to stimulate general mental development and to provide experience out of which interests can be built. Even when grouping is introduced, there should be sufficient overlapping between groups to make transfer up or down easy, and of course sufficient common activities in a school or college to discourage the formation of barriers. In other words, the process should be one of gradual approximation in accordance with the principles of educational guidance rather than one of selection or irreversible decision.

Inevitably this is a vague kind of framework and the psychologist must always remember that his prescriptions are liable to be upset by social prejudices and traditions, financial shortages, increasing birthrates, and innumerable other factors.

The American type of school organization seems to meet the prescription set forth in this paper more nearly than does the British, though it may, of course, show weaknesses in other respects. Some means should be devised of giving greater and earlier recognition to individual differences in general educability and of avoiding, if possible, some of the mistakes that have arisen in England as a result of the strangle hold of tradition and the well-intentioned but short-sighted policies of educational planners.

COMMENTS ON INTELLIGENCE TEST VALIDITY

Many textbooks avoid controversy. However, if the students can grasp the basic issues involved, it may be well to let them know that educational and psychological problems are more complex than textbook presentations may indicate, and that even the experts do not always agree. The "proper" use of standardized tests (for example, for intelligence, aptitudes, achievement, personality) has always been an issue. When the objective testing movement reached its zenith of popularity before World War II, students were routinely subjected to batteries of tests. The school personnel who administered, scored, and interpreted the tests frequently knew little about their construction and inherent limitations. Test scores became sources of divinely revealed truth. The IQ tests particularly were enshrined, and a students's score became one of his indelible identifying characteristics. With the current national talent hunt there has been a resurgence of testing in the schools, and a students's educational advancement or college admission often hangs on the scores that he receives on standardized achievement and ability tests. The ease with which tests can be administered and scored, and the superficiality with which they can be interpreted, have made them popular rituals in the schools. Somehow the test becomes more important than the student who takes it and the test results more valued than the empirical realities of Johnny's behaviour.

Littell's criticism of Ebel's view of validity and the use of tests is that it may perpetuate this state of affairs. Littell does not want the test-taker subordinated to the test. Nor does he want the psychological interpretation of the student's behaviour to rest solely on the results of the test. The choice of appropriate test batteries must be tailored to individual need and rest on professional judgment. Even then the results are not revealed truth; but they do furnish the psychologist with some hypotheses about the nature and cause of an individual's behaviour, and these hypotheses must be checked in a specific set of circumstances. In this latter sense, test validity (or the particular usefulness of a test in given circumstances) remains an important concept.

In considering the matter of validity, Littell has expressed a view about the present state of psychological knowledge which may differ from what Ebel has at least tacitly assumed. At present, we have much more theory in psychology than we have experimental tests of theory. Psychological theory often gives us "images" of behaviour to which we become subjectively attached. When this occurs, we no longer trust the feedback that we can obtain when we try to apply the theory to particular individuals and situations. The rationale upon which tests are built is often such a body of untested theory or assumptions. To use the tests without checking them against the observable facts of Johnny's behaviour is to have purely subjective faith in tests and theory. In the present state of our science, psychological tests often lack the valid theoretical under-pinnings assumed in their indiscriminate use. Until we have much more specific information about how well the tests do their jobs under particular conditions, little trust can be placed in test scores. It should be clear, however, that Littell is not demeaning psychological theory and tests; he is simply urging a more realistic view of their present limitations.

It might be of some interest for the student to organize two testing programmes : one should follow the suggestions of Ebel and the other the suggestions of Littell. How would you "test" the programmes to discover which was more effective? Also , how does Littell's view of testing technology or practice agree with Melton's view about the present state of educational technology.

The concept of test validity has been subjected to increasingly close scrutiny over the past few years (e.g., A.P.A., 1954; Cronbach, 1960; Littell, 1960). This scrutiny has reflected and indeed is an outgrowth of the growing understanding of the process of theory development, use and evaluation within science in general. This particular discussion has been stimulated by Ebel's recent articles

(1961) which questions very seriously the concept of validity as it is currently employed by test developers and users. Certainly, as Ebel points out, the concept of validity as it is currently applied and discussed, is confused and contradictory and based on an outmoded philosophy of naive realism; it is of great concern to test developers, but difficult to apply and often receives only lip service. If the case were closed at this point, the test user would be left in a real and very serious "validity dilemma."

Ebel proposes a way out of the dilemma through the concept of "meaningfulness" which he suggests should replace validity as the primary factor to consider in evaluating a test. Meaningfulness, for Ebel, arises from knowledge of:

(*a*) an operational definition of the measurement procedure;
(*b*) the relationship of the scores to other measures (validity coefficients, predictive and concurrent, and other correlation coefficients or measures of relationship);
(*c*) a good estimate of the reliability of the scores;
(*d*) appropriate norms of examinee performance.

This factor or meaningfulness, along with convenience in use and, a third criterion, "the importance of the inferences that can be made from the test scores" constitute the basic criteria offered by Ebel upon which one should base his choice and use of a psychological test. Five and one third pages are devoted by Ebel to the discussion of the limitations of the current concepts of validity, a little more than one page to the presentation and discussion of "meaningfulness" and only two short sentences to the mention of what the writer sees as the critical issue of test validity, *the inference from test scores.* In this sense, Ebel has really not taken up the issue of *validity* at all. With a casual reading , one might be left with the impression that somehow by knowing how a test was developed and administered and a variety of correlation coefficients with other measures (usually other tests), the process of inference is clear and unambiguous, and needs no further thought or evaluation.

The following discussion takes up the issue of inference and compare some of the implications which emerge with some of the points Ebel has made. In general, this discussion takes a position which reflects several basic ideas about psychological test validity:

1. Test validity is best understood and the issues are most clear when considered within the context of the choice and use of psychological tests by those actively engaged in using them.

2. All matters of test construction (convenience, reliability, norms, "meaningfulness," etc.) are important only in so far as they bear on the process by which the test user formulates, applied, and evaluates the inferences he makes from the test scores.

3. In the last analysis the value of a test depends upon the degree to which it aids the user in reducing his error in anticipating other behaviour more relevant to his professional activities.

4. While this article is written with the standard psychological test in mind, the issues brought out and the positions taken are equally applicable, although perhaps with different emphasis, to any situation in which one chooses to measure or identify a variable in a conceptual system in a particular way.

The Use of the Psychological Test

Whether the user of a psychological test is operating within a clinical, educational, industrial, or research setting, he engages the use of a psychological test for specific reasons highly related to his professional activities. Aside from those thousands of tests administered merely to fill in blanks on forms which have become functionally autonomous, the user employs a given test because he wants to know more about the person than simply his score. He wishes to be able to infer, to generalize, to gain information about a person that would not be available as easily, or cheaply, or efficiently, or quickly had he not administered the test.

In the usual situation, the professional psychologist or educator is faced with the necessity of formulating and selecting from among possible plans of action through which he hopes to achieve his therapeutic, remedial, educational, or advising goals. His effectiveness as a professional rests very heavily on his ability to formulate and select the "best" plan. The plans he makes and the bases for his choice among them depend in part on such practical considerations as the problem presented, his professional purpose, the facilities available, ethics, etc. The factors having to do with the specific people involved, however, are the ones which rightly demand his deepest consideration; he must know as accurately as possible how the *people themselves will respond to them*, and as an aid to this end he employs the psychological test. He chooses to give a test rather than to gather information in some other manner, and to give this particular test (or tests) because he has reason to believe that in this way he can maximize his efficiency in gathering information that will be relevant and helpful in formulating and choosing from among these alternative courses of action open to him.

This approach has interesting implications. One should give a test only if he cannot select with a *sufficient degree of certainty* from among the alternative courses of action on the basis of information already at hand; if nothing the test could show would alter his choice, then giving the test is a waste of time and money. Tests should be given for a specific purpose growing out of the user's need in *that particular instance* for specific information. (The valid "exploratory" use of tests must be recognized, of course, when indeed one does not have enough information to begin even to formulate alternative courses of action.)

The problem remains of how a test user is to assess the ability of a particular test to do a specific job in any given situation. At present this is at best a very complex and often unrewarding task.

The Basic Need for Empirical Validation

Apparently central to Ebel's approach is the suggestion that there is some way *other* than through empirical validation by which a test may be established as truly useful. Responsible use of a test *must*, in the last analysis, be tied to empirical observation. Somewhere along the line in his use of a test the user must make some statements that can be checked by direct observation. The final question as to the validity of the test as used is answerd only through these observations. If there is no way to tell whether one is right or wrong (even though this evidence may be quite distant in time and connected only by inference) then one might as well let his fantasy run unchecked and answer only to his aesthetic and/or libidinal impulses in his choice and use of a test. (Better still, he can fall back on common usage: "I may not be right, but no one will dare tell me I'm wrong.") Ethically, however, he is committed to make it clear to others what he is doing.

For the test user the problem of test validity is relatively simple when he has a clear idea of what he wants to predict and has available sound empirical evidence that bears directly on the ability of the test to do in fact what he wants it to do under his particular set of circumstances. Very seldom is this the case, however, and usually the test user is forced (or even prefers) to infer beyond any clearly applicable predictive studies. He does this usually by finding a test that will (apparently) measure some supposed enduring characteristic of the individual which is not directly observable and for which no one observable criterion exists, but which his theory (or "understanding") tells him is important (i.e., related to the behaviour he ultimately wishes to predict). We assume, of course, that the user is interested in something more than achieving subjective "closure," something more than filling in the gaps in his own subjective understanding of his client, subject, or student. We suspect that this feeling of subjective understanding *can* come about, for instance, simply by fitting the phenomenon into an old, familiar context which may, if judged on subjective criteria alone, be not only objectively misleading but quite wrong.

The question of the ability of the test used in this manner to do what the user wants it to do must be dealt with in terms of some level of construct validation. At present this is to open a Pandora's box of problems, for under these circumstances the user's faith in the inferences made from the test must rest upon his assessment of the "validity" of *both* the test as a measure of the variable and of the *whole conceptual system* in which the variable takes on the meaning from which future predictions of behaviour are made. This puts the psychological test user in a very dangerous situation, for at present under the best of circumstances he is forced to operate with a conceptual system in which clinical, personal, educational, and cultural folk lore combine in almost unknown quantities with the little objective evidence available.

At some future date the term "validity" might be used to refer to the confidence with which one can substitute the score of a particular psychological test for a term in a pre-existing, well substantiated, internally consistent theory or set of laws. At present, however, psychology, especially in the applied fields, has only the barest beginning of such theories of sets of laws. Strictly speaking, under current conditions, it is meaningless to look for the construct validity of a test measure expect in the most gross terms. The situation is difficult enough when we speak of the construct validity of a measure of intelligence (e.g., Littell, 1960); consider the problems involved in assessing the construct validity of a measure of such concepts *as social presence* or *extraversion.*

For the test user, this means that he cannot look upon his theory as more than a guide, a source of hypothesis to be tested. He must approach these measures of an hypothetical construct with extreme caution, and continue to investigate critically the "validity" (internal consistency, agreement with facts, etc.) of the conceptual system (s) he uses in his professional endeavor. The long term goal for psychology as a science is to develop theoretical structures of sufficient definity, etc., that their "validity" and the validity of the measures of the constructs they involve can be investigated. The present goal for the users of psychological tests must be to compensate for this lack of easily generalized validity by sticking as closely as possible to short term, "checkable" unglobal, uses of tests.

The Problem of the Criterion

Many people appear to share Ebel's concern over the failure to find "adequate" criterion measures by which to establish a test's validity. At this stage of theory development we would be surprised if in, fact the situation were other than this. Whenever one wishes to measure a variable that has meaning beyond that which can be contained in any one observation (and this is the usual case), one must deal with the process of construct validation. While this is especially true with "psychological" variables, it is true even with such supposedly obvious terms as *arithmetic ability, immediate recall, achievement in social studies,* etc. The search for an "ultimate" criterion is bound to fail.

When a criterion against which a test is to be validated is chosen, of course its reliability, relevance, etc. must be investigated, and of course at this stage of development of psychological theory and measurement the criterion will be found to be just as lacking as any test in the degree to which it is isomorphic with the rich, involved (and usually somewhat contradictory and ambiguous) cognitive structure behind the behaviour of the investigator. But one cannot throw in the sponge and selectively *avoid* this disappointing but *essential* empirical anchoring of any scientific theoretical structure.

A mistrust of observation result primarily when one expects too much from observation; the observation of the relation between the test and one criterion event can establish the final "validity" of the test only when one is interested in predicting *that* particular event. As long as test users continue to operate on the basis of "folk lore" theory (be it personal, clinical, or educational) no appeal to data will really capture the essence and full meaning of the concept sought.

The Essential Mistrust of Appearances

Ebel chooses to reject the suggestion of the disillusioned naive realist that we mistrust appearances. It is the writer's opinion that the only way to make healthy use of a test is to have a firm and enduring mistrust of appearances. The validation of a test is not the final discovery of what the test (really) measures, no matter how it is phrased (e.g., the abilities it taps, the personality factors it reflects, the skills it measures, etc.), but is more the accumulation of enough empirical information about the test (e.g., factors which influence the scores, necessary conditions to be met in administration, the relationships into which it enters with other *behavioural* measures, etc.) to have reason to suspect that it will in fact do what we want it to do. Its use is to be based on this information, and not on the label it is given, or the classification into which it is placed by its appearances, whether these appearances are superficial and naive evaluations of its content or detailed and complex descriptions of the development of the test.

There need be nothing "mysterious" about the use of a psychological test. In a very real sense the psychological test should be a tool for the professional psychologist or educator much like a hammer is a tool for the carpenter. One does not speak of the "validity" of a hammer; as one learns the trade, one finds out what can be done with it and how to use it in order to obtain the best results. Only for the novice must one label a hammer "an instrument for pounding." In other words, the test user also should base his use of a test on what he knows from experience (his own or that of others) the test can do.

The use of a test is in a very basic sense arbitrary; that is, unrelated to its name, its "classification," or any associations the psychologist might have to its content, development, etc. The same basic questions of validity must be dealt with no matter how the test is used. For example, an intelligence test could be used "validly" as a clock; a very rough and inefficient clock to be sure, but a clock none the less. We administer the intelligence test to a person at time *t* and then readminister it at some time Δt later. By reference to appropriate data (diminution of practice effects over time) a rough estimate of Δ t could be inferred from the difference between the two scores. Certainly it would be rough and inaccurate and very inefficient as a measure of time, especially when compared with other more standard time measures. But it could be expected to render an estimate more accurate than would be obtained by merely guessing at random from all possible times. As a measure of time the "difference between two intelligence test scores" should be rejected because it is less efficient and reliaible and less useful than other measures; not because "an intelligence test does not measure time."

The Operational Definition of a Test

Ebel suggests that the operational definition of a test ("critical procedures in test construction, in test administration, and in scoring") be included as an important aspect of what he terms test "meaningfulness." There is no question as to whether this information should be available to any user of the test. There is a question left unanswered by Ebel's discussion, however, as to how the psychologist should make use of this information. An operational definition in and of itself, aside from aiding competent administration of the test, means very little. Once a measure is devised one need not know how or by what method unless there is reason to suspect that such information will be of help in the use of the test. The test could be distilled from the residue at the bottom of a witch's caldron if it were convenient and inexpensive to use, reliable and entered into a large number of significant relationships with other behavioural variables important to the psychologist. We suspect, of course, that there are some ways of devising a test to do a certain task that will have a greater chance of being fruitful than others, and many texts have been written about these suspicions. Once devised, however, it must stand only on the evidence which shows that it can *in fact* do what it was devised to do.

For the test user, an operational definition is perhaps best understood as a check point, an attempt by the developer of the test to spell out in as much detail as possible all of the factor which might bear on the test score. There are no hard and fast rules as to what should be included although, of course, there is considerable agreement. What is included in the operational definition of any test is left up to the judgment of the test constructor as to whether from his knowledge, background, etc. any particular factor should be considered important to include. Few test constructors would bother to include a minute description of the colors of the shirts of the subject upon which the test was developed, simply because there is no reason to suspect that this variable could have any effect on the test score. If he felt it were important and, better still, had evidence, then shirt color would become a legitimate part of the operational definition of the test.

Test Reliability and Standardization as Possible "Distractors"

Considerable effort and skill has gone into the development of techniques for increasing the reliability of psychological measuring devices. This is all well and good. Care must be taken, however, that due to the effort expended on it, reliability does not assume a position in the evaluation of a test out of keeping with its actual contribution to the user's faith in the test. A test can be used only to the degree that it is reliable. A sufficient degree of reliability is an *essential but completely insufficient* condition for the use of a test. It is a condition which must prevail *before* one can begin on the basic task of finding what in fact the test can do.

Tests are highly standardized and systematized methods of observation, and as such there is a great potential for strength and efficiency in their use. This usefulness must be built into the test and assessed empirically, however, for these tests also provide highly systematized patterns of behaviour, for the user, and therefore apparently may come to achieve the status of the compulsive ritual, an act which, it is well known, tends to be perseverated in spite of any and all feedback. In fact, it is just in such situations in which feedback is ambiguous and anxiety is high that we expect these magical rituals to tend to develop.

CONCLUSION

There is in fact a "validity dilemma" in common psychological test usage today. When the test user departs from directly applicable empirical data he is on tenuous ground; conclusions from available studies are overgeneralized and the psychological theory in use is all too often little more than a rough guide. Perhaps the best course of action for the test user is to recognize the essentially limited contribution of psychological tests to professional endeavor and to use them realistically as they are. One can face this fact and still find sufficient reason to involve tests as still another source of information (with many unique and helpful features) *the usefulness of which must be evaluated under any specific set of circumstances.*

In this light perhaps the best thing a test constructor or test company can do is to provide a convenient, inexpensive and highly reliable measure of behaviour which evokes a rich set of associations (inferences) in the professional test user and which therefore provides a large number of hypotheses regarding the possible use of the test to be then checked in any specific set of circumstances. The test user has only one course of action open to him: to be continually aware that he is working with hypotheses to be tested. At no time can he stop and trust appearances, subjective certainty or current theory.

9

Disadvantage and Education

In this final chapter we look at the part played by families, by schools and by society itself in the linguistic development and academic attainment of children, with particular emphasis on those from less advantaged environments. Why are some children at a disadvantage in the educational system? How significant a factor is social class or membership of an ethnic minority? What effects does poverty have on a child's intellectual development? Can schools compensate for deprivation in the home? How does the wider culture shape the direction of a child's aspirations and achievements? None of the answers is simple since these questions concern the complex interaction of many factors, from the parent-child relationship to the social context within which the child develops.

In trying to answer them, it may help to consider Bronfenbrenner's ecological model of human development. In advocating this model, Bronfenbrenner is warning of the dangers of focusing on the individual without taking into account the context within which he or she exists or the processes of interaction through which the behaviour of individuals in a particular system evolves. He is arguing that when psychologists try to understand the many factors influencing development, they should use methods which are ecologically valid. They should be aware of the effects on the subject of removal from the natural environment to a strange setting (for example, a university laboratory or a psychological testing room). It is useful to bear Bronfenbrenner's ideas in mind as you consider the issues raised in this chapter. But first, let us look at the idea of disadvantage itself.

The Concept of Disadvantage

We have all had unfavourable experiences which we would say 'put us at a disadvantage' in some way, perhaps socially or intellectually. To the psychologist, however, disadvantage usually means a relatively enduring condition that results in lower academic achievement at school and reduced opportunities in the wider society; this tends to refer to social or cultural characteristics, for example being a member of an ethnic minority group, living in an inner city area, or having a low income. Passow (1970) defined the disadvantaged child as one who 'because of social or cultural characteristics, for example social class, race, ethnic origin, poverty, sex, geographical location, etc. comes into the school system with knowledge, skills and attitudes which impede learning'. Wedge and Essen (1982) defined the disadvantaged as 'that group of children who failed to thrive, who failed to mature as much or as quickly physically, or who have failed to achieve as well in school as other British children'. Important social factors which served to identify such children included family composition (a large number of children in the family, or only one parent figure); low income; and poor housing. Each of these factors was related to poor physical and academic development and less acceptable behaviour.

Historically, this concern coincides with the advent of a universal free education system and the corresponding philosophy of 'equality of opportunity' which arose in most Western societies, including Britain and the USA, in the years following the Second World War. As the Newsom Report (1963) put it, 'all children should have an equal opportunity of acquiring intelligence, and developing their talents and abilities to the full'. It was assumed by many that this would also result in an equality of achievement amongst different social class and racial groups. Yet, surveys over the past 20 years have consistently shown that children from lower social class groups, ethnic minorities and adverse social conditions, such as those described by Wedge and Essen, have on average achieved poorly in the school system.

For example, one nationwide survey of school achievement in the USA, the Coleman Report (Coleman *et al*, 1966), showed that the best academic performance was obtained by white children from cities in the north-east of the country. As Table 9.1 shows, children from other areas, especially the rural south, and of non-white ethnic origin, under-achieved on average by anything up to six grades (six years) by the end of secondary schooling.

Table 9.1

Average Under-achievement, in Grades (Years), of Different Groups of American Children in Standardized Scores of Verbal Ability and Mathematics, from the Coleman Report of 1966

	Verbal ability	*Mathematics*		*Verbal ability*	*Mathematics*
White children, western cities	0.5	0.8	Mexican/American children	3.5	4.1
White children, rural south	1.5	1.4	Puerto Rican children	3.6	4.8
Black children, NE cities	3.2	5.2	Indian American children	3.5	3.9
Black children, rural south	5.2	6.2	Oriental-American children	1.6	0.9

White children from north-east urban communities are taken as the standard.

The Rampton Report (1981) provides large-scale statistical evidence about the educational attainment from ethnic minority groups in the UK. The report examines CSE, Ordinary and Advanced level results, and destinations, of school leavers from six local education authorities with high concentrations of ethnic minority children—a sample which typified around half the ethnic minority school leavers in the country in 1978/1979. In Table 9.2 figures are given for Asian, Afro-Caribbean, and other school leavers. Also given are comparative figures for all maintained school leavers in England during the same period. It is clear from these findings that Afro-Caribbean children are achieving much less well in the educational system than S. Asian or white children.

Table 9.2

Evidence of Academic Under-achievement by Young Black Students

	Asians	*Afro-Caribbeans*	*All other leavers*	*All school leavers in England*
Five or more passes at 'O' level or CSE Grade I	18%	3%	16%	21%
One or more 'A' level passes	13%	2%	12%	13%
Went to university	3%	1%	3%	5%
n =	527	799	4,852	6,93,840

Source : Rampton Report, 1981.

In the UK the National Child Development Study, a longitudinal study of all children born in one week of March, 1958, found that social class was a strong predictor of school achievement in reading and arithmetic. The children were the subjects of a socio-medical survey soon after birth. At 7, 11, and 16 years, detailed information was obtained about the children's educational progress, psychological development and home circumstances.

The study found a marked relationship between social class, defined by father's occupation, and the children's educational attainment (Davie *et al.*, 1972). Figure 9.1 shows the percentages by social class of those children from the cohort who performed badly on a test of arithmetic at the age of 7. It shows that 41 per cent of children from unskilled families (social class V) had a poor test score as compared to 12 per cent of children from professional families (social class I). Figure 9.2 shows a similar pattern of scores on the Southgate reading test : 48 per cent of children from social class V made low scores compared to 8 per cent of children from social class I. If the criterion of poor reading is made more stringent, the disparity is much larger. The chances of a social class V child being a non-reader are fifteen times greater than those of a social class I child. Teachers were

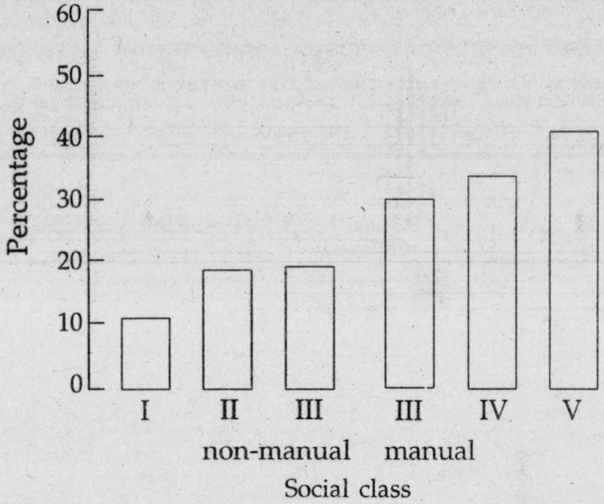

Fig. 9.1: Percentage of children with 'poor' problem arithmetic test scores (0-3) at age 7 (adapted from Davie *et al.*, 1972)

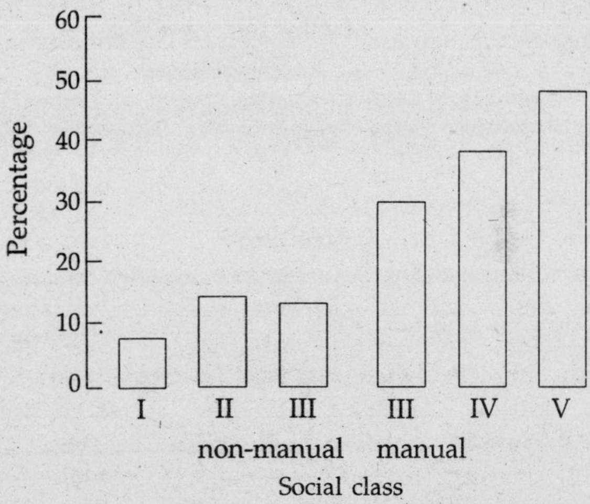

Fig. 9.2: Percentage of children with 'poor' Southgate reading test scores (0-20) at age 7 (adapted from Davie *et al.*, 1972)

also asked to say whether the children would benefit from special educational treatment. Figure 9.3 shows that around 25 per cent of children from social class V were said to be receiving or in need of specialist teaching; only 3 per cent of children in social class I fell into this category. The gap between children of different social class background remained at the age of 11, as can be seen from the reading scores presented in Table 9.3

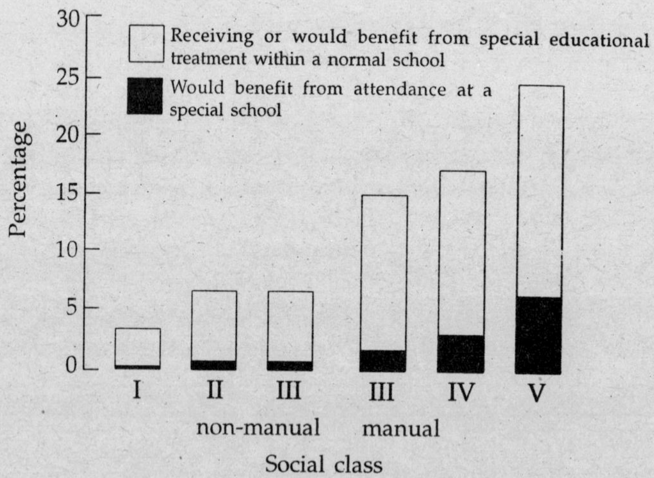

Fig. 9.3: Percentage of children needing special educational treatment by social class at age 7 (adapted from Davie *et al.*, 1972)

Table 9.3

Reading Comprehension Scores in Percentages by Social Class at 11 Years

	Social class					
Reading score	*I and II*	*III (non-manual)*	*III (manual)*	*IV*	*V*	*Total*
0-12	12.0	15.7	33.2	41.8	52.2	29.5
13-19	37.5	40.8	43.7	40.4	35.6	40.9
20-35	50.5	43.5	23.1	17.8	12.2	29.6
Total	100	100	100	100	100	100

n = 11,961.

Source : Davie, 1973

This survey, and others, have therefore identified a strong relationship between social class and educational attainment in reading and arithmetic. There seems to be a clear division in educational attainment between children from non-manual or middle class homes on the one hand and those form manual or working class homes on the other.

Causes of Educational Disadvantage

In the 1960s and early 1970s many psychologists and educational researchers thought that the reasons for the relative failure in school of children from lower social class groups, and ethnic minorities, must lie in psychological factors such as the quality of parent-child language in the home, or parental attitudes to school. It was felt that parents of these children did not provide the intellectual stimulation which children needed. In the UK the Newsom Report (1963) identified linguistic disadvantage in some home backgrounds; the abilities of boys and girls, it stated, were often unrealized because of their 'inadequate powers of speech'. These ideas came to be known as the 'deficit' model which places blame on the home for failing to give an adequate socialization experience for the children; as a result children have poor language skills, and/or inadequate intellectual skills to cope at school.

The term 'cultural deprivation' became popular in this period to describe what was thought of as a lack of 'cultural' stimulation in the homes of 'deprived' children. Such a perspective led naturally to the idea of programmes of 'enrichment' or of 'compensatory education' to remove these children's supposed psychological deficits.

We shall examine the effects of such enriched environments or compensatory education shortly. In certain circumstances, for example, institutional rearing, enrichment programmes can have very substantial effects. However, the outcome of compensatory education programmes has seemed more modest, at least at first. The apparent failure of these programmes to remove educational disadvantage led to explanations other than the deficit model being seriously considered.

Advocates of an alternative approach, known as the 'difference' model, argue that schools are essentially white, middle class institutions in terms of their values, the language used by teachers and the content of courses. Hence, children from different backgrounds achieve less well. Difference theorists would wish to see greater tolerance of the values, attitudes and behaviour which the children bring to school from their home background; or even separate kinds of schooling for ethnic minorities. For example, Labov (1969) demonstrated the verbal skills which American ghetto children can display in the right context, but also argued that educators seldom value or encourage the non-standard English of inner city children. Writing about American Indian children, Wax and Wax (1971) argued that educators have been too quick to classify them as 'deprived' or 'lacking in culture' because their homes are without books, radio, newspapers or television. Such, an attitude ignores the rich customs, ritual, language, mythology and medical knowledge which is part of the American Indian child's heritage. These authors suggest that the value and meaning of minority groups' culture should be an important part of the educational experience of all children.

Another approach is something of a compromise between the deficit and the difference positions. This emphasizes the 'social disadvantage' of lower social class and ethnic minority groups. Usually, such families have lower income, poor housing and more difficult family circumstances. These factors may be responsible for some real deficits in children's development, which may then show up in psychological or educational tests but which are not primarily psychological in origin. In common with difference theorists, this perspective would not expect too much from compensatory education programmes which did not deal with social and material inequalities. Moreover, such deficits produced by the culture might be exaggerated by actual discrimination against lower class or ethnic minority children in schools, as difference theories suggest.

From a very different and controversial standpoint it has been argued that children from lower social class backgrounds or certain ethnic minorities have, on average, genetically lower potential for intelligence and hence for education. One well-known proponent of this view is Arthur Jensen (1969). This hypothesis naturally raises considerable indignation amongst members of minority groups. Although its supporters argue that it is scientifically valid to present it as a hypothesis, to advance it seems insensitive to the prolonged injustice and discrimination suffered by many ethnic minority groups in Britain and the USA. Much of the early research on race and intelligence was biased and unsound (see Gould, 1981), while more recent research is against the hypothesis. For example, Scarr and Weinberg (1976) studied 130 black children adopted by middle class white families in the USA. These children achieved comparable levels of intellectual achievement to adopted white children in similar families. These and other studies (Scarr, 1984) suggest strongly that, while individual differences in intellectual ability may indeed be partly genetic in origin, racial differences in intelligence test scores are overwhelmingly due to environmental factors. Whether these environmental factors are best seen as due to psychological deficits in the home environment, educational prejudice against cultural/subcultural differences, or the consequences of social and material disadvantage, is still actively under debate.

The Effects of Severe Deprivation and Institutional Rearing

The deficit model of disadvantage supposes that some children experience a deprived or impoverished rearing environment. This is contentious as applied to the homes of lower social class or ethnic minority children. However, it is not contentious in certain extreme circumstances. These include the experience of children reared in orphanages or children's homes in the years before and early after the Second World War. At that time children's institutions provided little stimulation of any kind. The children had few toys or playthings, little conversation with staff, and experienced extreme multiple caregiving. As a result, institutionally reared children scored very poorly on tests of cognitive or linguistic development, as well as showing problems in later social adjustment. It was the work of Bowlby and other psychologists which drew attention to these consequences of institutional rearing, and hence led to great improvements in the quality of the institutional environment. The success of these efforts was one factor contributing to the broad popularity of the deficit model in the 1960s, and the enthusiasm for compensatory education and enrichment programmes.

Two early studies showed dramatically the effects that could be achieved by enriching the environment for institutionally reared children. Skeels and Dye (1939) chanced to notice the effect of environmental change on two apparently retarded children who had been transferred at 18 months from an orphanage to the women's ward in an institution for the mentally retarded , with an associated school. Their new environment was in fact an enriched one in comparison to the orphanage. Both staff and patients lavished attention and affection on them, played with them and took them on outings, and the children were given a much more stimulating experience than they had previously. The gains were dramatic and after 15 months of this experience the children were considered to be within the normal range of intelligence. Children who had remained in the unstimulating environment of the orphanage did not make progress in this way.

Skodak and Skeels (1945) then carried out a more systematic longitudinal study in which 13 mentally retarded infants from the orphanage were transferred in the same way as the earlier two. The infants were aged 11-21 months, and had a mean IQ of 64. Again the children made dramatic gains; after an average of 19 months' stay the mean IQ was 92. By the age of 3 or 4 most were adopted by families and went on to attend normal school. A similar, control group of 12 children who stayed in the orphanage, however, actually decreased in IQ from a mean of 87 to 61 over this period. More than 20 years later, a follow-up study (Skeels, 1966) indicated that the gains made by the experimental group of children were lasting. They had obtained significantly more grades at school than the control group, had formed stable partnership, and had a varied range of occupations (*e.g.* teacher, beautician, airline stewardess, sales manager). In the control group, all but one were in unskilled occupations, were unemployed or still living in the institution. These dramatic findings suggested that intervention at an early age had crucial effects on later educational and vocational success.

Kirk (1958) advised caution in interpreting Skeels and Skodak's results. Was it the intervention alone which had the effect, or was it the long-term stimulation and care from the adopted families? Kirk followed groups of retarded children during the preschool and first school years. Twenty-eight of his sample were given an enriched preschool experience in the community; 15 remained within the institution but attended an institution nursery school; 12 in a different institution had no preschool education. In terms of intellectual level the community preschool group made an average gain of 12 IQ points, the institution preschool group made an average gain of 10 IQ points, while the institution control group had an average *loss* of 6-7 IQ points. However, some of the differences became smaller after the children had entered school. Much of the intervention effect 'wore off' or 'washed out' after the experimental period was over. The reason for this could have been acceleration on the part of the control children once they experienced the stimulation of school or deceleration on the part of the experimental children once their enriched experience was over. The Kirk experiment suggested that early intervention could have immediate effects, but needed to be reinforced by a continuing experience of enrichment, warmth and stimulation (like that of the adopted children in Skeels and Skodak's study) if the gains were to be permanent.

It was clear from studies such as these that orphanage care for children could be improved. The benefits of better institutional conditions have been shown in a study of London children by Tizard and Rees (1974), discussed in box 3.2. The study started with 65 children who had been placed in the care of institutions by the age of 4 months. Tizard followed up the children at the ages of 2, 4.5 and 8 years. By the age of 4.5 years, 26 remained in the institution, 24 had been adopted and 15 restored to their mothers. There was no evidence of intellectual impairment or language retardation in the institutionalized children; their environment was stimulating with plenty of books and toys, and the staff made efforts to talk with the children. However, the adopted children were more advanced intellectually than those remaining in the institution; they were, in addition, friendlier, more talkative, more cooperative and more relaxed with strangers. The Institutionalized children in this study were functioning within the normal range of cognitive and linguistic abilities, but they still showed some problems of social adjustment (see box 3.2). In modern institutions with a more stimulating environment there do not seem to be the adverse effects on cognitive and linguistic development found in earlier studies. The residual effects on social adjustment are probably related to the extreme multiple caregiving which is still an almost inevitable consequence of institutional rearing.

There have also been some case studies of the effects of extreme deprivation and neglect on young children. There have, for example, been anecdotal accounts of 'wild children', that is children discovered in the wild with apparently no form of human contact. When rescued, these children tended to display behaviour more characteristic of animals, such as running on all fours, and this led some to believe that the children had survived through being reared by and among animals. Such cases are generally poorly documented. Whatever the circumstances of their rearing, the prognosis for wild children has been poor. Their linguistic and cognitive attainment has tended to remain low, and their social behaviour strange. However, we cannot be sure that such children were normal when they were abandoned by their parents, and some investigators have suggested that wild children may have been psychotic or retarded in the first instance.

We do have a few more reliable case studies of children who have been reared in conditions of extreme deprivation in their own homes and who have subsequently been rescued. These accounts can help answer the question of how far an enriched environment can compensate for the effects of very severe neglect in the early years.

Koluchova's (1972) case study of Czechoslovakian twins born in 1960 gives evidence to support the argument that these effects need not be irreversible. The twins' mother died when they were born and they spent the next 11 months in an institution where they were said to be making normal progress. The father then took them back into his home but, on his remarriage, they were again put into care until the new household was formed. From around the age of 18 months until 7 years the twins lived with their father and his new wife. However, the stepmother kept them in conditions of extreme deprivation. She forbade her own children to talk to the twins and denied them any affection herself. They spent their time either in a bare, unheated room apart from the rest of the family or, as a punishment were locked in the cellar. They never went out and lacked proper food, exercise and any kind of intellectual or social stimulation apart from what they could provide for themselves . The neighbours did not know of their existence but from time to time heard strange, animal-like sounds coming from the cellar. By the age of 7, when the authorities became aware of the twins' existence, they had the appearance of 3-years-olds; they could hardly walk because of rickets, they could not play, their speech was very poor and they relied mainly on gestures to communicate. On their discovery, they were removed from the family and placed in a home for preschool children.

They had experienced such severe emotional, intellectual and social deprivation that the prognosis seemed very poor, but once placed in a supportive environment, they began to make remarkable gains. After a year they were ready to be placed in a school for mentally retarded children. There they made such progress that they were transferred the next year to the second class of a normal infant school. At the same time, they were placed in the care of two sisters who gave them the emotional security and intellectual stimulation which had been so lacking in their own family environment. As a result, in the next 15 months, the twins' mental age increased by three years, showing clearly how the environmental change had compensated for early neglect. A follow-up found the twins completely normal in their language development at the age of 14; school performance was good and motivation high. They were now functioning at an average academic level in a class of children who were only 18 months younger than they. They were socially adjusted and had realistic aspirations to go on to take a vocational training. Figure 9.4 indicates the intellectual progress made by the twins from three months after intervention began. Prior to that, Koluchova had estimated their intelligence to be around an IQ of 40 , although no formal assessment was possible because of their unfamiliarity with any of the tasks that appear in intelligence tests.

Koluchova's study indicates how removal from an extremely impoverished environment can reverse the effects of deprivation. It could be argued of course that the success of the intervention was only possible because the twins had experienced some normal nurturing in the first few months of their lives; in addition, they were not totally isolated since they had the support of one another. Finally, the twins were discovered when they were still relatively young . A less favourable outcome was found in another case study, that of a girl called 'Genie', where two of these ameliorative factors were absent (Curtiss, 1977).

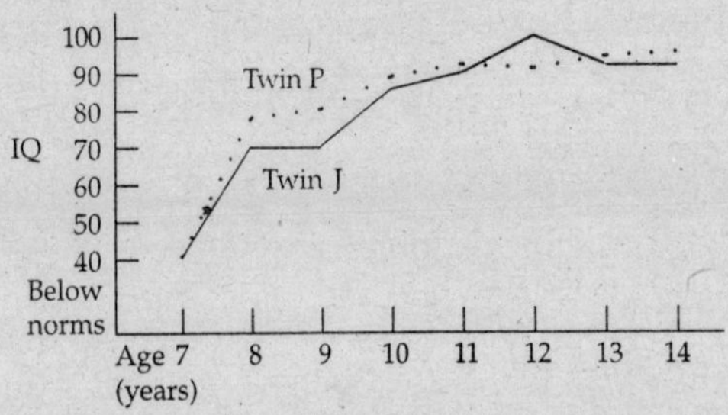

Type of intervention	The twins are placed in institutional care; they are timid; lack trust, and react with fear to stimuli such as TV traffic, mechanical toys. They tend to use gesture rather than language	They go to a school for retarded children, they learn to walk	They attend the second class of a normal infant school	They progress through normal school; they learn to ski, swim; enjoy playing the piano,	At 14 they are in a class of children only 18 months younger than they are
		They are placed in the care of two sisters who in time adopt them; they experience a warm, loving, secure family environment			

Fig. 9.4: Changes in the IQ score of the Koluchova twins, measured by the WISC, after intervention began

Genie's isolation was even more extreme than that of the Czechoslovakian twins and lasted for a longer period of time. From the age of 20 months until she was 13 years old she was imprisoned alone in a darkened room. By day she was tied to an infant potty chair in such a way that she could only move her hands and feet; at night, she was put in a sleeping bag and further restrained by a sort of wire straitjacket. She was beaten by her father if she made any sound and he forbade other members of the family to speak to her. She lived in an almost silent world, deprived of warmth, proper nourishment and normal human contact. She was kept in these conditions until her mother, who was partially blind and dominated by Genie's father, finally escaped with her. At this point, Genie could not walk, she was emaciated, weighing only 59 pounds, she spent much of her time spitting and salivating , and was virtually silent apart from the occasional whimper. When tested soon after admission to hospital, she was functioning at the level of a 1-year-old.

Curtiss (1977), a graduate student of linguistics at the time, has given a moving and detailed account of Genie's development after she was taken into care. Despite the terrible conditions she had endured, Genie did respond to treatment. She soon learned to walk. Her level of intellectual functioning (measured by a non-verbal intelligence test developed for use with deaf children) increased (see Figure 9.5) and in some perceptual tasks, such as the Mooney Faces Test which required subjects to distinguish between real and distorted faces, she performed well above average. She also became able to form relationships with other people.

In the area of language, however, Genie's development proved puzzling. During the first seven months in care she learned to recognize a number of words and then began to speak. At first she produced one-word utterances like 'pillow'; later, like any normal toddler, she produced two-word utterances, firstly nouns and adjectives (*e.g.*' big teeth') and later verbs ('want milk'). She was even able to use words to describe her experience of

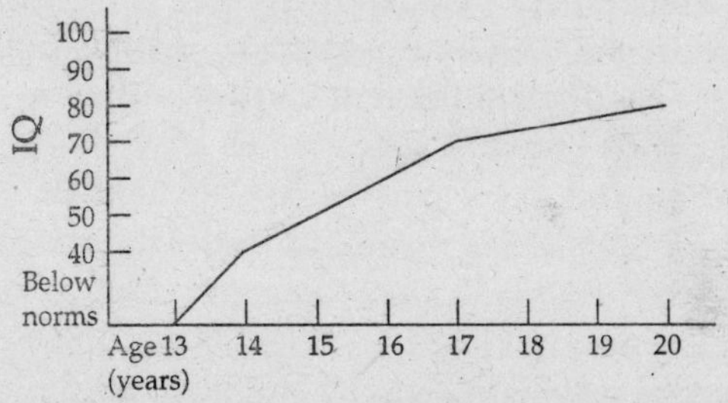

Type of intervention	Genie arrives in children's hospital tiny emaciated under nourished unsocialized silent	she is placed in nursery class for normal children	She attends special elementary school for mentally retarded children	She attends high school for mentally retarded pupils

Fig. 9.5: Changes in Genie's IQ scores, measured by the Leiter International Performance Scale (a non-verbal test), after intervention began

isolation and neglect (Curtiss records Genie as saying , 'Father hit arm. Big wood. Genie cry'). However, there were unusual aspects to her language development. She never asked questions, she never learned to use pronouns and the telegraphic speech did not develop into more complex sentences. In fact, she was more inclined to use gestures in order to convey meaning.

Thus, although Genie showed great interest in language and developed some competence, she did not catch up with other children of her own age. Curtiss speculated that Genie was using the right hemisphere of the brain for language use not the left as is usual. Since the right hemisphere is not predisposed to language, this would explain some of the strange aspects of Genie's speech. Such an interpretation is confirmed by Genie's competence at discriminating faces, which is a right hemisphere task. Curtiss' explanation of Genie's unusual language development is that if language is not acquired at the right time, the cortical tissue' normally committed for language and related abilities may functionally atrophy'. If Curtiss is right, Genie provides support for the idea that there is indeed a critical period for the development of left hemisphere functioning.

Some of the questions remain unanswered since all research into Genie's development stopped in 1978 when a court allowed her mother to become her legal guardian. At this point Genie's mother filed a lawsuit claiming that Curtiss and others had used Genie for their own personal gain.

Intervention did have a considerable impact on Genie's development, but apparently without such dramatic success as was obtained with the twins in Koluchova's study. A review of these and similar cases has been made by Skuse (1984). In general, it would seem the results of these recent case studies of extreme deprivation, and the improvements made in institutional care of young children, point to the great positive benefits which intervention, based on knowledge of children's psychological needs, can have.

The Quality of Language in the Home

One of the factors implicated in producing the unstimulating environment of the orphanages of the 1930s was the lack of linguistic stimulation. Infants were largely left to their own devices, with little interaction or conversation with staff or caregivers. Yet, there is a large body of evidence to suggest that children's language flourishes, in an environment where adults and siblings use rich, varied language themselves, and where they respond with sensitivity to the language which the child produces.

Some deficit theorists have extended this finding to suggest that children in lower social class or ethnic minority groups have also been deprived of an adequate linguistic environment in the home. If so, this might explain their later educational disadvantage. One of the early theorists of this kind was Basil Bernstein, who examined social class differences in the speech of London children.

Bernstein (1962) proposed a distinction between two kinds of conversational language, or code : These are a public language, or 'restricted code', and a formal language, or 'elaborated code'. The restricted code is colloquial and context-dependent. Phrases such as 'Do as I tell you', 'Lay off that', 'It's only natural, isn't it?', or 'I wouldn't believe it' are given as examples. These are idiomatic phrases of a fairly simple grammatical type which can be understood in context but not fully out of context (for example, with 'Do as I tell you' we have no idea, out of context, what the child is being asked to do).

By contrast, an elaborated code is more formal and context-independent. The meaning is made explicit for the other person, rather than aspects of meaning being taken for granted. Sentences such as 'I've asked you not to put dirty hands in your mouth since it may make you sick', or 'I know many children are brought up to like sweets, but I believe you can educate them to prefer other more healthy foods', might be examples of elaborated code. You know what the person is meaning, without being present. The sentences also tend to be more complex.

Bernstein proposed that children from middle class backgrounds could use either restricted or elaborated codes, depending on which was most appropriate in the circumstances; but that children from working class backgrounds could only use the restricted code. The restricted code had disadvantages, in that it 'limits the range of behaviour and learning', and leads to 'a low level of conceptualization—an orientation to a low order of causality, a lack of interest in processes'. This could contribute

Class structure of society → Defferent parent child socialization practices in different social class groups → Different accessibility of language codes and hence modes of cognitive experience

↓

Differental educational attainment by social class

Fig. 9.6 Schematic diagram of Bernstein's early model.

to the educational disadvantage of lower class children in school (see figure 9.6).

Bernstein (1971) also distinguished between 'person-orientated' and 'position-orientated' communications. A person-orientated message uses personal appeal, such as 'I know you don't like kissing grandpa, but he is unwell, and he is very fond of you, and it makes him happy'. A position-orientated message appeals to status roles of a general kind, such as 'I don't want none of your nonsense; children kiss their grandpa,. Berstein thought the latter to be more characteristic of traditional working class families.

Bernstein and other researchers provided some evidence to support their position. In laboratory or test situations differences in the speech of middle class and working class children seemed to be somewhat along the lines Bernstein's theory suggested. However, this could be either because working-class children lacked the competence to use elaborated code, or because the test environment was more threatening to them and this context did not encourage their use of elaborated code. Lawton (1968) assessed the written and spoken language of 12 and 15-year-olds from different social class groups. In written work the middle class children produced more elaborated essays; but in individual interviews, there were much smaller differences and many examples of abstract thought and generalized content in the conversation of the working class sample.

This and other research suggested that any differences in the language of middle class and working class children in Britain are not so much a matter of competence (the deficit model) as one of the contexts in which particular kinds of language may be used, contexts that are facilitating or threatening to the child (the difference model). In later writings, Bernstein himself went some way to agreeing with this view, thus modifying aspects of his early theories. He also has more recently laid greater stress on the direct effects of social disadvantage and inequalities in society. However, his early work was influential in the USA, where it was generalized to racial as well as social class differences.

A much-quoted study by Hess and Shipman (1965) appeared to prove that black children from 'deprived' backgrounds in the USA lacked crucial stimulation from their mothers in the early years so that they failed to acquire the basis for linguistic and cognitive development. This apparently objective study of the effects of deprivation on the intellectual development of children is now seen to have serious flaws in its design and interpretation (see box 9.1). Nevertheless, other language deficit theorists (*e.g.* Bereiter and Engelmann, 1966) have written about children from ghetto backgrounds as if they had virtually no language which could be of use outside their local environment, and attributed difficulties in reading and writing to the children's deficient, non-standard version of English.

The inadequacy of this sort of conceptualization of lower class black children in the USA was vividly demonstrated by William Labov (1969). He recorded the spontaneous language of black children aged 8-17 years in a ghetto area in Harlem, New York. Many of the boys were gang members, most were failures at school. Labov used black interviewers. Two examples of transcripts follow. In the first, the interviewer, Clarence Robins (C.R.) is talking to an 8-year-old called Leon.

C.R.	What if you saw somebody kickin' somebody else on the ground, or was using a stick, what would you do if you saw that?
Leon	Mmmmm
C.R.	If it was supposed to be a Fair fight—
Leon	I don't know.
C.R.	You don't know? Would you do anything..... huh? I can't hear you.
Leon	No

C.R. Did you ever see somebody got beat up real bad?
Leon ...... Nope???
C.R. Well-uh-did you ever get into a fight with a guy?
Leon Nope.
C.R. That was bigger than you?
Leon Nope.
C.R. You never been in a fight?
Leon Nope.
C.R. Nobody ever pick on you?
Leon Nope.
C.R. Nobody ever hit you?
Leon Nope.
C.R. How come?
Leon Ah 'on' know.
C.R. Didn't you ever hit somebody?
Leon Nope.
C.R. [incredulous] You never hit nobody?
Leon Mhm.
C.R. Aww, ba-a-a-be, you ain't going to tell me that.

(Labov, 1969).

Although the interviewer is also a black person raised in Harlem, in the formal interview situation he elictis very little from Leon. Is Leon'deprived of language', of just clamming up in this context? The following extract proves it is the latter.

C.R. Is there anybody who says *your mamma drink pee?*
Leon [rapidly and breathlessly] Yee-ah!
Greg Yup!
Leon And your father eat doo-doo for breakfast!
C.R. Ohhh!! (laughs]
Leon And they say *your father-your father eat doo-doo for dinner!*
Greg When they sound on me, I say CBM.
C.R. What that mean?
Leon Congo-booger-snach! [laughs]
Greg And sometimes I'll curse with BB.
C.R. What that?
Greg Black boy! [Leon-crunching on potato chips] Oh that's a MBB.
C.R. MBB. What's that?

Greg Merican Black Boy!
C.R. Ohh ...
Greg Anyway, Mericans is same like white people, right?
Leon And they talk about Allah.
C.R. Oh yeah?
Greg Yaah.
C.R. What they say about Allah?
Leon Allah-Allah is God.
Greg Allah-
C.R. And what else?
Leon I don't know the rest.
Greg Allah -Allah is God, Allah is the only God Allah-
Leon Allah is the *son* of God.
Greg But can he make magic?
Leon Nope.
Greg I know who can make magic.
C.R. Who can?
Leon The God, the *real* one.

(Labov, 1969)

Clarence Robins changed the context here by bringing along potato chips, by inviting along Leon's friend Cregory, by sitting down in Leon's room, and introducing taboo words and topics. Leon is transformed from a suspicious non-verbal child into one who is actively competing to speak. From this example it is also apparent that Leon is using a distinct dialect of 'non-standard English' (or NSE) which is different from standard English (SE). NSE used by black American children differs from SE in systematic ways, for example copula deletion (omission of 'is' or 'are'), and the use of double negatives (*aun't* with *no*; *don't* with *nobody*). These are surface structure differences which reflect a similar deep structure of meaning. There is nothing inferior in these features, and many languages use them. For example, the double negative is used in French (*e.g.*, 'will ne comprend rein') Another interview, between interviewer John Lewis (J.L.) and 15-year-old Larry, a gang leader, shows that NSE has just as much potential for formal argument and abstract thought as SE, and Larry is fully capable of it.

J.L. What happens to you after you die? Do you know?
Larry Yeah, I know.

J.L. What?
Larry After they put you in the ground, your body turns into-ah-bones, an' shit.
J.L. What happens to your spirit?
Larry Your spirit-soon as you die, your spirit leaves you
J.L. And where does the spirit go?
Larry Well, it all depends ....
J.L. On what?
Larry You know, like some people say if you 're good an' shit, your spirit goin' t' heaven ..... 'n if you bad, your spirit goin' to hell. Well, bullshit! Your spirit goin' to hell anyway, good or bad.
J.L. Why?
Larry Why I'll tell you why. 'Cause you see, doesn'' nobody really know that it's a God, y 'know, cause I mean I have seen black gods, pink gods white gods, all color gods, and don't nobody know it's really a God. An 'when they be sayin' if you good, you goin 't' heaven, tha's bullshit, 'cause you ain't goin't' no heaven, 'cause it ain't no heaven for you to go to.

(Labov, 1969)

Labov thus stressed 'difference' rather than 'deficit' in analysing the language of children from disadvantaged backgrounds. Lower class black children acquire NSE at home and with peers, but are faced with SE at school or in psychological test situations. There is no intrinsic deficit in NSE, but its difference from the SE required in the school, and the biased attitude of educators to NSE, puts lower class black children at a disadvantage.

Criticism of the deficit model also comes from a study by Wells (1983) on social class differences in the UK. He collected a large amount of data in naturalistic settings at home and in school of children's conversations both with adults and with other children. He was especially interested in differences between talk at home and at school, aiming to investigate the claim that 'a major cause of differential success is the difference between children in their ability to meet the linguistic expectations of the classroom as a result of their preschool linguistic experience at home'. His Bristol Longitudinal Study followed a representative sample of children through the preschool years into the infant school with recordings of the children's spontaneous talk in the two contexts of home and school. Wells found that there were very few homes which did not provide richer opportunities than are found at school for learning through interaction with adults.

However, Wells pointed out that differences in 'habitual use of language' between home and school could lead to difficulties. Here is an example. One 5-year-old girl, Rosie, from a working class family, already experienced learning difficulties at school because she did not seem to be tuned in to the teacher's expectations of appropriate questions and answers. But Wells did not blame the home. His recordings of interactions between Rosie and her mother indicated that at home she had greater control of language than in class; her difficulty at school stemmed from 'remoteness from direct, personal involvement in a shared or self-initiated activity'. The formality of the schools setting was unfamiliar and threatening to her, so she was put at a disadvantage in her ability to respond to the school environment. Wells argues that teachers should be more flexible in their interactions with children so as to minimize the gaps between home and school. This can happen when the goal of the task is open-ended and where there is an area of negotiation, so that pupils and teachers can share meanings and use language in an exploratory way. Furthermore, Wells argues that it is simply false to suggest that working class children are linguistically 'disadvantaged'; his observations did not identify clear-cut social class differences in the use of language by parents and their children. He stresses the need for teachers to provide opportunities for children to continue the process of learning through the active conversation which has been their experience in the pre-school years.

Compensatory Education Programmes in the USA

We have seen how, in the later 1960s, a deficit or cultural deprivation model had become the most accepted hypothesis to explain the educational disadvantage and under-achievement of lower social class and ethnic minority children. The early work of Bernstein, and Hess and Shipman (see box 9.1), combined with what psychologists had found out about the successful consequences of early intervention with children reared in orphanages, suggested that the answer to this deficit was early intervention with disadvantaged children, particularly focusing on their language where much of the supposed deficit was thought to be located. This led to a large number of programmes of compensatory education for preschool children in the USA (and also in the UK, see below).

One of the earliest examples, in Illinois, USA was a highly structured language programme for 4-year-old black children devised by Bereiter and Englemann (1966). This aimed to teach English to non-standard English speakers as if it were a foreign language, by drilling and repetition. Here is a typical interaction between a teacher and a group of children :

Teacher What's this? This is a ....?
Child Gun.
Teacher Good. This is a gun. Now everybody say, 'This is a gun.' This is a gun. This is a gun.
Children [in unison] This is a gun.
Teacher Good. [trying to hold their interest] Now, what is this? Let's say it one more time. This is an alligator.
Child That ain't no alligator. That a gun.
Teacher That's what I said. This is a bulldog.
Child It ain't neither. It a gun.
Teacher Well, what did I say?
Children You said that a bulldog.
Teacher You're just too smart for me, I can't get away with a thing. I'll start again. This is a gun. Is that correct?

(Bereiter and Engelmann, 1966)

The aim was to change the children's non-standard speech patterns through many repetitions of dialogues and exercises like the one above. Bereiter and Engelmann thought that 'the language of culturally deprived children is not merely an underdeveloped version of Standard English, but is a basically non-logical mode of expressive behaviour'. The viewpoint has since been exposed by Labov, and other difference theorists, as biased and completely insensitive to the different features of black American culture or dialect.

Another early example was the work of Blank and Solomon (1969). They did not require the children in their programmes to speak standard English, nor did they use drilling or repetition. Instead, 'a specialised language program was devised to facilitate abstract thinking in young deprived children through short, individual tutoring sessions on a daily basis.' They involved the children in conversations that arose naturally out of the child's own interests and experiences. Here is an example of a typical conversation;

Teacher	Look! I've got some nice toys for you. Do you remember what you wanted to do with them today?
Child	[Looks at doll and smiles] Give a bath.
Teacher	Yes. That's just what you said yesterday. Now, what do we need to do?
Child	Give her a bottle and then she sleep.
Teacher	Sleep? We could do that but you said you wanted to give her a bath. What do we need for that?
Child	A big bath to put her in.
Teacher	Right. Now, where could we give her a bath?
Child	There's no bath tub here.
Teacher	That's right. There is no bath tub but there is something we could use instead. What is the name of the place where we get water?
Child	The Sink.
Teacher	That's a great idea. [Holds up doll] What do we need to do first?
Child	Take off these things.
Teacher	Yes. Take off her clothes. Now you say, 'I have to take her clothes off'.
Child	I have to take her clothes off.

(Blank, M. 1972)

If you read back through the conversation, you will notice that the teacher confirms that the child remembered from the previous day what they had both planned to do with the doll; the sequence which the child suggests is in the wrong order so the teacher corrects her by suggesting 'bath' before 'sleep'. She helps the child focus on the search for an object which will serve for a bath—the sink. When the child gestures the removal of the doll's clothes, the teacher directly asks her to make the statement. 'I have to take her clothes off', while at the same time continuing with the game. Blank and Solomon found that children experiencing this programme increased in terms of IQ scores more than did control children, which suggested the programme was having some benefit, and subsequently the Blank language programmes were quite widely used.

Following the apparent success of these kinds of compensatory education programmes, a much more massive policy of intervention occurred in the USA with 'Project Head Start'. This started in the summer of 1965 and built up over the next few years until millions of preschool children across the USA had participated in some form of Head Start programme. The general goal was to give 'deprived' children a head start in schools by some form of early intervention to stimulate cognitive and linguistic development. Up to the 1960s, nursery schools had tended to be more orientated towards the needs of the middle class child. Much of the emphasis was on social and emotional development through free play, and unstructured imaginative activities. Preschool programmes of compensatory education, by contrast, aimed directly to prepare children for entry into infant school and to give them skills which, it was felt, their homes had failed to provide. Programmes were often based on the assumption that the children's language was deficient, that they lacked cognitive strategies appropriate for school learning , and that their parents used ineffective modes of control. However, no detailed syllabus was laid down and the exact nature and length of programmes varied widely.

Compensatory Education in the UK

The Plowden Report of 1967 advocated a policy of positive discrimination in favour of children from poor areas throughout Britain which were to be designed 'Educational Priority Areas' (EPAs), through the provision of more resources, more teachers and better school buildings. In response to the recommendations of the Plowden Report, Halsey (1972) mounted a large project, the Educational Priority Area Project, to initiate and evaluate compensatory education programmes in exceptionally deprived communities in London, Birmingham, Liverpool, Yorkshire and

Dundee. Each area formulated its own programme within the wider framework of the Project in order to take account of the particular needs of the region. We describe one programme which was mounted in conisborough and Denaby, a Yorkshire mining community with high levels of unemployment, low wages among the employed and a great deal of ill-health among the general population. The research team developed two major programmes in this community : the establishment of preschool education in the area (there had been none before) and intervention with families in their homes.

To establish the first programme, the local education authority set up nursery classes for 3 and 4-year-olds in two schools. Three different curricula were compared : 'normal' nursery provision, *i.e.* an unstructured approach; the Peabody Language Development kit; and the language programme developed by Blank.

The children were assessed on the English Picture Vocabulary Test at the beginning and end of the first year in nursery school and during the first year of infant school. The groups that had experienced a structured approach—the Peabody and the Blank programmes—showed most improvement. Average scores were above those of groups who had not experienced the programmes; gains were maintained into the infant school.

The second programme involved home visits. Families of children aged 18 months and over were visited with the aim of helping them develop an active learning climate in the home. Thirty-five families were visited each week for 1-2 hours by a researcher who brought toys, books and equipment and who helped mothers to play with their children. Mothers were encouraged to see the educational value of play and helped to extend their children both intellectually and socially. This project was highly successful in the sense that it was appreciated by the families involved, but its effects were not evaluated objectively.

In addition, an educational resource centre called Red house was established. This ran special courses for children at local primary and secondary schools, provided a base for preschool groups and a centre for student teachers. This too was felt to be a success although it was not formally assessed.

The other projects which ran parallel to the programmes based in Conisbrough and Denaby were evaluated in the project report. Halsey's overall conclusion was a positive one. He argued that the concept of Educational Priority Areas was a useful one which enabled positive discrimination to be made in favour of underprivileged children. He advocated the use of structured programmes which are flexible enough to accommodate to local needs and he recommended the development of community schools as one means of bridging the gap between home and school. Although he did not claim that programmes like his could fully compensate for deprived social conditions, he argued that education could play an important role in extending young children's cognitive and linguistic abilities.

Compensatory Programmes Evaluated

Some of the early evaluation studies showed disappointing results for the compensatory programmes. The first national evaluation of Project Head Start was carried out in 1969 in Ohio University by the Westinghouse Learning Corporation. This research study showed that the intervention programmes had very little, if any, effect on the children who had taken part. Any benefits seemed to be very transient, disappearing after a year or so at school. Some psychologists, such as Arthur Jensen (1969), took this to confirm their view that children from poor families had inherited low academic ability which no amount of compensatory education could make up for. Others thought there should be *more* intervention. This might mean more intensive intervention, involving parent as well as child education; or starting intervention earlier or following through into the early school years. At an extreme, this might virtually involve removing a young child from a 'deficient' home environment. Yet others—the difference theorists—argued that the whole premise of intervention was biased or racist. As Baratz and Baratz (1970) put it, 'Head Start has failed because its goal is to correct a deficit that simply does not exist'. By now the ignorance and insensitivity which many white researchers had shown to black culture and to the thoughts and feelings of black mothers and children had become more obvious. Baratz and Baratz claimed that the 'Head Start programs may inadvertently advocate the annihilation of a cultural system which is barely considered or understood by most social scientists.'

However, the Ohio—Westinghouse study took place only five years after Project Head Start began. By 1976, researchers who were following the long-term effects of intervention programmes began to report encouraging results. One major research project (Lazar and Darlington, 1982) was a collaborative study in which 11 preschool research teams came together to pool their results for a group named the Consortium for Longitudinal Studies. Each researcher had independently designed and carried out preschool programmes in the 1960s; the children who had participated, mainly black children from low-income families, were followed up in 1976 when their ages ranged from 9 to 19.

For example, one project, organized by Weikart *et al.* (1970) in Ypsilanti, Michigan, involved 123 children from low-waged black families. Half of them, selected at random, experienced an intervention programme; the other half, the control group, had no preschool educational provision. The programme children spent 12.5 hours per week for two years in a special preschool intervention programme which stressed active learning and a great deal of communication between child and adults and between child and child. There were also home visits by the teachers.

The results for IQ scores from the project and later follow-ups are shown in Table 9.4. The programme group children showed an initial increased (more than the control group) in the year or so immediately following the intervention, but through the middle school years this showed a familiar falling-off or wash-out effect. However, some long-term effects of the intervention were found in other areas. By the age of 15, the programme group scored on average 8 per cent higher on reading, arithmetic and language tests than the control group. By the end of high school, only 19 per cent of the programme children had been placed in remedial classes compared with 39 per cent in the control group. Socially too there were effects. The programme youngsters were less likely to be delinquent (36 per cent as compared to 42 per cent of the control group). Ten per cent of the programme group went on to college but none of the control group did. These findings were fairly typical of the other ten projects in the survey.

Table 9.4

Changes in IQ with Age, for Programme and Control Group Children, in Weikart's Preschool Programme

	Pretest	*3*	*4*	*5*	*6*	*7*	*8*	*9*	*10*	*14*
Programme group	79.6	79.9	92.7	94.1	91.3	91.7	88.1	87.7	85.0	81.0
Control group	78.5	79.6	81.7	83.2	86.3	87.1	86.9	86.8	84.6	80.7

Source : Lazar and Darlington, 1982

As discussed in box 9.2 , the Consortium for Longitudinal Studies concluded that early intervention programmes could have significant, long-term effects (Lazar and Darlington, 1982). The interpretation of achievement test scores was difficult because of variability in the tests themselves. However, the authors reported some evidence that children who had experienced early intervention performed better on school attainment tests than controls. But perhaps more important were the non-cognitive differences—the changes in attitudes towards themselves as learners, in aspirations and beliefs in their own competence (box 9.2).

A Continuing Debate

The apparent failure of Project Head Start around 1970 led many workers, such as Baratz and Baratz, to reject the idea of compensatory education and to replace the deficit model with the difference model. The deficit theorists had certainly been naive in their assumptions. Nevertheless, the difference model too may be naive if taken to the extreme of supposing that all kinds of rearing conditions are equally valid. Poor material conditions, inadequate housing and poverty, may well affect the quality of a child's development. Lower social class groups, and many ethnic minorities, tend to suffer from these material and social disadvantages, as well as possible prejudice or bias within and outside the educational system.

Another perspective sees disadvantage as involving both genuine cultural or subcultural differences (as *e.g.* in standard English and non-standard English dialects) which may be discriminated against in the educational system or wider society; and also more psychological deficits stemming from poor material conditions. As Tulkin (1972) expressed it :

> Subcultural influences may represent a legitimate explanation for some of the behaviour observed in particular low-income or minority populations, but these influences should not be regarded as the sole determinant of life styles in these groups. Social scientists must also consider the way in which the majority culture, by its tolerance of social, political and economic inequality, actually contributes to the development, in some subgroups, of the very characteristics which it considers 'depriving'.

From this perspective the evaluation of compensatory education programmes is more difficult than from either a purely deficit or purely difference model. They might have some part to play in the amelioration of genuine deficits, as indeed the long-term success of Head Start seen to indicate. However, they should be sensitive to the cultural or subcultural differences involved, and to the actual wishes of the parents and the community. In this respect, some of the British projects may have been better designed than many of the early American projects.

In a review of American compensatory education programmes, Bronfenbrenner (1979) argued that the best schemes are those that involve the families, since those that focus on the child alone tend to have only short-term effects. If the parents are involved throughout, they can sustain the effects after the programme is over. He recommends child care education for young people before they become parents, and support for them once the children are born, as well as a network of community support services amongst parents and other members of the community. However, he concluded that programmes of compensatory education are not effective for the most deprived groups if they concentrate only on the parent-child relationship. He calls also for intervention at other levels to alleviate the desperate conditions in which some families are forced to live. Removal of educational disadvantage requires that the families themselves have adequate health care, reasonable housing, enough food and a sufficient income. Programmes of compensatory education cannot by themselves undo the inequalities that continue to exist in our society, and should not replace efforts to tackle poverty and racial prejudice.

More recent research shows that material disadvantage, and discrimination in the educational system, remain convincing explanations of much educational under-achievement. There is plenty of evidence to show that poor children perform less well at school than children from better-off families, are less healthy and have a narrower range of opportunities in later life. As we saw earlier, reports from the National Child Development Study (Wedge and Essen, 1982) defined social disadvantage in terms of family composition, poor housing and low income. Children experiencing all three of these were defined as 'disadvantaged' in their analyses. Figure 9.7 shows the populations of children experiencing each of these three kinds of adversities separately, and those defined as disadvantaged, at ages 11 and 16. The number of children included in all three categories amounted to 4.5 per cent at age 11. At 16, the figure was 2.9 per cent. This means that amongst all 16-year-olds in Britain in 1974, there were 46,000 who were socially disadvantaged by these criteria.

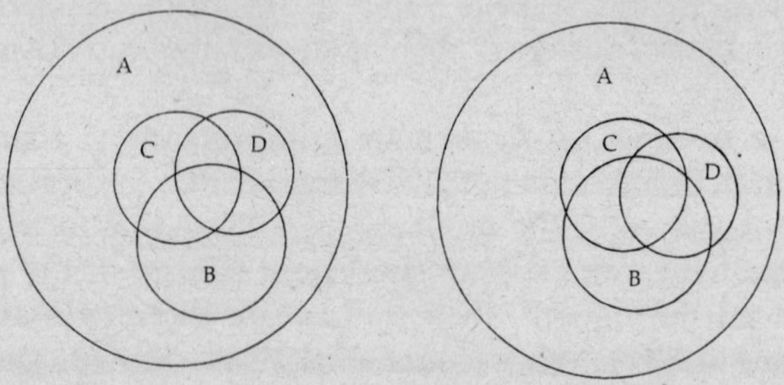

	(a)			(b)	
A	No adversities	71	A	No adversities	73
B	One parent/large family	20	B	One parent/large family	19
C	Poorly housed	15	C	Poorly housed	12
D	Low income	13	D	Low income	10
E	Disadvantaged	4.5	E	Disadvantaged	2.9

Fig. 9.7: An analysis of social adversities among british children at (a) age 11 and (b) age 16 in percentages (from Wedge and Essen, 1982)

These children had more difficulties than ordinary children, besides their poor housing and income, the fathers were more likely to be unemployed, and both parents were more likely to be chronically sick. In school these children were less motivated; at 16 only 41 per cent hoped to continue their education as compared to 71 per cent of their peers. Teachers were asked to say whether the 16-year-olds in the survey were able to do all the calculations normally required of an everyday shopper, and whether they were able to read well enough to cope with everyday needs. Again, the largest proportion of those unable to do these tasks were pupils from disadvantaged homes (Figure 9.8).

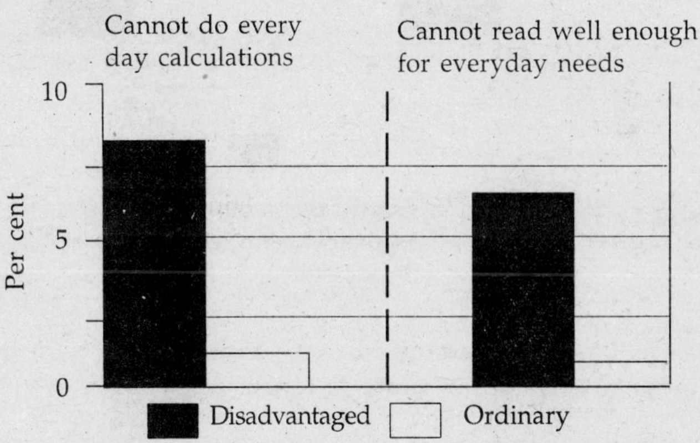

Fig. 9.8: Percentage of 16-year-olds assessed by their teacher to be without basic arithmetic and reading skills (from Wedge and Essen, 1982)

Was the poor attainment solely attributable to home conditions? Wedge and Essen argue that 'the particularly poor exam records of the disadvantaged could to quite a large extent be attributed to the tendency to enter them for fewer exams, and not necessarily to their performance in those exams'. Figure 9.9 shows that disadvantaged children, even when they scored in the top range on attainment tests in reading and mathematics, were less likely to be entered for examinations in English and mathematics than others in their year group with similar scores. The author recommended a policy of positive discrimination to

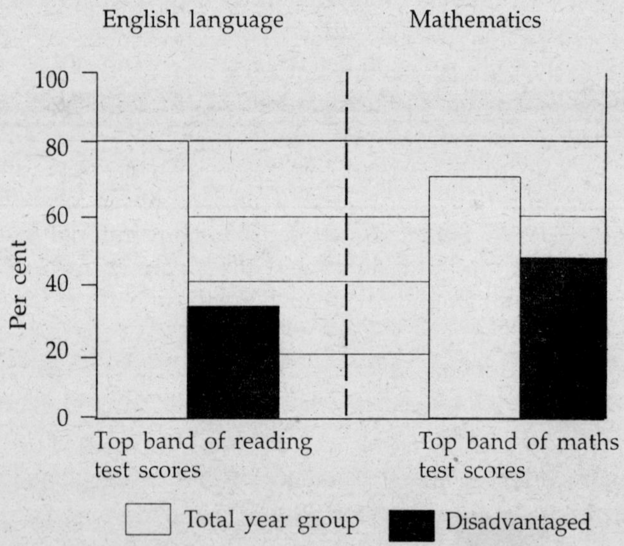

Fig. 9.9: Entry for 'O' level examinations among children with the same range of scores in reading and mathematics (from Wedge and Essen, 1982)

encourage the disadvantaged to take examinations which will give them a better opportunity in future life.

Ethnic Minorities

Similar results seem to emerge from recent studies of the achievements of young people from ethnic minorities in Britain. Eggleston (1985) carried out an investigation into the educational and vocational experiences of 15 to 18-year-old young people of ethnic minority groups. He studied 593 young people, of whom 157 were South Asian, 110 were of Afro-Caribbean origin and the rest white. In public examinations whites and South Asians did equally well. Afro-Caribbean girls performed as well as white boys, but Afro-Caribbean boys obtained fewest passes in the whole sample. The Eggleston Report suggests that Afro-Caribbean children suffer most from the system of streaming and banding which at present exists in comprehensive schools and that pupils should be assessed more carefully before they are entered for examinations to ensure that they achieve the maximum of which they are capable. As the report states : 'In schools, both at and below sixth-form level, ethnic minority pupils may be placed on courses and entered for examinations at levels below those appropriate for their abilities and ambitions'.

A self-fulfilling prophecy seemed to be operating with teachers expecting less of Afro-Caribbean boys in particular, and the latter then being alienated from conventional schooling. Nevertheless, black students and their parents have academic aspirations and ambitions which, according to the Eggleston

Table 9.5

Examination Marks in English Language (Eng.) and Science (Sci.) and Allocation to Upper (U) and Lower(L) Bands for All Asian, All Afro-Caribbean and a Random Sample of white Pupils in the Same Year Group

	Asian			*Afro-Carribean*			*White*		
	Eng.	*Sci.*	*Band*	*Eng.*	*Sci.*	*Band*	*Eng.*	*Sci.*	*Band*
Number of pupils with Eng. marks over 43	5		U	3		U	6		U
Indivdual pupils at upper-lower band boundary(%)	43	50	U	43	35	L	42	45	U
	42	27	U	42	48	L	42	15	L
	41	36	U	37	33	U	37	27	L
	39	27	U	36	31	L	37	19	L
	36	34	U	36	23	L	36	43	U
	34	41	U	35	24	L	34	37	U
	27	33	U	27	17	L	33	49	U
	27	21	L	24	34	L	31	24	L
	25	26	L	21	26	L	30	44	U
	23	16	L	21	23	L	28	27	L
	23	43	U				27	52	U
	21	44	U				24	35	U
	21	43	U						
Below 21% in English, absent or remedial	6		L	6		L	5		L

Source: Wright, 1985.

Report, are not being met by the present educational system. Cecile Wright (1985), a member of the research team which produced the Eggleston Report, has provided some evidence that bias exists in the allocation of pupils to streams or bands for examination purposes. In Table 9.5, for example, Wright presents examination results in English and Science for all black pupils and a random sample of white pupils in one year group of a comprehensive school . She points out that the allocation of some Afro-Caribbean pupils to lower bands is puzzling (*e.g.* the Afro-Caribbean pupil who gains 42 per cent for English and 48 per cent for Science); white pupils with comparable marks were placed in the upper band. Wright suggests that teachers may be making their decisions about placement on the basis of behaviour and 'cooperation' as well as ability. For example, one Afro-Caribbean girl with quite high examination performance was allocated to a lower band because, as her teacher explained : 'This pupil is not one of the pleasant Form members. She tends to be arrogant and very insolent. Unless her attitude changes immediately she will not have an enjoyable time in the Upper School'.

The Swann Report (1985), an investigation into the education of children from ethnic minority groups, reached a similar conclusion. Swann also noted that S. Asian children show a pattern of academic achievement which is broadly similar to that of white British children; by contrast, children of Afro-Caribbean origin on average under-achieve at school. He argues that some ethnic minorities are disadvantaged in both social and economic terms and that this is due to racial prejudice and discrimination, especially with regard to housing and employment. Under-achievement at school is also, Swann claims, due to discrimination within the educational system which bears directly on the children:

> Under-achievement may have its origins in the very beginnings of schooling—whether in nursery schoolor infant school—where preconceived attitudes to children's ability, racist or ethnocentric reading books and the treatment of misdemeanors can give a child a negative picture of himself and his place in the wider society. And these disadvantages become cumulative as the child progresses through the system.

As one black child quoted in the report puts it :

> In a lot of books you find lovely, pretty pictures, but the pictures are white postmen, white businessmen. You never see a black postman, you never read about black scientists, black whatever. It is always white. If you can't identify yourself with something that you are learning then it is going to kill the incentive in you to learn or go further.

Swann's solution is a long-term policy—a pluralist approach to the curriculum :

> We believe it is only through reaching a consensus on the overall task for education both in meeting the needs of ethnic minority pupils and in preparing *all* pupils, both ethnic minority and ethnic majority, through a common educational experience, for life in today's multi-racial Britain, that our aim of a truly pluralist society can be achieved. (Swann Report, 1985)

Macdonald (1989), the barrister who chaired the inquiry into the murder of Ahmed Ullah, a pupil at Burnage School, Manchester, argued the case for 'glasnost and power-sharing' to combat racism in schools. His inquiry team recommended principally that schools should create means for pupils' views to be properly heard and opportunities given for pupils to report incidents like racist name-calling and to know that schools have, and operate, an effective anti-racist policy.

Cowie and Rudduck (1991) argue that cooperative learning strategies can make a contribution to the task of creating equal opportunities for *all* pupils and fostering the kind of social climate in the classroom where learning will flourish. American studies (*e.g.* Johnson *et al.*, 1984; Kagan, 1986) and an Israeli study (Hertz-Lazarowitz *et al.*, 1989) have consistently found that cooperative learning, by reorganizing the social structure of the classroom, can make radical improvements in the interpersonal relationships amongst children from different ethnic backgrounds. As Cowie and Rudduck (1991) point out :

> Pupil roles in cooperative classrooms are quite different from those in traditional classrooms. They are more likely to be active, self-directing and communicative. Pupils helps one

another and have relationships which are more often characterized by equal status.

A dilemma facing educators is that if the curriculum is changed to accommodate to the knowledge and values which the child brings from home, there is no guarantee that what is taught will still be valued by society, *e.g.* by employers or examining boards. However we know that there is a danger that a *laissez-faire* attitude may block the avenues that help children from poor backgrounds gain access to mainstream culture. By failing to take action, educators help to perpetuate injustice in our society. Clearly this is a topic in which the values of society and the political possibilities of the times must be considered together with our psychological knowledge of the processes of children's development.

Further Reading

R. Davie, N. Butler and H. Goldstein 1972 : *From Birth to seven,* London : Longman (National Children's Bureau) is the report of the National Child Development Study at the first follow-up of the 1958 'cohort' at the age of 7. There are many useful analyses of educational attainment, health and environmental conditions in different sectors of British society. A very readable account of the impact of disadvantage is P. Wedge and J. Essen 1982 : *Children in Adversity,* London : Pan Books. This looks at the experiences of the same sample of children up to the age of 16, and in particular the consequences of living in disadvantaged circumstances. It is a disturbing book with important implications for educational policy and practice.

A collection of useful articles can be found in A.M. Clarke and A. D. B. Clarke 1976 : *Early Experience,* London : Open Books. The authors challenge the belief that the early years have an irreversible effect on later development. The book includes chapters on the effects of parent-child separation, effects of institutionalization on children's cognitive development, and the case study of severe deprivation in the Czech twins. For a detailed account of the Genie case, see M. Pines 1981: The civilizing of Genie. *Psychology Today,* 15, (September), 28-34. This describes the effects which an intensive programme of intervention had on the social, intellectual and linguistic development of Genie. A number of important theoretical and practical issues are raised about deprivation and the extent to which its effects can be reversed.

Discussion Points

1. Discussion the meaning of the team 'disadvantage'.
2. How useful are the concepts of 'deficit' and 'difference' in explaining educational disadvantage?
3. Consider the problems involved in evaluating the effects of a programme of compensatory education. How would you attempt to do this?
4. 'Black students and their parents have academic aspirations and ambitions which are not being met by the present educational system' (Eggleston, 1985). Discuss how educators might change this state of affairs.
5. What effects do family composition, poor housing and low income have on a child's school performance, and why?

Practical Exercises

1. Collect examples on tape of individuals speaking in a variety of dialects and accents. Play them to the class and discuss responses to the speakers. How are they perceived? What status do you think they would have in our society? How might they fare in the educational system?
2. Try to teach your classmates a new skill (*e.g.* understanding some technical language, becoming familiar with computer jargon) using the drilling and repetition techniques advocated by Bereiter and Englemann. Afterwards, compare their subjective impressions of the experience.
3. (*a*) Look at a selection of textbooks or reading books used in school. To what extent do they acknowledge the existence of ethnic minority groups in our society? Can you find examples of middle class bias or racism in them? (*b*) Discuss how a teacher might try to develop the pluralist approach to the curriculum which is recommended in the Swann Report.

Box 9.1

Early Experience and the Socialization of Cognitive Modes in Children

This study, carried out in the USA, is often quoted in the literature on disadvantage. Hess and Shipman claimed their study showed conclusively that there were striking differences in the ways in which mothers from various social class backgrounds operated as teachers and agents of socialization. They suggested that these differences lay at the very root of the child's social, linguistic and cognitive development and, as a result, were crucial for the child's future educational prospects. Children from 'deprived' backgrounds lack crucial stimulation in the early years and so fail to acquire an adequate basis for language and cognitive development. They demonstrated these differences by analysing the content of interviews carried out in the families' homes, and by observing the mothers as they helped their children solve three tasks in a university laboratory, namely sorting toys by colour and function, sorting blocks by two characteristics simultaneously, and copying designs on an 'Etch-a-sketch' pad.

The participants were 163 black mothers and their 4-year-old children. The social class backgrounds of the mothers were classified as follows :

Group A	college educated : professional and managerial.
Group B	skilled blue-collar workers; had gone no further than high school.
Group C	unskilled or semi-skilled occupational level.
Group D	unskilled or semi-skilled occupational levels with father absent and families supported by public assistance.

The researchers recorded the conversations between mother and child while carrying out the tasks in the laboratory. They analyzed the data on the basis of Bernstein's theories, looking at restricted and elaborated codes, person versus status orientation, mode of classification and maternal teaching style.

Based on material in R.B. Hess and V.C. Shipman 1965 : Child development, 36, 869-86.

The authors reported that the middle class children and their mothers (from group A) performed significantly better on the tasks than the others, and the difference was explained as being due to varying teaching and language styles. The lower class mothers were seen as making more use of restricted and less use of elaborated code than the middle class mothers. For example, mothers in group A were said to use more abstract nouns and verbs than mothers from the other groups. Hess and Shipman give examples of abstract and non-abstract word usage: 'The lion is an animal' shows 'animal' used as an abstract word: 'This animal in the picture is sitting on a throne' does not. The abstraction scores—calculated by taking the proportion of abstract noun and verb types to total number of noun and verb types—are shown in box Table 9.1.1. Hess and Shipman give no levels of significance so it is difficult to interpret the importance of these differences among the four groups.

Box Table 9.1.1

Some Social Status Differences in Language Usage

	Social status group			
	A	*B*	*C*	*D*
Abstraction (use of abstract words)	5.60	4.89	3.71	1.75
Syntactic structure elaboration	8.89	6.90	8.07	6.46

Another measure used by the authors used was syntactic structure elaboration, that is , the use of subordinate clauses ('when I came home...'), participial phrases ('continuing the story, the lion...') and unusual infinitive phrases ('To drive well you must be alert'). The score was the proportion of these complex structures to the total number of sentences. Results are also shown in box Table 9.1.1. The differences among the four groups are small yet Hess and Shipman interpret the results as confirming their hypothesis about the superior quality of middle class communication patterns.

Similarly, they noted differences in the modes of control which the mothers used. The middle class mothers were more likely to be 'person orientated' and to explain actions and ideas to their children. For example, they would use explanations like 'if you are tardy or if you stay away from school, your marks will go down'. Working class mothers were more likely to be 'status orientated' and use an imperative mode of command which demanded unthinking obedience, such as 'Mind the teacher and do what she tells you'. The authors also reported that lower income mothers and children were less mature in their use of concepts for classification tasks, and less successful in maternal teaching style due to an inability to give sufficiently clear and specific instructions.

For a time the Hess and Shipman results were taken to prove the hypothesis that children from working class and low-income families experienced an impoverished intellectual and linguistic socialization in the preschool years. In their words, 'the meaning of deprivation is the deprivation of meaning'. However, criticisms have since been levelled at this study to their analysis of the data the authors do not give us the levels of statistical significance and for some of the variables (*e.g.* syntactic structure elaboration) there is no clear trend at all. Working class mothers in the sample did show that they could use abstract nouns and complex syntactical structures. The results did not warrant the conclusion that the working class mothers were 'deprived of meaning'; in fact, the result could equally well have suggested that the mothers had access to meaning but did not always choose to use it.

The linguistic analysis was superficial and did not tap the underlying meaning at all, or the potential complexity of the mother-child dialogues. Labov's work was to demonstrate that interactions in non-standard English could be articulate and complex when they took place in naturalistic settings.

This leads to a most fundamental criticism. In this study no allowance was made for the context in which the experiment took place—a university laboratory with white, middle class investigators speaking middle class dialect. Even the tests themselves could be described as being culturally biased in favour of the middle class participants. This is a setting in which the middle class, college-educated mothers might well feel more at ease than the others.

Indeed, Hess and Shipman themselves wrote that 'in our testing sessions the most obvious social-class variations were in the total amount of verbal output in response to questions and tasks asking for verbal response.' This would support the idea that the lower class black mothers and children adopted a defensive strategy in an unusual and potentially hostile setting. In retrospect, many psychologists would say that this study reveals more about how the values and expectations of the researchers can lead to lack of awareness and sensitivity on their part, than it does about any deprivation in the development of low-income children.

Box 9.2

Lasting Effects of Early Education : A Report from the Consortium of Longitudinal Studies

Lazar and Darlington attempted an impartial evaluation of the longer-term effectiveness of 11 compensatory education programmes. The individual projects differed; six and used preschool centres, two were home-based and three combined the two methods. The programmes also varied in the content of their curriculum. But what they had in common was that all were concerned with the acquisition of basic cognitive concepts and many stressed language development. All were well-designed studies which had compared the programme children with a control group, and which tested the children before, during and after the intervention began. As many as possible of the children (about three-quarters of the original samples) were traced, assessed on a range of educational and psychological tests, and both they and their families were interviewed. Four main sets of dependent variables were examined :

1. School competence : *e.g.* whether the child had ever been assigned to a remedial class, or retained in grade (held back to repeat a year in school).
2. Developed abilities : performance in IQ tests and standardized tests of achievement in reading and mathematics.

Based on material in I. Lazar and R. Darlington 1982 : Monographs of the Society for Research in Child Development, 47 (nos. 2-3).

3. The children's attitudes and values : their self-concept, achievement orientation, and aspirations and attitudes towards education and a career.
4. Impact on family : the effect which participation in an intervention programme had had on the families, how the parents thought about children and what their aspirations were for their children.

Two samples of results are shown in box Table 9.2.1 and 9.2.2. (The number of projects varies, as not all the original projects had data on all the dependent variable.) Box Table 9.2.1 shows that in seven out of eight projects fewer programme children were ever held back a year in school, compared to control children. Box Table 9.2.2 shows that in six out of six projects more programme children gave achievement—related reasons for being proud of themselves in interview.

Box Table 9.2.1

Percentage of Students Retained in Grade, in Programme Versus Control Groups from Eight Early Intervention Programmes

Location of programme	*Programme group*	*Control group*	*Significance level*
North Central Florida	27.6	28.6	n.s.
Tennessee	52.9	68.8	n.s.
New York	24.1	44.7	$p<0.01$
Ypsilanti, Michigan	4.0	14.9	n.s.
Philadelphia	42.9	51.6	n.s.
Long Island, NY	12.9	18.8	n.s.
Louisville, Kentucky	7.8	0.0	n.s.
New Haven, Connecticut	26.6	32.3	n.s.
Median all projects	25.4	30.5	$p<0.05$

Source : Lazar and Darlington, 1982.

These tables show the strength of combining the results of independent studies. Most of the comparisons for individual studies are not statistically significant, but the pooled data are significant and the consistency of individual studies is convincing.

Box Table 9.2.2

Percentage of Students Giving Achievement-related Reasons for being Proud of themselves, in Programme Versus Control Groups from Six Early Intervention Programmes

Location of programme	*Programme group*	*Control group*	*Significance level*
North Central Florida	88.2	76.5	n.s.
Tennessee	75.8	52.9	n.s.
Ypsilanti, Michigan	86.2	77.1	n.s.
Philadelphia	65.7	60.0	n.s.
Louisville, Kentucky	78.9	71.9	n.s.
Harlem, NY	77.8	52.4	p<0.05
Median all projects	78.4	66.0	p<0.01

Source : Lazar and Darlington, 1982.

The overall conclusion was that these intervention programmes did have an effect in the long term on the capacity of low-income children to meet school requirements. Other significant findings were that those who had experienced a programme of compensatory education were significantly less likely to be assigned to special education. Scores on intelligence tests did improve among the programme groups but the differences between the programme and control groups became insignificant over time (*cf.* Table 9.5). However, the authors reported some evidence that programme children performed better at mathematics than at reading in relation to controls. More striking were the differences in attitudes towards education. In all groups, children's aspirations far exceeded those of their parents : but the programme children were significantly more likely than controls to give reasons related to school success when asked to described ways in which they felt proud of themselves. The parents too seemed to have changed as a result of the programmes. Mothers of the programme group children were more likely to report higher educational aspirations for their children than control mothers, and they also reported more satisfaction with their children's performance at school. Interestingly, the authors did not find any significant differences in the long-term effects of early intervention programmes among subgroups of their samples. There was no difference reported between boys and girls, between single-parent families and two-parent families, nor did family size appear to be a significant factor.

The long term effects of intervention programmes were found to be not so much on developed abilities (academic test achievement) as on school competence, attitudes and values. The authors conclude that there may be 'mutual reinforcement processes' in that children who take part in early intervention programmes may raise their mothers' expectations of them. The mothers' encouragement may in turn spur them on and furthermore, positive attitudes towards school are rewarded by teachers. Thus, they argue, high quality programmes can be effective for a number of different types of low-income families. The benefits are measurable; some of the qualitative changes are harder to assess objectively but can be inferred from interview material and from self-evaluation reports.

The quality of the Consortium report rests on the quality of data from the individual projects. The main reservation here is that not all the investigators were truly able to assign children randomly to programme or control groups. Thus (to varying degrees) some of the projects are best described as quasi-experiments rather than true experiments. Nevertheless, the findings rank among the most important and substantial in the area of compensatory education and early intervention.

10

Personality Determinants

The teacher has an obvious interest in the determinants of personality. Only by knowing where personality comes from can he decide the extent to which the personalities of the children in his class are fixed by what happens outside school, and the extent to which they can be altered by what happens inside it. Personality is the result of interaction between inherited and environmental factors, and we need now to look at the evidence for this view, taking heredity first.

THE INFLUENCE OF HEREDITY UPON PERSONALITY

Common observation has always led people to believe that we each inherit something of our personalities. We say that Mary has her father's calmness, that John has his mother's love of music, that Peter has his grandfather's determination. We describe people as born optimists or pessimists, as born teachers or nurses or comedians. But common observation could be wrong in ascribing these things to inheritance. They could just as easily be acquired through the close contacts which children have with their parents during the early formative years of their lives. Many may have learnt the value of calmness from the calm way in which her father treated her, Peter may be determined because his mother admired this quality in her own father and sought to encourage it in her son, and the 'born' comedian may simply have found that making people laugh was the one sure way to get their attention when he was a boy.

The difficulty of separating the relative influence of heredity and environment in any area of psychological development is considerable (witness, for example, the continuing debate over the origins of measured intelligence). From the moment of birth onwards—indeed from the moment of conception, since the inter-uterine environment is itself important—heredity and environment interact with each other in a highly complex way. Many of the experiments which might help the psychologist to distinguish their relative importance, such as keeping the individual in a strictly controlled environment from birth, and denying him certain kinds of potentially valuable stimuli, are unacceptable for ethical reasons (which is one of the reasons why the psychologist so often falls back upon experiments with animals), and more often than we care to admit, the limited experiments that we can carry out produce conflicting results.

Some of our strongest evidence for the role of heredity in personality comes, therefore, not from psychology but from our knowledge of the biological mechanisms of inheritance. A good, simple account of these mechanisms is given in Mussen, Conger and Kagan (1974), and all that we need to say here is that at conception each normal child, with the exception of indentical twins, receives his unique complement of forty-six chromosomes, twenty-three from each parent, and that these chromosomes contain the genes responsible for the transmission of attributes from the parents to the child. Our biological knowledge is not yet sufficiently advanced to tell us which precise genes transmit which precise attributes, but it is known that physical characteristics such as potential height and weight, colour of hair and eyes, sizes of feet and hands and so on, are all in some way genetically determined. Importantly for our purposes, there is also evidence that genes play a part in determining individual differences in behaviour.

Much of this evidence comes from studying people who have inherited chromosomal, and therefore genetic, abnormalities of one kind or another. For example, Down's syndrome (mongolism), which accounts for some fifteen per cent of patients in institutions for the subnormal, is present in individuals who have inherited an extra chromosome. Turner's syndrome, which produces abnormal shortness together with diminished mental ability, attention span, and memory, shows itself in girls who lack the normal complement of sex chromosomes. And choreoathetosis, a disease in which children exhibit spastic symptoms, self-mutilation, and extreme aggression, seems likely also to be due to an inherited defect. Finally, Price and Whatmore (1967) have produced evidence suggesting that among men who have inherited an extra male sex chromosome, there is a greater than normal incidence of instability and severe personality disorder, of early conviction for delinquent offences, and of eventual committal to institutions for the mentally subnormal and violent offender.

Of course, the fact that chromosomes are implicated in certain kinds of abnormal behaviour does not mean that they are necessarily also implicated in normal behaviour, but it does provide useful pointers in that direction. Following a similar clue, we can also look at those children who inherit identical chromosomes at conception, i.e. identical twins, and see if their personalities are any more alike than are those of fraternal twins. Identical, or monozygotic twins (M2 for short), are formed from a single ovum and a single sperm which, in the course of normal cell division split completely into two separate embryos, while fraternal, or dizygotic (D2) twins, are formed from two separate ovums and two separate sperms and are no more alike genetically than are any other siblings.

Assuming that the twins in each M2 and D2 pair are brought up in similar environments, if M2 twins do prove to resemble each other more closely than do D2 we would be justified in seeing this as evidence for heredity. Research, in fact, shows the existence of just such a resemblance. Eysenck (1956) found closer similarities between M2 than D2 twins on two measures of personality which he calls neuroticism and extraversion while Stagner reports them to be more alike on occupational interests and free association responses. In a comparison between ordinary siblings as well as twins, Cattell and his colleagues (1955) concluded that heredity weighs more heavily than environment on such personality traits as warmheartedness and sociability.

So far so good, but the problem has further complications. M2 twins and D2 twins may not enjoy similar environments. M2 twins, who are always of the same sex, and who resemble each other closely physically, are often treated consciously much more alike by their parents than are D2 twins. They are also treated more alike by other adults and by school friends, many of whom cannot tell them apart. The only way to avoid this problem is to look at instances where M2 and D2 twins have been separated at birth and each brought up in a different home. An early study by Newman, Freeman and Holzinger (1937) concluded that even here M2 twins resembled each other on personality measures more closely than did D2, while Shields (1962) found that on Eysenck's measures of extraversion and neuroticism, the resemblance between M2 twins was so much greater than that between D2 that even M2 twins reared apart were more alike than D2 reared together.

Fortunately from a humane point of view, but unfortunately from that of the researcher, instance of M2 twins reared apart are rare, and we cannot regard the samples in the above studies as large enough to put the matter beyond dispute. Taking the whole range of twin studies however, and applying statistical techniques, Eysenck has attempted to answer the question as to *how much* of the measurable personality differences between people is due to heredity and how much to environment, and has concluded that for his own measures of neuroticism and extrauersion at least, the balance in favour of heredity may be as high as three to one (Eysenck and Eysenck 1969).

More evidence for the role of heredity comes from studies which seek a relationship between physique and personality. We know that the former is genetically strongly influenced, and if it can be established that certain kinds of physique usually go with certain kinds of personality, this might argue a genetic basis for the latter as well. If we go back to common observation again, we find that people have long claimed the physique-personality relationship to exist. The ancient Greeks, who studied man almost as keenly as the modern psychologist, held that people resembled in temperament those animals they most closely resembled in appearance (perhaps there are still echoes of this when we describe people as sheepish, or bovine, or wolfish, or owl-like) while Shakespeare's reference to men with a 'lean and hungry look' as being more thoughtful and dangerous than those who are fat has passed into popular speech , along with many other examples of his acute observations about his fellow men.

Whether the modern psychologist can improve very much upon the Greeks and Shakespeare in this field is open to question, but extensive work in it has been carried out over the last quarter-century and more by the American William Sheldon. On the basis of studies with male college students, Sheldon has postulated the existence of three basic types of body-build, the *endomorph,* who is round and fat, the *mesomorph,* who is hard and muscular, and the *ectomorph,* who is lean and delicate. Personality tests with the same sample revealed that each body build seems to have a corresponding set of personality characteristics:

> *the endomorph* is tolerant, complacent, sociable, easy-going, affectionate, and dependent
> *the mesomorph* is aggressive, tough-minded, competitive, energetic, and dominating
> *the ectomorph* is restrained, withdrawn, intellectual, and anxious.

Nobody belongs exclusively to only one of these types. We each of us have elements of all three in us, and in measuring a person's physique Sheldon assigns him a score from one to seven on each of them (known as his *somatotype).* Thus an extreme endomorph might score 7-1-1, an extreme mesomorph 1-7-1, and an extreme ectomorph 1-1-7. In practice, such extremes are rare, though in most people one of these scores will predominate over the other two.

Subsequent studies have shown a similar situation to exist for women, and for both women and men it has been asserted that the somatotype can be assessed reliably from age six onwards, and that it remains relatively constant throughout life (e.g. Sheldon 1954). True, many people put on weight or get more muscular as they grow older, but since endomorphs put on more weight than do people with other builds, and mesomorphs more muscle, the somatotype remains, in comparison with other people in the same age group, more or less the same.

Unfortunately, Sheldon's findings have not been fully confirmed by other investigators. Some claim not to have found the same three physical types, while others doubt the relationship between them and personality. However, more recent work by Sheldon (Sheldon *et al.*, 1969) has uncovered further corroborative evidence, and his assertions seem, partially at least , to be well founded. It would be nice to leave it at that, and to move on to our next point, but once again we must admit to a snag. Sheldon's findings might have nothing to do with heredity at all. Muscular people may be more aggressive and competitive than fat or thin people simply because life has taught them that with their physical strength aggression and competitiveness pay off, while thin people, who find the reverse to be true, retire discreetly to their books. Alternatively, though less likely, child rearing practices may be responsible, with the fat person developing both his broad waistline and his love of comfort in response to an over indulgent mother.

Sheldon keeps an open mind on these matters, and the most reasonable conclusion is that both heredity and environment lie behind the physique-personality relationship. From an educational point of view, Sheldon's work is of added interest because correlations have been found to exist between the somatotype and, respectively, personality disorders and educational achievement. For example, samples of delinquent youths have been shown to contain a significantly large percentage of mesomorphs (Glueck and Glueck 1956), while samples of good honours degree holders have been found to show a significant tendency towards ectomorphy (Parnell 1958). Eysenck has suggested in the past that if the somatotype does give us an insight into inherited personality characteristics, it would be of use to take a simplified measurement of it, based upon height-weight ratio and chest girth, as a part of the routine school medical examination. This would give us a clue, from an early age, to the trend of a child's future personality development, and would help us to avoid making demands upon him which he is temperamentally unable to fulfill. However, it might have the corresponding disadvantage of serving as a self-fulfilling prophecy.

Another approach to the relationship between heredity and personality is the longitudinal study. We look for any evidence of temperamental differences between babies in the early days of life, when environment has had little chance to exert any influence, and then follow them through into later life to see if these differences are still apparent. One of the best longitudinal studies is that of the American researchers Thomas, Chess and Birch (1970). Taking a sample of 141 children, initially aged eight to twelve weeks, the researchers obtained ratings for them from parents and social workers on such items of behaviour as activity levels, regularity of bodily functions (feeding, sleeping, etc.), adaptability, sensitivity to stimuli, and disposition (cheerful, cranky, etc.). Results showed that sixty-five per cent of the children could be assigned unequivocally to one of three groups:

the easy group, characterised by regular body functioning, adaptability, a positive approach to new people and objects, low reaction levels, and cheerfulness of mood (forty per cent of sample)
the difficult group, characterised by irregular body functioning, low adaptability, a negative approach to new people and objects, over-reaction to stimuli, and negativity of mood (ten per cent of sample)
the slow to warm-up group, characterised by low activity levels, low adaptability, some withdrawal in the face of new people and objects, mild reaction levels, and slight negativity of mood (fifteen per cent of sample).

The sample has now been followed through childhood and into adolescence, and membership of the groups has remained markedly constant. Not surprisingly, the *easy group* have presented fewer problems. When they started school, they proved readily adaptable, joined in activities, and learnt rules quickly. Only eighteen per cent of them have developed behaviour problems, as opposed to seventy per cent of the *difficult group.*

Obviously environmental factors will by now have played some part in heightening or diminishing these temperamental characteristics, but that environment is not the *cause* of them is evidenced by the fact that the researchers have found parental behaviour styles to be evenly distributed across the three groups of children. Where these styles have been an important variable, however, is in the success with which each group of children has come to terms with these characteristics. Easy children have flourished under most parental styles (this would probably not have been so had there been any really bad parents in the sample), but the difficult children have become increasingly awkward and negative if reared by inconsistent, impatient or excessively punitive parents. Difficult children, it seems, need extra skilful, objective and painstaking handling. And the same appears to be true of those who are *slow to warm-up.* The last named children have shown a particular need for encouragement and parental support. Without it, or in the face of abrupt precipitation into new experiences, they have tended to withdraw even further into themselves. The key to success with them seems to have been to present them with plenty of new and interesting stimuli, but to allow them to tackle this stimuli at their own pace, providing plentiful praise and guidance, and encouraging them not to give up in the face of difficulties.

Thomas, Chess and Birch's findings that early temperamental characteristics provide a reliable guide to future personality development confirms the work of earlier researchers such as Escalona and Heider (1959). It puts us in a position (taken together with the other areas that we have mentioned in this chapter) to agree with Allport (1961) that what we seem to inherit is the raw material of our personality ('temperament' is as good a word for this raw material as any). Environment, in ways which we shall be examining in the next section, then moulds this raw material into its mature form. The importance of this to the teacher is emphasised by Thomas, Chess and Birch themselves. They point out that temperament affects a great deal of what child does in school, from the way in which he relates to his teacher and other children, to the way in which he tackles the learning task. A child with high activity levels is likely to become frustrated and fidgety if made to sit still for too long, a child with a short attention span may respond well only in an environment with plenty of variety, a slow to warm-up child may need repeated and patient exposure to a learning task before he becomes confident enough to be able to tackle it, and a child with a negative and whimsical disposition may become worse if his own mood is matched with a similar one, or with anger and a battle of wills, by the teacher.

Of great relevance to the more general debate on teaching methods. Thomas, Chess and Birch found that an over-permissive atmosphere was particularly unsuitable for the difficult child, who did better on clear and patient guidance from the teacher in a more formal and structured classroom. It seems probable that the slow to warm-up child might well also flourish more in such a classroom, and might run the risk of passing unnoticed in a particularly open and active environment.

This doesn't mean that we are entering a plea for formal teaching methods. Far from it. But it does mean that there is no single set of methods which is of optimum benefit for all children. An active, outgoing, sociable child may do much better in an informal than in a formal setting, and the opposite may be true of a more withdrawn or hesitant child. So whatever methods the teacher uses, he must be alert to children as individuals, which is very difficult in a large class, but which is an essential aspect of the teacher's role. We shall be returning to this point at greater length in the next section.

ENVIRONMENT

Having established the importance of heredity in personality, we now turn to environment. The obvious place to start is in the home, where the child spends all his early years and a large proportion of his later ones. Within the home, most research interest has focused on the mother-child relationship. It is the mother who normally supplies the child with much of his stimuli. It is she who feeds him, cares for him, plays with him, and decides what behaviour is acceptable and unacceptable from him. It is she who provides him with love, and with an audience for much of his early activity. It is she who takes him to school when he grows older, and she to whom he tells his problems. This not to minimise the role of the father, nor is it to ignore the fact that some of the mother's role is often shared with other adults. We shall have more to say about this later. It is simply to stress that for the majority of children, the mother provides the main human link with the outside world in the early years of life.

One way of seeing how important this link actually is in the formation of the child's personality is to look at those instances where the child has been deprived of it through maternal death or neglect. In a series of studies, Goldfarb (e.g. 1955) compared two groups of orphans, one of whom had been brought up in institutions for the first three years of their lives prior to fostering, and the other of whom had been placed in foster homes at a much earlier age. At adolescence, the children in the first group were found to be far less mature and emotionally stable than the second. Although making many demands upon their foster parents, they seemed incapable of relating warmly to them or to anyone else. They were relatively apathetic, and showed signs of linguistic and mental backwardness.

This study seems to show two things. Firstly that maternal deprivation in the first three years of life leaves a permanent mark upon the personality, and secondly, that as the group who had been placed early in foster homes seemed to be developing normally, a good foster mother is a satisfactory substitute for a natural mother. Other studies have produced similar findings. To take just one example, Williams (1961) found that eight per cent of a sample of children in care aged between five and eleven who could not relate satisfactorily to their foster parents had been deprived of mothers or of mother substitutes during the first two years of life.

What these studies don't tell us is which aspects of maternal care are the most important, or whether indeed these aspects differ from child to child dependent upon temperament. It is also fair to point out that some institutions offer a good level of substitute care, and that some children from even the worst kinds of institutions have turned out well. Our point of emphasis must be, I think, that with most children, the absence of the warm and supportive relationship which normally exists between the child and his mother (or mother substitute) makes it much more difficult for them to form satisfactory relationships as they grow older.

Before we leave this quick survey of research evidence into maternal deprivation we ought to see what happens when the child remains with his mother but is neglected by her. Robertson (1962) produces a number of case studies which dramatically illustrate the point. She found that children who were brought up with adequate physical care but by mothers who, through emotional problems of their own, seemed unable to respond to them with real warmth or affection, demonstrated 'less reaching out to the environment' (to use Robertson's own phrase) than did normal children. They tended to be docile, to cry less than usual, and to show less animation and less signs of real pleasure. At nursery school, they showed a lack of muscular tone, their 'flabby limpness' and 'clumsy unco-ordination' contrasting markedly with the 'strong sturdiness' and 'directed and skilful movements' of the children from good homes.

These findings fit in well with an earlier study by Sears, Maccoby and Levin (1957), whose research showed that even amongst mothers who appeared well adjusted, a generally cold, strict and partially rejecting mothering style led to a higher level of feeding problems, of over-dependency, of poor socialisation, and of weak initiative amongst young children than did a warm and more permissive approach. They also fit in well with studies with animals, and in particular with the work of Harold Harlow at the University of Wisconsin. We shall refer to animal studies in this book only rarely, but Harlow's work seems to have such obvious relevance for human behaviour, that it cannot very well be left out.

What Harlow did was to raise several generations of rhesus monkeys under conditions of varying degrees of maternal deprivation, and study the results. In an early experiment, infant monkeys were taken away from their mothers at birth and kept isolated in individual cages equipped only with artificial *surrogate mothers*, simple wire models provided in some cases with feeding bottles and in others with a covering of a towelling material that provided the young monkey with soft tactile contact. Harlow found that this tactile contact seemed of great importance to the monkeys. Where a monkey was in a cage with both kinds of surrogate mother, he would have to feed at the wire one, but he would voluntarily spend most of his time with the towelling one, clinging to her soft surface with every sign of contentment and pleasure. When he was challenged by the introduction of a frightening stimulus into his cage, he would invariably run to the latter for comfort, viewing the stimulus with apparent curiosity from the safety of his perch.

These findings led Harlow to conclude that it is the actual tactile contact between a mother and her child that plays the major part in the growth of love between the two, and that allows the latter to develop satisfactorily. These findings seemed to be strengthened by the fact that monkeys who were raised with only a wire mother surrogate, and without the towelling one, showed every sign of emotional disturbance and withdrawal. They spent most of their time in the corner of their cages, rocking quietly to themselves, and cowered in terror when a frightening stimulus was brought near them. They fed at the wire mother surrogate, but spent little time with her otherwise. When taken outside their cages, they showed no confidence in exploring their environment, in marked contrast to the towelling reared monkeys, who as long as their surrogate mother was present to provide a refuge in case of threat, took great interest in the toys and the building blocks that had been placed there for their use. Harlow was even prompted to conclude that the towelling mothers were in some ways better than real ones, since they were always available, and never became impatient or scolded their young!

However, no doubt to the relief of mothers generally, Harlow was forced to revise this opinion when his infant monkeys grew older (Harlow and Harlow 1962). From the age of three to five years, monkeys raised with towelling mothers turned out to show many of the behaviour problems of those raised with wire ones. When allowed to mix with other monkeys, they were unable to relate to them satisfactorily either socially or sexually. Those females who eventually became mothers (entirely, it seems, through the patience and persistence of a group of normally reared males), proved themselves to be in Harlow's words 'hopeless, helpless and heartless' at the job, either ignoring their offspring or abusing them cruelly.

What Harlow's work seems to show is that although certain things like the provision of tactile contact are an important part of mothering, mothering itself is a very complex function, and unless the child receives an adequate amount of it (what represents an adequate amount may, of course, differ from child to child), then his chances of normal development, or indeed of becoming a satisfactory parent himself in adult life, are likely to be permanently blighted. Later experiments by Harlow (Harlow and Harlow 1966) lead him to suggest that the major damage is done if deprivation takes place for the first six months of the infant monkey's life, which is roughly equivalent to the first two or three years of human life. Deprivation for the first sixty days of a monkey's life—the first six months or so of human life—is in Harlow's opinion probably reversible in its effects, given adequate subsequent care and attention. By one year of age, Harlow concludes, the deprived human child may have sustained 'enduring emotional scars, and by two years (may have) reached the point of no return'.

Evidence for the importance of environment in personality development does not come only from the home. Numerous studies have shown that children brought up in a middle class culture tend to have measurable differences in personality from those brought up in a working class one. McCandless (1969) has it that middle class standards and values lead children to espouse hard work, ambition, cleanliness and self-control (particularly in relation to aggression and sex), while those of the working class result in children who are more open and uninhibited, and more inclined towards the immediate gratification of needs and impulses. The greater incidence of aggressive, violent and delinquent behaviour amongst working class children is argued to be directly attributable to the poorer training in social control and to the greater economic and social deprivation and frustration that these children experience (e.g. McDonald 1968). Sociological research shows that some working class sub-groups develop their own sub-cultures which espouse forms of behaviour that are at variance with what is taught at school and by the law of the land. Often these sub-groups lay positive emphasis upon toughness, quick wits, excitement and the desirability of resisting restraint, and whether he likes it or not, the child grows up believing that such things are the norm until he starts school and comes into conflict with a quite different order of things.

On a wider canvas still, anthropologists have shown us that identifiable personality differences exist between national or tribal groups. One of the most celebrated of all such investigations is that by Margaret Mead. Mead (1935) found that three primitive new Guinea tribes, although similar ethnically, differed markedly from each other in behaviour . The Arapesh were co-operative gentle, unassertive and friendly, while the Mundugumor appeared violent, aggressive, competitive and suspicious. The third tribe, the Tchambuli, seemed to have reversed the sex roles, with the women doing the hunting and the trading (though not the fighting), while the men concentrated on artistic and non-utilitarian pursuits. Mead's findings are regarded nowadays as something of an over-simplification, but they are by no means out of keeping with more modern ones, such as those of Caudill and Weinstein (1966) on the personality differences between Japanese and American adolescents. It seems, then, that our social class and our national culture, as well as our more immediate environment within the family, can all influence the way in which our innate temperament develops.

From the point of view of the teacher, the particular importance of the findings quoted in this chapter on personality determinants is that the child who appears awkward or difficult, violent or aggressive, withdrawn or sullen, should not automatically be blamed for it. In our chapters on personality and learning theory, we shall be looking at how far psychologists hold us to be responsible for our own behaviour (and incidentally seeing that there is a fair measure of disagreement amongst them), but for the present we need to stress that a child's personality is not his own wilful creation. Teachers and others who are concerned with the alleged decline in standards of behaviour amongst the young are sometimes prone to blame it upon the influence that psychologists have had upon child-rearing practices. This is unfair. As we shall be saying throughout the book, the psychologist emphasises the importance of clear and consistent standards in the education of the young as much as, perhaps more than, the most ardent exponents of outmoded Victorian discipline. Where he differs from them is that he suggests that before we start trying to 'correct' a child, we first take the trouble to understand why he is as he is. Only then are the methods that we use to change him likely to be well chosen, and the changes beneficial to him as well as to us.

11

Personality Development

The first three years of life, during which, as we have seen, the effects of maternal deprivation seem particularly hard to reverse, are an example of what he psychologist calls a *critical period* in the development of the child. A *critical period* is, in fact, any stage in human or animal development during which the organism is maximally sensitive to the presence of certain kinds of stimuli. Denied these stimuli, behaviour which is regarded as characteristic of the species concerned does not develop, even though there is often a considerable gap in time between the critical period and the age at which the behaviour normally occurs. Thus, deprived of mothering themselves in infancy, Harlow's monkeys grew up incapable of mothering their own young, and the same may well hold true for humans, as any veteran social worker who has watched the depressing cycle of aggressive and violent mothering styles pass from one generation to the next will readily attest.

One question that is sometimes asked is why should children who are shamefully treated by their mothers during this critical period often show great affection for them, even though they are incapable of showing it to anyone else? One answer is that proposed by Hess (1970), namely that in the early years of life children may have a natural tendency to seek proximity to other people, and that whoever happens to be proximate during the critical period becomes the object of an enduring attachment. The point Hess is making is that this attachment is a mechanical one. The child attaches himself to his mother simply because she happens to be there. There is no element of choice in the matter. Such an attachment would have obvious survival value, and may be akin to imprinting in animals, that instinct that prompts some creatures to attach themselves to the first moving object they see during the early hours of life, and to remain attached to it through thick and thin (however embarrassing this may prove to the object concerned, should it happen to be the research psychologist himself).

In an attempt to study the influence of the first three years of life upon subsequent development more closely, Bronson (1962) has conducted research which suggests that the extent of our involvement with other people may be particularly influenced by experiences in the first year of life, while our ability to behave independently and to cope with problems may be influenced by experiences in the third. Whether it is possible to be as precise as this with all children is by no means clear. It is probably safer to go in the opposite direction and to say that the whole of childhood is a critical period and that, so complex is human psychological development, there may be great variation between children as to which particular years of childhood are critical for which particular kinds of development. There may, as we indicated above, even be children who can survive severe maternal deprivation in the first three years or so of life, and yet still appear, on the surface at least, unscarred, but they are probably very few in number.

What we must stress is that what happens to the child during the critical period and sub-periods of childhood is not really analogous to the rational experiences of the adult, which happen to a physiologically mature organism and which can be viewed by him objectively and within the context of extensive previous experience. To the child, with his immature emotional and cognitive systems, the things that happen are assimilated at a much more fundamental level, and help define, for better or worse, the very meaning of being alive. A child brought up by a rejecting mother will see the world as a much more hostile place than will the child raised in happier circumstances. The child who always has to yell his head off to get attention will have a different idea of human relationships from the child whose wants are respected and satisfied. The child who is brought up in the shadow of his parents' unhappy marriage, or who constantly has demands made upon him that he is temperamentally unable to meet, will see the world as a more threatening place than will the child who enjoys more social harmony.

Though we need not dwell upon it, since there is no proof that it applies equally to humans, there is evidence that animals brought up in environmental impoverishment may even suffer physiological impairment. For example, Teyler (1975) reports evidence that rats raised in social isolation have a thinner cerebral cortex, less developed neural connections, and secrete less brain chemicals than do rats raised in a stimulating and enriched environment. Not surprisingly, the unfortunate creatures also perform less well on the kinds of discrimination problems that in humans are normally regarded as signs of intelligence. Such physiological impairment seems to be permanent. Because of their social isolation, the rats have been deprived of the possibility for physiological growth which is only open to them during the critical period concerned.

ERIKSON'S DEVELOPMENTAL STAGES

One approach to the subject of critical periods in human development is to see each of them as dominated by certain learning tasks which must be completed properly if the individual is to move satisfactorily on to the next period. One of the main proponents of this theory in the field of personality is Erik Erikson (b. 1902), until recently professor of human development in the University of Harvard. Erikson hold that in personality there are eight critical periods, or stages, spread out over the whole of the individual's life span, and he defines them in terms of the positive learning that takes place if they are successfully negotiated, and the negative learning that takes place if they are not (e.g. 1959). These eight stages are:

		Positive *Negative*
1	early infancy	— trust versus mistrust
2	late infancy	— autonomy versus shame and doubt

3 early childhood. — initiative versus guilt
4 middle childhood — competence versus inferiority
5 adolescence — identity versus role confusion
6 early adulthood — intimacy versus isolation
7 middle adulthood — generativity versus stagnation
8 late adulthood — self-acceptance versus despair

Erikson isolated these stages as a result of his experiences in clinical psychology both in Europe and America, and they are strongly influenced by psychoanalytical ideas. However, Erikson does not propose that these stages represent all the critical learning tasks that the individual has to face if his personality is to develop successfully. All the suggests is that they are a useful way of looking at childhood and adulthood, and of isolating the point at which the child or the adult may go astray in his development. The eight stages are by no means hard and fast ones, and even though the individual may apparently come through each one satisfactorily, some negative learning will almost certainly take place, and may remain within the personality as a potential source of insecurity.

Erikson's ideas have proved very influential in the field of education, an his eight stages provide a convenient way for us to examine personality development. Let's take each one in turn, and discuss it within the context of the work of the teacher.

1. Trust versus Mistrust

Erikson accepts the critical importance of the child-mother (or mother substitute) relationship in the first three years of life. He divides these years into his first two developmental stages, *stage one* covering the first year, and *stage two* years two and three. In year one, Erikson sees all the various aspects of good mothering as combining to produce in the child a sense of trust. From his mother's love and care, from the attention which she devotes to his needs, from her ready provision of food and of tactile comfort, in short, from her consistent presence as the satisfier of all his various needs, the child learns that the world around him is a place he can trust, a secure place in which he can safely consign his physical and emotional well-being to the good offices of others, in consequence becoming free enough to turn his attention to all the other interesting things that surround him.

Denied this sense of trust, the child is likely to become fearful and anxious, and, dependent upon temperament, either to have little energy or confidence for relating to the outside world, or to feel that he must take what he wants from it by aggression and hostility.

2. Autonomy versus Shame and Doubt

If he comes through this first stage successfully, the child's urge to reach out and explore the world is aided from the second year of life onwards by his growing physical competence. From the secure base of his trust in those around him, he sets out on a voyage of discovery. Inevitably, this voyage involve experimenting to find out the extent of his powers over the people and objects in his world, and just as inevitably, this involves him in the increasing exercise of his own will. Many psychologists (e.g. Valentine 1956) testify to the child's going through a particularly negative phase during the third year of his life, in which he appears deliberately to defy those around him. If thwarted, he may show temper tantrums and be aggressive and destructive. This seems to be a necessary part of his experimentation, and a necessary sign that he is beginning to see himself as a distinct, autonomous person, differentiated from those around him. The long term consequences of adult reaction to the child during this phase may well be considerable. If the adult meets him head on in a conflict of wills, then, dependent upon temperament, the child may become increasingly difficult, determined to make his own will prevail even at the cost of the feelings of conflict that this arouses in him, or he may abandon his attempt at asserting his autonomy, and become inhibited and full of doubts about himself.

Often it is difficult for adults to avoid this conflict of wills. The child seems to be threatening adult authority, and that's not an easy thing to take from a two-year-old. But Valentine also reports evidence which seems to show that children who, probably for temperamental reasons, do not go through this negativistic phrase are frequently rated by their parents when they get to adolescence as lacking in initiative and spirit, and too easily led by others. The role of the adult should, therefore, be one of patience and understanding, a role in which the child's autonomy is respected and encouraged where practicable, and limited consistently and with gentle firmness where it is not. Thus the child will learn that the world is a place in which certain laws and standards obtain, within the limits of which he can do things for himself and take decisions for himself. By learning that control is not something that is always exerted upon him from outside, he will also begin to learn that he has responsibilities for self-control. Just as he can influence the behaviour of people and things in the world around him, so he can influence his own behaviour, and gain in consequence the rewards of adult approval which such self-control brings.

Erikson himself (1963) sums up the stage of *autonomy* versus *shame and doubt* by saying that it is decisive for the ratio within the child's future behaviour of 'co-operation and wilfulness, self-expression and its suppression. From a sense of self-control comes a lasting sense of good will and pride; from a sense of loss of self-control and of foreign overcontrol comes a lasting propensity for doubt and shame.'

3. Initiative versus Guilt

This stage, which begins at the age of about three or four, is the first one in which the teacher is directly concerned. If the child has successfully consolidated his autonomy, he is now free to find out the extent to which he is allowed to put this autonomy to good effect. Increasing physical agility on the one hand, and increasing linguistic skills on the other, allow him to communicate more fully with the people and things around him, and to give more scope to his powers of initiative. In his expanding world, which now embraces the nursery school or the play-group as well as the home, he discovers the extent to which he can exercise this initiative, and extent to which it is to be restricted by others.

Since this period of development also marks the growth of moral behaviour and of the conscience, such restrictions, dependent upon the language in which adults express them, may lead to the child's feeling worthless and guilty for being as he is, and for wanting to do the things that he wants to do. He is also likely to be increasingly influenced by the behaviour of those around him, in particular of those older than him. His most important models of behaviour (*role models*) are usually his parents, and from this age onwards, the father often becomes an increasingly important influence in the child's life. Up to now, the father may have acted as a very efficient mother substitute, but from now on he begins to take up a more distinct role, as a provider of different kinds of experiences from those of the mother, and as the source of overall authority in the home.

From both parents, but particularly from the parent of the same sex, the child begins at this time to learn his definitive sex role. Some part of this sex role is, of course, biologically determined. Smith (1974) reviews evidence to show that in other primates besides man the male is more prone to engage in aggressive and in boisterous physical activity from infancy onwards than is the female, and that this difference disappears if the female's mother has been injected with male hormones during the pregnancy. But a significant part of it is learnt from parents, teachers, and the adult world in general. Violent activity is more readily countenanced in boys in our society than it is in girls. Certain pastimes are regarded as boyish, certain others as girlish. Books, toys, games, even colours are usually chosen for a child with his or her sex in mind.

What this means is that boys and girls have different kinds of limits placed upon their initiative. A boy who engages in girlish pursuits is made to feel uncomfortable and guilty about it, as is the girl who engages in boyish ones. Perhaps because of their traditional role in the home, girls have their initiative further curbed in that they are encouraged to be more dependent than boys. Lewis (1972) shows that this dependency training in girls is often evident from the second year of life onwards, and appears to continue right through into adolescence, and Davie and his colleagues (1972) show that girls are more anxious for parental approval than boys, while boys are more concerned with the approval of other children. Older siblings also help the child to learn his sex role. Koch (1956) has shown that boys with older sisters take more interest in girlish activities than do boys with only older brothers, while girls with older brothers show a corresponding interest in boyish things.

The growth of initiative has obvious implications for the kind of education that we ought to be offering to children at this stage in their lives. Assuming that we want to encourage this initiative, assuming that we want children to develop their sense of independence, assuming that we want them to grow in responsibility, and to be capable of taking decisions and of using their imagination, then the school or play group must give them opportunities to do these things. This means, of course, having the right kinds of equipment, the water and sand, the crayons, paints and clay, the building blocks and the constructional toys, the climbing frame, the home corner, the cooker, the dressing up clothes, the books, the musical instruments and the animals. But more than any of these, it means having the right kind of relationship with children. Teachers of the very young are dedicated people, and it would be quite wrong to talk of such a thing as 'teacher neglect' analogous to parental neglect, but there is a danger that in their relationship with children teachers may unwittingly be inclined to exercise the wrong short of control over them.

Dependent upon the language which adults use to enforce them, the restrictions that are laid upon a child may make him feel worthless and guilty for being as he is. Obviously, there are many things that children must be prevented from doing. What is important, though, is that the child should not be made to feel at odds with himself for wanting to do them. But it cannot be stressed too strongly that it is very damaging for a child to be made to feel that he is wicked or bad for wanting to behave as he does. These wants may stem from deep biological drives over which the child has no control. Labels like' good' or ' bad' are quite inappropriate for these drives, and belong only to the way in which the child learns to control them and to channel them into socially acceptable forms.

This means that the teacher should always focus attention upon a child's action, rather than pass moral judgement upon the child himself. It is the action that is unacceptable, not the child. 'That wasn't a very kind thing to do,' rather then 'you are an unkind boy'. That was a thoughtless thing to say' rather than 'you are an ungrateful girl'. The child's self-concepts, as we shall see later, are immature, fragile things. He gains his idea of the kind of person he is from listening to what the adults in his life tell him about himself. If they are constantly censuring him, and thus assuring him of his lack of worth, he may incorporate this negative picture into his own self-image, and not only feel guilt in consequence, but often come to produce the very sort of anti-social behaviour that he feels adults expect of him.

The teacher, like the parents, also acts as a role model for the child. The warmer the relationship between teacher and child, the more effective a model will she be. Any discipline which relies upon harshness, or upon the constant deprival of privileges, is likely to alienate the child, and dependent upon his temperament and home background, to frighten him, to antagonise him, or simply to make him withdraw his attention elsewhere. In all these cases, the teacher's function as an agent in the child's socialisation will be greatly diminished. The most satisfactory deterrent that the teacher has for unwanted behaviour is to withdraw her approval of it in the manner mentioned above, preferably at the same time suggesting an alternative, more acceptable activity.

As far as the child's developing sex role is concerned, it is important that all school activities are open to both sexes, and that different standards of behaviour are not demanded of them. However, the teacher's influence in this sphere is not all embracing. The child will quickly learn his sex role outside school, and it would be wrong for the teacher to impose a form of unisexualism upon children that will expose them to ridicule in the home! The best that the teacher can hope for is that the child will grow up respecting the opposite sex.

4. Competence versus Inferiority

Having learnt initiative, which frees the child to *do* things, he now faces the task of learning competence, which frees him to do them *well*. This stage, which lasts approximately throughout the primary school years, is marked by the child's growing physical and linguistic skills. In a few short years he moves from the world of infancy to something approaching an adult's physical co-ordination and verbal fluency. As he does so, he vastly increases his capacity for experience. As Piaget has shown us, he also develops new cognitive skills, in a relatively fixed order of progression, and uses them to comprehend and manipulate this experience.

These maturing skills profoundly influence the picture he builds of his environment. He asks questions, he interprets the answers, he watches how things behave, he tackles problems. And as every teacher knows, he goes about all these things in his own unique way. Further, not only is there a wide variation between different children, the same child has a pretty broad repertoire of responses himself. However well the teacher may know his class, he will be hard put to it to predict how individual children will react to many of the stimuli of everyday classroom life. At times, it seems as if the child is trying out different kinds of responses to the same stimulus simply to see which one works best, and often this is precisely what he is doing, experimenting, in fact, to see how the world behaves and to determine the extent to which his own skills allow him to influence this behaviour.

Sadly, as every teacher also knows, many children by this time are already showing signs of slipping inexorably behind the others in this business of acquiring skills. Sometimes they seem innately less able to ask the right kind of questions, and to comprehend the answers when they come. Others seem to have missed the kinds of stimulation that we have been talking about in the last chapter and in this. Failing to gain trust, autonomy, or initiative—or sometimes all three—the child is handicapped in his attempts to make use of his innate potential. The older he becomes, the worse things often get. His failure to master early skills renders him less able to master later ones. Failure, like success, breeds upon itself. With each experience of failure, he becomes less and less sure of himself, less and less ready to tackle new things, less and less confident of his own abilities. Conversely, the child who is developing competence has the constant reassurance that his skills are an effective way of dealing with the world, and of keeping a balance between its demands and his own needs. With this competence comes the increasing conviction of the world's consistency and predictability, and of his own status and prestige within it. He develops a defined personality, within an environment which he comprehends. And as he watches and identifies with his teachers and his parents, so he can see that his own skills are a successful version of the way in which they themselves go about the business of living.

During the primary school years, the child discovers other role models besides his parents and teachers of course. And this discovery highlights more sharply than ever his developing competence, or the lack of it. Principally, he discovers these models amongst other children, and becomes increasingly aware of their levels of competence in relation to his own. Other children do things better or worse than he does, other children get better or worse marks, get more or less praise from the teacher, are more or less popular with the rest of the class , get into trouble more or less often. And whether we like it or not, as teachers we help this process of comparison along. We draw attention to good work, we withhold approval from bad, we assign classroom jobs, we give extra help. The very uniqueness of children makes it impossible to treat them all alike.

Unfortunately, little research has been carried out on the influence that teachers have on the child's concepts of competence and mastery. But significant evidence of the role which parents play in this area comes from the work of Stanley Coopersmith in the USA. Coopersmith (e.g. 1968) has followed a group of boys through from age ten to early adult life, and has found that on the basis of psychological tests and of self and teacher ratings they have divided consistently throughout into three groups which he has labelled *high, medium* and *low* self-esteem. *High* self-esteem boys were from the beginning active and expressive; they enjoyed joining in, and were generally successful academically and socially. They were confident, not unduly worried by criticism, and had an accurate picture of their own abilities. *Medium* self-esteem boys shared many of these qualities, but were more conformist, more anxious for social acceptance, and less sure of their own worth. The *low* self-esteem boys were, by contrast, what Coopersmith calls a sad little group, isolated, fearful, self-conscious, reluctant to participate, and very sensitive to criticism. They were prone to underrate themselves, and were pre-occupied with their own problems.

What was of particular interest was that membership of these three groups did not appear to be particularly correlated with physical attractiveness, intelligence, or affluence (all came from middle class homes). But in examining their backgrounds Coopersmith found that the high self-esteem boys came from homes in which they were regarded as significant and interesting people, and in which their views on family decisions were invited and listened to. Parental expectations were more consistent and were higher than in the other two groups, and discipline was less permissive, though it depended more upon rewards than upon withdrawal of love or upon corporal punishment. The boys praised their parents' fairness. The low self-esteem boys, on the other hand, often rated their parents as unfair. There was little sign that their parents were interested in them or gave them clear guidance, and standards of discipline were inconsistent, veering unpredictably from extreme permissiveness to extreme strictness.

These findings are of interest to teachers not only for the light which they throw on children's backgrounds, but because they can be applied equally well to the classroom. The high self-esteem boys were generally successful in what they did, set themselves high goals, and worked more nearly to their potential, because they were not inhibited by the fear of failure, or by uncertainties as to their worth. If one has a realistic knowledge of, and confidence in, one's own skills, one is less wounded by the occasional failure, less deflated by the odd criticism, less anxious for the unqualified approval of all and sundry. One is readier to participate, less overawed by things, less daunted by possible pressures. The high self-esteem boys knew they counted as people because their parents, directly and indirectly, told them so. By the same token, the teacher can show his children that they count. He can encourage them to use their abilities, urge them on when they fail instead of punishing this failure by word or deed, take a close interest in their day to day progress, share their pleasure in success. It is one of the golden rules of the remedial teacher that the classroom must be so structured that each child can experience this success, no matter how low his personal level of ability happens to be, and the same rule should apply with equal strength in the normal classroom.

Interestingly, the high self-esteem boys had parents who set standards, and applied them consistently, and who were not unduly permissive. We have already mentioned the importance of consistency when dealing with children, and this is perhaps the point at which we should give it particular stress. It is through his experience of consistency in others that the child gradually learns that the world is a predictable place, and that the skills he acquires today will be of some value tomorrow as well. The infant's sense of trust, the older child's sense of self-esteem, are all based upon the security of knowing that the things in the world around us have patterns and laws. Water isn't dry today and wet tomorrow . People aren't kind to you one minute and cruel the next. The presence of standards in the classroom, standards that are related to the individual child's potential, gives the child a pattern against which to measure his own progress, something to aim for, proof of his own growing competence.

By setting standards, the teacher emphasises even further to children his interest in them. In all walks of life, if we are interested in anything, whether it be gardening or the local football team, we usually show this interest by a concern for standards of performance. Our garden, or mine at least, will never be like Kew, and our football team may never win the European Cup, but nevertheless, within the limits of what are possible, we have standards for them. An absence of any standards is often an indication that the thing, or the person, concerned, is really not worth bothering about. In the classroom, the presence of standards shows the child that we believe in him and want to see him make progress, and shows him also that the thing we are asking him to do, the skill we are asking him to master, the knowledge we are asking him to acquire, is worth something as well.

None of this implies an absence of classroom democracy. It is significant that the high self-esteem boys came from homes in which they were encouraged to express their views, were consulted over family decisions, and were generally make to feel that they were important people. The boys praised, remember, their parents' fairness. Nor does it imply a harsh discipline. Parents relied upon encouragement rather than upon corporal punishment or the withdrawal of love. The withdrawal of love, or in the teacher's case the withdrawal of concern and of interest, are never likely to produce self-esteem in a child. He need to feel that he matters enough to be always given these things, and that they are no more subject to change or withdrawal than are the natural laws that make the world a reliable place in which to live.

At the risk of extending this section too far, there are three other factors that have bearing upon the development of competence in a child. The first is sex. We have already looked at some of the differences in personality between boys and girls, and there is ample evidence to show that these differences are reflected in academic achievement. One of the most exhaustive longitudinal studies ever carried out, that of Davie and his colleagues (1972), shows that girls tend to talk earlier than boys, and to remain more verbally fluent than boys even after starting school. Perhaps because of this fluency, they are generally more successful than boys in learning to read. Even though the gap between the sexes has narrowed by the age of nine, there are known to be more backward readers amongst boys than amongst girls at all stages of compulsory schooling. Girls are also less likely than boys to suffer speech defects, are less likely to be accident prone (at least outside the home), and are less likely to be referred for special help to the child guidance clinic. Boys on the other hand are generally better at number work than are girls, and they tend to take a wider interest in events outside the home, and in how things are made and in how they work.

The precise reasons for these differences between the sexes are not known. Girls may, for cultural reasons, spend more time in the home and in conversation with their mothers than do boys, and they may spend more time in reading because they have fewer outlets in organised sport. We have seen from the reference to Davie's work in the last section that they are more anxious to please their parents, and this again may mean that they spend more time with them, and more time doing the things of which parents approve, such as school learning. But there are probably genetic reasons as well. In many areas, girls seem to mature physically more rapidly than boys, and this may mean that they are able to tackle certain skills at an earlier age than are boys.

The second factor that still need to be mentioned is social class. One gap in the work of Coopersmith is that his sample consisted only of boys from middle class homes. It tells us nothing about self-esteem in working class children . However, evidence from elsewhere (e.g. Rosenberg 1965) tells us that working class children, especially working class boys, are lower generally in self-esteem than are those from the middle class. And if we return to Davie's work again, we find that both working class girls and boys show more of the personality characteristics normally associated with low-self-esteem, such as aggression, withdrawal, depression, and hostility to adults, than do middle class children. Davie also shows that for all the areas of competence in school which he tested (oral skills, creativity, reading and number), working class children trail significantly behind their more socially favoured peers. The inescapable conclusion is that working class children are handicapped in their search for competence, doubtless by the higher level of maternal and paternal deprivation, the poorer amenities and facilities, the less clearly defined standards and values, that go with membership of their class.

We have to be careful here of course. It would be quite wrong to suggest that *all* working class children have poor backgrounds, or that *all* middle class children come from stimulating and loving homes. Many working class homes are excellent, and many middle class homes are barren alike of material and of emotional support. Coopersmith, remember, found many low self-esteem boys in middle class homes. It would also be wrong to suggest that middle class values are in all cases *better* than working class ones. All we are saying is that the incidence of deprivation is statistically higher in working class homes than in middle class ones, and that middle class values are closer to most of those that lead to success in school and in society generally. It is up to the reader to decide for himself whether this is a good or a bad thing.

The third factor to which we must make brief reference is family size. Back in the 1930s, the psychoanalyst Alfred Adler put forward the theory that family size and one's birth order within the family have a significant influence upon personality. Adler's theory was a somewhat elaborate and fanciful one, but some part of it at least seems to be supported by modern research. Several studies, most recently Davie, show an inverse relationship between family size and both school attainment and personality adjustment. Since this relationship holds good irrespective of social class, it rather looks as if the unavoidably reduced amount of parental attention, guidance, and verbal communication which the individual often receives in a large family has a deleterious effect upon a wide range of his behaviour. This effect becomes increasingly noticeable as family size increases beyond two children. Davie also noticed that in these families it seems to be the oldest child's school attainment and social adjustment that are the most heavily penalised, presumably because, being the oldest, he or she is left to fend for themselves by the parents more than are any of the others.

Before we leave the question of competence and personality development, perhaps we could take up just one point that we mentioned a few paragraphs ago. We said that, amongst other things, a high level of *hostility to adults* is a characteristic of some children, particularly working class children, who are low on self-esteem . This might seem strange, but the reason for it is not hard to seek. If a child finds that in everything he does in the school and at home he is reminded of the fact that he is just not as good as most other children of his age, he can either accept this knowledge and become one of the sad little children to whom Coopersmith refers, or he can try to protect what is left of his self-esteem by fighting back. If he is no good at the things he is asked to do at school, he can either accept that this means *he* is no good, or he can reject the things themselves, and announce to the world, with hostility or with bravado, that *they* are not worth doing. If he fails to measure up to the standards of the school, he is in effect saying, it is not I who am incompetent, it is the standards that are wrong.

5. Identity versus Role Confusion

Erikson sees all the stages through which the personality passes in its development as really stages in self-discovery. By finding out about his place in the world, by listening to what other people have to say about him, by identifying with adults and with other children, by comparing himself with his peers, the child gradually builds up a picture of the person he is. He forms an *identity*. This process comes to a head in adolescence, and by the end of adolescence Erikson sees the personality as basically formed. In the developmental stages which remain in adult life, the individual is faced with coming to terms with, and making best use of, the kind of person he has become. The more successfully he weathers the crisis of adolescence, the more sure and realistic will this 'person' be, the clearer and better defined its identity. Should the individual fail in the self-discovery tasks that face him in adolescence, he will suffer from what Erikson calls *role confusion.* He will have no clear idea of the person he is, a prey to the many diverse and conflicting pressures of adult life, clinging for security to a rigid and artificial picture of himself that leaves no room for change.

The most important biological feature of adolescence is the arrival of physical and sexual maturity. This abrupt transition from childhood to adulthood causes all kinds of problems. It takes girls approximately four years, from the onset of the adolescent growth spurt at about twelve and a half, to reach adult stature, with boys starting and finishing about eighteen months later. The adolescent has learned to cope with the business of being a child, now he finds himself called upon to cope with the business of being an adult, and to cope with it in a complex industrial society which, partly because of the lateness of the school leaving age, is reluctant to accord him adult status. More primitive societies than ours, where the child is automatically granted the rights and responsibilities of adulthood at puberty, experience far fewer problems with this age group than we do. Sociologists have suggested that these problems are therefore more a product of our 'artificial' culture than of the biological changes of adolescence itself.

Be that as it may there is no denying that these problems exist. Obviously, they vary in intensity from individual to individual, but most adolescents find that many of the concepts which they have built up during childhood seem suddenly outdated. What they now have to learn is whether the naughty boy necessarily becomes the bad man, whether the good boy necessarily becomes the good one. Naughtiness, which once may have seemed a downright nuisance to one's peers, may now come to be regarded by them as an admirable rejection of authority, while goodness may come to be seen as a furtive attempt to gain adult favours. To make matters worse, partly because of changes in hormonal balance, many adolescents are prone to wildly fluctuating moods. Love and affection towards those around them may suddenly change to irritation and even active dislike. Not surprisingly, this causes the adolescent great perplexity (to say nothing of what it causes to the adults in his life!). Who, hidden within this confusion, is the real person?

To complicate things still further, the adolescent often finds himself taking on the colour of his surroundings. He behaves one way with his friends, another way with his parents, another way with his teachers. Each of these ways seems to involve a quite different set of values, and to impose quite different demands upon him. If he belongs to a minority group, such as an immigrant community or a minority social group, these conflicting demands may be even worse. And whoever he is, he often seems to be faced with having to make important decisions without clear guidance, because there appears to be no experienced person who really understands his position.

Intellectually, the majority of adolescents achieve what Piaget calls the stage of formal operations, a major landmark in cognitive development. As a result, they are now capable of abstract and deductive reasoning, and it is this, together with his frustration at the adult world, that makes the adolescent so prone to question things. Abstract concepts like freedom, justice and equality now begin to mean something to him, and before the realities of adult life catch up with him, he often goes through a phase of intense idealism during which he wants to set the world to rights. It is partly this that often makes him espouse political and social causes, but there is another reason too, namely that in spite of his outward assurance, the adolescent is far from certain that his opinions, particularly when they are at variance with his teachers or parents, are really correct. The doubts that he has over his own identity stretch to these as well. He is still experimenting with himself, still trying out his adult clothes so to speak, and by supporting causes and joining things he experiences a sense of kinship that gives him confidence. If other people are rebelling against authority, and are prepared to let him become one of them, then his personal battles against teachers and parents must be justified too, or so he reasons.

The adolescent's partial rejection of the authority of his parents and teachers also makes him less inclined than hitherto to see them as role models. He finds alternatives, sometimes in cult heroes like sportsmen and pop stars, sometimes in his peer group. Indeed, the peer group becomes increasingly important to him, especially in matters of dress, speech and behaviour. Acceptance by the peer group is of great moment to him. He finds himself excessively concerned to conform to its norms, excessively on show to it in all he does. He may be acutely embarrassed by anything, such as late physical development, which sets him apart from these norms. The sex drive, which in males reaches its peak at about sixteen to eighteen years of age, also makes the adolescent take an increasing interest in the opposite sex, and to be unsuccessful in relationships with it may be a profound blow to both boys and girls, and may lead to negative self-concepts that will crucially affect decisions later in life about such things as vocation, friends, life style and marriage partner.

Adolescence is also a peak age for delinquent activity. Although delinquency, as we have already suggested, is a multi-causal phenomenon, whose origins stretch back into faulty adjustment early in childhood, the majority of delinquent acts tend to occur in children who are in or near the final year of compulsory schooling, precisely the time when they are most irked by their continuing lack of adult status. Their lower levels of aggression, their greater dependency, their more effective socialisation, and their earlier reconciliation to their role in life make girls less prone to delinquent activity than are boys, though over the last ten years delinquent acts in girls, particularly those involving violence, have been increasing proportionately faster than in boys (in America the ratio of one such act in girls to every five in boys is now reported to be down to one to three). This is probably a reflection of the changing status of women in our society.

Evidence from both Britain and America suggests that the personality of the delinquent adolescent is characterised by hostility, suspicion, impulsiveness, and low self-control. Usually there are poor self-concepts, feelings of inadequacy and rejection, and of confusion and conflict (e.g. Conger and Miller 1966). In addition to maternal deprivation, parental styles in delinquent homes usually show those features noticed by Coopersmith in the background of low self-esteem boys, i.e. they are erratic, unpredictable, and contain little evidence of any genuine interest in children. Frequently the father is rejected as a role model by the son because of the former's weakness, drunkenness, or harshness (Andry 1960). The incidence of delinquency increases sharply as we move down the social classes, and typically the delinquent comes from a deprived urban area in which, as we see in chapter 13 the community approves such values as toughness and a rejection of authority.

In delinquency there is probably also a temperamental factor at work. We mentioned in chapter 13 that Glueck and Glueck have found a high proportion of mesomorphs amongst delinquents, and it may be that the high leadership and aggressive qualities that mesomorphs have, when denied socially acceptable outlets, turn to the gang sub-culture which features so prominently in delinquent activity. Further evidence for a temperamental factor comes from the work of Eysenck, who finds that delinquent samples are significantly extraverted, which again suggests a high level of aggression and an innate need for external stimuli and excitement.

Enough of the negative side of adolescence. It is not difficult to make adolescence seem a very unattractive stage in human development. In fact many teachers much prefer working with this age group to any other, and welcome the adolescent's potential for idealism and involvement. They also find it exciting to watch the personality develop in such a brief span from a childish to an adult one, and find great reward from the help that they can give to the process. Part of their secret in dealing successfully with adolescents is that they seem aware of the experimental nature of much of what the adolescent does. By their tolerance, but at the same time by the clear and consistent standards which they maintain in areas where such standards are not negotiable, they help the adolescent to answer the questions which he is posing of his environment, and to understand the limits that exist in the new grown-up world that he is about to enter.

They also seem aware of the depths of feeling and the vulnerability that underlie the sometimes brash and cynical adolescent exterior. Faced with the problem of achieving an identity in which the various parts of his personality enter into a consistent relationship with each other and are not lost in role confusion, the adolescent feels profound self-doubts, and needs the security of knowing that his teacher has confidence in the kind of person that he is becoming. The brashness and the cynicism are often no more than a defensive screen erected to hide inner sensitivities and to impress the peer group. The teacher sees through the screen, though he is careful not to puncture it, particularly in front of the rest of the class, because this kind of humiliation can only lead to shame and loss of face for the adolescent, and often to a subsequent unforgiving hostility towards the teacher.

Teachers who understand adolescents also seem aware of the continuing need to show an interest—though never an intrusive one—in the adolescent's activities. This means his activities outside school as well as inside, and in his future prospects and ambitions as well as in his present performance. Such teachers also show an interest in his likes and dislikes. They listen to and respect his opinions, they tolerate his desire to be different from his elders, and they don't make glib judgements about his personality from such externals as fashions in appearance, speech, or dress. They encourage him to bring into the classroom as a fit subject for discussion his problems over personal and sexual relationships and they are prepared to give clear answers to his questions, and to indicate the difference in the field of values between fact and belief, both of which have their place but which involve different kinds of issues.

They also understand the conflict, now often brought into sharper focus than ever in some children's lives, between the standards of school and those of the home. Any direct conflict between home and school can greatly increase the pressures towards role confusion in the child. Often the school can best reconcile these pressures by avoiding the unnecessary rules and restrictions which give the child the impression that school is out of touch with the real world. In any community, rules are necessary if people are to live together in harmony, but these rules should exist clearly and obviously for that end, and not to serve outmoded customs, or the prejudices of one small group. The more democratic the process that can be used to arrive at rules, the more point everyone sees in them, and the more likely they are to be obeyed. Bad rules, which are inevitably ignored as soon as those responsible for them have their backs turned, lead only to a loss of respect for authority, and consequent flouting of many other rules that are there for a much better purpose.

There is some evidence that by a policy of rejecting the least able children in its own midst, a school can also cause its own kinds of conflicts and sub-cultures. Hargreaves (1967) and Lacey (1970) discovered (independently of each other) that secondary modern and grammar schools were instrumental in creating similar 'A' and 'C' stream mentalities, the former characterised by acceptance of the school, of its staff, and of its values, and the latter by their rejection. This is not the place to enter the debate about streaming, which has implications beyond those associated with personality, but the point is that where schools feel the need to separate children by ability, this should be done in a way which protects the self-esteem of the less able as well as of the more able.

Finally, teachers who work well with adolescents seem to understand that it is no good looking for the obedience and dependency in them which they had when younger. It is a failure to show this understanding that leads to many of the conflicts which parents have with adolescent sons and daughters. Refusal to accept that the adolescent is growing up only makes him assert his right to independence all the more strongly. Teachers who recognise this right take care to give him every reasonable opportunity to demonstrate his growing ability to take adult responsibility. Such opportunities are of far more value than any number of homilies directed at him by the adults in his life on the *need* for him to develop this responsibility. Too often when we lecture adolescents, and indeed younger children, on the desirability of their acquiring a maturer approach to life, we mean that they should acquire it only when it suits us, and at other timers revert to the subordination of an earlier stage in their development. This is misguided practice, and perhaps if we all realised it we would have less reason in education to bemoan the 'irresponsibility' of the young.

6. Intimacy versus Isolation

This stage, which occurs in early adulthood, is more the direct concern of teachers involved in higher and further education, but it is of relevance to all teachers in that it is the culmination of the years of childhood and adolescence. Intimacy is the ability to have full and satisfying personal relationships with other people of both sexes, relationships which culminate in marriage, in life-long friendships, and in close and sustaining contacts with the people with whom one works, and with the people in one's community.

Perhaps the best way of discussing this stage is to merge it with the wider discussion of the mature personality, that is with a discussion of those personal qualities that mark people out as having attained a balance and a richness in their development that allows them to live full and satisfying lives. Erikson has himself written widely on the mature personality, but the psychologist who has centred most attention on it is probably

Gordon Allport (1897-1967). Allport (1961) sees the acquisition of a real sense of personal identity in adolescence as meaning that the individual has developed from being essentially a number of different people to being a single, or whole person. In the early stages of our personality development, Allport sees us as possessing a wide range of *traits,* such as friendliness, honesty, bookishness, which we use somewhat inconsistently and arbitrarily in our dealings with other people (e.g. we are honest with our friends but not with our teachers, bookish at school but not at home). As we grow older, many of these coalesce into a smaller number of better integrated units which Allport calls *selves* (e.g. we have one recognisable self for school, another for home), and, with the discovery of identity, these come together in turn to form the single unit of the mature personality.

To Allport, the mature personality is, therefore, characterised by co-ordination and consistency. If a person is mature, we know that whatever the situation in which we meet him he remains identifiably the same person (within reasonable limits at least; every personality may break down under extreme stress). He is not honest at home and dishonest at work (or honest and dishonest at both home and work in different circumstances), or pious at church and amoral at the local club, or humorous with his friends and a wet blanket with his family, or confident with men but a pitiful stammerer with women. He does not, in fact, still have several different selves, each one of them capable of its own separate codes of behaviour and of values. An extreme example of people who had failed to achieve this mature integration were the nazi concentration camp officers who were reputedly good husbands and fathers in the evenings, but spent their days sending innocent people to a hideous death.

Of course, this is not all there is to maturity. Usually when we talk of the mature personality we imply a value judgement in that we expect his integrated personality to have qualities that make him desirable to the community as a whole. It is possible, in theory at least, for a person to be entirely integrated in doing evil, which might mean that he meets Allport's criterion, but is hardly the sort of person we would want to have as a neighbour or as a teacher of children. We also usually think of the mature person as being an effective person, as being good at getting things done within his chosen field. This is supported by such studies as those of Barron (1954), who found that graduate students rated most highly on maturity of personality by their teachers seemed to be particularly good at organising their work, at judging themselves and others, and at resisting stress. They also seemed to be high on integrity, and to be energetic, adaptable, resourceful, and well adjusted.

Allport recognises the need for a definition of maturity which takes into account these questions of value and, in summarising the views of a number of psychologists on the subject, he suggests that the mature personality manifests the following qualities:

1. *An extended sense of self,* that allows him to transcend the self-centredness of childhood, and to identify with the concerns and problems of others.
2. *A warm relationship with others,* that allows him to love them for their own sakes as well as for his own.
3. *Emotional security,* that allows him to withstand the problems and fears of daily life.
4. *Self-insight,* that allows him to laugh at himself without loss of self-esteem. (There is *some* correlation between self-insight and intelligence, though the one by no means necessarily implies the other.)
5. *A realistic orientation towards the world,* that allows him to exercise sound judgement of people and things and to take necessary decisions.
6. *A unifying philosophy of life,* either religious or humanistic, that allows him to interpret life's purpose and to decide on long-term goals and on standards of behaviour.

This makes the mature person sound like a paragon of perfection, but this is misleading. To feel a respect for others, for example, does not stop him from sometimes feeling angry or impatient with them. Sound judgement does not mean that he never makes a mistake. Emotional security does not mean he never feels depressed or inadequate. Self-insight does not mean he never feels depressed or inadequate. Self-insight does not mean he never feels surprised at himself, or never feels disappointment at failing to achieve a cherished ambition. The basic point about maturity is that the mature person is not constantly at the mercy of his own weaknesses, or constantly vulnerable to people and events in the world outside. He has a degree of self-knowledge and of self-control that allow him to make the most of himself, a respect for those close to him that allows him to love them without smothering them, a tolerance for the world in general that allows him to respect the rights of others, and a sense of purpose and of aspiration that give substance and direction to his life.

Many of these qualities may not develop of course, until the individual is well past early adulthood. Erikson still sees the personality as having to face major problems of learning and of adaptation in middle and later life. He describes these as *generativity,* which is the ability to innovate, to bring in new ideas, and, in particular, to influence the next generation through parenthood and teaching, and as *self-acceptance,* that is the ability to review one's life in old age with a sense of fulfilment, with a knowledge that one has done what one could to enhance the lives of others and to use productively whatever abilities one was fortunate enough to possess.

12

Learning Theory and Personality

We must now look at the contributions that the last of the three main forces in psychology, behaviourism, has made to the study of personality. It claims to be the most objective and scientific of the three, since it concerns itself not with what people have to tell you about their own states of mind, but with what they actually *do* (i.e. with their behaviour). It rejects all reference to the sort of mechanisms that psychoanalysis and humanistic psychology see as underlying personality, and has shown no particular enthusiasm even for such devices as attitude measurement. The trouble with all these things, say the behaviourists, is that they rely largely upon pure theory. Nobody can observe the unconscious at work (or even test its workings as we can with something like remembering), and no one knows for sure whether the attitudes that people express have very much to do with their subsequent behaviour towards the object of these attitudes.

On the other hand, under controlled laboratory conditions at least, we can all agree on a man's (or an animal's) behaviour. Does he respond quickly to a particular stimulus, or does he take a long time? Do his physiological responses (raised heart rate, blood pressure, etc.) show him to be tense and angry, or calm and relaxed? Does he take three tries before he picks up a simple learning task, or does he take four or five? It is these things, say the behaviourists, that turn psychology into a science, not the speculations of men like Freud and Maslow. And of course, as to Kelly's first principle that someone with personality problems might just know what is wrong with himself, they would answer that we have no way of knowing whether he does or not until we have observed his behaviour carefully enough.

Behaviourism was first proposed by the American psychologist J. B. Watson in 1913, and has enjoyed great popularity in the USA and, to a somewhat lesser extent, Europe. It refers to units of behaviour as *responses,* and sees these as consisting partly of innate reflexes (e.g. sucking, crying), but mostly of learnt reactions. It is this stress upon learning that causes behaviourism to be known by its alternate title of *learning theory,* which we have used as our heading for this chapter. To understand man, say the behaviourists, one has to study the way in which he acquires his repertory of responses. That is all.

Learning theory is much too extensive to be discussed fully here, We shall simply look at its main two sub-divisions, *classical conditioning* and *operant conditioning.*

Classical Conditioning

Classical conditioning, first discovered by the Russian physiologist Ivan Pavlov (1839-1936), occurs when an innate reflex (called unconditioned response or UR) becomes elicited not just by its natural or unconditioned stimulus (US) but by an unnatural stimulus (a conditioned stimulus or CS) as well. This happens if the CS and the US occur close together frequently. Thus, if a light is flashed (CS) every time we get an electric shock (US), the wince (UR) normally elicited by the shock in time becomes elicited by the light alone. The wince is now called a *conditioned response.*

Pavlov believed that the whole of the complex activity of man is simply a collection of conditioned responses. The baby's love for his mother, for example, would thus be explained by the fact that the mother is present as a CS every time the baby receives his milk (US). Over a period of time, the pleasure which is the UR to the milk becomes elicited as a conditioned response (CR) by the mother as well, even when it is not feeding time. Evidence that stimulus-response bonds, as they are called, of this kind can be set up was produced by Watson himself (Watson and Rayner

1919), who found that the natural fear which a baby boy called Albert had for loud noises could become associated as well with the previously innocuous stimulus of a white rat, if rat and noise were produced together often enough. Through what Watson called *stimulus generalisation*, it was then found that Albert had also become afraid of anything that looked like a white rat, such as a white rabbit or even Watson himself in a long white Santa Claus beard.

It is now known, of course, that although some behaviour can be explained through classical conditioning, it is inadequate as an explanation of all behaviour. The learning which it accounts for seems to be largely confined to responses which occur in the autonomic nervous system (i.e. to involuntary rather than to consciously mediated responses), and in any case, conditioned responses tend to weaken and disappear (become extinct) as soon as the US and the CS finally cease to occur together. Behaviourism, nowadays, tends therefore to pay much more attention to operant conditioning.

Operant Conditioning

Operant conditioning differs chiefly from classical conditioning in that instead of concentrating upon the stimulus which *precedes* a response, it concentrates upon the consequences that follow *after* the response. Operant conditioning theory holds that if a response has pleasant consequences (is 'rewarded' or 'reinforced') it tends to be repeated, if it has unpleasant consequences (is 'punished' in some way), it tends not to be. This principle was originally stated, at somewhat greater length, by one of the pioneers of behaviourism, the American psychologist E.L. Thorndike (1874-1949) in his 'Law of Effect', but it is now particularly associated with the work of perhaps the best known of all American psychologists, B.F. Skinner (b. 1904).

Skinner, in a number of publications (most recently 1972), takes up Thorndike's view that since human behaviour most frequently occurs in the absence of any precedent stimulus, classical conditioning, even if it was not subject to extinction and covered learning in the central nervous system as well as in the autonomic, could not explain most of human behaviour. He also maintains that we should give up the idea that behaviour is prompted by instincts, needs, or drives such as those suggested by the psychoanalysts or the humanists. Instead, we should 'shift to the environment a causal role previously assigned to a person's feelings, states of mind, purposes, or other attributes' (1972). This does not mean that Skinner rejects the idea of innate differences. People differ from each other in their physiological endowments, and therefore must differ from each other in the level of the responses which they make to the environment. What he does reject is the idea that man's habits, his likes and dislikes, his beliefs, his moral judgements, in sum his personality, is anything more than a set of learned responses to the particular environmental circumstances he has encountered during his life to date. Thus the belief that man has free will, or autonomy, or control over his individual destiny, is an illusion.

Skinner has amassed a great deal of evidence, working with both men and with animals, in support of this view. The details of this evidence belong more to a book on learning than to one on personality, but we can see how they can be applied to personality if we take the example of a child who is consistently misbehaving in class. Skinner would say that the child is misbehaving not because he 'feels' like it (i.e. as the result of a freely taken decision), but because of the experiences that he has had in his life so far. These experiences have rewarded (reinforced) his disruptive behaviour, have stamped it in and make it a part of his personality. He may be a child with an unstimulating home background, who has tended, only to be reinforced with adult attention when he behaves badly. Good behaviour goes unnoticed, and therefore has tended to disappear from his behavioural repertoire. Or he may be a friendless child, who is only rewarded with the approval of his peers when he enlivens things by cheeking the teacher. Or he may be a child who is backward in class and who is largely ignored by the teacher unless he becomes disruptive.

If we take the opposite example of a child who behaves well, Skinner would say that this good behaviour is a result of the frequent and sympathetic adult attention with which such behaviour has been reinforced at home. Where we have a well behaved child who, for example, becomes difficult on the birth of a baby sibling, Skinner would deny that this has anything to do with regression and would say it is simply because the mother is now too busy to notice him when he is good, and only turns her attention to him when he does something wrong.

Note that what Skinner is saying here is that the very *fact* of adult attention can be rewarding to a child, even though it be angry attention. Adults often assume that simply because they are speaking crossly to a child he is actually experiencing punishment, whereas in truth the real punishment might be to ignore him altogether. By speaking crossly to him, one is at least acknowledging his existence, and, by showing him that he is important enough to make adults angry, one is demonstrating that he has power over the immediate environment. We shall return to this point later in the chapter, but what Skinner is in effect saying is that often we make children's behaviour worse by inadvertently reinforcing it when we imagine ourselves to be doing the opposite.

It can probably be deduced from what we have said already that Skinner's attitude to psychoanalysis and humanistic psychology is a very antagonistic one. He sees on reason for postulating the existence of id, ego, or super-ego, or meta needs, or ego defence mechanisms, or for the various processes that psychoanalysts and humanistic psychologists advance to account for the existence of neuroses. People become neurotic, Skinner argues, because their environment makes them so, in particular through reinforcing them in a haphazard and unpredictable way, and by handing our harsh punishments. It is quite possible to make a laboratory animal 'neurotic' by this kind of treatment, and no one suggests that laboratory animals have id, ego and super-ego.

Skinner is very much less at odds with Eysenck and with the nomothetic approach to personality than he is with the psychoanalysts and humanists (and indeed Eysenck is very much less at odds with Skinner). He would accept Eysenck's attempt to relate the personality to such physiological systems as the hypothalamus and the reticular formation areas of the brain. He would also accept Eysenck's view that a large percentage of attributes like anxiety and introversion may be inherited, if by inherited we mean that some people develop the conditioned responses that are described as 'anxiety' and 'introversion' more readily than do others.

Of course, Skinner does not pretend that is always possible

to point to the precise cause in a person's environment of each item of his present behaviour. The consequences of a particular learning experience, especially in a complex society such as ours, are often long delayed. But the rule remains that all behaviour is caused. Thus when we observe an activity that seems to us to be spontaneous and creative, we are simply witnessing the consequences of a piece of experience that may have taken place much earlier. 'Consequences', says Skinner (1972) 'take over a role previously assigned to an antecedent creative mind.' Embedded in this line of reasoning is Skinner's emphasis upon *performance* as well as upon learning. We are learning new things all the time, but this learning may not be very apparent in our performance until it is suddenly reinforced by our environment. Thus a child may learn to discriminate between musical notes, but show little sign of this skill until he is suddenly re-inforced by teacher approval when he starts taking music lessons.

Skinner recognises the existence of both primary and secondary re-inforcers. The former (e.g. food, warmth, shelter) have intrinsic value, the latter (e.g. money) have not, but have become desirable through their association with the former. In our complex society, a great deal of social behaviour is the result of secondary re-inforcement. Since a school is a particularly artificial environment, in which children have to learn in a few years information that has taken centuries of research and discovery, Skinner accepts that it cannot help but rely upon secondary re-inforcement (such as teacher approval, good grades, examination success). Usually these secondary re-inforcers are built into what Skinner calls 'chains,' with each re-inforcer associated with the next and so on back to a primary re-inforcer. Thus a child values good marks (secondary re-inforcer) because they are associated with parental approval (secondary re-inforcer) which is associated with improved creature comforts (primary re-inforcer). As might be predicted from his extreme environmentalist viewpoint, Skinner places great emphasis upon the importance of education, and deplores the fact that, partly through teachers' misapplication of re-inforcers, it is generally so inefficient.

We will now look at another set of learning theories, somewhat related to operant conditioning by virtue of their similar emphasis upon the environment, namely social learning theories.

Social Learning Theories

Social learning theories are associated particularly with the work of the Canadian psychologist Albert Bandura (b. 1925). Bandura has been much influenced by the behaviourists, but he differs from them in insisting that much behaviour takes place in the absence of any kind of re-inforcement at all. The child, he claims, has an innate propensity for copying the behaviour of others, even when he receives no reward for doing so. Much learning, therefore, takes place by *imitation* (or *modelling*). It is strange that before the work of Bandura and of other social learning theorists, psychologists had tended to neglect imitation as an important element in shaping human behaviour.

Imitation, Bandura claims (e.g. 1969), explains both broad culture movements (fashions, fads, mass hysteria, etc.) and the individual socialisation of the child. The child's personality is, therefore, largely an imitation, within the limits laid down by innate differences, of those around him. In a sense, Bandura helps span a small part of the gap between the behaviourists and the psychoanalysts, since he would accept the latter's emphasis upon the child's acquisition of role bahaviour from his parents, though he has shown little enthusiasm for the idea of various systems within the personality, or for meta needs. As for self-actualisation, Bandura would claim that the child's basic need to copy those around him is sufficient explanation of the origin of many of the goals and aims that he develops in life.

Bandura's emphasis upon the possibility of learning taking place in the absence of re-inforcement does not mean that he sees the latter as unimportant. A child is more likely to imitate a model who is being rewarded for his actions than one who is being punished, and once having imitated his behaviour, this imitation is more likely to persist if it is rewarded in its own turn. Bandura also accepts Skinner's distinction between learning and performance. A child need not necessarily *perform* the actions of another at the moment he is learning them. He can store up these actions mentally and produce them at an appropriate time later on, as when a boy watches a cowboy film and next day at school acts out the role of the hero.

Bandura also considers that the more prestigious the model, the more likely the child will be to imitate his behaviour (hence violence on the football field by a star player is more likely to spread to the watching crowd than violence by a lesser known one). Since this imitation goes on in the absence of rewards and punishments, this means that the child may well be learning many things from a prestigious model like, for example, the teacher, which the model himself has no idea he is teaching. This is particularly true of emotions. The child may have all kinds of emotional behaviour modelled unwittingly for him by the teacher, such as sympathy towards those in difficulties, or impatience and anger. Bandura has made a special study of aggression, which he feels lends itself especially well to a social learning theory interpretation. In a number of research studies, he has shown that children who witness adult aggression are much more likely to behave aggressively themselves than are children who do not. It is as if the adult aggression sanctions similar behaviour in children. And of course if the children find that this aggression pays off in helping them to get their own way, then it may become an established part of their behaviour.

Innate differences and the child's own previous experiences will obviously affect the extent to which social learning takes place. Jakubczak and Walters (1959) show that dependent children imitate prestige figures more readily than do those who are less dependent, and that timid or anxious children take over fearful responses vicariously more frequently than do secure and confident ones. Similarly, children who have learnt to respond warmly to teachers in the past will be far readier to take them as models in the present, while someone who has learnt, e.g. to despise the opposite sex, will be less likely to accept a member of that sex as a model than will someone who has learnt to respect it. Similarly again, a child who has seen someone behaving ineffectually in the past, or receiving frequent punishment, will be less likely to accept them as a model than he will be to accept someone who has been behaving with success.

Techniques for Modifying Children's Behaviour

If, as the behaviourists believe, personality problems such as neuroticism or maladjustment are simply caused by the wrong kinds of stimulus-response bonds or by the wrong kinds of reinforcement, it follows that if we want to cure people of these problems, all we have to do is to break these bonds or to reverse this reinforcement. This, indeed, is the principle behind *behaviour therapy*, which is the behaviouristic equivalent of psychoanalysis or Rogerian therapy. It has the advantage of extreme simplicity, and in certain circumstances at least, it seems to work. To see how it does, perhaps we could first go back to Watson's experiment with little Albert. Once having conditioned Albert to feel fear for the white rat by associating it with the unpleasant stimulus of the loud noise, we can remove this fear (in other words, *de-sensitise*, Albert) by now associating the white rat with something pleasant. This means presenting the rat to Albert along with something of which he is very fond, say jelly. Each time Albert sees the rat, he gets his plate of jelly. This has to be done discreetly, with a respectable distance at first between the rat and Albert while he eats his jelly, otherwise his aversion for the former could just end up by being associated with the latter.

Similarly, by *aversion* therapy, it is possible to turn somebody against something (a bad habit, a deviant activity), just as Albert was turned against the rat in the first place, by pairing it with something unpleasant. Thus, for example, a smoker can be given an electric shock every time he opens his cigarette packet, or a finger nail biter can have his nails coated with a foul tasting substance.

De-sensitisation and aversion therapy have been used extensively to treat a wide range of anxieties, phobias, and deviances. It will be noted that they waste no time probing the subject's previous experience to find the exact situation that gave rise to his unwanted behaviour. Nor do they see this behaviour as a symptom of some deeper, unconscious malaise. They see the symptom and the anxiety, or phobia or whatever it happens to be, as essentially the same thing, with the cure of the former necessarily also curing the latter.

De-sensitisation and aversion therapy are based, of course, on classical conditioning techniques. The operant conditioning approach to behaviour therapy is somewhat broader. It focuses upon consistently re-inforcing the wanted behaviour, while at the same time, if possible, withholding reinforcement from the unwanted. Thus to cure a man of smoking by operant conditioning, we would not rely upon the, often impractical business of associating his smoking with something unpleasant, we would concentrate instead on rewarding him for *not* smoking. As long as our reinforcement of his non-smoking is consistent and thorough, the operant conditioning theorists hold that this will be a much more effective way of getting him to stop smoking than by treating his smoking as a sign of oral fixation (as the Freudian might), or by giving him any number of lectures on the evils of smoking.

Social learning theorists accept this operant conditioning approach, but also lay stress upon providing the subject with models of the reformed behaviour we want from him. Thus, to continue with our example of smoking, the smoker would be exposed to prestigious non-smokers, instead of, as happens more frequently at the moment, to prestigious smokers.

All the above techniques, and particularly those associated with operant conditioning and social learning, are now in wide use, especially in the USA. Since they are used to change all kinds of behaviour, and not just the behaviour of those in need of therapy, the collective title of *behaviour modification* is usually assigned to them. Our interest in these techniques lies chiefly in what they can achieve in the classroom, and it is in this context that both Skinner and Bandura have put forward many of their ideas. Perhaps we can best start by taking the example of an isolate child in the infant school, who refuses to mix with the other children. The natural reaction of the sympathetic teacher is to spend much of her time approaching him solicitously and attempting to draw him into group activities. The net result of all this is that often by the end of term he is no more sociable than he was at the beginning. The teacher may redouble her efforts the following term, but with no better results. What has gone wrong? Well, argue the exponents of behaviour modification, the teacher has actually been *re-inforcing the* child's isolate behaviour. She has rewarded him for being an isolate by paying attention to him every time he is on his own. And doubtless, on the occasions when she has succeeded in drawing him into a group, she has then withdrawn her attention from him thinking it was no longer needed. What she *should* have done is the exact opposite, i.e. to withhold her attention from the child while he is behaving as an isolate, and to give it to him every time he makes an approach response to other children. In this way, he will learn that instead of getting teacher's attention by being on his own, the way to get it is to be with others.

We can take this model and apply it to other kinds of behaviour. Just as the isolate child was being rewarded for being an isolate, so a child who is not very good at his work may find that the only way he can get his teacher's attention is by playing about. Another child may find that by showing contempt for a subject he can always draw the teacher's attention away from the lesson and into a fruitless attempt to 'convert' him to a better attitude. Another may find that by using bad language he can offend (and therefore strike back at) a teacher he dislikes. Another that he can get more attention from a popular teacher by getting his work wrong than by getting it right. In all cases, the logic of the situation remains the same. The child is being rewarded for the very kinds of behaviour that the teacher wishes to eliminate in him. Defects of personality, Skinner argues, are caused by a misapplication of re-inforcers. Study the situation, apply the re-inforcers differently, and the defects will be cured (or, more technically, *modified*).

There are several texts available which go into the techniques of behaviour modification exhaustively (e.g. Poteet 1974). But basically these techniques can be reduced to a few simple rules:

1. The teacher lists each of the behaviours in a particular child that he wishes to modify. This must be done in detail—e.g. it is not enough just to write down 'rowdiness', one must break this down into such things as 'entering class noisily', 'banging desk lid', 'scraping chair on floor'. These are called *target behaviours*.
2. The teacher lists against each of these the target behaviours that are to be aimed for (normally the exact opposite of those in the first list).
3. The teacher analyses precisely how target behaviours in list one have been re-inforced in the past, and withdraws this re-inforcement.
4. The teacher systematically re-inforces the target behaviours in list two.

All this requires skill and patience. It also requires self-control, as when the teacher deliberately ignores a child's noisy entrance into the class, and praises him when he takes his seat quietly. Bandura claims that the teacher can help things along still further by modelling the desired behaviour himself (e.g. not shouting in class if he doesn't want the children to do so), by drawing favourable attention to children who are modelling the desired bahaviour (but only if they are prestigious models), and by always stressing in his instructions to the class the desired rather than the undesired behaviour (e.g. 'work quietly' rather than 'stop the noise').

It is also claimed that behaviour modification techniques can be used to produce less tangible kinds of behaviour such as patience, self-control, determination. This is done by what is called *self-contracting,* a kind of course in self-management. Tharp and Wetzel (1969) report a successful attempt to employ self-contracting in a large secondary school and the surrounding community. Once target behaviours had been listed for individual children, *mediators,* such as parents, local trades-people and so on, who could provide the children with suitable rewards, were contacted and their help enlisted. Children were then asked to contract to produce desired target behaviours in return for specific rewards. Each time they produced the behaviours (e.g. truthfulness, co-operation, perseverance) they were awarded notations which could be accumulated and then exchanged for the rewards (e.g. extra time watching TV, outings, horse rides, helping in a garage, extra pocket money). Within two to six weeks, Tharp and Wetzel claim that seventy five per cent of the undesired behaviour had been converted (*turned round)* into desired behaviour. The children had learnt, many of them for the first time in their lives, that things like honesty actually pay off. In the course of this learning, they had also acquired a range or other secondary re-inforcers as a result of their good behaviour, such as improved school performance, better relationships at home, more teacher approval, more prestige. It is these other secondary reinforcers that prevented the desired behaviour from collapsing once the experiment was over.

Tharp and Wetzel's experiment is really an example, in the normal school setting of the *token economy* which behaviour modifiers employ in many closed communities such as approved schools, institutions and hospitals, and in which desired behaviour is rewarded with tokens which are exchanged for treats and privileges (e.g. Lovitt 1970). It also indicates to us that rewards must be things that children genuinely desire, and demonstrates that while children are gaining these rewards they are also acquiring more long term secondary reinforcers that will sustain their improved behavior in the future.

Criticism of the Learning Theory Approach

A whole literature, for and against, has grown up around Skinner's work (e.g. Wheeler 1973), and in the short space available here we cannot hope to review it. All we shall try to do is to suggest ways of resolving some of the main areas of disagreement between Skinner and the theorists.

The least controversial part of Skinner's argument, and one that is acceptable to most psychologists, is that we often unwittingly re-inforce the very behaviour in children that we wish to discourage. Behaviour modification techniques provide a very useful way of identifying when this is happening, and of doing something to put it right. It is generally accepted that these techniques work best when they are practised throughout the whole of an institution, which means that if they are tried in a school all the staff should be involved in them, and should work out together a common and consistent programme.

Where Skinner is on more controversial ground is in maintaining that behaviour modification techniques can correct all personality problems. His opponents argue that these techniques tackle the symptoms and not the causes of personality malfunction, and that, in the long run, new sets of symptoms are likely to occur in their place. His supporters deny that *symptom substitution* of this kind does happen, as long as all the relevant symptoms in a given category of behaviour problems are tackled in the first place. But of course it is often impossible to do this. In a highly anxious person for example, particularly one with free floating anxiety, anxiety is a generalized reaction to pretty well every aspect of his life.

Another point of criticism in Skinner's work is that much of it (though admittedly by no means all) has been carried out with animals, and it is doubtful how far the results of this work can usefully be applied to humans. Because, for example, we can make an animal behave neurotically, this in no sense demonstrates that anxiety cannot be caused in man through the existence of such a thing as a super-ego. The super-ego is a collection of ideas, values, and beliefs acquired and sustained largely through the use of language. Language gives man a much wider and more complex range of experiences than have animals, and allows him to brood on these experiences, to plan future behaviour, to suffer guilt.

Through the thought processes to which it gives rise, language also helps man to be *aware of the fact that he is being re-inforced*. If he needs the re-inforcement, he produces the appropriate bahaviour to obtain it, if not, he withholds the behaviour.

Skinner, of course, denies that man can choose whether to produce behaviour or to withhold it, since this would imply that man has free will, a point that Skinner is not prepared to concede. Here, inevitably, Skinner is straying into a field beset with all kinds of philosophical hazards where 'proof' is not possible one way or another. Indeed it is surprising that Skinner, who prides himself on being a scientist, should allow himself to become involved in a debate of this kind, or to make the kind of categorical statements concerning it that appear so frequently in his work.

From our point of view, and surely from the point of view of any rational person, the important thing is that man thinks and acts *as if* he has free will. Even Skinner, by exhorting mankind to adopt his operant conditioning techniques as the only way to make the world safe for future generations (1972), is behaving *as if* man has the freedom to choose whether to accept his advice or not.

Finally, Skinner's rejection of the notion that man's behaviour can ever be traced to such things as meta needs, raises great problems in the explanation of human motivation. It is not easy to see how a simple operant conditioning model can ever be stretched to explain satisfactorily the work of a Beethoven or a Shakespeare, still less, perhaps, the pleasure that this work has brought to the rest of mankind.

13

Personality and Cognition

Personality and Intelligence

To speak of personality and intelligence is somewhat misleading, since it suggests that the two are quite separate categories of human psychology. If we accept one of the currently popular operational definitions of intelligence—e.g. that it is the ability to overcome difficulties in new situations—we realise that it is very much a part of that general reaction to life that we call personality. When we speak of children as bright, or alert, or dull, it is usually this general reaction that we're talking about, not just the fact that they do well or badly in tests of intelligence. The point is well taken by Cattell, who includes intelligence as one of the factors measured by his personality tests and by Kelly.

Perhaps what we should be talking about is the relationship between intelligence and other factors of personality therefore. Certainly, intelligence seems to influence some areas of personality more strongly than others. Often there does not seem to be any straightforward link between intelligence and a person's beliefs and values (though it will normally affect the manner in which he can defend them). On the other hand, there will be an obvious connection between intelligence and the level of the goals which a person sets himself in life, and between intelligence and the kind of interpretations that he puts upon his life experiences.

Not surprisingly, since intelligence tests are themselves nomothetic devices, most of the research into the relationship between intelligence and other factors of personality has been carried out by nomothetic rather than by idiographic personality theorists. With the exception of the correlations between low intelligence and 'N' scores, neither Eysenck nor Cattell have found, however, that intelligence correlates *consistently* with any of the dimensions or factors of personality measured in their tests.

One very interesting line of research is that carried out by the Fels Institute in the USA into samples of children who, between the ages of six and ten, showed either a marked increase or a marked decline in I.Q. scores (Kagan *et al.* 1958). It was found that boys were twice as likely as were girls to be in the group that had shown an increase, while there were more girls than boys in the group that had declined (this may be an indication that boys tend to mature later in measured intelligence than do girls, just as they mature later in speech and in reading skills. Alternatively it may be a cultural thing, with boys receiving more challenge and encouragement once they reach school age than do girls). Children in the increased I.Q. group, both boys and girls, were more independent, more competitive, and more verbally aggressive than were those in the declined I.Q. group. They were also readier to work hard, showed a stronger desire to master intellectual problems, and were less likely to withdraw in the face of challenge.

What this research seems to show is that the possession of certain personality characteristics helps children to make full use of their intellectual potential. If we think back to chapter 11, it will be remembered that in higher education as well, Barron found that resourcefulness, energy, and adaptability correlated well with satisfactory levels of achievement. In one of the most ambitious studies of its kind ever attempted, Terman and Oden (1947) followed up 750 children with I.Q.s of 140 plus into adult life, and found that those who fulfilled their early potential were more interested in their work, more persevering, more self-confident, and better integrated in their life goals. They people are more autonomous, self-sufficient, self-assertive, and resourceful. They are also more introverted, more inclined towards feminine interests, more aware of their impulses, and more open to the irrational in themselves. At the risk of lengthening this list too far, we can add that other investigators have found creative people to have a high tolerance of ambiguity (they enjoy puzzling over things that have many possible solutions), and to be capable of a high level of abstract thought. As with intelligence, most studies indicate that people who make effective use of their high levels of creativity are generally strong on achievement motivation. They have a single mindedness which enables them to work hard in their chosen field and to show a high level of interest and involvement in the things that they do.

We must stress, however, as we did with intelligence, that creativity should not be seen as something distinct and separate from personality. The creative person is creative in his whole approach to life. Many of the personality characteristics that we mentioned above are not just things that the creative person happens to have, they *are* his creativity as it reveals itself in the business of everyday living. When it comes, therefore, to discussing how best the teacher can encourage creativity in children, much of what we have said already earlier about the teacher's role in helping the child towards maturity and self-actualisation of personality will still apply. Rogers stresses that positive regard and empathic understanding are, as with other areas of personality, the most important contribution the teacher can make towards fostering creativity in children, and to these he adds a *freedom from external evaluation.* This means that although the teacher is free to *react* to children's creative work (i.e. to say whether he likes it or not), he should refrain from passing categorical judgements upon it (i.e. saying it is 'wrong' or 'bad'), since by its very nature divergent activity contains no immutable rules of correctness.

The important part that the teacher can play in allowing the child sufficient freedom to develop his creative powers is evidenced by a number of studies (e.g. Haddon and Lytton 1968) which show that children in informal primary schools perform better on divergent thinking tests than do children in formal schools, and that this enhanced performance persists when the children transfer to secondary schools, irrespective of the type of secondary school involved (Haddon and Lytton 1971). What we are really saying is that if the teacher wishes to encourage the creative side of a child's personality, the child must not be taught to reject this side of himself, and to adopt only a conventional approach to thinking. Hudson (1966) found a tendency amongst boys specialising in science subjects at sixth form level to think convergently, while those specialising in the arts tended to think divergently, and this could well be evidence that some teachers of science subjects are not prepared to allow as much self-expression in their pupils as are some teachers of arts subjects. (Mistakenly, we might add, as there is just as much need to think creatively about science as about the arts.) It seems that when children who are highly convergent are encouraged to be freer and less judgemental in their responses, their ability to think divergently increases markedly.

Jerome Bruner and his colleagues, in a number of studies (e.g. 1956), speak of *holistic* (creative) thinking and *algorithmic* (rational) thinking, and consider that our western educational system encourages the latter at the expense of the former. We lay stress upon conformity, upon children always arriving at the same conclusions as the teacher, upon children always using the 'right' method for solving problems in mathematics and science, upon children not guessing solutions (frequently *guessing*, Bruner argues, is evidence of creative effort, or a sudden flash of insight), upon children not tolerating ambiguity. It is not that Bruner, or indeed any psychologist, argues against the need for convergent, algorithmic thinking, but simply that this kind of thinking should not be the only form of thought encouraged in children. McKellar (1957) puts the case well when he talks of holistic (or, as he chooses to call it, 'autistic') thinking as being the *author* of any worthwhile creative act, while rational thinking is the *editor* who sifts through the ideas generated by holistic thinking, isolates those which are most relevant, and puts them to use.

There is evidence that teachers sometimes find it harder to relate to children high on creativity than to other children . Getzels and Jackson (1962) certainly found this to be the case in their, admittedly rather narrow, sample of teachers and children. They suggest that the creative child's non-conformity and apparent self-sufficiency can make him less immediately sympathetic to teachers than are children with more conformist attributes.

If Getzels and Jackson are right, this means that teachers may sometimes have to take particular care not to allow the creative child's independent outlook to count against him. But this probably applies to all gifted children, whether their giftedness lies in very high creativity, very high intelligence, or both. It is probably another of the failing of our national educational system that we pay insufficient attention to helping the gifted child to live with, and to make good use of, his gifts. Sometimes, though probably not as often as writers in the national press have taken to claiming, the highly gifted child can feel as isolated from other children as can the child of correspondingly low ability. He can also feel as misunderstood and unappreciated. With his high level of curiosity and activity, and his boredom in the face of unchallenging work, he can be a generally uncomfortable member of the class, and some teachers, not surprisingly, feel threatened by his precocious knowledge, and are convinced that he is setting out to score off them in front of the class.

Perhaps because of their very feeling of separateness, there is some evidence that gifted children (particularly, it seems, gifted girls) play down their gifts to avoid antagonising the teacher, and to avoid unpopularity with the rest of the class. Such self-rejection may be potentially as damaging to the personality as are the other forms of self-rejection. The cost to the nation in terms of lost potential needs no emphasising.

Cognitive Style

Cognitive style theorists start from the accepted fact that we are bombarded by so much data from the environment every moment of our lives that we cannot possibly attend to them all without enormous cognitive strain. They then ask *how* do we sort these data out and decide what to attend to and what not, and suggest that we do it by *coding* them, that is by placing each of them into one of a range of categories which carries its own rating of importance. In any situation, things belonging to categories relatively high in importance gain our attention, those belonging to categories relatively low do not.

The way in which we assign things to categories will be partly determined by previous experience, and partly by innate factors, including how we actually *perceive* things (e.g. some people are innately more sensitive to certain stimuli, such as loud noises, bright colours, subtle differences in shape, than are others). We can get a good example of coding from a child tackling a problem.

First he studies and categorises the information it contains. Next he hunts through the information in his head until he finds data coded into a similar category. Finally, he forms an hypothesis and sees if it will solve the problem.

Cognitive style theorists claim that we carry out this coding process in our own characteristic and consistent way. We don't change our method drastically from problem to problem. Since our whole contact with the outside world, including our social behaviour, is influenced by the way in which we code, it must be seen as a part, and an important part, of our personalities.

Cognitive style theory is not, however, an alternative to the theories of personality. It does not concern itself with motivation, or with the possible systems within the personality, such as the ego and the super-ego, which help to determine why people differ in the degrees of importance which they attach to various categories. For the most part, it seems content to accept that neurotic people may put things into categories which have to do with their worries, and then attend to those which they find the most threatening. It accepts that the extravert may tend to code in terms of his preferences as an extravert, and the introvert in terms of his preferences as an introvert. It accepts that coded categories may become built into personal constructs and so on. It is not so much a theory of personality, as an attempt to explain the actual mechanism that the personality uses to interact with the world. It is concerned with the way in which we think, and not with why we think in this way or with the content of our thoughts.

We can explain this by going back to our example of a child tackling a problem at school. One child may characteristically read quickly through the problem, get an overall, and perhaps inaccurate, picture of what it is all about, and immediately start trying to solve it. Another might characteristically read it through slowly, word by word, before starting work. These different methods of tackling the problem are part and parcel of the children's respective cognitive styles. However, such things as the level of enthusiasm which they bring to bear upon the task, the degrees of importance which they assign to the respective categories which it contains, and the amount of anxiety which they feel if they get it wrong, belong not to their cognitive styles but to those areas of their personality and of their learning.

Obviously, from an educational point of view, cognitive style is an important aspect of personality. We often find ourselves saying that one child tends to rush things, that another always seems to miss the essentials in an argument, that another is disorganised in his thinking, that another is precise and methodical, and so on. The characteristics represented by those labels are evidenced not only in the way in which children solve problems, but also in the way in which they relate to other people, and in such things as the amount and depth of consideration which they give to their selection of short term and long term life goals.

However, terms such as 'disorganised', 'inconsistent', 'methodical', are somewhat vague and subjective, and various attempts have been made by psychologists to see if there are any more precise—albeit broad—categories of cognitive style into which people can be divided. The results of this research have proved to be rather similar to those produced by the nor   ntic approach to personality theory, in that they have tended to identify bi-polar dimensions. These dimensions are still very much in the experimental stage, and the tests upon which they depend are still crude. It is not clear, either, to what extent or in what way they relate to each other, or to personality theories. Nevertheless, three of them are of sufficient interest to be looked at closely, namely *field dependence-independence, focussing-scanning* and *reflectivity-impulsivity.*

1. *Field Dependence—Independence.* In one way it is a little unfair to talk of the dimension of field dependence-independence as being still in the experimental stage, since it has been the subject of a formidable amount of research over the last fifteen years, chiefly by the American psychologist Herman Witkin and his colleagues. The impetus for Witkin's work came from the discovery by the United States Air Force that many pilots, on losing visual contact with the ground (as e.g. when they flew into a dense cloud bank), lost all sense of the vertical, and, if unaided by instruments, would often end up unwittingly flying upside down (with consequent increase in combat vulnerability!).

Witkin attempted to study this phenomenon experimentally by constructing the Body Adjustment Test, in which subjects were seated in a tilting chair facing into a small box-like 'room' which could also be tilted (Witkin 1959). When taking the test, some subjects proved able unerringly to say whether they were upright or not irrespective of the angle of the chair and of the 'room' while others lost their sense of the vertical completely as soon as the 'room' in front of them started to tilt; some of them even claimed to be upright when room and chair were both tilting through an angle of thirty degrees. What seemed to be happening was that the first group of subjects was able to sort out the pull of gravity (the relevant stimulus) from the visual experience of the 'room' in front of them (the irrelevant stimulus), whilst the second group was not. Witkin termed the first group field independent (f.i.), and the second group field dependent (f.d.).

Witkin then established that dimension has interesting applications in everyday life. For example, f.d. people seem less able to pick out and remember the details in a given situation than can f.i. When presented with a battery of projective techniques, they also disclose themselves as less perceptive in dealing with life, and more easily influenced (Witkin *et al.* 1954). Witkin sums this up saying that the f.d. person has a *global* cognitive style, while the f.i. has an *articulated* one (these terms, global and articulated, together with the group label *psychological differentiation*, are tending to replace field dependence-independence).

Since correlations have been found between extraversion and field dependence (Witkin 1959), it is tempting to suggest that the latter is to some extent an expression of the former. The extravert, with his greater social involvement, his greater need for frequent and varied stimuli, and his slower rate of conditioning, pays less attention to each unit of experience, is more readily swayed by group opinion, and gives himself less time to be perceptive about which are the most relevant units of experience in any given situation. He is therefore logically somewhat more likely to be f.d. than is the introvert.

However, it would be wrong to regard the dimension of field dependence-independence as lying precisely along the same dimension as extraversion-introversion. Though there is a correlation, it is far from being a perfect one. Many extraverts are f. i., just many introverts are f.d. For field independence also seems to go with certain things that extraverts possess as frequently as do introverts, such as a more developed sense of personal identity (which in Erikson's terms, remember, indicates maturity of personality—chapter 11), and with higher self-esteem and self-confidence. Interestingly, it also goes with a particular style of ego defence mechanism. Bertini (1961) demonstrates that when f.i. people employ repression, they seem able to repress selectively, whereas f.d. people are likely to repress indiscriminately, blotting out large chunks of their past experience in a way which suggests they are much less able, consciously or unconsciously, to single out the precise causes of their anxiety. F.d. people are also better able than are f.i. to keep their feelings separate from their thoughts and perceptions, which could be one of the reasons why field dependence correlates more strongly with women than with men.

It is important to stress that although much of what we have been saying seems to favour field independence over dependence, Witkin is at pains to point out that, as with something like extraversion-introversion, neither is 'better' than the other. The f.d. person might be more sensitive to the needs of others than is the f.i. more gregarious, more socially involved, perhaps less likely to withdraw. *Extremes* at either end of the dimensions are equally adverse, with the f.d. person tending to suffer from identity defusion and over dependence upon others (alcoholics and compulsive over-eaters are often field dependent), and the f.i. person from a too rigid defence of personal identity which leads him to lay the blame for his problems always upon others rather than to blame (and try to change) himself.

Field dependence-independence has obvious implications for the teacher in terms of children's inter-personal relationships and their approach to problem solving. Although it throws little light on creativity (different kinds of creativity may possibly demand different kinds of style), it does have bearing upon intelligence. Studies show that f.i. children perform better on analytical items in I.Q. tests than do f.d., though there is no difference on verbal items. Witkin (1965) argues that as many ESN children also score more highly on analytical items than they do on verbal, and that as many children with low analytical scores are often not diagnosed as ESN because this poor performance is disguised by high verbal ability, I.Q. tests should be replaced by those for cognitive style, since the latter are more comprehensive and 'recognise the rooting of intellectual functioning in personality'.

2. *Focussing-Scanning* is associated particularly with the American psychologist Jerome Bruner, now at the University of Oxford. Unlike Witkin, the main impetus behind Bruner's work comes from research with children. Again unlike Witkin, this research has concentrated upon observing the coding systems (called by Bruner *strategies*) which are adopted in a problem solving situation. One of Bruner's best known tests is to present the child with a number of pairs of cards, one pair at a time, each card consisting of varying arrangements of squares, circles, lines and colours. The child is then told that one card in each pair is 'correct' and the other 'incorrect', and as more of the pairs are presented to him, he is asked to determine what particular features of the squares, circles, etc., denotes 'correctness' and 'incorrectness' (Bruner *et al.* 1956).

Research of this kind appears to indicate that children are distributed along a dimension, at one end of which are those who examine the relevant features in each of the pairs until they have amassed enough information to advance an hypothesis (the *focussers*), and at the other end are those who form an hypothesis on the basis of the first pair, stick to it until eventually enough subsequent pairs have been examined to show it to be untenable, and then have to go back to the beginning and start again (the *scanners*).

What seems to be happening is that focussers characteristically delay hypothesis-making until they have enough evidence, while scanners characteristically form an hypothesis on slimmer evidence, and have no option but to begin afresh if subsequently they are shown to be wrong. If the same strategies are applied in social situations, we might say that the focusser makes up his mind about other people only when he has got to know them well, whereas the scanner makes up his mind more quickly, sometimes only to have to abandon this opinion altogether (and along with it, perhaps, a friendship), when the evidence against it becomes too strong.

The importance to teachers of the focussing—scanning dimension is considerable. Children who scan, it seems, have a particular need to be allowed to go back and check earlier clues if their original hypothesis becomes untenable, and therefore may be at a disadvantage in mentally presented problems. Children who focus, on the other hand, may delay too long over forming their hypotheses, and thus be handicapped in work involving quick responses. On the teacher's own part, there is the risk that the scanner may make snap decisions on children, and then have to recant later (e.g. with such remarks in a school report as 'has deteriorated this term, must do better next', which may confuse the child as much as it worries his parents), while the focusser may be over-cautious in giving praise, or good marks, or in writing an enthusiastic report or reference.

Ideally, people should be able to focus or to scan, depending upon the nature of the problem they are called upon to tackle, the amount of time in which they have to do it, and so on. Sometimes a quick hypothesis is called for, sometimes a more cautious one. Extreme focussing can be a sign of insecurity (if you never reach a decision about anything, you can never be proved wrong), and may lead to sitting on the fence until the opportunity has been lost (e.g. someone else proposes to the girl). Extreme scanning on the other hand can mean an early commitment with little hope of retrieving the situation later (the wedding bells sound too early). When solving each problem, one should be a good judge of how long one can delay one's decision while awaiting further evidence.

Again there are no clear correlations between focussing-scanning and creativity (or between it and intelligence). Probably extremes of either are less helpful than a judicious combination of the two. There is also little link between Bruner's dimension and Witkin's (scanners are not, as one might suppose, f.d. and focussers f.i.), though it is not unreasonable to hope that future research, with more sophisticated measuring devices, may reveal a relationship of some kind between them.

3. *Reflectivity-Impulsivity.* The third dimension that we are to examine is proposed by another American psychologist, Jerome Kagan. If we think back to the beginning of this section, it will be remembered that there are typically three stages in problem solving, firstly categorising the given information, secondly sifting, mentally through one's own knowledge to find similar categories, and thirdly forming an hypothesis with which to proceed to the solution. Kagan considers that cognitive style particularly influences the first and last of those stages. Some people, he claims (1966), characteristically act *reflectively* in categorising the

information and producing their hypothesis, whilst others behave *impulsively.*

Kagan also claims to have discovered another dimension, *visual analysis*, which relates to the extent to which people break down the information in stage one. Some people, at least with a visually presented problem, tend to break it down into small units, whilst others prefer to work with much larger chunks of it. Perhaps oddly, there is no strong correlation between visual analysis and reflectivity-impulsivity. Some reflective people work with large chunks of information and some with small, and the same is true of impulsive people.

Kagan has devised a number of tests to explore these two dimensions. In the Delayed Recall Design Test, which is a test of reflectivity-impulsivity, the child is presented with a simple black and white design for a few seconds, and is then asked to pick it out from a number of similar designs. The test is scored for response time and for accuracy, and typically, reflective children take longer over their responses and make fewer errors than do impulsive children. In the Visual Analysis Test, the child learns to associate respectively four nonsense syllables with four complex designs, each containing several components, and is then asked to produce the correct syllable when he is shown only single components abstracted from each design. The visually analytic child, who has had no difficulty in analysing each design into its separate components, makes far fewer mistakes than does the unanalytic child, to whom each of the designs exists only as a complete unit.

As with Witkin and Bruner, Kagan's work has important potential implications for education. At present, most of these implications must be drawn from the reflectivity-impulsivity dimension, as the visual analysis dimension is still very much in the experimental stage. Leaving aside a small group of highly anxious children who have a long response time and still make many errors, it seems clear that on challenging and difficult problems at least, reflective children make significantly fewer errors than do impulsive ones. Kagan (1966) claims that they show a strong desire to be right first time, and seem able to tolerate the ambiguity of a long silence (not easy if perhaps both teacher and class are waiting impatiently to see if they know the answer of not) while they weigh each possibility before responding. Impulsive children, on the other hand, adopt a 'shotgun' approach, firing out several answers, either in the hope that one will prove correct or because they rely upon feedback from the teacher rather than upon their own internal reflections to tell them if they are getting 'warm' or not. Kagan says that reflective children have a slow, and impulsive children a fast, *conceptual tempo*.

Conceptual tempo also seems important in serial learning tasks. For example, when learning vocabulary lists, impulsive children tend to make more errors of commission (i.e. including extra words in the recalled list) than do reflective children, and the more critical the teacher becomes, the more of these errors they make. When reading, they tend to make more orthographic errors, typically by misreading simple three letter words (e.g. 'log' for 'dog' 'cat' for 'pat'), even when they are perfectly familiar with the individual letters concerned.

Like Witkin and Bruner, Kagan resists the conclusion that it is necessarily 'better' to be reflective than impulsive, though the former does seem associated with maturity in that as children grow older their reflectivity scores tend to increase (though the *relative* differences between impulsive and reflective children may remain the same). He suggests that whereas high reflectivity may be advantageous in academic subjects like maths, it may be a disadvantage in the visual arts and in some aspects of the humanities and social sciences. However, Kagan does concede that the highly impulsive child's frequent experience of selecting the wrong hypothesis may be a source of discouragement, and lead to increased anxiety and greater impulsivity as he tries to put things right.

Further Research into Cognitive Style

It is by no means clear whether it is possible to change a child's cognitive style on any of the dimensions mentioned. Relative positions on each of them seem to remain markedly stable over the years and Kagan concludes that cognitive style may be a 'basic component of the individual's behavioural organisation' (1966). More research is needed before the point is proved, and hopefully such research will also show whether tests of cognitive style are the improvement on tests of intelligence that Witkin claims them to be, and whether they can be usefully used by teachers when deciding how best to structure the learning situation to suit individual children.

We also need to know more about the relationship between the various dimensions of cognitive style so far discovered, more about their relationship to intelligence and creativity, and much more about their relationship to the causal factors in personality development. As we have seen, a start has been made in relating cognitive style to ego defence mechanisms, to personal identity, and to particular forms of personality problems. But what part does an individual's sense of security, of confidence, of self-esteem, etc. have to play in his style? And is style more a product of, or a cause of, these things? And how does cognitive style affect the way in which one forms one's personal constructs, or the freedom with which one locomotes through one's life space, or the methods which one employs to deal with cognitive dissonance? The subject is rich in research possibilities.

Index